Dignity in Movement

Borders, Bodies and Rights

EDITED BY

JASMIN LILIAN DIAB

**E-INTERNATIONAL
RELATIONS
PUBLISHING**

E-International Relations
Bristol, England
2021

ISBN 978-1-910814-59-8

Production: Michael Tang
Cover Image: Ekkapop Sittiwantana/Shutterstock

A catalogue record for this book is available from the British Library.

E-International Relations

Editor-in-Chief and Publisher: Stephen McGlinchey
Books Editor: Bill Kakenmaster
Editorial Assistance: Simon Hilditch, Eleanor Pearson, Leo Lin, Farah Saleem
Düzakman, Bárbara Campos Diniz.

E-International Relations is the world's leading International Relations website. Our daily publications feature expert articles, reviews and interviews – as well as student learning resources. The website is run by a non-profit organisation based in Bristol, England and staffed by an all-volunteer team of students and scholars. In addition to our website content, E-International Relations publishes a range of edited collections, monographs and textbooks. Each of our books is available in print and digital versions. As E-International Relations is committed to open access in the fullest sense, free electronic versions of our books, including this one, are available on our website.

Find out more at https://www.e-ir.info/

Abstract

This book brings together a diverse range of contributors to offer interdisciplinary perspectives on developments across the forced migration sphere – including reflections on international migration and refugee law, global health, border management, illegal migration, and intersectional migration experiences. The chapters address subjects ranging from the Global Compact for Migration, migration laws, fundamental human rights discourse and principles, colonial violence, environmental migrants, and internal displacement. The book additionally delves into the interplay between such notions as the role of women in migration trends, the Kafala System, unaccompanied minors, and family dynamics. Along with tackling border practices, transnational governance, return migration, and complementary protection, the chapters featured in this volume discuss the notions of belonging, stigma, discrimination, and racism.

Acknowledgments

This edited collection would not have been possible without the brilliant insights from its contributing authors, and their incomparable experience and grasp of the human spirit. I would like to take the opportunity to thank Stephen McGlinchey and Bill Kakenmaster at E-International Relations, and the wider E-IR Team. Without your support and platform, this book would not have materialized.

Jasmin Lilian Diab is an Assistant Professor of Migration Studies at the Lebanese American University (LAU)'s Department of Social Sciences. Previously, she served as the Refugee Health Program Coordinator at the American University of Beirut's Global Health Institute (GHI) and as a Research Associate under GHI's Political Economy of Health in Conflict Workstream. Prior to assuming her roles at AUB and LAU, she served as the Research and Project Manager of the Lebanese Research Center for Migration and Diaspora Studies at Notre Dame University-Louaize's Faculty of Law and Political Science, as well as the MENA Regional Focal Point on Migration of the UN General Assembly-mandated UN Major Group for Children and Youth. She is a Senior Consultant on Refugee and Gender Studies at Cambridge Consulting Services, a Research Affiliate at the Centre for Refugee Studies at York University, a Junior Scholar in Forced Displacement at University of Ottawa's Human Rights Research and Education Centre, and a Junior Fellow and Program Lead at the Global Research Network's 'War, Conflict and Global Migration' Think Tank. Dr. Diab is a Founding Member of the 'Migration and International Law in Africa, Middle East and Turkey International Network' (MILAMET), and has served as an International Consultant to UNHCR, WHO, Danmission, KAICIID Dialogue Center, Terre des Hommes, ECODIT, AMURT, the Arab Foundation for Freedoms and Equality, the International Domestic Workers Federation, Justice Without Frontiers and Relief & Reconciliation for Syria. She has been a Reviewer to the Journal of Internal Displacement, a Reviewer and Copy-Editor to the journal 'Refugee Review', and an Editorial Board Member of the Journal of Applied Professional Studies at Marywood University since 2020. She holds a PhD in International Relations and Diplomacy with an emphasis on Asylum, Refugees and Security from the Center for Diplomatic and Strategic Studies of the School of Advanced International and Political Studies at INSEEC U. in Paris, and is the recipient of the CLS 2021 Bursary Award to complete her Postdoctoral research at LAU-University of Oxford's Centre for Lebanese Studies.

Contributors

Fiore Bran Aragón holds a Master's with honors in Latin American Studies from the University of New Mexico (USA). Since 2016 she has worked as a researcher and humanitarian affairs officer for migrant and refugee issues in Central America and Mexico, and more recently in the United States. She is co-founder of the Migration narratives project "Me lo contó un migrante" and has served as a South America focal point and research staff member at the United Nations Major Group for Children and Youth (MGCY) on Migration. Her research interests include forced migration, migrant women's rights, and wellbeing, and integration policies in Central America and Mexico.

Sabrina Andrea Avigliano holds a law degree from the University of Buenos Aires (Argentina) and is a Master's student in Criminal Law at the University of Palermo (Argentina). She has published analytical pieces on migration law and gender-based violence.

Keshav Basotia is a Master's graduate of Diplomacy, Law and Business from Jindal School of International Affairs (India). He currently works as a Geopolitical Intelligence Analyst for a multinational bank. He is interested in South Asian Geopolitics and World Foreign Policy, with particular interests in the geopolitics of Israel in the Middle East and its implications when linked with Indian Foreign Policy.

Hadjer Belghoul is a Lecturer of English Literature and Didactics at the Abdelhamid Ibn-Badis University (Algeria) and a researcher at the University of Mustapha Stambouli-Mascara (Algeria).

Pat Rubio Bertran is an LLM Candidate in Human Rights Law at the University of Kent, specialising in legal research and advocacy regarding migration and border violence. Simultaneously, Pat is the Program Lead at the search and rescue NGO Refugee Rescue, working in the Mediterranean.

Anna Closas Casasampera holds an M.A. in International Conflict Studies at the Department of War Studies, King's College London (UK). She has collaborated with and worked for various NGOs, particularly on gender and migration issues. She previously studied Philosophy, Politics and Economics at Pompeu Fabra University, Carlos III and Universidad Autónoma de Madrid (Spain). Her research interests focus on Political Theory, International Relations, Migration Studies, as well as Gender and Critical Security Studies.

Diotima Chattoraj is currently working as a Research Assistant at the department of Public Health in National University of Singapore. She holds a

PhD from the Department of International Development Studies (IEE), Ruhr-University Bochum (Germany). She is a social scientist with over 8 years of research experience in the field of Migration and Development Studies. Her areas of research interests include Asia, Sociology of Migration, Theories of Migration, Refugee Studies, Trafficking, Globalization, Climate Change, Development, Gender Studies, Security, Border Studies and International Relations. She serves as a peer reviewer for a number of international refereed journals including, *South Asia Research* and *Comparative Migration Studies*.

Guadalupe Chavez is a PhD student at the Department of Politics and International Relations at the University of Oxford (UK). She previously worked for the Center for Migration Studies (CMS) as the Interim Editorial and Production Assistant, where she managed the administrative and editorial process of CMS's peer-reviewed journals including the International Migration Review and the Journal on Migration and Human Security. Guadalupe is also a recipient of the 2018–2019 Fulbright-García Robles Research Fellowship in Mexico City. Her research interests include the Politics of Post-deportation in Latin America, Comparative Citizenship Studies, and Border Politics.

Manuela da Rosa Jorge is a Leverhulme Doctoral Scholar in the School of Politics and International Relations at Queen Mary, University of London (UK). Manuela holds a BA in International Relations from the Universidade do Sul de Santa Catarina in Brazil and a MSc in Human Rights and International Politics from the University of Glasgow, which was funded by the University of Glasgow Trust International Leadership Scholarship. Through a de-centred and postcolonial approach, Manuela's doctoral thesis explores European migration policies that are designed to regulate and control non-European human mobility. She is particularly interested in expulsion policies and discursive strategies that work to legitimise and justify such policies. Her research is informed by the intersection of critical migration studies, critical IR theory and policy analysis.

Mitxy Meneses Gutierrez is a PhD candidate in the Department of Politics and International Relations at Goldsmiths, University of London (UK). She is affiliated with the Centre for Postcolonial Studies and funded by the Mexican Consejo Nacional de Ciencia y Tecnología (CONACYT). She has been an Associate Lecturer in the Department of Politics and International Relations at Goldsmiths. Her research focuses on Transborderism and its policy implications at the US-Mexico border, specifically transborder students living in the Cali-Baja region. Her research critically engages with Contemporary Border Studies, Migration, Transnationalism, Transborderism and International Cooperation. She previously worked with the UN International Organization for Migration (IOM) stationed at the Mexicali-Calexico border.

Kensiya Kennedy is a Master's graduate in Diplomacy, Law and Business from the Jindal School of International Affairs (India). She is currently an analyst for an international risk management firm. Her interests lie in studying the dynamics of political economies around the world and in understanding the nuances of a post-colonial world order. Her prior works have explored issues such as the impact of Covid-19 from a gendered perspective on migrant help and the politics of State infrastructure.

Anne-Cecile Leyvraz is a Research Fellow at the University of Applied Sciences and Arts Western Switzerland (HETSL | HES-SO). Her research addresses Refugee and Migration Law from an international law perspective. She holds a PhD from the Graduate Institute of International and Development Studies Geneva (Switzerland). Her latest publication is a co-edited collective book addressing the performative role of 'the fight against abuses' in the Swiss asylum system. For several years, she has worked as an immigration lawyer in Geneva.

Kendra Morancy is a joint MA/PhD student in African and African Diaspora Studies and International Relations at Florida International University (USA). Her research areas include Human Trafficking, Sex Tourism, Migration, and Global Health and Development Studies. Her major fields include Latin American and Caribbean foreign policy and global governance systems. She seeks to use her analytical writing skills to effectively solve societal issues and serve as an advocate for women, children and other disadvantaged groups.

Oanh K. Nguyen is a PhD Candidate in the Political Science Department at the University of Minnesota, Twin Cities (USA). Her work examines the politics of migration governance in Southeast Asia.

Hannah Owens is an ESRC-funded LISS Doctoral Training Partnership Scholar in the School of Politics and International Relations at Queen Mary, University of London (UK). Having begun the PhD in 2019, she holds an MRes in International Relations from Queen Mary and an MA in American Studies from the University of East Anglia (UK). Hannah is the 2020/21 Co-convener of the International Political Sociology (IPS) PhD seminar series, and the Co-convener of the Politics of the Middle East (POME) seminar series for early career researchers. Hannah's current research looks at the realities of displacement in hosting spaces next to large-scale humanitarian structures, and their interaction with local and humanitarian governance. Through the study of movement, infrastructure and socio-political relations, Hannah investigates the concept of living (in)security.

Lorcán Owens is a consultant in global and strategic risk, podcaster, writer, researcher and teacher. Holding an MA in Political Communication from Dublin City University, his main areas of interest are political risk, democratisation in the MENA region, minority & LGBTQ rights and OSINT as a tool for activism. Lorcán hosts and produces a podcast called Nazra: Politics, Society and Extremism. He has travelled and worked between Ireland and the MENA region since 2014, where his research to date has focused on the growth of secular political movements in Lebanon since 2018.

Sara Riva holds a PhD from the Gender, Women and Sexuality Studies Department at the Ohio State University (USA). She is currently a Marie Skłodowska-Curie Research Fellow with the Spanish National Research Council and the University of Queensland (Australia). Sara's research interests include Migration, Feminism, Colonialism, Punishment, Confinement and Border Abolition. She puts refugee issues in the United States in conversation with Europe and Australia and theorizes the border as a transnational sovereign assemblage.

Chiara Scissa is a PhD student in Law at Sant'Anna School of Advanced Studies, DIRPOLIS Institute, in Pisa (Italy) where her research focuses on Environmental Migration in the context of EU Law. She holds a Master's with honors in International Cooperation and the Protection of Human Rights from the University of Bologna (Italy), where she worked as a Project Assistant throughout the course of her studies. Chiara serves as the Focal Point for Migrant Protection and Human Rights at the United Nations Major Group for Children and Youth (UNMGCY).

Alma Stankovic is an Attorney in the states of California and New York as well as the District of Columbia and has previously worked as a practicing attorney for high level NGOs, including the Clinton Foundation in New York and Public Counsel Law Center in Los Angeles, where she conducted legal advocacy, policy development, and litigation on behalf of immigrants and persons living in poverty. She holds a Bachelor's Degree in Political Science from the University of California Los Angeles (USA) and a Juris Doctor from the University of Southern California (USA). She is currently completing her PhD thesis on Human Rights of Refugees at the University of Graz (Austria). Her research focuses on the topics of Human Rights, Migration, Transnational Governance, Citizenship, and Refugee Law.

Flo Strass has been working with Mare Liberum (Germany) both on- and off-board the ship since 2018. She holds a Master's degree in Theatre from the University of Arts Berlin (Germany) and a B.A. in History and Political Science. She has been working for different NGOs and activist groups around the Mediterranean, mainly on the ground and in advocacy projects.

Monica Trigos Padilla is an MPA Candidate at Columbia University (USA). She has a BA in International Relations from the Instituto Tecnológico Autónomo de México (ITAM) (Mexico). She has also completed studies in Public Policy, Public Diplomacy, and Immigration and Refugee Policy. She has worked in the private, public, and social sectors in Mexico. She is the Co-Founder and Deputy Director of the collective *'Sin Palabras'* dedicated to giving art, theater, and introspection workshops to migrants and refugees. She also serves as the Regional Focal Point of North America and the Shaping Narratives Lead in the Migration Working Group of the United Nations Major Group for Children and Youth (UNMGCY). She is an Associate and Member of the Board of Directors of the Youth Program of the Mexican Council of Foreign Affairs (COMEXI).

Domiziana Turcatti is a Clarendon Scholar and DPhil Candidate in Migration Studies at the Centre on Migration, Policy and Society (COMPAS), University of Oxford (UK). Domiziana's doctoral research focuses on the experiences of the families of onward Colombian migrants who moved from Spain to London. This research emerged from her previous study on the experiences of social reproduction of Latin American migrants in London, conducted during her MPhil in Sociology at the University of Cambridge (UK) as a Gates Cambridge Scholar. Prior to moving to the UK, Domiziana was awarded an Honors BA in Liberal Arts and Science at Amsterdam University College (Netherlands), where for three years she looked into the educational experiences and the peer culture of Moroccan-Dutch youth in Amsterdam and Rotterdam. Her research interests lie at the intersection of Migration, Family and Childhood Studies, and the role of migrant-led organizations in advancing migrants' rights and visibility.

Meredith Veit worked onboard the Mare Liberum (Germany) ship in August and September 2019. She is an American writer, multimedia storyteller, and researcher who principally works with human rights organizations and activists. She holds an MA. in Human Rights and Democratisation from the Global Campus Human Rights Europe program and a BA in Communications from The George Washington University (USA).

Alexander Voisine is a PhD student in the Department of Spanish and Portuguese at the University of Texas, Austin and completed his Masters in International Relations at the National Autonomous University of Mexico (UNAM) with a Fulbright García-Robles Graduate Degree Award (2018–2020). He most recently worked as a consultant for the United Nations Development Program in Mexico and has collaborated with various NGOs in the US and Mexico, including Project Citizenship in Boston, HIAS Pennsylvania in Philadelphia, and, most recently, Programa Casa Refugiados in

Mexico City. Alexander's research interests include Queer Migration, Human Mobility in Latin America, Geopolitics and Cultural Studies.

Meltem Yilmaz Sener is an Associate Professor of Social Work at Nord University, Norway. She holds a PhD in Sociology from the University of Illinois, Urbana-Champaign, USA. Previously, she worked as an Assistant Professor of Sociology at Istanbul Bilgi University, Turkey. She aims to perform theoretically informed analyses of inequality at the global and country levels. Her research areas include social policy, migration, transnational studies, development, racial and ethnic studies, social inequality, and gender.

Benedetta Zocchi is a Leverhulme Trust Doctoral Scholar in the School of Politics and International Relations, Queen Mary University of London (UK). She previously completed a BA in Politics, Philosophy and Economics at LUISS University (Italy) and an MPhil in International Relations at the University of Oxford (UK). Benedetta is interested in post-colonial legacies, de-colonial thinking and critical migration studies. Her past work explored the social and political construction of colonial amnesia in Italy and the discursive re-activations of colonial consciousness in Italy, France and the UK. Her current research focuses on practices of European coloniality at EU borders, with particular attention to the different realities of exclusion and marginalization on the frontier between BiH and Croatia. Her intellectual approach is informed by the intersection between political activism, social engagement and critical scholarship.

Contents

Introduction

Bodies, Borders and Rights

JASMIN LILIAN DIAB

Today, hundreds of millions of people live outside the borders of the country in which they were born. And migration trends continue to rise. By 2019, the number of global migrants reached an estimated 272 million individuals, 51 million more than in 2010 according to International Organization for Migration (IOM) data (IOM 2019a). While many individuals migrate intentionally, many others migrate involuntarily. By the end of 2020, the number of forcibly displaced people globally reached 70 million for the first time in the history of the United Nations High Commissioner for Refugees (Refugees International 2020). This number is comprised of approximately 26 million refugees, 3.5 million asylum seekers, and over 41 million internally displaced persons.

While international legal frameworks, human rights debates, and international discourse has almost exclusively been focused on the rights of migrants and forced migrants, definitions across the migration spectrum have struggled to center on a unified scope. The IOM defines a migrant as any person who is moving or has moved across an international border or within a state away from his/her habitual place of residence, regardless of the person's legal status, whether the movement is voluntary or involuntary, what the causes for the movement are, or what the duration of the stay is (IOM 2019b). However, when counting migrants and analyzing the consequences of migration, who counts as a migrant, and a particular category of 'migrant' more specifically, is of pivotal importance in understanding the scope of their rights, and states' duties. There remains no consensus on a single definition of a 'migrant'. Within different contexts, states, and legal frameworks, migrants may be defined by foreign birth, by foreign citizenship, or by their movement to a new country to temporarily reside – whether for a short period of time, or for long-term settlement. In many instances, minors who are state-born or even nationals whose parents are foreign-born or foreign-nationals, are counted and governed under the migrant population.

While more technical linguistic definitions make a distinction between 'immigrants' – people who are or intend to be settled in their new country – and 'migrants', who are temporarily resident, both terms are often used interchangeably in public and policy discourses and even by practitioners and experts. In a number of scholarly and legal usages, people who move internally within national boundaries are also referred to as migrants. As this distinction remains overlooked and unclear, so does the more troublesome definition of a 'forced migrant' and all the sub-categorizations this definition entails.

The European Commission for instance, defines a 'forced migrant' as an individual subject to a 'migratory movement in which an element of coercion exists', including threats to life and livelihood, whether arising from natural or man-made causes (European Commission n.d.). In their definition, the European Commission includes the movements of refugees and internally displaced persons, as well as people displaced by natural or environmental disasters, chemical or nuclear disasters, famine, or development projects. And while the European Commission provides for a more modern and comprehensive definition than the generally 'outdated' one provided by the 1951 Refugee Convention, it still falls short in connecting this definition to migration, asylum, and refugee policies within the European Union and its borders.

Though it would seem imperative for a discussion that focuses on 'migrants' and 'forced migrants' – refugees, asylum seekers, internally displaced persons, etc. – to reach a consensus on what each of these terms actually denotes, since the terms have come to be used in such a large number of intersectional contexts, disciplines, and legal frameworks, one comprehensive definition remains difficult to attain. And while legal, sociological, anthropological, and even historical definitions continue to develop and zero-in on these definitions, the international community, international conventions and treaties, and international agencies have yet to develop a definition vague enough or specific enough to serve the purpose of including each and every person involved in movement.

And so, the question persists: Do the variances in definitions indicate that we have simply not attained adequate definitions? Or can definitions from across contexts, disciplines, and legal frameworks differ without contradicting one another? As the definitions across the migration discourse develop and we continue to move closer in our understanding of the intersections, overlapping circumstances, and internal and external forces that govern these definitions, this book discusses a combination of various migratory contexts and their implications. This book provides a collection of pieces that serve to enrich the debate amid the evolution of definitions, our understanding of human movement, and, most importantly, our understanding of human rights, human dignity, and the human spirit.

References

European Commission. n.d. 'EMN Glossary Search: forced migrant'. https:// ec.europa.eu/home-affairs/what-we-do/networks/european_migration_ network/glossary_search/forced-migrant_en

IOM. 2019b. 'Glossary on Migration'. Geneva: International Organization for Migration.

IOM. 2019a. 'World Migration Report'. Annual Report, Geneva: International Organization for Migration.

Refugees International. 2020. 'COVID-19 and the Displaced: Addressing the Threat of the Novel Coronavirus in Humanitarian Emegencies'. Issue Brief, Report, Refugees International.

1

A Foucauldian Reading of the Global Compact for Migration: How 'The Migrant' is Represented and Rendered Governable

ANNA CLOSAS CASASAMPERA

This chapter first emerged in the midst of what was pervasively declared to be a 'migration crisis'. Exodus, drowning ships, desperate mass escapes, people storming the walls – from Venezuela to the United States to Algeria, passing through Myanmar and Bangladesh, people seemed to be overwhelmed by what they deemed to be a number of asylum applications they thought was too high. In the media, in political discourses, and in policy interventions, one could see this generalized concern about the burden of an excess influx of migration, which triggered pervading talks about fingerprinting, Frontex missions, wall-building, and exhausting migrant relocation. Through all these performances and enactments of emergency, migration arose again as a matter of risk, as a security concern. Responding to this *problematique*, or indeed problematization, the United Nations (UN) General Assembly passed in September 2016 the 'New York Declaration for Refugees and Migrants' as a declaration of political commitment to strengthening the international refugee and migrant protection system.

This chapter explores one of the documents that emerged from this declaration, namely the Global Compact for Migration (GCM). Understood together with the Global Compact on Refugees (GCR), this piece looks at what the GCM does, how it is framed, and how it fails, if it fails at all. As a way to approach the analysis, and drawing from literature that has revisited Michel

Foucault's notion of governmentality, it asks how migration is governed through the GCM. More accurately, it asks how 'the migrant' is represented and rendered governable. The task here is to unpack the ways whereby, through an unproblematized migration-development nexus, the GCM reproduces, or rather reinforces, two different categories – i.e., migrant and refugee– informing two ways of governing. This differentiation works to reproduce a hierarchy of lives between the refugee and the migrant, as well as between the regular and irregular migrant, normalizing such rigid distinctions.

After laying out the conceptual framework upon which this analysis is based, this chapter moves to disseminate how, in and through the GCM, 'irregularity' and 'the migrant' are (re)produced. Second, the chapter looks at what these processes of naming and labelling do, how representation works to order human mobilities through a myriad of techniques of government, and what forms of knowledge production these foster. Lastly, it discusses the state-centrism laying at the basis of this document to underline the seeming incapacity to conceptualize mobility beyond security and borders.

The aim of this chapter is not solely to point to the fact that such rigid distinctions, informing two different compacts, are not accurate to capture human mobilities and displacement. The goal is also not to criticize the efforts behind the GCM or to claim that cooperation is not needed. Rather, it attempts to render visible the power dynamics enabling this document as well as the forms and techniques of government it fosters – a set of processes informed by a framework, which fails to conceptualize mobility beyond migration and borders, and politics beyond citizenship. In doing so, this chapter hopes to hint a way in which public discourse can move beyond the narrative of risk that monopolizes the political space of contestation, in turn precluding discussions of solidarity, equality, or mobility, which are not mediated through citizenship, security, and (il)legality.

This analysis is relevant even after the European Commission declared this 'migration crisis' to be over (Rankin 2019). Beyond lockdown and mobility restrictions, the Covid-19 pandemic has left us with some dreadful images of pushbacks and increased levels of violence at the borders of countries such as Greece and Turkey. Hence, this global pandemic has brought the topic of human mobility/ies back to the forefront of the conversation. For that, the analysis of the documents, conferences, and declarations that govern the everydayness of human mobilities has not lost its relevance.

What is the Global Compact for Migration?

The Global Compact for Safe, Orderly and Regular Migration is an intergovernmental agreement that was formally adopted in a conference held in Morocco in December 2018. It was endorsed through a vote in which 152 countries voted in favor, five countries – the United States, Israel, the Czech Republic, Hungary, and Poland – voted against and 12 countries – Austria, Australia, and Libya among them –abstained.

Reaffirming the 'New York Declaration for Refugees and Migrants', the GCM describes itself as addressing international migration 'in all its dimensions' (GCM 2018, 2) and as a 'roadmap to prevent suffering and chaos' (UN News 2018). Clearly set out in the Preamble, the GCM rests on the principles of the United Nations Charter and the Declaration of Human Rights to establish a non-legally binding cooperative framework while upholding states' sovereignty over border control. That is, even though the goal was to reinforce the need for cooperation, dialogue, and consensus, there is a commanding state-centrism informing this document. Migration and borders remain a matter of the sovereign state.

The GCM also outlines the need to strengthen knowledge of migration as a way to advance policymaking. It argues for improving data collection and analysis systems, as well as registration and statistical collection processes, in order to achieve better evidence-based solutions. Hence, through this document, migration emerges as an object of knowledge, data, and graphs, and as a space to govern, a sphere within which one can intervene, reinforcing the nexus between government and knowledge, or indeed government through knowledge.

Conceptual Framework

The work of Michel Foucault has inspired a vast body of scholarship, giving rise to new research, sets of questions, and points of inquiry, among which we can highlight the emergence of so-called 'governmentality studies'. As a style of analysis, governmentality draws our attention to the techniques and knowledge that underpin attempts to shape the conduct of selves and others in diverse settings (Walters 2012, 30). Put differently, to govern is 'to structure the possible fields of action' through a complex ensemble of institutions, procedures, analyses and reflections, calculations, and tactics (Foucault 1982, 790). It designates 'the way in which the conduct of individuals or of groups might be directed' (Foucault 1982, 790). As such, it is inherently linked to the exercise of power – power as governmentality, or governmentality as the exercise of power. However, this is not an all-pervasive, one-way, only-destructive power. Understanding governmentality as a conduct of conduct, as the activity of (self)conducting an individual's behavior and relationality, sheds light on the immanent possibility of resistance or counter-conduct (Foucault 2009, 195), complicating the question of control.

More concretely, in the *Birth of Biopolitics*, Foucault describes the ways in which the word 'liberal' can be understood as a governing practice, as a set of techniques of government. To him, this liberal way of governing is not the respect or imperative for freedom. Differently, the liberal organizes and produces freedom, managing the conditions under which one can be free (Foucault 2010, 63–4). Yet, this management of freedom 'entails the establishment of limitations, controls, forms of coercion, and obligations relying on threats' (Foucault 2010, 63–4), namely, security. Hence, for Foucault, security is not merely a compensatory to freedom, not is it a value or a reality, but rather the way through which society is ordered and managed, and freedom is produced.

Applied to the field of migration, governmentality helps us understand the ways in which mobility has been managed and conducted, and the subtle and complex games involved in the 'biopolitics of otherness' (Fassin 2011, 214). As the anthropologist Dider Fassin has claimed, migration, located at the heart of the three pillars of governmentality – i.e., economy, police, and humanitarianism – is deeply implicated in the construction of borders and boundaries of sovereignty and identity/ies (Fassin 2011, 221). Similarly, the sociologist Didier Bigo has tried to illuminate the reasons behind the ever-present framing of migration as a security issue, related to crime, (un) employment, and integration. The state-centric metaphor of the 'body politic', embedded in the myth of national sovereignty, creates the image of 'immigration associated with an outsider coming inside' together with the presupposition that it is possible to control the flow of individuals at the state borders (Bigo 2002, 67).

The GCM (2018, 2) conceptualizes migration both as a problem that 'undeniably affects our countries and communities' in unpredictable ways and as a 'source of prosperity, innovation, and sustainable development' that can be optimized and therefore governed. Hence, Foucault's liberal art of governing, together with some of its contemporary mobilizations, provides a powerful tool to inquire into the ways in which migration becomes an object of government, emerging at once as a problem and a source of prosperity.

Governing through Representation: 'Migrants' and 'Refugees'

To be governed, one must be represented as governable. As a starting point, this compact for migrants, not refugees, normalizes the already rigid distinction used by administrations and border controls to regulate, disseminate, and differentiate between the desirable and undesirable, between the refugee, carrying a 'forced-to' sense of helplessness and inevitability, and the migrant, carrying a sense of voluntarism. Furthermore, this document reproduces the binary between the regular and irregular migrant, a binary loaded with moral assumptions of worth and even criminality and lawlessness.

As we can read from the title, and repeated over 20 times throughout 34 pages, this is a compact for *safe, orderly, and regular* migration. Using the framework provided by literature on governmentality, this section unpacks the logics of representation framing the GCM that reproduce migration as an international, or indeed transnational, problem to be managed. It tries to disseminate how 'the migrant' is re-produced vis-à-vis 'the refugee' and how 'irregularity' re-emerges with a strong moral connotation, as something bad that needs to be prevented. Altogether, what 'migrants' are, or indeed how they are represented, informs the way one should respond to them and their claims for protection, bringing to the foreground the politics that come with the naming.

From the outset, one finds in this document a commitment to manage the problem posed by refugees and migrants through two separate processes. In other words, while recognizing that 'migrants and refugees may face many common challenges and similar vulnerabilities' and 'are entitled to the same universal human rights', they 'are distinct groups governed by separate legal frameworks', and 'only refugees are entitled to the specific international protection' (GCM 2018, 2). The exercise of this labelling power creates a need for the to-be-migrant/refugee to conform to these two framed-elsewhere categories of being as if they were real, already-there forms of subjectivity. In turn, this classification of types of mobility is employed as a form of intervention for either humanitarian or security purposes, or indeed both at once, and so must be understood within 'the proliferation of dematerialized spatial and moral borders' (Mai 2014, 175).

Such a rigid distinction forecloses the ambivalence and ambiguity, and more generally the epistemic crisis, around the very labels by which various forms of mobility are presumed to be knowable as governmental contrivances (De Genova 2017a, 8). Consequently, such nuances as the 'migrant-ization of refugees' (Garelli and Tazzioli 2017, 170), the structural violence that might constitute the root cause for displacement for 'mere economic migrants' (De Genova 2017a, 9), and more generally the ways in which these categories are lived-in, claimed and/or resisted are left unframable.

Differently, and as if the UN were a fully-fledged humanitarian actor, bound by the principles of humanity, neutrality and independence, the GCR (2018, 1–2) defines itself as 'entirely non-political in nature'. This claim reflects a seeming obliviousness of the politics of labelling, of what this naming does, or allows. Beyond that, this is a claim that does not appear in the GCM, as if you could be political with migrants. What is more, the GCR employs more strongly and widely the vocabulary of vulnerability and protection, accompanied with claims for further and distinct support (GCR 2018, 15). Altogether, these compacts reinforce 'the migrant' vis-à-vis 'the refugee' as subjects and objects of government through a suggested variety of policy plans allowing for constant monitoring of mobility routes and diaspora communities. In doing that, they work to sort and rank mobilities and claims of protection, which translate into who gets to make what claims and how valid they are (De Genova 2017a, 8).

Moreover, in the employment of the lexicon of (ir)regularity, the GCM participates in the reproduction of the legal/illegal binary, which in turns constructs 'irregularity' as something that, because of its negative impact, needs to be prevented (De Genova 2017a, 3). Even if it purposely avoids the term 'illegal' and repeatedly states the importance of eliminating discrimination, by reinforcing the regular/irregular binary and referring it to the receiving country – which will juridically determine this (ir)regularity – the illegality of the irregular migrant unavoidably emerges (GCM 2018, 4). Preoccupied with 'identity fraud and document forgery' (GCM 2018, 11), the GCM perpetuates such discrimination and forecloses a reading of the ways in which (ir)regularity is produced through already existing and institutionalized racial and colonial dynamics (see Andersson 2014; De Genova 2004, 2017a, 2017b; or Mc Cluskey 2018). This production is apparent in sections that read certain spaces in need of special attention as 'geographic areas from where *irregular migration* systematically originates' (GCM 2018, 17). Hence, the irregular migrant arises, in the base of its risky/at risk condition (see Aradau 2013), as a non-desired subject.

Governing through Representation: A Human Rights Approach

The employment of governmentality as a position of inquiry illuminates the ways in which movement and displacement, successfully framed as risk, are governed. It also underlines what security does, and how the imaginary promise of a knowable future is 'subtended by practices in the present that represent problems', or migration as a problem, 'in order to intervene and manage them, act upon subjects, and attempt to conduct their actions in view of the projected future' (Aradau 2008, 6). Following Foucault (2009, 20), the specific sphere of security then refers to a series of potentialities, 'to the temporal and the uncertain, which have to be inserted within a given space'. In this light, security emerges as the art of governing and ordering the uncertain.

In a more contemporary reading of this liberal art of government, and under the term 'liberal cosmopolitanism of government', Vivienne Jabri (2013, 3) captured the latter's claims to a critical and emancipatory agenda in which 'theory and practice meet in advocacies around international law and its transnational reformulations of human rights'. This mode of governance operates through a liberal understanding of solidarity and, in the name of peace and human security, permeates the social through pedagogic and developmental practices of policing. Through this cosmopolitan imperative to bring law 'into force with every instance of intervention to uphold rights in the name of humanity' (Jabri 2013, 117), this 'humanity' arises as a location of legal and political structure, a sphere of intervention. This is the case with the GCM, which undertakes humanity within its purview of operations, trans- forming mobility into a global procedural problem in need of management and resolution. Yet, this *a priori* benevolent definition of solidarity is based on a twofold understanding of humanity, reinforcing a hierarchy of lives separating those who have the legitimacy and the means to save from those in need to be saved.

The GCM brings forward this hierarchy between the agents of change and those who must be changed, managed, or governed. In the name of human rights and cosmopolitan law, the former (self-)proclaims its authority to intervene over the latter. As previously stated, even if the GCM is concerned with fighting discrimination and racism, there are some instances that reproduce spatial hierarchies by labelling some zones as problematic or 'deteriorating' (GCM 2018, 8). Additionally, by unproblematically referring migration to development, and the GCM to the 2030 Agenda for Sustainable Development, it fills up the deceptive generality and emptiness of 'the receiving countries' – 'making us all countries of origin, transit and destination' (GCM 2018, 2) – with those appearing as recipients of development and risk- reduction programs in the 2030 Agenda.

In Jabri's work, one also finds claims of liberal cosmopolitanism's complicit participation in the reproduction of already institutionalized forms of domination, such as neoliberal markets. These claims help us recognize the depoliticizing reading of migration found in the GCM as something, which, following the neoliberal logic of demand and supply, serves the market needs. That is, it claims that migration needs to be governed in ways 'reflecting demographic and labor market realities' (GCM 2018, 11), 'in accordance with national priorities, national labor market demands, and skills supply' (GCM 2018, 23) to 'ensure market responsive contractual labor mobility through regular pathways' (GCM 2018, 12).

Additionally, reading the GCM through these conceptual remarks reveals that the document's goal is not to stop mobility, quite the opposite. In line with Foucault's (2010, 28) claim of liberalism being 'the art of the least possible government', the compact aims to facilitate migration by 'offering accelerated and facilitated visa and permit processing' (GCM 2018, 12) and 'flexible modalities to travel, work, and invest with minimal administrative burdens' (GCM 2018, 27). Informed by a language of resilience, autonomy, and emancipation, the GCM is not about direct, bodily intervention, but self-regulation. Simply put, the aim is not to block mobility, but to manage, accelerate, and flexibilize it. Yet, for this acceleration to happen, some forms of movement need to be deemed undesirable, irregular, and therefore to be stopped. That is to say, the GCM encourages speed and derogation of bureaucratic procedures for some, while keeping others in place through development programs and policies, alternatively named 'deterrence' (see Andersson 2014 and Brown 2010).

Lastly, reading the GCM through governmentality brings to the foreground the forms of knowledge production it pretends to foster. The GCM (2018, 4–5, 9–10, 14–15) aims to promote a pervasive knowledge economy, which reifies not only the migrant but also the route, or indeed 'all stages of the migration cycle' as data variables. Parallelly, this knowledge production involves everyone, from consulates, diaspora communities, and academia, to the private sector, trade unions, and the media (GCM 2018, 5). The data gaps, the unregistered and more broadly the unknown, and so the future, become a problem. Hence, through advanced techniques of knowledge production, the future must be rendered predictable or governable (Ansems de Vries 2013; Bigo 2014) in order to 'monitor and anticipate the development of risks and threats that might trigger or affect migration movements' and develop evidence-based policies (GCM 2018, 8).

The GCM as a Question of National Sovereignty

As a final remark, this paper underlines the state-centrism informing this compact and the ways in which it is supposed to be implemented. In the 'Implementation' and 'Follow-up and Review' sections, one finds a lot of 'we invite', 'we allow', and 'we encourage' formulations. The word 'voluntary' is also abundant. That is, it states that the financial and human resources in charge of applying the points of this compact are a mere invitation or encouragement to voluntarily elaborate a 'national implementation plan' (GCM 2018, 34).

Yet what, to this analysis, looks like a state-centric document is also regarded as derogating the sovereignty of a country over its borders. Especially on the political right, some received this compact with outrage, believing that it would 'encourage more illegal migration' and work to erode national sovereignty over the states' territory (Goodman 2018). Consequently, five countries – the United States, Israel, the Czech Republic, Hungary, and Poland – did not ratify it. Hungary's Minister for Foreign Affairs and Trade, Péter Szijjártó, declared that the General Assembly was committing a serious mistake by endorsing 'this unbalanced, biased and pro-migration document' (United Nations, Meetings Coverage and Press Releases, 19 December 2018). Migration is 'a dangerous phenomenon', he stressed, and endorsing this document could 'prompt new migratory movements, which in turn would put transit and destination countries at risk' (United Nations, Meetings Coverage and Press Releases, 19 December 2018). In a not too different line, the United States' representative said that his government could not endorse the compact because 'decisions about how to secure its borders and whom to admit for legal residency or to grant citizenship are among the most important sovereign decisions a State can make and are not subject to negotiation or review' (United Nations, Meetings Coverage and Press Releases, 19 December 2018).

Having said that, the fact that the GCM is not legally binding raised opposing concerns among non-governmental organizations and human rights advocates who feared that countries would never fully implement the measures detailed in the document. However, the issue with state-centrism, which this chapter raises, goes beyond the impossibility to fully implement a compact that can only be encouraged. Differently, this paper brings to the foreground the incapacity to conceptualize mobility beyond migration and borders, and politics beyond the categories of 'citizenship', 'refugee', and '(ir)regular migrant', the impossibility to think about mobility beyond the framework of the sovereign state. The GCM remains a question of national sovereignty.

Conclusion

Overall, this chapter does not pretend to be an exhaustive analysis of the GCM, but an attempt to use governmentality to underline the power dynamics disguised by the human rights discourse of protection. It wants to problematize the assumed neutrality of the process of naming and bring to the foreground the political agenda behind labelling and the use of categories such as 'migrant' or 'refugee', which the compact assumes to be state-dependent. In other words, through the GCM, the state emerges as legitimate to make claims about who gets to be named what and how.

Using both Foucault and contemporary scholarship that finds in his work a productive point of inquiry, this chapter unpacks the ways in which, in the GCM, migration re-emerges as a problem to be managed. By understanding liberal governance as an effort to make reality knowable, or to make reality visible as knowledge (Ansems de Vries 2013), it sheds some light on the practices of government the GCM legitimizes and the hierarchies of life it perpetuates. It is worth clarifying that, by having two sections – one focused on techniques of representation and another on practices of governing – this chapter does not suggest that one can understand them separately. Contrarily, and as it tries to show, logics of representation inform techniques of government and vice versa.

Lastly, this chapter also acknowledges that its concern with state-centrism is by no means accepted by all. As mentioned above, some, especially on the right, received the compact with outrage or simply refused to ratify it, stating that it would 'encourage more illegal migration' and erode national sovereignty over states' territory and borders (see Goodman 2018 and Rieffel 2018). Yet, this research is driven by a personal conviction that employing governmentality can provide productive insights into the conditions of possibility of this document and the state-centric power dynamics behind it. In other words, it tries to argue that understanding security in its larger function of ordering the social illuminates the exceptionality surrounding human mobilities. More generally, doing so can help challenge the pervasiveness of concepts and terminology such as 'border', 'citizenship', or 'irregularity' that still clog and exhaust the debate on human mobilities.

References

Andersson, Ruben. 2014. *Illegality, Inc. Clandestine Migration and the Business of Bordering Europe.* University of California Press.

Ansems de Vries, Leonie. 2013. 'Political Life beyond the Biopolitical?', *Theoria,* Vol. 60, No. 134, 50–68.

Aradau, Claudia. 2008. *Rethinking Trafficking in Women: Politics Out of Security.* London: Palgrave Macmillan UK Ltd.

Bigo, Didier. 2002. 'Security and Immigration: Toward a Critique of the Governmentality of Unease', *Alternatives,* 27, 63–92.

Bigo, Didier. 2014. 'The (in)securitization practices of the three universes of EU border control: Military/Navy – border guards/police – database analysts', *Security Dialogue,* 209–225.

Brown, Wendy. 2010. *Walled States, Waning Sovereignty.* New York City: Zone Books.

De Genova, Nicholas . (ed.). 2017a. *The Borders of 'Europe': Autonomy of Migration, Tactics of Bordering.* London: Duke University Press.

De Genova, Nicholas. 2017b. 'Anonymous Brown Bodies: The Productive Power of a Deadly Border'. *Presented to the Global Migration Working Group.* Chicago: University of Illinois.

De Genova, Nicholas. 2004. 'The Legal Production of Mexican/Migrant "Illegality"', *Latino Studies,* 160–185.

Fassin, Didier. 2011. 'Policing Borders, Producing Boundaries. The Governmentality of Immigration in Dark Times', *Annual Review of Anthropology,* 213–226.

Foucault, Michel. 2009. *Security, Territory, Population.* New York City: Palgrave Macmillan.

—. 2010. *The Birth of Biopolitics.* New York City: Palgrave Macmillan.

Foucault, Michel. 1982. 'The Subject and Power', *Critical Inquiry,* 777–795.

Garelli, Glenda, and Martina Tazzioli. 2017. 'Choucha beyond the Camp: Challenging the Border of Migration Studies', in *The Borders of "Europe": Autonomy of Migration, Tactics of Bordering*, by Nicholas De Genova, 165–184. London: Duke University Press.

Goodman, Jack. 2018. *BBC News: What's the UN Global compact on migration?* https://www.bbc.co.uk/news/world-46607015

Jabri, Vivienne. 2013. *The Postcolonial Subject: Claiming Politics/Governing Others in Late Modernity.* New York City: Routledge.

Mai, Nicola. 2004. 'Between Embodied Cosmopolitism and Sexual Humanitarianism: the fractal mobilities and subjectivities of migrants working in the sex industry', in *Borders, Mobilities and Migrations, Perspectives from the Mediterranean in the 21st Century*, edited by Anteby-Yemini, Virginie Baby-Collin and Sylvie Mazzella, 175–192. Brussels: Peter Lang.

McCluskey, Emma. 2018. 'Freedom, Technology and Surveillance: Everyday Paradoxes on the EU- Morocco Border'. *Presented at the European International Studies Association.* Prague.

Rankin, Jennifer. 2019. *The Guardian: EU declares migration crisis over as it hits out at 'fake news'.* March 6. https://www.theguardian.com/world/2019/mar/06/eu-declares-migration-crisis-over-hits-out-fake-news-european-commission

Rieffel, Lex. 2018. *The Global Compact on Migration: Dead on arrival?`.* December 12. https://www.brookings.edu/blog/up-front/2018/12/12/the-global-compact-on-migration-dead-on-arrival/

Torpey, John. 2000. *The Invention of the Passport: Surveillance, Citizenship, and the State.* Cambridge: Cambridge University Press.

UN News. 2018. *UN News: General Assembly officially adopts roadmap for migrants to improve safety, ease suffering.* December 19. https://news.un.org/en/story/2018/12/1028941

UNHCR. 2018. *Part II: Global compact on refugees.* New York City: United Nations.

United Nations, General Assembly. 2018. 'Global Compact for Safe, Orderly and Regular Migration'. *United Nations Web site: Refugees and Migrants.* July 13. https://refugeesmigrants.un.org/sites/default/files/180713_agreed_outcome_global_compact_for_migration.pdf

United Nations, Meetings Coverage and Press Releases. 2018. 'General Assembly Endorses First-Ever Global Compact on Migration, Urging Cooperation among Member States in Protecting Migrants'. https://www.un.org/press/en/2018/ga12113.doc.htm

Walters, William. 2012. *Governmentality: Critical encounters.* London: Routledge.

2

The Compliance of Argentina's Migration Law with Fundamental Human Rights Discourse and Principles

SABRINA ANDREA AVIGLIANO

The Argentinian Republic is, at its core, a country of migrants. The last decades of the 19th century were marked by a period described as the Alluvial Era, in which important contingents of European people began to arrive at the port of Buenos Aires motivated by the war and economic and social chaos. So why did they choose a country in the southernmost tip of South America, and across the Atlantic Ocean? Probably because of the lenient migration policies enacted by the state that encouraged the entry of foreigners. The 1853 Constitution had granted protection to aliens and extended them the same civil rights as nationals. It also encouraged European immigration under the pretense that European characteristics were convenient and desired for the rising nation. The Immigration and Colonization Law (commonly known as Avellaneda Law) was passed in 1876. It promoted the reception of foreign farmers as settlers on lands contributed by the state. It is no surprise then that, by 1889, about 261,000 immigrants had entered the Argentinian Republic, and that the capital city harbored 100,000 foreigners out of a total population of 214,000 (Romero 1951, V). As a result, this first wave of immigration changed the social structure of the country, leading to the construction of a national identity that merged diverse customs and traditions. According to the results of the census in 1914, a third of the country's inhabitants were foreigners. World War I eventually interrupted the massive European migratory flow and, since then, migratory currents have come mostly from neighboring Latin American countries and, to a lesser extent, Eastern Europe, Asia, and Africa (Modolo 2016, 208).

Between 1976 and 1983, Argentina lived through a military dictatorship. Migration policies became regressive – as evidenced by the 1981 General Law on Migration and Immigration Promotion (also known as Videla Law). It contained clauses that affected constitutional rights and guarantees, such as the power to detain people and expel them without legal or judicial control over the administrative decision of the immigration authority. It also contained clauses outlining the obligation of all public officials and of people in general to denounce the presence of irregular immigrants and restrictions on the rights to health and education, among other restrictions. It took 21 years – even long after democratic order had been restored – for the Congress to approve a new migration law.

The Sanction of the National Migration Law No. 25.871

Under President Kirchner's center-left administration, there was a change in legislation when the Migration Law No. 25.871 was developed at the beginning of 2004. This implied a paradigm shift at the national level, as it complied with the international commitments assumed by the Argentinian Republic regarding human rights, mobility, and integration of aliens into society. The law defines a migrant as 'any foreigner who wishes to enter, transit, reside or settle permanently, temporarily, or incidentally in the country' (Article 2, Law No. 25.871). It expressly establishes the fundamental right to migration, determining that the 'right to migration is essential and inalienable for the person and the Argentinian Republic guarantees it on the basis of the principles of equality and universality' (Article 4, Law No. 25.871). Its primary focus is on the migrant as a subject of rights. Therefore, it acknowledges equal rights and treatment for both nationals and foreigners, as well a series of actions that facilitate admission, income, stay, and their access to basic social services in health, education, justice, work, employment, and social security. This is granted regardless of the person's immigration status, making the application of the principle of non-discrimination based on any criteria indisputable (Articles 6 to 13, Law No. 25.871). One of the general principles guiding the law is to 'promote the labor integration of immigrants residing legally for the best use of their personal and work capacities to contribute to the economic and social development of the country' (Article 3, subsection H, Law No. 25.871). Other obligations are outlined in Article 17 of the law, which foresees that the state will provide 'whatever is necessary' to adopt and implement measures aimed to facilitate the regularization of foreigners' immigration status.

There is no recognition at the international level of a person's right to settle in a country of their choice, other than that of their nationality. At most, the rules provide for freedom of movement, which does not necessarily imply the right to choose the place of residence. For this reason, according to Hines (2012, 309–310), the Migration Law represents 'a great step forward in the rights of immigrants, not only for Argentina, but worldwide,' both for repealing a restrictive law – the previously mentioned Videla Law – and for declaring migration as a human right. Because migration is now held as a human right, then all human rights principles such as non-discrimination, *pro homine*, reasonableness, non-regressivity, and others, apply to the right to migration.

The body in charge of applying migration policy throughout the Argentinian Republic has been the National Migration Directory. It was created in 1949 and falls under the executive branch. It has the aptitude and jurisdiction to act in the admission and granting of residents, to establish new delegations all across the country, to control the entry and exit of people to the country, and to exercise control over permanent residents in the entire territory of the Republic (Article 107, Law No. 25.871). It also has the authority to intervene whenever the Migration Law is violated. Upon detecting a foreigner with an irregular immigration status, the immigration authority can decide to expel or deport them – a measure that is generally accompanied by a temporary or permanent prohibition of re-entry to the country.

This regulates the administrative procedures regarding the admission, permanent residence, and expulsion of foreigners and incorporates reinforced guarantees for the judicial review of the decisions of the immigration authority. Consequently, it provides for a system of both administrative and judicial appeals when the admission or residence of a foreigner is denied; the authorization of permanent, temporary, or transitory residence is canceled; a foreigner is ordered to leave the country, her expulsion is decreed or the application of fines and sureties, or her execution is resolved (Article 79, Law No. 25.871). About restrictions or impediments to entering the country, the rule determines causes linked mainly to criminal matters and administrative irregularities at the moment of entering the territory (Article 29, Law No. 25.871).

Although it is the power of the state's authorities to establish mechanisms to control the entry into and departure from its territory in relation to individuals who are not nationals, these devices must be compatible with the human rights protections to which the state has committed itself. As such, it is evident that foreigners are unaware of the country's legal system and are in an aggravated situation of vulnerability, which is why the Inter-American Court of Human Rights (IACHR), in the case of Velez Loor v. Panama, acknowledged that the states have to guarantee individuals' effective access to justice, regardless of their immigration status, and must provide legal counsel to satisfy the requirements of procedural representation. It also acknowledged that the accused is to be advised about the possibility of other remedies against acts that affect individual rights. This obligation was materialized in Article 86 (ACHR, 2021) that read:

> Foreigners who are in national territory and who lack economic means will have the right to free legal assistance in those administrative and judicial procedures that may lead to the denial of entry, return to their country of origin or expulsion of the Argentine territory. They will also have the right to the assistance of an interpreter if they do not understand or speak the official language. The regulations to the present, that in its case are dictated, must protect the exercise of the Constitutional Right of defense.

For that reason, in all cases where a migrant makes a written objection at the time of being notified of the expulsion order, the National Migration Directory must give immediate intervention to the Public Ministry of Defense, ordering the suspension of any procedure and of the current deadlines in the administrative actions, until the Ministry becomes involved or the interested party receives the legal assistance necessary to safeguard their interests.

Another aspect of the law is that it incorporates as a standard of residence, the relation to an Argentinian relative or another permanent resident (Article 22, Law No. 25.871). As well as the traditional filing factors, such as work, study, and medical treatment, the Migration Law recognizes Argentina's commitment with the Southern Common Market (MERCOSUR) in order to harmonize the legislation to achieve the strengthening of the integration process by allowing as criteria the residence by nationality of MERCOSUR country or associated countries (Article 23, subsection I, Law No. 25.871). This is so anyone in the region can establish residence in Argentina for that fact alone. This has constituted an important step towards the free movement of people in the region, as they are permitted to exercise their labor rights on equal terms with nationals. It additionally generates an increasing commitment to mutual cooperation between the states that are part of MERCOSUR.

Family constitutes an important aspect of the Migration Law, as does the objective to 'guarantee the exercise of the right to family reunification' (Article 3, subsection D, Law No. 25.871). Argentinian Law additionally ensures that 'the State shall guarantee the right to family reunification of immigrants with their parents, spouses, minor unmarried children, or older children with different abilities' (Article 10, Law 25.871). The National Migration Directory may waive entry impediments because of family unity or humanitarian reasons (Article 29 and 62 in fine, Law No. 25.871). This means it is possible to annul an expulsion order when the existence of a family with strong emotional ties is verified, as it is considered that this protected asset is superior to the crime committed or administrative infraction that originated the expulsion proceedings.

In light of all this, there is no doubt that the Migration Law lies at the forefront of respect for the human rights of migrants and reflects the open-door policy enshrined in the Argentine Constitution.

Modifications Introduced by Decree of Need and Urgency No. 70/2017

After more than a decade of the center-left administration of the Kirchners, in December 2015, a liberal conservative government with a center-right ideology led by Mauricio Macri assumed the presidency. In 2017, the executive branch issued the Decree of Need and Urgency No. 70/2017 (DNU), which modified several aspects of Law No. 25.871, on the basis of alleged increase in crime at the hands of foreigners. The law highlights that 'the population of people of foreign nationality in the custody of the Penitentiary Service has increased in recent years until reaching 21.35% of the total prison population in 2016'. Currently, foreigners represent only 4.5 percent of the population of Argentina. Nevertheless, when analyzing exclusively the total number of people arrested for drug trafficking, the number of foreigners rises to 33 percent (Recital No. 15 and 16, DNU No. 70/2017). This reasoning clearly associates migration to delinquency and reinforces the thought that migrants are dangerous and a threat to nationals. Therefore, the proposed solution is to deport them at a more rapid pace. This approach holds all people who come from other countries under permanent suspicion even after formalizing their immigration status.

The DNU affirms that each state has 'the sovereign prerogative to decide the criteria for the admission and expulsion of non-nationals' (Recital No. 8, DNU No. 70/2017). In this regard, it says that this capacity is currently hindered by the duration of the administrative and judicial processes that could 'reach seven years of processing' to expel someone from the country (Recital No. 13, DNU No. 70/2017). Instead of detecting the bureaucratic obstacles or other hassles that could have caused these delays, it was decided to modify the expulsion procedure, reducing the time limits and the instances of appeal, imposing more requirements to access to free public aid, and restricting the application of exemptions from expulsion orders, among other changes.

Even if there were an actual need to reform the Migration Law, no justifiable reason can be invoked to resort to the use of such special mechanisms as the DNU, especially when the decree is much more restrictive, overriding human and fundamental rights of migrants, which makes the state capable of generating international responsibility. The fact that the executive branch issued a decree that modified the procedure created by a law and produced another, vastly different procedure, invades the powers and competencies of the legislative branch and constitutes a serious violation of the division of powers and the republican principle of government as stated by the Constitution.

As previously mentioned, the most critical aspects of the DNU are related to the setbacks in terms of guarantees of due process, access to justice, and access to regular immigration. On the subject of these guarantees, the American Convention on Human Rights provides in Article 8 that:

> Everyone has the right to be heard, with due guarantees and within a reasonable time, by a judge or competent, independent and impartial court, previously defined by law, in the substantiation of any criminal accusation made against it, or for the determination of its rights and obligations of a civil, labor, fiscal or any other nature.

In addition, Article 25 of the same instrument states that

> Everyone has the right to a simple and quick recourse or to any other effective recourse before the competent judges or courts, which protects them against acts that violate their fundamental rights recognized by the Constitution, the law or this Convention, even when such violation is committed by persons acting in the exercise of their official functions.

Inter-American jurisprudence has been emphatic in stating that immigration procedures must be developed in accordance with the guarantees of due process, regardless of whether they apply to regular or irregular migrants. Therefore, any judicial or administrative procedure that may affect a person's rights must be followed in such a way that people have the necessary means and can adequately defend themselves from any act emanating from the state (Case of the Constitutional Court v. Peru, 69).

However, the summary procedure originated by the DNU implies a unilateral alteration of the rules of the game and means a substantial reduction in the procedural deadlines – from 30 days to three business days for the event of filing of appeals – which significantly damages the person who must exercise his defense in such a meager time, and in practice, makes it impossible for the migrant to have his right to be heard, to offer and produce all the evidence that he needs, and that in general implies an impairment of the right to defense in court. To that effect, the DNU states that rights and guarantees of migrants are recognized, but the deadlines that are imposed turn them into a clear illusion and make it extremely difficult to comply with them. The requirements contained in the norm invalidate any defense instrument that the migrant seeks to use, which implies a substantial limitation on the right of defense. The increase in expulsion orders and the short appeal period have reduced the possibilities of providing an effective and efficient service from public defense offices and private legal assistance. On that subject, the DNU exclusively admits the right to free legal aid to those foreigners who expressly request it and, at the same time, accompany supporting documentation that proves their lack of financial resources. If these requirements are not met, the procedure will continue without the migrant having legal representation during the expulsion process, which not only includes the exit from the territory, but also the establishment of a re-entry ban that may be permanent (Article 86 Law No. 25.871, modified by DNU 70/17).

Additionally, the decree interferes with the orbit of the judiciary by setting up deadlines within the issue must be resolved. Regarding judicial control, the exemption of expulsion for reasons of family unity and humanitarian reasons is limited to a small group of impediments and cannot be subject to judicial review, as it is the exclusive and discretionary power of the National Migration Directory (Articles 29, 62 and 63 Law No. 25.871, modified by DNU 70/17).

In this manner, the impediment to the judiciary of reviewing and granting the dispensation for reasons of family unity undermines both the rights of the person subjected to the expulsion process, their family, and their children in particular. The right to family life constitutes a limit on the power of the state to determine its immigration policy and to define the requirements for entry, stay, and expulsion of non-nationals from their territory as it is displayed in Article 17 of the American Convention on Human Rights, as well as in Article VI of the American Declaration of the Rights and Duties of Man, both of which articulate the right to protection of the family, recognizing that the family is the natural and fundamental unit of society and must be protected. This does not imply that the state cannot exercise its power to expel a non-national resident based on a legitimate interest, but that this capacity must be balanced in light of the due consideration of deportation procedures in relation to the family connections of the deportee and the hardships that deportation can cause to all its members (UN Human Rights Committee, Stewart v. Canada, 12.10).

Another matter of concern is that the DNU allows the expulsion order to be issued in the mere beginning of the migrant's criminal process. That is to say, before a judicial verdict that indicates the commission of the act and its responsibility. This violates the principle of innocence (Article 8.2 of the

CADH) as it equates criminal record to 'any firm indictment, closure of the investigation, preparatory or comparable procedural act' (Article 29 Law No. 25.871, modified by DNU 70/17) without the need for the person to have a final judgment. The modification also broadens the range of crimes as a cause for expulsion to include infractions, misdemeanors, and minor felonies, such as manslaughter and other negligent crimes.

The administrative authority may request a judge to order the retention of the alien until their expulsion from the country can be materialized. Given that the retention, whether preventive or executive, implies an affectation of the physical freedom of the foreigner, in all cases the previous judicial order is necessary to be issued. Regarding preventive retention, it is provided that 'recursive actions or processes will suspend the counting of the retention period until its final resolution' (Article 70 Law No. 25.871, modified by DNU 70/17). Consequently, the deprivation of liberty of the migrant, which should have the sole purpose of making the expulsion order effective, becomes in practice an arbitrary detention due to the long duration of these procedures.

Under these new rules, the Committee Against Torture (CAT) has expressed concern about the sanction of the DNU and has urged the state to 'repeal or amend the provisions of the Decree of Necessity and Urgency No. 70/2017 so that people subject to expulsion can have enough time to appeal it at the administrative and judicial level and have access to immediate free legal assistance during the expulsion process in all instances' (CAT 2017, 34b) and 'ensure that immigration legislation and regulations only resort to the detention for immigration reasons only as a measure of last resort... for the shortest possible period of time' (CAT 2017, 34c). On the whole, the DNU has implemented changes in the Migration Law that resulted in a generalized obstacle to access to justice for migrants and despite the objections of international entities, social organizations, and members of the current government, it continues to be in force as of today.

Concluding Reflections

The 2010 census showed that 4.5 per cent of the inhabitants of Argentina were foreigners: 1,471,399 come from neighboring countries plus Peru; 299,394 were born in Europe; 31,001 in Asia; 2,738 in Africa; and 1,425 in Oceania (INDEC 2010). That is to say, Argentina's history as a nation has been shaped by migration flows and cannot be understood separately from migration.

By and large, most public policies in Argentina change according to who is in government at any given moment. Immigration policy is no exception. Initially conceived as an instrument to populate the territory and build a concept of the nation with European overtones, it was restricted during the last civic-military dictatorship. Despite the return of democracy in 1983, it was not until 2004 that the Migration Law was developed and enacted. It recognized migration as a human right. Moreover, it implemented more flexible requirements to access residences, especially for those foreigners from MERCOSUR, as well as the impediments to income and permanent residence. The powers of the National Migration Directory regarding the retention and expulsion of migrants were defined. Lastly, it established that judicial control of the expulsion order was to be exercised by the Federal Administrative Litigation jurisdiction and the Federal Justice based in the provinces, until the specific Immigration Court was created (Article 98, Law No. 25.871 original version), which obviously has never happened to date.

However, immigration policy became regressive again when former President Macri issued the DNU, which modified the aforementioned Migration Law. Although the Migration Law had been considered a role model across the world, through an exceptional executive order, various aspects of a regulation emitted by the National Congress were amended on the basis of an alleged wave of crime caused by non-nationals (Recital No. 13, 15 and 16, DNU No. 70/2017). The DNU presents a substantial reduction in guarantees of the rights of migrants. Among other measures, the conditions and requirements for entry and permanent residence in the country were limited, the possibility of judicial control of the measures taken by this public body were reduced, access to free legal aid was hampered, and an immigration regularization process was created that excessively delayed and bureaucratized the obtaining of Argentine documentation. Finally, it also produced a special summary procedure for the expulsion of foreigners which, as already explained, clearly violates the principles and guarantees enshrined in human rights instruments, such as the guarantees of due process, the principle of family reunification, and the best interests of the child, and it 'allows the possibility of holding a person in detention throughout this summary expulsion procedure regardless of the fact that no one may be deprived of liberty on grounds of immigration status' (Committee 2019, 10e). The establishment of the summary procedure not only implies the material impossibility of preparing an adequate defense, but also prevents access to free legal assistance, since the procedure and the resources become illusory.

For the aforementioned reasons, it is clear that this decree places the migrant in a situation of complete defenselessness and vulnerability in the face of the punitive state power. That is exactly why the Committee for the Protection of the Rights of All Migrant Workers and their Families (2019, 11) urged Argentine authorities to 'take immediate steps to have Decree No. 70/2017 repealed by the relevant body and, pending the completion of this process, to suspend its implementation.'

The center-left administration returned to power in 2019 under the leadership of Alberto Fernández, with Cristina Fernández de Kirchner as vice president. The abolishment of Decree 70/2017 finally occurred in March 2021 through Decree No. 138/2021 which restored the validity of Law No. 25.871 in its original wording. However, it did not determine what would happen with cases effectively executed during this time span or the ones that are still pending. As a result, the migration process will now again last years, violating the reasonable time period guarantee and bringing uncertainty to foreigners while they wait for a final decision on their immigration status. Therefore, it is relevant to notice that additional modifications are needed to be made about migration policy as a whole, and specifically regarding the mobility of children and adolescents – which will be effectively respectful of the commitments assumed by the Argentine state in order to prevent incurring international responsibility.

References

Inter-American Court of Human Rights . 2010. 'CASE OF VÉLEZ LOOR V. PANAMA. Preliminary Objections, Merits, Reparations, and Costs'. November 23. https://www.refworld.org/cgi-bin/texis/vtx/rwmain/opendocpdf. pdf?reldoc=y&docid=4d9accbb2

Comité contra la Tortura CAT. 2017. 'Observaciones finales sobre el quinto y sexto informe conjunto periódico de Argentina'. May 10. https://tbinternet. ohchr.org/Treaties/CAT/Shared%20Documents/ARG/INT_CAT_COC_ ARG_27464_S.pdf

Hines, Barbara. 2012. 'El derecho a migrar como un derecho humano: La actual ley inmigratoria Argentina'. *Revista Derecho Publico.*

Instituto Nacional De Estadísticas y Censos . 2010. *Migrations.* Accessed August 16, 2020. https://www.indec.gob.ar/indec/web/Nivel4-Tema-2-18-78

Inter-American Court of Human Rights . 2001. 'Case of the Constitutional Court v. Peru. Merits, Reparations and Costs'. November 31. https://iachr.lls. edu/sites/default/files/iachr/Court_and_Commission_Documents/ Constitutional%20Court%20v.%20Peru.Merits.01.31.01.pdf

Modolo, Vanina. 2016. 'Análisis histórico-demográfico de la inmigración en la Argentina del Centenario al Bicentenario'. *Papeles de POBLACIÓN* No. 89, 201–222.

Organization of American States. 1969. 'American Convention on Human Rights. Adopted at the Inter-American Specialized Conference on Human Rights, San José, Costa Rica, 22 November 1969'. *Inter-American Commission on Human Rights*. Accessed August 28, 2020. https://www.cidh.oas.org/basicos/english/basic3.american%20convention.htm

—. 1948. 'American Declaration of the Rights and Duties of Man. Adopted by the Ninth International Conference of American States, Bogotá, Colombia, 1948'. https://www.oas.org/dil/access_to_information_human_right_American_Declaration_of_the_Rights_and_Duties_of_Man.pdf

Romero, Jose Luis. 1951. *Historical guide to the Rio de la Plata*. Accessed August 16, 2020. https://www.jlromero.com.ar/tematica/inmigracion

Stewart v. Canada. 1996. CCPR/C/58/D/538/1993 (UN Human Rights Committee (HRC), November 1). https://www.refworld.org/cases,HRC,584a90807.html

United Nations, Committee on the Protection of the Rights of All Migrant Workers and Members of Their Families. 2019. 'International Convention on the Protection of the Rights of All Migrant Workers and Members of Their Families.' September 13. http://docstore.ohchr.org/SelfServices/FilesHandler.ashx?enc=6QkG1d%2FPPRiCAqhKb7yhsmZh886bo4a4Xtk2VOCOZARc3bM%2Fhb3bWkfXQPahkMnY71mfIzPd7cP6jlbw4vMTd8WEaGf%2BPsJIYeYitRdI%2BVwOvMXCIYG2KQ%2BSOEnxY0

3

On the Margins of EU-rope: Colonial Violence at the Bosnian-Croatian Frontier

BENEDETTA ZOCCHI

The reflection that will follow in this contribution can be traced back to one moment and one place. The place is a huge warehouse named Bira, in Bihac, Bosnia and Herzegovina (BiH). Bira used to be a refrigerator factory and is now managed by the International Organization of Migration (IOM) as a Temporary Reception Centre (TRC) for asylum seekers. The moment is 23 March 2018, when I first visited it. I was there with a group of activists and researchers and we were interested in understanding the dynamics of pushback and deportation that prevent people traveling on the Western Balkan Route (FRONTEX 2018) to cross the European Union (EU) border between BiH and Croatia.

Bira was not the first TRC I visited, but something about it made violence particularly explicit, undeniable and impossible to hide. The first time I entered Bira, an IOM operator gave me gloves and a mask. 'It is protocol,' he said, 'there have been plenty of diseases spreading in the camp and we shall take all the necessary precautions'. I looked around me. Nobody apart from visitors and camp staff was wearing masks or gloves. In a very visible way, those were precautions intended to protect us from them. The construction of an 'us' in opposition to a 'them' was pretty clear. The color of our skins, the quality of our clothes and the freedom of our bodies inscribed the undeniable acknowledgment of the different positionality that European staff and non-European hosts of the camp occupied in that space.

When IOM first arrived in Bihac, in 2016, Bira was set up to accommodate the unexpected deviation of thousands of people aimed at crossing the Western border with Croatia. However, because of the continuous pushbacks on behalf of Croatian police forces, many travelers ended up blocked in Bira for months, some even for a year. As their passage became more permanent, Bira was not re-adapted, but its existence as a camp was normalized. What used to be a storage of refrigerators and machines now looked like a storage of living bodies, forced into a paradoxical space, created to accommodate their temporary passage in the form of imprisonment.

As I walked within the building, escorted by IOM staff, I could sense the inevitable violence that act came with the space. In that space, my bodily existence as a white European woman inevitably shielded me from experiencing the camp in the way its hosts were experiencing it. My body performed that violence unconsciously and non-purposely, just for the categories of privilege it displayed. A white woman, whose white body could move freely in and out the camp, in and out the frontier, without being observed, monitored, or subject to suspicion. A European citizen, with papers that legalized her existence. A free individual, with a right to choose how to nourish her body, how to self-determine her identity. As a white European citizen, I entered in Bira performing my rights to freedom, legality, and mobility. However, these rights were not granted to me because of my humanness. On the contrary, they were strictly attached to my Europeaness.

> Bodies are shaped by histories of colonialism… (they) remember such histories, even when we forget them (Ahmed 2007, 153–154).

Decades after the end of the European colonial enterprise, and miles away from the geographical sites where it took place, my body vividly signaled the physicality of the colonizer as their body vividly signaled the physicality of the colonized. I was standing on European soil, within a United Nations managed facility, 18 kilometers away from the European Union. Symbols and labels inscribed in promises of universal human rights, freedom of mobility, and rights to self-determination. However, on this border, it was clear that those promises applied to some and not to others. They applied to us and not to them.

In the past decade, enormous amounts of funding and resources have been destined to securitize the external borders of the EU. Inevitably, the 'EU/non-EU borders became the favored arena for testing, developing and shaping the policies of fortress Europe' (Dalakoglou 2016, 183). The walls on the Spanish-Moroccan and Hungarian-Serbian borders, the intensification of police control in Greece, Turkey, and Serbia, and tensions between the Italian government and rescuing non-governmental organizations' boats in the Mediterranean Sea contributed to turning points of crossing into points of immobility, where thousands of people remain blocked for months, repeatedly attempting to cross and constantly pushed back.

As a Balkan nation with a complicated past of conflict, BiH has often been observed as both within and excluded from Europe (Balibar 2012). As the Eastern margin of the EU, its transformation into a new peculiar point of immobilization shows how one part of Europe is transforming another part into an internal post-colony where 'all the excluded to the project of modernity are gathered and confined' (2012, 447).

Since 2015, the Bosnian-Croatian frontier has turned into a site of struggle over who has a right to enter EU-rope. The struggle results in the systematized and normalized illegalization, immobilization, and racialization of non-European travelers who, stuck on the frontier, are forced to face the reproduction and legitimation of forms of violence, inscribed on their bodies and on their minds as they 'are watched, channeled, documented, obliged, commanded and pressured' (Goldberg 2006, 355). Eventually, 'their presence, if not indeed their very being, is discussed, negotiated, ordered, and recorded' (Goldberg 2006, 355).

This contribution starts from the assumption that violence perpetuated on the margins of the EU cannot be disconnected from European legacies of colonial domination, and that these legacies are echoed by EU border securitization. Conceived after several fieldtrips, this chapter results from a combination of theoretical and empirical engagement with observing violence experienced by travelers stuck on the Bosnian-Croatian frontier in line with European action as a colonial force.

In order to understand how a space like Bira came to exist a few kilometers from an EU border, we must take a step back. It only took me a three-hour bus drive to go from Zagreb to Bihac. I fell asleep in the EU and woke up at the Croatian-Bosnian frontier, where they checked my passport and registered my arrival. After twenty more minutes of traveling, I could notice two main differences. Outside, I could no longer hear bells or see the bell towers of Croatian churches. Instead, I could hear the Muezzin coming from the Minarets of Bosnian mosques. Inside, I no longer had connection on my phone, because my roaming was limited to EU territory. As I arrived at Bihac bus station, I caught myself staring at a writing on the wall of a building: 'Bosnia = graves of the doomed'. I notice that the building was covered in bullet holes.

Bihac is the capital of the Una Sana Canton. This area is part of a region called Bosniaka Krajina. In Bosnian language, *kraij* means end, and the name of the area can be translated as Bosnian Frontier. Since the Ottoman Empire, this was considered the last zone before the West, geographically beginning on the opposite side of Mount Plješivica. Today, the same mountain sets up the institutional border between BiH and Croatia. This zone has a century-long historical legacy as a place of passage, clash, and encounter between peoples, ideologies, and cultures. In this area, Christians and Muslims have coexisted and interacted for centuries (Bergholz 2016). From 1992 to 1995, during the bloody conflict that succeeded the dissolution of the former Yugoslavia, the city of Bihac was under a siege by the Serbian army. Memorial monuments celebrating those who lost their life in the conflict can be found across the area, and many of the locals today suffer from post-traumatic stress disorder.

In the last two years, this frontier has become one of the central waiting zones for people arriving from the Western Balkan Route (Agier 2016). Most travelers come from Iran, Iraq, Syria, Afghanistan, Pakistan, and Bangladesh, but since the route on the Mediterranean has become less accessible, it is not rare to find people coming from Algeria, Tunisia, and Morocco, or even from Sub-Saharan Africa. Most of them travel on foot, and it might take months on the road to arrive here. Today, this border remains one of the hardest to cross.

Following a series of EU and bilateral containment agreements that succeeded the 2015 Syrian crisis (Seeberg 2015), this route was one of the last to be securitized in Europe. However, because of the constant pushbacks of the Croatian police forces, the majority of travelers remain stuck here for an indeterminate amount of time, until they are able to collect the resources to cross again. Once they arrive in Bihac, it takes at least 10 days to reach Italy on foot. During the journey, people avoid villages, hide and sleep in the woods, and must carefully ration food and water. However, most of them will be caught on the Croatian or Slovenian borders, and will be pushed back to Bosnia. This situation condemns them to a paradoxical displacement, where they are prisoners and fugitives at the same time; not wanted in that country, with no desire to remain and no possibility to move forward. Border police violence, camping and squatting, and social marginalization are constant reminders to people stuck here that their lives are somehow less worthy than those of their European counterparts.

To address the humanitarian situation, IOM set up four camps. Bira and Miral are set up in two former factories and now host single men. Borici and Sedra, respectively, used to be an abandoned student house and an abandoned hotel. Today, they host minors and families. Notwithstanding IOM intervention, as both the arrivals and pushbacks increased, people began to occupy abandoned and bombed buildings or sleep on the streets around town.

As soon as they are able, they arm themselves with backpacks and food supplies and hit the road on the mountains to continue their journey. Until that moment, they have no other possibility than to remain where they are. They cannot work and are not included in public life. They sit in groups on the green grass of the shores of the river Una, or on the benches of the city center. Some of them prefer to remain in the camps, as most cafes and shops do not allow them in.

And so it begins, the preparation of what travelers call the game. The expression of the game grew to describe the long trekking that would bring travelers from one country to another. The game consists of days and nights walking and sleeping in the woods, exposed to cold temperatures, rain and snow, wild animals, and with the constant risk of being captured and pushed back by border police forces.

After days of walking in the woods, most of the people in the game will be caught by the Croatian police and pushed back into Bosnia. Some of them will manage to arrive to Slovenia and will be captured there. Those who make it to Italy and the Schengen Zone can hope to move forward. The rest of them will find themselves at the point where the game started, forced to attempt it again. The game has roles, characters, strategies, enemies, and obstacles. Forced to make many attempts, those who have been in the game often use the term as a metaphor to portray their role on the frontier as actors playing with their life.

As I reached the Bosnian-Croatian frontier, I found myself in a space of suspension, a space that was European without responding to the main narratives I had learned to associate with the idea of Europe. That space did not participate in the unilateral emanation of the universal character that Europe had for centuries imposed out of its borders. It did not participate in the collective amnesia of war, conflict, and darkness that Europe brought on itself. The dark side of Europe was not hidden. On the contrary, signs of a dark past were more visible than ever. This was the Europe not wearing an EU-ropean costume, where violence was visible and legitimate.

In his infamous theorization of necropolitics, Achille Mbembe recognizes a number of similarities between colonial and frontier spaces. He observes that both spaces exist as peripheral zones detached from a core. This core is geographically located far away and for as much as the physical presence of the central authority might be enforced through the imposition of similar educational, cultural, and political inputs, the implementing strategies are inevitably less rigid as they overlap with similar forms of local authorities. As a result, both frontiers and colonies are spaces of suspension.

They are inhabited by savaged; they are not organized in a state form... their armies do not form a distinct entity and their wars are not wars between regular armies. They do not imply the mobilization of sovereign subjects. They do not establish a distinction between soldiers and civilians or again between enemies and criminals (Mbembe 2003, 35).

As no one in the core looks this way, on the frontier, violence returns to be a legitimate mean of enforcement. Today, in the Una Sana Canton, local authorities are increasingly making decisions independently of both Sarajevo and European institutions. For example, Kljuc's local police has orders to stop buses coming from the hinterland before they arrive in Bihac and force travelers to stop their journey. In February 2020, I took a ride on one of these buses. As we stopped in Kljuc, two police officers got on the bus. They walked around the seats rows and started asking documents to certain passengers. Not surprisingly, the passengers selected for the check were those not looking European. Four young boys and two adult men were asked to get off the bus. They kept showing officers a document granting them permission to travel in BiH, which was given them by IOM in Sarajevo. However, there, on the frontier, the legal value of those documents was suspended. A different authority was enforced. Those commanded to stop found themselves in the middle of a country road. From the core in Sarajevo, they had the imperative to move closer to the border. However, they were stopped before they could reach the frontier.

Another example of autonomous management of the crisis is the one of a jungle camp. During the summer of 2019, Bihac municipality independently set up an open camp managed by the Red Cross in an area called Vucjak. Travelers were arbitrarily caught in town by the police and deported there. The health and living conditions in the camp were so bad that people forced to live there were calling it the jungle or jungle camp, and several organizations reported it as not conforming to the European Convention of Human Rights (Council of Europe Commissioner for Human Rights 2019).

These examples are useful for beginning to observe the way in which conventional dynamics, rules, laws, prescriptions, and discourses are suspended to make space for a language of constant emergency. On the frontier, the status quo is eventually reorganized around the issue of travelers' undesirable presence, and new unconventional, violent, and de-humanizing measures become legitimate in the name of security (Ahmed 2007b).

It is in this suspension that we find the connection between frontiers and colonies. According to Mezzadra and Nelson (2013, 84), the colonial frontier is imagined precisely as the 'qualitative distinction between European space and those extra-European spaces which are by definition open to conquest'. As such, it naturally 'tends to superimpose itself over other divisions (colonists and natives)' (Mezzadra and Nelson 2013, 243). The colonial frontier is also strictly connected with what Ahmed would call a space oriented towards whiteness (Ahmed 2007a, 158–159), i.e., a zone where 'non-white bodies become hyper-visible when they do not pass, which means they stand out and stand apart'. In Bihac, the inevitable detachment from European cores blurred the lines between justice, human rights, and security. This is something that highly connects with a series of debates that are today central in critical migration studies.

The immobilization and illegalization of migrants at European frontiers captured the attention of a plurality of activist scholars in the post-colonial tradition. Reflecting on the reproduction of the post-colonial migrant as a neo-colonial subject and criticizing the overarching attention towards the language of a migrant crisis, new studies emerged combining the scholarly and activist effort to challenge classical epistemologies and re-think discourses and practices (Mbembe 2003; Mezzadra and Nelson 2013; Tazzioli 2015; De Genova 2016; Isin 2018).

Undoubtedly, the language of the colonial (post-colonial, de-colonial, neo-colonial) has today reached well beyond the historical experience of land conquer and domination on behalf of European imperialist forces (Bhambra 2014). Thanks to intellectual inputs of distinguished scholars, such as Said, Fanon, Du Bois, and Cesaire, arguments are increasingly detached from treating colonialism as a circumscribed historical fact, highlighting how the histories of colonialism result from Europe or the West's self-proclaimed entitlement to modernity.

Following these theoretical inputs, I understand the colonial as relational before historical. In this sense, I believe we can find the colonial within hierarchies among peoples, ideologies, cultures, class, and race (Goldberg 2006; Bhambra 2014).

In turn, reading on this relational understanding of the colonial, I dedicate the rest of this chapter to conversations with travelers I met in Bihac. There, my aim is to identify different forms of violence performed on the frontier that can be connected to colonial violence.

My first preliminary fieldtrips in Bihac were primarily aimed at observing and exploring the context to assess its potential as a case study for my PhD research. I did not know what I would find, and I did not plan to conduct formal interviews. The material I gathered at the frontier was supposed to form an archive to reflect on positionality and methodology issues. Consequently, most of the data I display here were gathered in informal contexts, as I reached out to people outside the camps or around towns. I presented myself as a researcher and briefly explaining what I was researching. I did not attempt to orientate them towards a particular aspect of their present or past experiences, but I let them decide what they wanted to tell me. However, I could not help but notice that violence was a recurring theme. In turn, I rely on images, description, situations, and conversations to tell a story about colonial violence on the Bosnian-Croatian frontier.

The main objective of this approach is to situate my argument within the specific spatiality and temporality of the European frontier without overlooking historical trajectories associated with colonialism, race, and migration.

Travelers captured and pushed back on the Croatian border tell very similar stories about the dynamics of capture. Often, police officers beat men, insult woman, confiscate food supplies and money, and break phones. Deported bodies come back from the game covered in scars, bruises, and in some cases more serious injuries. A crucial and dramatic example is Ali, a 30-year-old man from Tunisia. Ali entered the game from the city of Velika Kladuša in the winter of 2018. The Croatian police captured him, beat him, and took his shoes, forcing him to walk back to Bosnia on his bare feet. Ali stayed in Bira for almost a year, with his feet completely necrotized, abandoned in one container where he lived isolated and immobile for seven months, until he died in September 2019. His story is both a story of physical and psychological violence. The trauma that Ali experienced highly affected his mental health. He refused to have his feet amputated, as he could have never been able to try the game again without being able to walk.

As with the case of Ali, violence is exercised on the body as much as it is on the mind. Many described the preparation for the game as invading their minds, dreams, and daily routines. They spent entire weeks studying routes and passages, and organizing supplies and groups. The trek is always dangerous. Wild animals, unexpected weather conditions, possible food or water shortage, and illnesses are inevitable risks. Yet, some people attempted the game 10, even 20 times. The constant perception of rejection, of risking one's life for nothing often leads to depression and anger. As a result, in the past year, there have been several suicide attempts. Many of the travelers who experienced pushbacks reported similar images about the way in which such experiences make one want to stop living. I remember a 16-year-old girl who came from Iran. She was traveling with her parents, and they had already attempted the game 15 times. She told me that she was tired of trying, but that they had no other choice, that this was not life, and that it was better to die attempting the game that to live like this. She said, 'At this point, death is the last thing I am worried about'.

Mbembe's (2003, 24) assertion that frontiers resemble colonial space highly relies on the understanding points of migrants' passages as death worlds where 'war and disorder, internal and external figures of the political, stand side by side or alternate with each other'. According to Mbembe (2003), the suspended temporality and interstitial status that travelers experience in these waiting zones prompt the development of latency and expectation, where the present, the being, and the self, fade into a status of constant alienation. The frontier looks like a purgatory, a middle way, a bridge between life and death, where the traveler has no choice but to struggle. A necropolis where bodies are left 'subjected to conditions of life conferring upon them the status of living dead' (Mbembe 2003, 32).

This also relates to forms of isolation and exclusion that permeate daily life on the frontier. Travelers are rarely called by their names. They are always observed, stop, and monitored as part of the mob, the multitude, or the migrants (Tazzioli 2020). Their body are physically re-oriented to spaces reserved for them, such as camps, TCR, abandoned buildings, or the woods. One day, I met a 16-year-old boy who lived with dozens of other travelers in an abandoned building just a few meters from Bira, on the way out of town. As many have done before him, he showed me the building as if it were his home, gave me a blanket to sit on, and invited me to stay for lunch. After the meal, we decided to go into town where we were supposed to meet another traveler he knew who was just back from the game and agreed to tell me his latest experience of pushback. To get into town, we had to pass in front of Bira. As we walked in front of the TRC, two police officers stopped us. They immediately divided us. One started talking to me, asking me for my ID and the reasons why I was walking with that migrant. I explained myself and showed my university card. Although he seemed to be satisfied with my explanation, he told me that I could not stay there and I had to go back to town. In the meantime, the other police officer took my friend by the arm and commanded him to go back to Bira. We both tried to explain that he was not living in Bira so he could not really go back to a place where he was not allowed to stay. But the officer seemed not to care. That was the dividing line. Within the frontier, that police checkpoint signaled the space designated for my white European body and the one reserved for his non-white and non-European one. The officer kept stressing that he could not move forward because there were too many migrants downtown. Therefore, I was told to go and he was told to stay. Even though there was not a place for him in that facility, he could not move forward. His body was confined to a space where it had no place.

In Fanon (1986), to be black in a white world means that one's bodily extension is diminished. 'In the white world, the man of color encounters difficulties in the development of his bodily schema. Consciousness of the body is solely a negating activity' (Fanon 1986, 110). Colonial violence is organized through the racialization of black bodies in a white space. In turn, the same form of subjectivities (Foucault 1972) applies to the field of the Bosnian-Croatian frontier. Although it experienced contamination with several cultures and religions, the Una Sana Canton remains a space of whiteness where black bodies are signaled, unexpected, watched 'hyper visible when they do not pass' (Ahmed 2007a, 159). On the frontier, the historical trajectory of the bodies that aim to cross is reconstructed on the lines of whiteness. Here, whiteness is a visual tool that signals the danger of the stranger body (Ahmed 2007b) just by looking at it. At the same time, it participates in the production of other layers of racialization. In conversation with Bihac residents, no one ever told me to be afraid of travelers because they were not white.

As noted by Du Bois (cited in Zuckeran 2004, 46),

> the global color line is not solely a matter of color and physical and racial appearance... [It] cuts across lines of colors of physique and beliefs and status... is a matter of cultural patterns, perverted teaching, and human hate and prejudice.

The expression 'economic migrant' is widely used on the frontier to convert racial and class issues into instruments of fear. As a person who is already in a condition of illegality, the traveler is subjectified as someone having nothing to lose and therefore is keener to engage in criminal activities, such as robbing or pickpocketing. The intersection between poverty, desperation, and race remains a fundamental lens to criminalize the traveler. As noted by Ahmed (2004, 132), it 'is through announcing a crisis in security that new forms of security, border policing, and surveillance become justified'. In her theorization of affective economies, Ahmed (2004) uses the two cases of burglary and asylum as connected matters participating in the discourse on the right to defense. Traveler are subjects one needs to be afraid of precisely because 'they are not part of the picture, and with their simple presence they are stealing something from the nation' (Ahmed 2004, 123).

This relies to another narrative recognized by Fanon, which identifies the black body in a white space as constantly out of place. They should not stay where they are, and do not have access to liberty. In *Black Skin, White Masks*, Fanon (1986, 170) argues that, for the colonial subject, 'it is solely by risking life that freedom is obtained... human reality in-itself-for-itself can be achieved only through conflict'. For the colonial subject, the right to liberty is not something that comes with humanness, but is something that must be earned and conceded by the white master. On the frontier, migrants' illegalization produces them as subjects who are arbitrarily deprived of liberty. Ballas, Dorling, and Hennig (2017, 28) observe this illegalization as part of a continuum in the criminalization of racialized subjectivities where 'every act, as long as it is made by a slave, an indigenous person, a colonized subject, or a black person... become a criminal act'. Thus, the stranger who appears on the frontier is not feared for being unknown, but for being a suspect (Ahmed 2004). The non-white traveler who attempts to reach Europe today is illegalized until the moment he/she is able to ask for asylum. During his/her journey, the condition of illegality forces him/her to hide, escape, and select routes that minimize the risk of being captured. His/her inferior status as a colonial subject is somehow re-framed in the form of illegalization.

> The first thing the colonial learns is to remain in his place and not overstep his limits. Hence the dreams of the colonial subject are muscular dreams, dreams of action, dreams of aggressive vitality... I dream I am jumping, swimming, running, and climbing (Fanon 1961, 22).

To be a colonial subject in the colonized world means having limited bodily extension, being checked, and being stopped (Ahmed 2004). On the frontier, immobilization is not just expressed in the impossibility to cross the border, but exists in the normalization of specific customs that eventually forbid people who are temporary on the frontier from entering certain spaces. Violence appears also in the form of segregation. In Bihac, most restaurant and cafes would not let migrants in. Some of them even have signs outside their door saying that migrants are not welcome. There are customs inscribing where migrants can and cannot go. As they are labelled migrants, they are immediately confined to certain ideas, places and imaginations. Wandering around towns, sitting in the camps, trekking in the mountains, hiding, making oneself less visible as possible become new strategies of survival.

Borders are constructed and indeed policed in the very feeling that they have already been transgressed: the other has to get too close in order to be recognized as an object of fear and in order for the object to be displaced (Ahmed 2004, 132).

Throughout this chapter, I proposed a dialogue between theoretical and empirical engagement to address violence perpetrated at the Bosnian-Croatian frontier as an expression of European colonial force. This should be read as an input (one among many) to challenge, problematize, and question conventional practices of EU bordering as directly connected with the colonial codification of difference between worthy and unworthy peoples. At the same time, it should also prompt discussion concerning the practice of internal EU bordering throughout which a part of Europe, mostly associated with EU member-states, is making another part peripheral, and for this reason expendable.

References

Agier, Michel. 2016. *Borderlands: Towards an Anthropology of the Cosmopolitan Condition.* Cambridge: Polity Press.

Ahmed, Sara. 2004. 'Affective Economies'. *Social Text* 22(2), 117–139.

Ahmed, Sara. 2007a. 'A Phenomenology of Whiteness'. *Feminist Theory* 8 (2): 149–168.

Ahmed, Sara. 2007b. *Strange Encounters: Embodied Others in Post-Coloniality.* London: Routledge.

Balibar, Etienne. 2012. 'The "Impossible" Community of the Citizens: Past and Present Problems'. *Environment and Planning D: Society and Space* 30 (3): 437–49.

Ballas, Daniel, Dorling, Dimitri. and Hennig, Benjamin. 2017. *The Human Atlas of Europe: A continent united in diversity.* Bristol: Policy Press.

Bergholz, Max. 2016. *Violence as a Generative Force: Identity, Nationalism, and Memory in a Balkan Community.* New York: Cornell University Press.

Bhambra, Gurminder K. 2014 'Postcolonial and Decolonial Dialogues'. *Postcolonial Studies* 17, no. 2 (3 April 2014): 115–21.

'Bosnia and Herzegovina Must Immediately Close the Vučjak Camp and Take Concrete Measures to Improve the Treatment of Migrants in the Country'. n.d. Commissioner for Human Rights. https://www.coe.int/en/web/commissioner/view/-asset_publisher/ugj3i6qSEkhZ/content/bosnia-and-herzegovina-must-immediately-close-the-vucjak-camp-and-take-concrete-measures-to-improve-the-treatment-of-migrants-in-the-country

Dalakoglou, Dimitri. 2016. 'Europe's last frontier: The spatialities of the refugee crisis', *City*, 20:2, 180–185.

De Genova, Nicholas. 2016. 'The European Question: Migration, Race, and Postcoloniality in Europe'. Social Text 34 (3 128): 75–102.

_____ 2018. 'The "Migrant Crisis" as Racial Crisis: Do Black Lives Matter in Europe?' Ethnic and Racial Studies 41 (10): 1765–82.

Du Bois, W.E.B 'The Negro and the Warsaw Ghetto' in 'the social theory of W.E.B. du Bois ed by Phil Zuckerman California: Sage Publications, 2004.

Fanon, Frantz 1986; 2008. Black Skin, White Masks. New ed. Get Political. London: Pluto-Press.

Foucault, Michelh. 1972. *The Archaeology of Knowledge.* New York: Pantheon Books.

FRONTEX European Border and Coast Guard Agency, 2018 Western Balkans Annual Risk Analysis Warsaw: Risk Analysis Unit.

Goldberg, David Theo. 2004 'Racial Europeanization' Ethnic and Racial Studies, 29:2, 331–364.

Isin, Engin. 2018. 'Mobile Peoples: Transversal Configurations'. Social Inclusion 6, no. 1: 115.

Mbembe, Achille, 2003 Necropolis, in Public Culture, Volume 15, Number 1 pp. 11-40.

Mezzadra, Sandro & Neilson, Brett. 2013. Border as Method, or, the Multiplication of Labor. Book, Whole. Durham: Duke University Press.

Seeberg, Peter. 2015. 'The EU and the Syrian Crisis: The Use of Sanctions and the Regime's Strategy for Survival'. Mediterranean Politics 20 (1): 18–35.

Tazzioli, Martina. 2015. 'Which Europe? Migrants' uneven geographies and counter-mapping at the limits of representation'. *Movements. Journal for Critical Migration and Border Regime Studies* 1, no. 2, 1–20.

_____ 2020. The Making of Migration: The Biopolitics of Mobility at Europe's Borders. Society and Space. London: SAGE.

Tazzioli, Martina, and De Genova, Nicholas. (no date) 'Europe/Crisis: Introducing new keywords of the crisis in and of Europe' *New Keyword Collective Zone*, 1–45. Zone Books, Near Futures, online.

4

Recognition and Protection of Environmental Migrants in International Law: A Long-Lasting Swing between Urgency and Postponement

CHIARA SCISSA

It was only in the 1990s that global concerns over environmental changes began to acquire the dimension of a humanitarian issue with massive effects on the well-being and safety of vulnerable populations. In the following decade, international experts and regional bodies provided different regulatory solutions aimed at recognizing and protecting people compelled to flee on environmental and climate grounds. However, these solutions have neither produced an internationally agreed definition of environmental migration nor common assistance and protection arrangements.

No groundbreaking policy element was introduced in the international debate on environmental migrants until 2015 with the adoption of the Agenda for the Protection of Cross-Border Displaced Persons in the Context of Disasters and Climate Change. The 2030 Agenda on Sustainable Development revitalized interest in and awareness of the causal nexus between environmental threats and migration, then reaffirmed in several United Nations (UN) soft law instruments. Despite this initial policy breakthrough, supported by relevant case law at all levels, the international regulatory process on environmental migration gets jammed again as a consequence of the overall lack of states' commitment to tackling climate change and granting protection to wider categories of forced migrants.

The Urgency of Raising Awareness

Human migration has always been linked to the environment, but political awareness of the importance of this factor is recent (IOM 2008). Indeed, only in the 1990s did global concerns of environmental changes begin to acquire the dimension of a humanitarian issue with massive effects on the well-being and safety of vulnerable populations. In the following decade, international experts and regional bodies provided different regulatory solutions aimed at recognizing and protecting people compelled to flee on environmental and climate grounds.

Still, the international community is far from reaching consensus on the definition to apply to this category of migrants and the protection status to which they should be entitled. Between the end of 20th century and the beginning of the 21st century, five proposals to define and assist environmentally displaced people gained particular attention. These were: 1) extending the 1951 Convention Relating to the Status of Refugees; 2) adding a protocol on climate refugees to the United Nations Framework Convention on Climate Change (UNFCCC); 3) adopting a new legal framework; 4) promoting the Guiding Principles on Internal Displacement; and 5) using temporary protection mechanisms. However, none of them succeeded in convincing heads of state to process them further.

Extending the 1951 Refugee Convention

UN Environment Programme researcher Essam El-Hinnawi (1985) proposed extending refugee status to people compelled to flee from environmental disasters. At the beginning of the 21st century, University of Oxford Professor Norman Myers (2001) supported the extension of the 1951 Refugee Convention to environmental refugees.

However, this proposal has been swiftly dismissed, since few requirements under Article 1A of the 1951 Refugee Convention would potentially be fulfilled by such a category (McAdam 2011). The traditional definition of a 'refugee' indeed requires the applicant to be outside the country of their nationality or of habitual residence. Firstly, it has been recognized that most people affected by the environment remain within their country of origin, thus not meeting this preliminary requirement (Nansen Initiative, 3). Secondly, it is difficult to prove the risk of persecution due to climate change or to qualify climate change as an agent of persecution pursuant to the 1951 Refugee Convention. In the well-known Teitiota case, the applicant's request for asylum in New Zealand was based on the fact that the international community, industrialized countries in particular, failed to limit greenhouse gas emissions, which, according to the claimant, led to drastic climate change effects in Kiribati. However, the High Court of New Zealand noted that 'there are many decisions rejecting claims by people from Kiribati, Tuvalu, Tonga, Bangladesh, and Fiji on the grounds that the harm feared does not amount to persecution, and there were no differential impacts on the applicants' (Teitiota v. Chief Executive of the Ministry of Business, Innovation and Employment 2015). Thirdly, even if the impacts of climate change could be considered persecutory acts, the 1951 Refugee Convention requires such persecution to be on account of race, religion, nationality, political opinion, or membership of a social group, while the impacts of climate change are largely indiscriminate, rather than tied to personal characteristics. Therefore, environmental threats and their drastic effects on human rights can be seen as a further reason to issue refugee status, but not the only one.

Adding a Protocol on Climate Refugees to the UNFCCC

Although some scholars (Biermann and Boas 2010), institutions (German Advisory Council on Global Change 2007), and non-governmental organizations (Environmental Justice Foundation 2017) support the use of the term 'environmental/climate refugees', they are reluctant to extend the scope of the 1951 Refugee Convention. Utrecht University Professor Frank Bierman, and Wageningen University Professor Ingrid Boas paved the way for an alternative proposal, concerning the establishment of an *ad hoc* climate refugee convention to be included as a protocol to the UNFCCC. However, they meant to distinguish strictly between climate change and environmental drivers of forced migration, thus impeding their proposal from gaining traction. Indeed, a conceptual and legal distinction between environmental and climate change disasters triggers multiple backlashes. For instance, science has so far not provided for a clear distinction between pure environmental and climate change threats. Even so, states might issue protection statuses more cautiously to the victims of disasters, in order to be sure that the applicant has been affected by pure climate change actions only. This would also lead to more categories and sub-categories of migrants, making efforts to address their vulnerability less efficient.

Adopting a New Legal Framework

Alternatively, other scholars have opted for the creation a new international instrument to protect environmental migrants, as suggested by a Resolution No. 1655/2009 and recommendation No. 1862/2009 of the Committee on Migration, Refugees and Populations together with the Committee on Environment, Agriculture and Regional Affairs of the Parliamentary Assembly of the Council of Europe. Other outstanding experts endorsed this third approach.

For instance, University of Limoges law specialists proposed to draft a new convention for environmentally displaced persons (Prieur et al. 2008), while Harvard Law School Professors Bonnie Docherty and Tyler Giannini (2009) promoted the establishment of a new, legally binding instrument based on human rights and shared responsibility in order to protect 'climate change refugees'. They defined a climate change refugee as 'an individual who is forced to flee his or her home and to relocate temporarily or permanently across a national boundary as the result of sudden or gradual environmental disruption that is consistent with climate change and to which humans more likely than not contributed' (Docherty and Giannini 2009, 378). In focusing purely on climate change threats, they reproduced the separation already introduced by Biermann and Boas, thus weakening the consistency and pragmatism of their proposal.

Nonetheless, University of New South Wales Scientia Professor of Law Jane McAdam (2011) has highlighted the reasons why environmental migrants may not benefit from a new international treaty or protocol. According to her, they might address neither their specific needs nor the causes of climate change in different regions around the world, given that climate change affects people differently, and the remedies or anticipatory strategies could diverge. To this end, she argues, local or regional responses would be better able to respond to their exigencies.

Promoting the Guiding Principles on Internal Displacement

The fourth proposal refers to the 1998 Guiding Principles on Internal Displacement (United Nations Office for the Coordination of Humanitarian Affairs 1998), a landmark development in the process of establishing a normative framework outlining protection, assistance, and rights for the protection of internally displaced persons (IDPs). However, the Guiding Principles only provide guidelines and lack of legal force. To produce binding obligations, they should be incorporated at the domestic level. For instance, the 2009 African Union Convention for the Protection and Assistance of Internally Displaced Persons in Africa (Kampala Convention) embeds relevant principles of international human rights and humanitarian law set out in the 1998 Guiding Principles. The Kampala Convention also explicitly refers to internal displacement due to natural or human-made disasters, including climate change. Moreover, it contains provisions not only for protection and humanitarian assistance for IDPs, but also legal and practical steps to avoid environmental displacement, as well as to provide satisfactory conditions for sustainable return, relocation, and local integration. To date, alas, only 27 out of 55 state parties have ratified the Kampala Convention and few tangible attempts to implement its provisions have been made.

An interesting effort to revitalize the Kampala Convention has been made by Narayan Subramanian and Johns Hopkins University Professor Johannes Urpelainen, who use game theory to study when regional treaties are feasible to address cross-border environmental displacement. According to their theory, two states benefit from mutual collaboration when both are affected by environmental threats and, therefore, when they find themselves in a condition of vulnerability (Subramanian and Urpelainen 2013). In their opinion, a regional treaty, such as the Kampala Convention, can provide cooperation and solidarity against a common threat. Nevertheless, when states do not have enough governance capacity to accept environmentally displaced from neighboring states, or are equally affected by climate change, regional treaties may not help either of them.

Using Temporary Protection Mechanisms

The last proposal concerns temporary protection measures to assist and protect those displaced by environmental events, combined with planned relocation and resettlement programs to reduce the vulnerability of affected populations. At the EU level, several countries have adopted various forms of temporary protection status in their domestic legislations that deal, or could deal, with environmental issues. A 2020 European Migration Network study shows that there are currently 60 national protection statuses, mostly based on humanitarian reasons, which, however, remain largely undefined in national legislation (European Migration Network 2020, 1). This leaves a significant margin of discretion to national authorities in assessing applications owing to environmental drivers.

Postponing Commitments: Recognizing Environmental Migration through Soft Laws

Although relevant, none of the previously mentioned proposals has been met with international consensus. This regulatory and policy limbo leaves a disproportionate number of people to struggle with environmental and climate disasters, exacerbating their vulnerability, poverty, and food and water insecurity. From the beginning of the 21st century, no ground-breaking policy element was introduced in the international debate on environmental migrants until 2015, when the adoption of the Agenda for the Protection of Cross-Border Displaced Persons in the Context of Disasters and Climate Change (Protection Agenda) and the 2030 Agenda on Sustainable Development revitalized interest in and awareness of the nexus between environmental threats and migration.

The Protection Agenda encourages states to identify measures for the protection and assistance of transnational disaster-displaced persons. Rather than negotiating a new international agreement, the Protection Agenda stresses the need for states to support the integration of effective practices at national and sub-regional levels into their own normative frameworks in accordance with their specific situations and challenges. In doing so, it seems to be in line with the fifth proposal, namely promoting domestic solutions to environmental migration. In providing a comprehensive, high-quality, and pragmatic legal and policy analysis of environmental migration, the Protection Agenda helps states also by giving effect to the 2030 Agenda on Sustainable Development, whose aim is to leave no one behind. The latter recognizes that the adverse impacts of climate change and environmental degradation represent a cause of forced migration. It therefore calls on states to provide adequate solutions to climate change and to protect people affected by it, both within and across their territories.

Similarly, the 2016 New York Declaration for Refugees and Migrants explicitly identifies environmental disasters as causes of forced migration (par. 1, and 7 of Chapter II in Annex II), and pledges signatory states to address their adverse impacts. The related Global Compact for Safe, Orderly, and Regular Migration (GCM) also represents a relevant breakthrough, as it is the first ever inter-governmentally negotiated agreement that simultaneously recognizes environmental disasters as drivers of forced migration as well as the urgency to provide protection to their victims (Scissa 2019). Most importantly, the GCM's Objective 5 calls on participating states to use protection mechanisms 'based on compassionate, humanitarian, or other considerations for migrants compelled to leave their countries of origin owing to sudden-onset natural disasters', as well as to devise planned relocation. In doing so, the GCM confirms the environment to be a cause of forced migration, but not of refugee movements. At the same time, the Global Compact on Refugees further stresses this conceptual and regulatory separation, by clearly asserting that environmental threats cannot be seen as valid grounds for the application of the Refugee Convention (Introduction, D8), but rather as an exacerbating factor of forced migration.

Despite this initial policy breakthrough, all these innovative UN instruments lack binding force, thus failing to generate strong binding commitments. What is more, several states have refrained from adopting the GCM, thus weakening its potential to foster cooperation in the realm of migration governance. The 2020 Sustainable Development Goals Report notes that only 54 percent of countries have established adequate migration policies to reduce inequalities and vulnerability (United Nations 2020), while feeble actions have been undertaken to tangibly tackle climate change. Remarkably, the last Conference of the Parties (COP25) in Madrid failed to produce common rules for implementing the 2015 Paris Agreement for Climate Change, with which the international community marked its commitment to reducing greenhouse gas emissions on the one hand, and to enhance concerted actions to limit the adverse impacts of climate change on the other. Given that the majority of states are also way off-track to meet the Paris Agreement's targets, it seems that national, short-term economic and political interests are making states reluctant to deal with two of the biggest challenges of our time. The overall lack of states' commitment in tackling climate change and in granting protection to wider categories of forced migrants is visible not only at the international level, with the United States withdrawing from the Paris Agreement, as well as at the EU level, where the negotiation process among member states on humanitarian visas, common resettlement programs, and an overdue reform of the Common European Asylum System has been in a deadlock for the past five years.

Beyond National Interests: States' Binding Obligations

As stated elsewhere, the common issue for the protection of environmental migrants should be the official recognition of the issue (Scissa 2019). Jurisprudence, international, and regional binding and non-binding instruments indicate that environmental threats represent both a breach of human rights and a driver of forced migration. They also suggest that states should combine their obligations under international environmental law to those related to international human rights law, as the two issues are inevitably interlinked.

Indeed, with regard to law enforcement, the UN Human Rights Council (UN Human Rights Council 2009), the African Commission on Human and Peoples' Rights (*SERAP v. Nigeria* 2012), the Inter-American Commission on Human Rights (Inter-American Commission on Human Rights 1997), and the European Committee of Social Rights (*MFHR v. Greece* 2006) found the environment to be a fundamental component of the right to life and health. Additionally, in the Urgenda climate case, the Supreme Court of the Netherlands has recently held that the Dutch government has binding legal obligations to prevent climate change damage, and by implication all governments do as well, under international human rights law (*Urgenda Foundation v. the Netherlands* 2019). Therefore, the next reasonable step should be to agree internationally on a comprehensive definition of environmental migrants to provide them with adequate protection mechanisms in full compliance with their human rights.

Protecting Environmental Migrants to Comply with International Law

In light of international human rights law, international customary principles, and international environmental law, states should overcome their attitude of postponement to comply with their international obligations. Environmental degradation, natural and anthropogenic changes in the climate and soil composition, and severe weather events are gravely affecting human rights, such as the rights to life, adequate food and water, health, housing, property, culture, the freedom of movement, and the principle of *non-refoulement*, among others.

In particular, the latter, enshrined in Article 33 of the 1951 Refugee Convention, prevents states from returning individuals to areas where they could face serious harm or where their life could be at risk. It is at the core of international and regional arrangements, as well as of discretional measures aimed at preventing the deportation of an individual whose life and freedom could be in danger. This *jus cogens* principle is also embedded in in the Convention against Torture and Other Cruel, Inhuman or Degrading Treatment or Punishment (Article 3), the International Covenant on Civil and Political Rights (ICCPR, Article 7) and the European Convention on Human Rights (ECHR, Article 3). Most importantly, in the case *Teitiota v. New Zealand*, the UN Human Rights Committee claimed that if the applicant's right to life is threatened because of the effects of climate change, s/he cannot be refouled (UN Human Rights Committee 2020).

The rights to life and to a healthy environment mutually reinforce one another. Indeed, protecting the environment is indispensable for the full enjoyment of the right to life, health, and an adequate standard of living, while human rights further foster the need of a safe and healthy environment. The right to life does not solely prevent states from deliberately taking life, but also obliges them to take positive measures to properly protect life under their jurisdiction. In this regard, the Inter-American Commission on Human Rights has recognized that the realization of the right to life is necessarily linked to and dependent on the physical environment (*Yakye Axa v. Paraguay* 2005). Similarly, the African Commission on Human and Peoples' Rights found a violation of the right to health and the right to life as a result of displacement from lands in Mauritania, which were confiscated by the government (*Malawi African Association v. Mauritania* 2000). The opinion that environment and human rights are inextricably linked has been further confirmed by the International Court of Justice Judge Christopher Weeramantry, who has stated that 'the protection of the environment is... a vital part of... the right to health and the right to life itself' (Office of the Persecutor International Court of Justice 2016).

Furthermore, the UN Commission on the Economic, Social, and Cultural Rights saw the right to water as essential for conducting a dignified life (UN Committee on Economic, Social, and Cultural Rights 2002). According to University of Bologna Professor Marco Borraccetti (Borraccetti 2016, 119), the right to water not only corresponds to one of the most fundamental conditions for survival, but is also crucial for the concrete enjoyment and realization of other key human rights, such as an adequate standard of living, food, clothing, and housing.

The right to health is enshrined in Article 25 of the Universal Declaration of Human Rights (UDHR) and restated in many other international arrangements, such as in Article 12 of the International Covenant on Economic, Social and Cultural Rights (ICESCR). At the regional level, neither the European Charter nor the European Social Charter contain provisions related to the right to a healthy environment. However, the European Committee of Social Rights (the Committee) has interpreted Article 11 of the European Social Charter, which specifically refers to the right to the protection of health, as including the right to a healthy environment. The Committee, in fact, found a complementarity between Article 11 of the Social Charter and Articles 2 and 3 of the ECHR. Consequently, in several conclusions regarding the right to health, the Committee explicitly stated that the provisions contained in Article 11 of the Social Charter should be duly considered in order to remove the causes of ill health also resulting from environmental threats. In the already mentioned decision on the Marangopoulos case, the Committee identified environmental protection as one of the key elements of the right to health under Article 11. The Committee also affirmed that states are responsible for activities that are harmful to the environment, whether carried out by the public authorities themselves or by a private company. Importantly, Article 16 of the African Charter deals with the right to health, whereas Article 38 of the Arab Charter explicitly recognizes the right to a healthy environment. Furthermore, Article 24 of the African Charter, by including a right to a 'satisfactory environment' favorable to development, has been interpreted as the first binding international obligation relating to the right to the environment (Ebeku 2003).

Protecting the environment and people living therein also leads to the promotion of the right to property as enshrined in Article 17 UDHR, Article 5 of the Convention on the Elimination of All Forms of Racial Discrimination, Article 14 of the African Charter, Article 21 of the American Convention on Human Rights, Article 31 of the Arab Charter, and Article 1 of Protocol No. 1 to the ECHR. In particular, these instruments affirm that individuals are entitled to peacefully enjoy their possessions. These instruments not only concern the unlawful deprivation, exploitation, and disposition of property, but also encompass the right to land and to land use. While there is currently no explicit reference to a human right to land under international human rights law, several international arrangements consider the enjoyment of land as strictly relevant for the full respect of other recognized human rights, such as the right to food, equality between women and men, the protection and assistance of IDPs, and the rights of indigenous peoples and their relationship with their ancestral lands or territories (UNHCR 2015).

Concluding Remarks

It has been no less than 30 years since the debate around environmental migration started flourishing. After two decades, scholars and institutions still refer to the protection of this still blurry category of migrants as an urgent and humanitarian issue to be managed with timely, well-planned responses. Several UN arrangements explicitly recognize environmental migration, but lack of binding force. Conversely, binding instruments that provide protection statuses to environmental migrants, such as the Kampala Convention, are too weakly implemented, while the Paris Agreement does not refer to people affected by climate change.

This chapter aimed firstly at summarizing the pros and cons of the most relevant advanced proposals, as well as recent international declarations, stepping up for ensuring protection to environmental migrants. Then, it pointed out that the fulfilment of certain human rights, essential to a dignified life, depends on a healthy and protected environment. Finally, it argued for the urgent need to overcome states' attitude of postponement in light of their international responsibility to protect human rights and fundamental freedoms.

References

Parliament Assembly of the Council of Europe. 'Resolution 2307/2019'.

Bierman, e Boas. Preparing for a Warmer World: Towards a Global Governance System to Protect Climate Refugees. 2010.

Borraccetti, M. 2016. 'The right to water and access to water resources in European Development Policies', In, *Natural Resources Grabbing; An International Law Perspective*, di F. Jacur, A. Bonfanti e F. Seatzu, 116–135.

Docherty, B., e T. Giannini. 'Confronting a Rising Tide: A Proposal for a Convention on Climate Change Refugees'. *Harvard Environmental Law Review*, 33 (2009): 349–403.

Ebeku, Kaniye. 2003. 'The right to a satisfactory environment and the African Commission'. *African Human Rights Law Journal*, 149–166.

El-Hinnawi, E. 1985. 'Environmental Refugees'. Nairobi: United Nations Environment Programme (UNEP).

Environmental Justice Foundation. 2017. 'Beyond Borders: Our changing climate – its role in conflict and displacement'.

European Migration Network. 2020. 'Comparative Overview of National Protection Statuses in the EU and Norway'.

European Parliament – Directorate General for Internal Policies. 2011. '"Climate Refugees": Legal and policy responses to environmentally induced migration'.

German Advisory Council on Global Change. 2007. 'World in Transition: Climate Change as a Security Risk'.

ICMPD. 2014. 'Policy Brief: Climate Change & Migration: What is the Role for Migration Policies?'.

Inter-American Commission on Human Rights. 1997. 'Report on the Situation of Human Rights in Ecuador'.

Ioane Teitiota v. The Chief Executive of the Ministry of Business, Innovation and Employment. (20 July 2015).

IOM. 2008. 'World Migration Report'.

Malawi African Association v. Mauritania. 2000. 'African Commission on Human and Peoples' Rights' 11 May.

Marangopoulos Foundation for Human Rights (MFHR) v. Greece. 2006. European Committee of Social Rights. 6 December.

McAdam, J. 2011. 'Climate Change Displacement and Intenational Law: Complementary Protection Standards.'

McAdam, J. 2005b. 'Complementary protection and beyond: How states deal with human rights protection'. UNHCR-Evaluation and Policy Analysis Unit, n. 118.

McAdam, J. 2011. 'Swimming against the Tide: Why a Climate Change Displacement Treaty is Not the Answer'. International Journal of Refugee Law 23, n. 2: 1–27.

Myers, N. 2001. *Environmental refugees: A growing phenomenon of the 21st century.*

New York Declaration for Refugees and Migrants. 2016. 19 September.

Office of the Persecutor – International Court of Justice. 2016. 'Policy Paper on Case Selection and Prioritisation'. 15 September.

Parliamentary Assembly of the Council of Europe. 2009. 'Recommendation No. 1862: Environmentally Induced Migration and Displacement: A 21st Century Challenge'.

Parliamentary Assembly of the Council of Europe. 2009. 'Resolution No. 1655: Environmentally Induced Migration and Displacement: A 21st Century Challenge'.

Prieur, M., et al. 2008. 'Draft Convention on the International Status of Environmentally-Displaced Persons'. *Revue Européene de Droit de l'Environnement*: 381–393.

Ramos, E.P. 2013. 'Climate Change, Disasters and Migration: Current Challenges toInternational Law', in *Climate Change: International Law and Global Governance*. Ruppel; Roschmann; Ruppel-Schlichting.

Scissa, C. 2019. 'A feeble light in the shadow: The recognized need to protect environmental migrants', *Comparative Network on Refugee Externalisation Policies*. 19 August.

SERAP v. Nigeria. 201. African Commission on Human and Peoples' Rights. 14 December.

Subramanian, N., e J. Urpelainen. 2013. 'Addressing cross-border environmental displacement: when can help?' *International Environmental Agreements: Politics, Law and Economics,* 14, n. 27.

The Nansen Initiative. 2015. 'Agenda for the Protection of Cross-Border Displaced Persons in the Context of Disasters and Climate', Geneva, 12–13 October.

UN Committee on Economic, Social and Cultural Rights. 2002. 'General Comment No. 15 on the right to water', 11–29 November.

UN Human Rights Committee. 2020. 'Views adopted by the Committee under article 5 (4) of the Optional Protocol, concerning communication No. 2728/2016, Case Ioane Teitiota vs New Zealand, CCPR/C/127/D/2728/2016'.

UN Human Rights Council. 2009. 'Human Rights Council Resolution No. 10/4, Human Rights and Climate Change'. 25 March.

UNISDR. 2018. 'Words into Action guideline: Man-made/technological hazards'.

United Nations Office for the Coordination of Humanitarian Affairs. 1988. 'Guiding Principles on Internal Displacement'. United Nations.

United Nations. 2020. 'The Sustainable Development Goals Report'.

Urgenda Foundation v. The Netherlands. ECLI:NL:HR:2019:2007. Dutch Supreme Court, 20 December 2019.

Yakye Axa v. Paraguay. 17 June 2005. Inter-American Court of Human Rights.

5

The Internal Displacement of People in South Sudan: Understanding Civil War and Forced Movement of People

KENSIYA KENNEDY AND KESHAV BASOTIA

In 2011, South Sudan gained its independence after a 22-year civil war between the predominantly Muslim northern Sudanese (now Sudan) government and the Southern rebels who mostly represented the Christian and indigenous religions. The peace agreement that brought forth South Sudan's independence was facilitated by the Intergovernmental Authority on Development (IGAD) and other countries like the United States, United Kingdom, and Norway. The Comprehensive Peace Agreement (CPA) signed between the Sudan People's Liberation Movement (SPLM) and the Sudanese President Omar al-Bashir in 2005 made way for a referendum that allowed the Sudanese people to decide if they wanted Sudan to be split in two. The referendum was held in January 2011 where an overwhelming 99 percent of South Sudanese people voted in the favor of independence of the South thus, forming the Republic of South Sudan on 9 July 9 2011. South Sudanese independence was celebrated, and many international organizations looked at the event optimistically.

This optimism was short-lived, as in December 2013, conflict broke out within factions of the Sudanese People's Liberation Army (SPLA). This plunged the recently formed country into a civil war that resulted in the death, abuse, and displacement of thousands of people. This chapter looks at the key turning points in the civil war in a bid to understand the internal displacement caused by the conflict, which is the largest forced migration event in recent African history. It uses empirical data to assess the movement of people and the trigger events that might have led to the movement in the three regions of the Equatorian states, Jonglei and Upper Nile.

Variables Defining the Conflict

Ethnic Diversity

Ethnic diversity is an inherent part of South Sudan, and the country comprises more than 60 different ethnic groups. The largest two groups are the Dinka and the Nuer tribes, which have been at the center of the civil war in South Sudan. Traditionally, both of these are rival pastoralist groups, which have competed over grazing land and water for cattle in the past. They, however, came together for the greater good to mount a resistance against (then) north Sudan. Keeping the rivalries aside did not make the problems go away, and the differences eventually surfaced after independence.

Differences in the Sudanese People's Liberation Movement

The country's first president, Salva Kiir, is from the Dinka tribe, a tribe that comprises around 36 percent of the population. In his Independence Day speech on 9 July 9 2011, he appealed to the people to view their cultural identities as a 'source of pride and strength, not parochialism and conflict'. Kiir emphasized the fact that the people were South Sudanese first. Kiir also appointed Riek Machar as his vice president. To understand the significance of this appointment, one has to realize that Machar is from the ethnic Nuer tribe, which is the second largest in the country. Machar was not merely a representative of the rival group, but also an important leader who was responsible for leading a brutal massacre in 1991 against Dinka civilians where around 2,000 civilians were killed. It is therefore clear how Kiir's stand on unity and the inclusion of a strong figure from a rival ethnic group seemed like a generous step towards inclusion.

Things turned sour when, in the beginning of 2013, Machar began vocalizing his criticisms of the way the government was being run under Kiir and on how the economy was being handled. Machar also expressed his intentions of contesting the presidency in 2015. This was not well-received by Kiir, and he fired Machar and all 28 of his cabinet members in July 2013.

The Civil War

On 15 December 2013, at a meeting, the conflict broke out between factions of the SPLA, each supporting Kiir and Machar. While who started the fight is still debated, one version of the events dictates that, at the meeting, presidential guards of the Dinka majority on Kiir's side tried to disarm the Nuer guards on Machar's side. The conflict escalated dramatically, and the violence spread and resulted in ethnic cleansing in the capital city of Juba.

The issue soon evolved from a political conflict to an ethnic face-off. Machar fled the capital city of Juba and the Nuer faction of the SPLA fled with him. President Kiir later stated that the fighting was a coup attempt by Machar and his allies, which Machar denied. In the first week of fighting, 1,000 people were killed and around 100,000 were displaced.

After Machar fled, the violence morphed into an ethnic conflict, spreading to other parts of the country, namely the then-Equatorian states, which are the Central, Eastern, and Western states (Juba is in central Equatoria), the Jonglei state, the Unity state, and the Upper Nile state.

In 2015, the two warring parties, the SPLA led by Salva Kiir and the SPLA-IO (Sudanese People's Liberation Army-In Opposition) led by Riek Machar, reached a peace agreement. The peace agreement was facilitated by IGAD and, as part of the agreement, Machar was supposed to return to Juba and resume his post as the vice president. Machar, however, was insecure about his safety in Juba and insisted on bringing his own fighters to Juba with him. In April 2016, the rival forces clashed again, re-igniting the violence, and Machar fled Juba. In this incident, around 300 people were killed and, in the following week, around 26,000 people fled the city.

In September 2018, a peace deal was signed between Salva Kiir and Riek Machar, officially ending the civil war. As part of the peace deal, Machar was supposed to return to Juba by May 2019, which was extended by six months as both parties had disagreements regarding the peace deal. The November date for the peace deal was pushed by a further 100 days due to concerns regarding the rebel leader Machar's security. This series of delays ended when both parties agreed to form a Unity government in February 2020.

Evolution from Community Clashes to Identity Politics

Events That Drew the Other Ethnic Communities into the Conflict

In October 2015, Kiir issued an order to increase the number of the states from 10 to 28. This move gave the Dinkas a majority in strategic locations and caused angst among the Equatorians and the Shilluk populations. This move was seen as a ploy by the Dinkas to grab land that belonged to the other ethnic communities. After these moves, new groups that were earlier relatively dormant in the fight began to rise up against the government.

In September 2016, Lam Akol of the Democratic Change party (the largest opposition party to SPLA) announced a new faction called the National Democratic Movement (NDM) in an attempt to overthrow Kiir. The fighting also spread to the relatively calm Equatoria region, where the SPLA-IO forces had sought shelter, and to the Upper Nile state.

Major Outbreaks in Jonglei, Equatoria, and Upper Nile regions

Post-December 2013, the magnitude of the prevalent community clashes increased. The common occurrence of clashes over resources between different tribes occupying and competing for the same natural resources evolved into something more. All empirical and event data used is dated through November 2019.

Jonglei

As a result, South Sudan witnessed its first major post-independence ethnic clash in January 2012 even before the civil war erupted between the Dinka and the Nuer factions of the governing SPLM. The government of South Sudan and SPLA had conducted disarmament, targeting the Lou Nuer people in particular after the CPA in 2005. This selective disarmament fueled the communal tensions between both tribes and resulted in armed confrontation backed by ethnic hatred. The state of Jonglei in South Sudan witnessed ethnic clashes between the Lou Nuer and the Murle tribes. Because of this, around 600 people were killed in Jonglei, and around 100,000 people from the area fled their homes. The reason for these clashes was primarily resource scarcity. However, the magnitude of this clash was much more intense than what had been witnessed before. The clash in Jonglei was bigger, more pronounced, and was backed by mistrust between major ethnic groups.

Equatoria

The second region in focus is the Equatoria region. Equatoria holds some of the best agricultural land in South Sudan and was known as the country's breadbasket. Ironically, the escalation of violence in the region has exposed around 6 million people to the risk of starvation.

The most focused-on ethnic tensions in South Sudan are those between the Nuer and the Dinka tribes, who form the major participants of the civil war, the former being associated with the SPLA-IO and the latter with SPLA. The people in Equatoria had lived in relative harmony for years before the civil war broke out in 2013. After the SPLA accused Machar of attempting a coup in 2013, Dinka troops were accused of carrying out house-to-house searches in the Nuer suburbs. Researchers from Human Rights Watch documented widespread killing of Nuer men mostly between 15–19 December 2013. This included the mass killing of 200–300 men in the Gudele neighborhood in Juba on 16 December 2013. This led to the targeting of the members of the Dinka tribe in other parts of the country, especially the ones controlled by SPLA-IO. This event is just one of the earliest examples of Dinka-Nuer clashes following the events of December 2013.

Despite this outbreak, the region managed to stay out of the conflict until the government army began purging the opposition in 2016. The peace agreement signed between Machar and Kiir sparked violence in this relatively immune region. The peace treaty of 2015 allowed the SPLA-IO to establish bases around the country, which allowed Machar's side to recruit in Equatoria. The government's deployment of the Mathiang Anyoor, a Dinka-dominated militia sought to curtail recruitment in the region. The Mathiang Anyoor, however, terrorized the local population and allegedly killed and arrested anyone suspected of having links with the SPLA-IO. They have also been accused of targeting civilians on ethnic lines.

Since 2015, there have been targeted killings in the region that has caused many citizens to flee to other parts of the country and south to Uganda. In a recent event on 3 July 2019, more than 100 civilians were killed, and a similar number of girls and women were subjected to sexual violence in the Central Equatorian region after the revitalized peace agreement in June 2019. This surge in violence itself caused more than 56,000 civilians to become displaced within South Sudan. The land in the region moreover is not being used for agriculture due to the inherent instability of the region causing a standstill in economic activity and food production in the region.

Upper Nile

In December 2015, President Salva Kiir, after a Christmas Eve broadcast, roped another stakeholder into the conflict when he announced that the then-existing 10 states would be divided into 28 new ones. He appointed 28 new governors who promised loyalty to him in exchange for being put in charge of the new states; these people were then sworn in five days later. This move was seen as a major power play by Kiir's opposition throughout South Sudan.

The Shilluk people in the country's oil-rich Upper Nile state denounced this move. The Shilluk have often viewed their land as their most valuable asset and therefore have chosen to tread politics carefully. The Shilluk never retaliated against the government and therefore did not have a reason to expect such a move. The group's main fighting force, called the Angwelek army, was also allied with the government. The carving up of the new states, however, was viewed by the Shilluk leaders as a deliberate attempt to carve up the Shilluk homeland. It was seen by the Dinkas as a move to remove the Shilluk community from their historic land. Therefore, the Shilluk community, along with the Angwelek army, switched sides to fight with Machar.

Another reason that might have contributed to this switch in loyalty is the presence of the Dinka Padong militia in the region. Dinka Padong were civilians armed at the beginning of the conflict (in 2013) to help protect the oil operations in the region, which the government was reluctant to disarm. The presence of such a strong militia in the Shilluk region further made the community insecure.

The Shilluk force was decently supplied with arms that were provided by their former allies, the SPLA. The common people in the region who earlier benefitted from the fragile balance of politics in the region suffered from this change in the power dynamics and, during the fighting between SPLA and SPLA-IO, the allied Upper Nile faction, many Shilluk people were forced to leave their homes. In the aftermath, the chairperson of the Commission on Human Rights in South Sudan claimed that the government was engaging in 'social engineering' after around 2,000 people, mostly Dinka, were transported to the abandoned regions.

Internally Displaced Population

The major brunt of the conflict has been borne by the people of South Sudan. The people barely got time to recover from the struggle for their independence before this conflict broke out. According to a 2018 report, around 400,000 people have lost their lives since December 2013; in addition, 4.5 million people have been displaced. Such conditions have led the people to move in order to look for better opportunities. South Sudan's refugee crisis is the largest in Africa and the third largest in the world. The internal displacement of the people is a pressing problem and is difficult to assess and monitor, mainly due to the many logistical, social, and psychological disadvantages associated with the problem.

One in every three people in South Sudan is an internally displaced person. The number of internally displaced people has risen from 76,000 at the onset of the conflict in 2013 to 2 million as of 2019. The major cause of relocation of people has been the ethnic conflict. The major stakeholders in this ethnic conflict are the SPLA, with a Dinka majority, and SPLA-IO, with Nuer majority. Other ethnicities, like the Shilluk and the Equatorian tribes, have also been affected. Ethnic cleansing by the Dinka-dominated government, lack of security due to fighting between the rebels and the SPLA, lack of economic opportunities, and natural disasters have also pushed people to move to other places in search for better living conditions.

The conflict left many sections of society vulnerable. Young men and boys were targeted because they were expected to join the struggle. Women and girls were exposed to sexual violence, such as rape and harassment.

According to the 2019 Humanitarian Needs Overview, there are currently 1.36 million internally displaced people in South Sudan. Out of these, 15 percent reside in protection of civilian (PoC) sites, 32 percent in collective centers, 7 percent in informal settlements, and 46 percent in other sites .

The United Nations (UN) bases have been a sanctuary for many of the people fleeing violence. The UN recognized its role as a protector, built fences, and set up sentry points to protect its bases. However, these spaces have not escaped the effects of ethnic divides. On several occasions, the UN bases have turned into conflict zones due to the big role that ethnicity plays in the everyday lives of the people. The bases are often divided into Shilluk, Nuer, and Dinka. Despite this, the base residents witness inter-ethnic fights, which are often stopped by UN peacekeepers.

The UN bases have also been targeted and on several occasions, and humanitarian workers have been part of the casualties. In one such incident on 17 February 2016 a UN base that housed 47,000 displaced persons was attacked by culprits wearing South Sudan military uniforms. The attackers killed 30 people, injured 120 more, and burned down most of the Shilluk and the Nuer sections of the base by the time UN peacekeepers pushed the attackers out of the camp.

The civilian population at the UN bases live under 24-hour armed guard. Some civilians leave the base during the day either to work or farm, but most stay in the camps due to the fear of being attacked. In bases like these, women have taken up the responsibility of stepping out of the bases for economic activities. The justification given is that men are more likely to be murdered by the soldiers than are women. Women of the families in the bases risk being sexually harassed on a daily basis when they step out of the bases, but they prefer this to putting the men in their family at risk.

Analyzing the Data

Data on Internal Displacement

The following section assesses the yearly humanitarian needs overview data compiled by the UN Office for the Coordination of Humanitarian Affairs (UNOCHA). Examination of the data aims to connect the dots between the empirical data and the events that took place in the region at different moments throughout South Sudan's history. The data on internal displacement also is affected by the sentiments of the people involved and the way they reacted to it.

Ceasefire Violations in these States

The Cessation of Hostilities Agreement (CoHA) was signed first in January 2014 with the aim of deterring ceasefire violations by providing a platform that could hold the involved parties accountable and hence vulnerable to international scrutiny. The IGAD Monitoring and Verification mechanism (MVM) was established to monitor the CoHA. Following is a table listing the ceasefire violations monitored by the MVM, which was renamed to the Ceasefire and Transitional Security Arrangements Monitoring Mechanism (CTSAMM) after the signing of the Agreement of the resolution of the Conflict in South Sudan (CTSAMM) in August 2015.

Connecting the Dots

Equatoria

Looking at the Equatoria region, one might notice the sharp ascent of the number of IDPs in the Central, Eastern, and Western Equatorian states. Between 2015 and 2016 (compare reports from 2016 and 2017), the number displaced people in Central Equatoria almost tripled. The numbers in Eastern Equatoria have risen by more than a factor of 37, and those in Western Equatoria have risen by around 30,000. Such numbers can be attributed to events that incited insecurity at a higher magnitude, like the ones that involved a face-off between the center's forces and rebels, and also to the amount of ceasefire violations reported in Jonglei, which is just north of the Equatoria region. The instability caused by Machar's return in July 2016 could also have been behind the rise of insecurity within the state itself.

Jonglei

The state of Jonglei witnessed a gradual drop in the number of IDPs over the years despite the drop in ceasefire violations. This could be puzzling, but if one looks at the magnitude of the ceasefire violations in Jonglei in 2014, that is the year following the outbreak of the civil war. It is clear that the intensity of insecurity in the state has been high. Jonglei also has been a hotspot for communal violence in the past and a major concern for the UN Mission in South Sudan (UNMISS) before the civil war broke out.

Upper Nile

The major strain in the Upper Nile state comes from the fact that it is an oil-rich state. Hence, violence to grab land should not come as a surprise, which could explain the number of ceasefire violations. The steady number of IDPs in the state, however, is puzzling, which is why one has to look at the indigenous community in the region too.

The government announced in 2015 that it intended to divide the number of states and then went on and gave the control of those states to governors who were favored by the Dinka community. Such a move raised a lot of insecurity amongst indigenous communities in the region, but at the same time also cemented the resolve of the indigenous communities to protect their historic land. The Shilluk community is one of the prominent communities in the Upper Nile who, despite a lot of friction with the ruling SPLM, decided to stay put. This was mainly because of the fear that, if they left, the community would leave their land unprotected. This presence of strong resistance chips away at any insecurity caused by other factors.

Lack of Contextual Considerations in the Peace Deals

In March 2018, nine opposition groups, excluding the SPLA-IO, formed the South Sudan Opposition Alliance (SSOA) to negotiate with the government. Following pressure from the international community, the Sudanese government succeeded in bringing Kiir and SPLA-IO to hold talks in Sudan's capital, Khartoum. A ceasefire was signed in June 2018, where both parties agreed to form a transitional government for the 36 months leading up to the national elections. Even though the ceasefire was violated hours after it was signed, and objections were raised regarding the extension of the president's term by three years (passed by a SPLM majority parliament), the SPLA-IO agreed to share power again with Kiir. According to the power-sharing agreement, 332 of the 550 seats in parliament would go to Kiir's faction, 128 to Machar's faction, and rest to other groups. Machar would also be one of the five vice presidents. The SSOA faction, however, was dissatisfied with this arrangement due to the skewed power sharing system as depicted in the table below.

Such an inconsideration has been evident in the peace processes since the CPA in 2005. An example is the composition of the pre-election national executive appointed to oversee the interim period after the CPA. According to the CPA the representation from South Sudan was as follows—28 percent from the SPLM and 6 percent from 'other Southern political forces'.

What the Future Holds

The February 2020 peace agreement is a welcome development for South Sudan's people and the country as a whole. Further, President Kiir's assurance to ensure the security of the opposition leaders and the reappointment of Machhar as vice president gives hope to an otherwise volatile country. This volatility, however, also warns one to tread carefully so as to not repeat the events of the past. It is therefore wise to keep in mind as the country moves towards a new future the plight and the social divisions caused by rifts between the minority communities. Such a consideration would go a long way in formulating sustainable peace processes.

A look at internal migration in South Sudan makes it evident that the situation does not just simply require a CPA—it requires an inclusive one. In a volatile and ethnically diverse community, like that of South Sudan, a strong leader motivated in the wrong way could tip the scales at any moment to restart the violence. It is also clear that, from here on, the peace process has to be sensitive to people's conditions, and focus should be given to providing people the basic right to work and live peacefully. The aim going forward now should be to improve basic infrastructure, secure economic opportunities, and promote equitable resource sharing.

Tables

Table 1: A timeline of the events in the region in focus (Equatoria, Jonglei, Upper Nile)

Date	Event
July 9	South Sudan gets its independence
January 2012	Ethnic clashes between the Lou Nuer and the Murle communities. 600 people are killed and 100,000 displaced
December 2013	Outbreak of civil war. 200–300 mostly Nuer men killed in Gudele neighborhood of Juba
August 2015	The original agreement on the resolution of conflict in the republic of South Sudan is signed. Machar agrees to return to Juba.
April 2016	Fighting begins again. 300 people are killed and 26,000 people flee Juba
August 2016	Machar flees Juba
August 2018	President Kiir and Riek Machar sign power-sharing agreement
July 2019	Central Equatoria; 100 civilians are killed and women and girls are subjected to sexual exploitation; 56,000 civilians are displaced
November 11, 2019	The formation of the Unity government is pushed by 100 days.
February 2020	Both parties agree to form unity government

Table 2: Internal displacement over the years; Source: Author's calculations of UNOCHA data

Years/ Regions	2015 report	2016 report	2017 report	2018 report	2019 report
Central Equatoria	80,688	53,415	143,950	168,438	142,475
Eastern Equatoria	7,566	4,654	158,206	107,235	41,671
Western Equatoria	14,742	93,276	124,103	126,384	160,124
Jonglei	623,898	502,209	378,821	363,399	382,906
Upper Nile	390,691	299,084	291,720	219,645	364,357

Table 3: Total number of ceasefire violations

Year/Regions	2014	2015	2016	2017	2018
Central Equatoria	1	-	-	-	1
Eastern Equatoria	-	-	-	2	-
Western Equatoria	-	-	1	1	-
Jonglei	6	-	-	1	-
Upper Nile	9	3	4	1	-

Table 4: Percentage of population in power sharing

Ethnic Community(ies)	Percentage of Population	Percentage in Power Sharing
Dinka	36	60.36
Nuer	16	23.27
Others	48	16.36

References

ABC news. 2017. *South Sudan: UN warns of 'social engineering' amid looming threat of genocide.* March 15. https://www.abc.net.au/news/2017-03-15/un-warns-of-south-sudan-27social-engineering27/8354958

Al Jazeera. 2014. *Profile: South Sudan rebel leader Riek Machar.* January 5. https://www.aljazeera.com/indepth/2013/12/profile-south-sudan-riek-machar-20131230201534595392.html

—. 2019. *Riek Machar back in South Sudan for rare talks with President Kiir.* September 9. https://www.aljazeera.com/news/2019/09/riek-machar-sudan-rare-talks-president-kiir-190909080210988.html

—. 2016. *South Sudan opposition replaces missing leader Machar.* July 24. https://www.aljazeera.com/news/2016/07/south-sudan-opposition-replaces-missing-leader-machar-160723144856580.html

BBC news. 2016. *South Sudan rebel chief Riek Machar sworn in as vice-president.* April 26. https://www.bbc.com/news/world-africa-36140423

Center for Civilians in Conflict. 2016. *A Refuge in Flames: The February 17–18 Violence in Malakal POC.* April 21. https://civiliansinconflict.org/publications/research/refuge-flames-february-17-18-violence-malakal-poc/#targetText=A%20Refuge%20in%20Flames%3A%20The%20February%2017,18%20Violence%20in%20Malakal%20POC&targetText=UNITED%20NATIONS%20(Apr.%2021%2C,of%20the%2

Checchi, Francesco, Adrienne Testa, Abdihamid Warsame, Le Quach, and Rachel Burns. 2018. *Estimates of crisis-attributable mortality in South Sudan.* London: London School of Hygiene and Tropical Medicine.

Council for Foreign Relations. 2019. *Global Conflict Tracker – Civil War in South Sudan.* October 21. https://www.cfr.org/interactive/global-conflict-tracker/conflict/civil-war-south-sudan

Cumming-Bruce, Nick. 2020. *South Sudan's Feuding Leaders Announce Unity Deal, Amid War Crimes Report.* February 20. Accessed July 2020. https://www.nytimes.com/2020/02/20/world/africa/south-sudan-peace-deal.html

Dockins, pamela. 2014. *What Triggered the Kiir-Machar Rift in South Sudan?* January 9. https://www.voanews.com/africa/what-triggered-kiir-machar-rift-south-sudan

Human Rights Watch. 2014. *South Sudan: Ethnic Targeting, Widespread Killings.* January 16. https://www.hrw.org/news/2014/01/16/south-sudan-ethnic-targeting-widespread-killings

Human Security baseline Assessment. 2016. *The conflict in the Upper Nile State.* Human Security baseline Assessment.

IGAD MVM. 2019. *Ceasefire and Transitional Security Arrangements Monitoring Mechanism.* Accessed December 3, 2019. http://ctsamm.org/about/background/

Kiir, Slava. 2011. *President Kiir's Independence Speech In Full.* July 14. Accessed July 2020. http://www.gurtong.net/ECM/Editorial/tabid/124/ctl/ArticleView/mid/519/articleId/5440/President-Kiirs-Independence-Speech-In-Full.aspx

Krause, Jana. 2019. 'Stabilization and Local Conflicts: Communal and Civil War in South Sudan, Ethnopolitics'. *Ethnpolitics* 478–493.

Kulish, Nicholas. 2014. *New Estimate Sharply Raises Death Toll in South Sudan.* January 9. https://www.nytimes.com/2014/01/10/world/africa/new-estimate-sharply-raises-death-toll-in-south-sudan.html

McNeish, Hannah. 2013. *South Sudan teeters on the brink.* December 17. https://www.aljazeera.com/indepth/features/2013/12/south-sudan-teeters-brink-20131217131843385823.html

Minority Rights. n.d. *South Sudan: Displaced again by conflict, the Shilluk community faces an uncertain future.* https://minorityrights.org/south-sudan-displaced-again-by-conflict-the-shilluk-community-faces-an-uncertain-future/

Patinkin, Jason, and Simona Foltyn. 2017. *The war in Equatoria.* July 12. https://www.thenewhumanitarian.org/special-report/2017/07/12/war-equatoria

Sawe, Benjamin Elisha. 2017. *Ethnic groups of South Sudan.* April 25. https://www.worldatlas.com/articles/ethnic-groups-of-south-sudan.html

Sperber, Amanda. 2016. *Just when a peace deal seemed within reach, President Salva Kiir is threatening to plunge the country back into bloody conflict.* January 22. https://foreignpolicy.com/2016/01/22/south-sudan-next-civil-war-is-starting-shilluk-army/

Tombe, Sandra. 2019. *Revitalising the peace in South Sudan.* June 24. https://www.accord.org.za/conflict-trends/revitalising-the-peace-in-south-sudan/

UN OCHA. 2019. *The Humanitarian Needs overview 2019.* UNOCHA South Sudan.

UNHCR. n.d. *South Sudan Refugee Crisis.* https://www.unrefugees.org/emergencies/south-sudan/

United Nations Peacekeeping. 2019. *Civilians deliberately and brutally targeted during surge in conflict in Central Equitoria.* July 3. https://peacekeeping.un.org/en/civilians-deliberately-and-brutally-targeted-during-surge-conflict-central-equatoria

United Nations. 2005. *Sudan Peace agreement Signed 9 January Historic Opportunity, Security Council Told.* https://www.un.org/press/en/2005/sc8306.doc.htm

UNMIS. 2005. 'The Comprehensive Peace Agreement between The Government of The Republic of The Sudan and The Sudan People's Liberation movement/ Sudan People's Liberation Army'. United Nations Mission In Sudan. January 9. Accessed December 2, 2019. https://unmis.unmissions.org/sites/default/files/old_dnn/cpa-en.pdf.

Yoshida, Yuki. 2013. *Interethnic conflict in Jonglei State, South Sudan.* July 12. https://www.accord.org.za/ajcr-issues/%EF%BF%BCinterethnic-conflict-in-jonglei-state-south-sudan/#targetText=In%20August%2C%20Murle%20retaliation%20killed,Arms%20Survey%202012%3A%203

6

Nineteenth Century Migration Trends and the Role of Women

KENDRA MORANCY

Gendered roles and the role of women within the international community and the international space has shifted for generations. These paradigms have been challenged by feminist movements and ideals, human rights activists, and international conventions and agreements – all to bring us all closer to notions of gender equality, equality of the sexes, and international and national standards that promote the dignity of each and every individual in society. In this chapter, I analyze how the shifts in migration trends have affected women globally. To answer this question, I conducted a literature review using three primary sources that answered questions, such as: how have women migration trends changed? What are the trends that influenced this change? What are the causes and consequences of female dominated flows of migration? And what are the patterns of labor market incorporation of women migrants?

Trends Defined

The most significant trend concerning women and international migration is that, by the last half of the 20th century, they dominated the largest of inter-national migration flows (Pedraza 1991, 304). This trend goes against the long-standing stereotype that the average migrant is a single male and that the women and their families follow. While studies do show that women generally have moved across international borders to reunite with their families, this is not always the case (Pedraza 1991, 304). By 1984, males who were of working age only accounted for one-third of all immigrants into the United States (Pedraza 1991, 304). It is clear that by the late 1980s, the demographic of immigrants had transformed. The next question is why? Why were more women migrating throughout the 20th century?

The question of 'why' can be answered through multiple factors. The first and most obvious is the purpose of family reunification. According to Pedraza (1991), family reunification is what accounts for the sex distribution of immigrants in the US, as well as the availability of jobs in the health care industry, the socioeconomic conditions of the state from which they are emigrating, and lastly the presence of a US military base. I did not find suitable evidence to argue that the presence of a military base had a major impact on women immigrating the US I did have substantial evidence to prove the role of family in women's migration trends. Often, migration is a part of survival for families, which then changes the dynamic between the individual and the household. Grasmuck and Pessar (quoted in Pedraza 1991, 308) state that, 'since gender is central to household decision making, then gender is also a key factor of immigration'. If we follow this line of thinking, then we would also think that women actually have some power within their households across the various groups of migrants. Pedraza (1991) uses various examples of different migrant women's experiences as immigrants into the US to highlight the impact of family reunification on the decision to move, which I discuss below.

In some cases, the act of migrating is a way of rewriting traditional family dynamics. In one study of the Dominican Republic, women had to stop contributing to their families through subsistence farming because of the rise in commercial farming (Pedraza 1991, 308). This economic transition ruined the structure of the traditional family in various ways. Sons were no longer seen as assets, but extra mouths to feed. Sons were then expected to emigrate to alleviate family concerns. The shift towards commercial farming also created a dependence on the husbands that the women had not experienced before. At that point, emigration was a way to escape complete dependency on their husbands (Pedraza 1991, 309). Immigration for women, in many cases, was a way of gaining more autonomy over their lives. This is evident in the way that women would often postpone returning to their home countries or to not return at all. Returning home was viewed as an early retirement from their jobs and a loss of their newfound freedom (Pedraza 1991, 310). This seemed to be the norm in women from developing countries overall, even in other regions of the world. In a 1989 study by Gugler, women in Sub-Saharan Africa also had to leave behind working the farms due to economic changes and the creation of job opportunities in the cities (Pedraza 1991, 310). In addition to job opportunities and newfound freedom, these women also gained higher life expectancies with the options of health care and even education.

These examples of women migration show that the second driving force behind the high rates of women migrating to the US is the transformation of social and economic structures in sending and receiving societies. This is evident in the cases that were presented, such as in the study on *maquiladoras* at the US-Mexican border. This 1983 study found that 85 percent of the workers in export-manufacturing plants along the Mexican border were female (Galhardi 1997). This trend of Mexican women flooding the US-Mexican border for work is a result of the new jobs that were generated in the service and manufacturing sectors in industrialized countries such as the US.

Another case of women emigrating due to social and economic changes is the plight of Irish women. A 1983 study by Hsia Diner says that Irish women were pushed by poverty, landlessness, social and economic dislocation, and the aftermath of the famine (Pedraza 1991, 320). This dislocation was an effect of the transition from an agrarian, feudal society to an industrial, capitalist one, much like the case in many other countries discussed above (Pedraza 1991, 313). Other factors that pushed Irish women to migrate were the lack of men to marry and a lack of jobs. Overall, Ireland held fewer and fewer attractions for women. One interesting trend involving the emigration of Irish women is that, once one emigrated to the US, that usually started a train reaction of others following suit. Sisters, mothers, nieces, and aunts would attempt to escape the 'interlocking relationship of land-family-marriage' to end up working as domestic service workers in the US (Pedraza 1991, 320).

Cuban women were different from Irish and the Mexican women in the way that they migrated. When these women immigrated to the US, they came to participate in the labor force as well, but they would eventually stop working to return to the Cuban value of women staying at home. Myra Marx Ferree calls this 'employment without liberation' (Marx Ferre 1985, 520). These women seemed to want to maintain the traditional Cuban household dynamic and worked only to help the family (Pedraza, 1991, 314). This may have been due to their original social class in their home country. Since these women would have experienced the luxuries that come with having a middle-class income in a developing state, they would obviously have aspirations to return back to this status.

It was evident that the type of work a woman immigrant did was influenced by several factors. One of the factors was her home life. Demanding jobs like domestic housework interfered with having a potential family life, but it did give them the consistency to save money. Domestic work was also safer than factory work, was not affected by economic downturns, and exposed them to middle-class American standards. The money that domestic workers earned allowed them to achieve upward mobility sooner and would include a potential future marriage, funds for a future business, or an education for them and their kids. These trends actually led to a quicker upward social mobility for Irish women than for Irish men. More importantly, there was also a trend of certain jobs being exclusively advertized to certain groups across racial, ethnic, social, and economic status. This reserved the unskilled, unprotected, and poorly paid jobs for women and people of color (Pedraza 1991, 315). A prime example of this was New York's garment industry. In the late 19th century, there was the inception of a market for ready-made and mass-produced women's clothing because of urbanization and the creation of a national market. Since this market demand began to grow around the time of a massive influx of Russian Jews and Italians, they were the main ones to enter these spaces. In addition to Russian Jews and Italians, Puerto Rican immigrant women also became a part of the garment industry. What made these three different ethnic groups flock to the garment industry was the level of skill required to fulfill this job in addition to the demand. Women who needed to work at home because of family obligations could do that by working as subcontractors (Pedraza 1991, 316). Today, the garment industry is still made up primarily of Latin American and Asian women migrants.

There are some notable differences between the different women migrant groups and their work status once they entered the US. This is seen with Cuban women and other Latin American women. Cuban women only worked to sustain the family until they reached American middle-class status and, once that was achieved, they would leave the work force. It is a known fact that a large percentage of Cuban refugees were already skilled and educated in their home country. Their goal was to help their husbands become self-employed in business. Mexican women immigrants would continue to work in their labor roles regardless of their marital status or family obligation. Mexican women would work the garment industry or in the other factories to help generate funds for their families, but there was also the possibility of supporting a home without a male head of household. As a result, Mexican women pursued personal fulfillment.

The more successful migrants come from English-speaking countries and have higher levels of education. These factors heavily affect their migration journey and job placement. English speakers with higher levels of education are able to assimilate into the US economy and potentially obtain jobs that require higher skilled workers. One key characteristic is that one extra year of education increased their labor market participation levels by 2.3 percent and their annual wages by between $3,000–4,000 (Pfeiffer et al. 2007, 171). Even though the majority of the literature I review focuses on migrants moving to the US, it is important to note that the receiving country of all migrants influences the genders flows in relation to their economic needs (Pfeiffer et al. 2007, 29). An example of this is the garment industry and the rise of factories during the 20th century being an opportunity primarily for migrant women. The variation in these women's earning power is also attributed to the political and economic statuses of their home countries. Latin Americans had lower levels of market participation and performance in correlation with lower levels of education. Women migrants from Western Europe would have a higher earning power and a smoother transition into the US than those from less-developed states. Africans and Eastern Europeans had higher levels of market participation. Education levels of migrant women who arrived in the US in the 1990s varied across countries and regions. Where they obtained their education was more important. This study demonstrates that the group with a larger portion of tertiary educated migrants were from Central America, Asia, and the Caribbean. These groups gained this education after they migrated to the US in comparison with European migrants who gained their higher education, if any, at home (Pfeifferet *et al.* 2007, 159). The need to gain further higher education once they migrated is linked to the need to obtain stronger English-speaking skills as well as to move up in socioeconomic status. Other notable factors concerning a migrant woman's success were the number of children they had, age, and experience.

Government policies play a noteworthy role in the gender imbalances in global migration (Pedraza, 1991, 310). These policies are what made farming so unsustainable in countries such as the Dominican Republic and along Sub-Saharan Africa. Pricing policies brought down the value of cash crops and made it hard for local families to compete with big agri-businesses. Government policy in Lesotho actually restricted the migration flows of men and women. A 1983 study by Wilkinson proves that influx control laws were put in place in South Africa to restrict the movement of women (Pedraza, 1991, 310). This caused a predominantly male flow of migrant workers crossing the border into South Africa. As a result, the migration of women in search of jobs was internal within Lesotho. In some cases, immigration laws can favor family reunification, which will attract migrants who have families or single daughter or sisters who want to send for their female counterparts. In 1986, the US Congress passed the Immigration Reform and Control Act, which was a positive for women and men migrants crossing the US-Mexican border (Schiff, Morrison, and Sjöblom 2008).

Illicit migration is also worth mentioning in discussing the shift of women migration trends. This is because illicit migration is a gendered way of migrating internationally. Especially in the case of human trafficking. Why? The social status of women and children. If we look at human trafficking in Latin America and the Caribbean, the majority of trafficking victims are young adult women between the ages of 18 and 25, and in many cases between 12 and 17. This migration can be internal, such as in the case of the Dominican Republic or from the Dominican Republic to Haiti and vice versa. The driving factors for the victims are similar to those of other migrants, which include economic necessity, lack of education, and their role as single heads of households (Langberg 2005, 5). These illicit migrants face far more barriers than other, more legal migrants because of the nature of their 'work'. They will neither take home the majority of their earnings nor have the possibility of upward social mobility all because of their line of work and the social stigma aligned with it whether they work voluntarily or not. These women are trapped in a cycle that many cannot escape.

Concluding Remarks

Whether legally or illegally, all of the trends in international migration concerning women are driven by the same factors. These factors include poverty, political and social transformations, gender inequalities, family reunification, and policy changes. The role that each of these groups fulfill in the US labor market differs according to the market needs of the receiving country, which in this case is primarily the US. The general trend is that the more educated English speakers have a more successful transition into the US market, which is evident in their higher earning capabilities and socioeconomic mobility. External factors that cannot change, such as race and ethnicity, also affect these immigrant women's abilities to emigrate and their assimilation within the US. The theme of self-realization and economic independence was very consistent across most groups that were mentioned except for Cuban-American women. That was due to their prior socioeconomic status in their home country and the way that they emigrated with the family wealth-building ideal. The illicit migrants do not get to enjoy the self-realization that the other migrant women do because of the social stigma and the dangers that come with sex work or labor trafficking. The wages are either too low, unsustainable, come with no safety, or provide no autonomy over one's life.

References

Galhardi, R. 1997. *Maquiladoras prospects of regional integration and globalization. Employment and Training Papers*, Geneva: International Labour Organization.

Langberg, L. 2005. 'A Review of Recent OAS Research on Human Trafficking in the Latin American and Caribbean Region'. *International Organization for Migration (IOM)*. Volume 43, Issue 1–2: 129–139.

Pfeiffer, L., S. Richter, P. Fletcher, and J. Edward Taylor. 2007. 'Gender in Economic Research on International Migration and Its Impacts: A Critical Review'. World Bank. https://elibrary.worldbank.org/doi/abs/10.1596/978-0-8213-7227-2

Marx Ferree, M. 1985. 'Between Two Worlds: German Feminist Approaches to Working-Class Women and Work'. Journal of Women in Culture and Society 517-536.

Morrison, A. R., Schiff, M., & Sjöblom, M. 2008. *The international migration of women*. Washington: World Bank.

Pedraza, S. 1991. 'Women and Migration: The Social Consequences of Gender'. *Annual Review of Sociology*, 17: 303–25.

Shelley, L. I. 2010. *Human trafficking: A global perspective*. (2010) Cambridge: Cambridge University Press.

7

The Sense of Home and Belonging: Northern Sri Lankan Tamils in Colombo

DIOTIMA CHATTORAJ

Migration is about people: their aspirations, fears, triumphs, and tragedies. The 26 year-long civil war in Sri Lanka forced hundreds of thousands of Sri Lankan Tamils to flee their places of origin in the northern part of the island and seek refuge elsewhere. As a result, a huge number of them migrated to the capital city of Colombo to find a way out of the island and secure a better future. Several succeeded in migrating abroad while the rest settled down and integrated in Colombo. This process of integration is the result of rural-urban dichotomies in income, employment opportunities, and a future free from uncertainties. This chapter thus aims to address the notion of 'home' among northern Sri Lankan Tamils: how they locate 'home' and their app-roaches towards returning to their places of origin. Drawing on their life exper-iences in Colombo, I show that, through integration, they have succeeded to adapt to the new lifestyle and view it as a more suitable place to live compared with their former homes. My main argument revolves around the idea that displacement has facilitated the recreation of 'home' in Colombo.

In general, the term 'home' is used to denote a material asset or a physical space in which to take shelter (Gureyeva-Aliyeva and Huseynov 2011). Geographically, displaced persons, who flee due to wars, view home as rooted in their places of origin. Walicki (2011) and Chattoraj (2017) presume that, many times, these persons view the abandoned places as their 'home' and want to return. The focus on either the material or geographical aspects of home underplays its more symbolic and existential dimensions. In addition, it results in a representation of home as an unproblematic and static space where culture and identity are rooted (Malkki 1995; Bakewell 2004; Jansen and Löfving 2011).

In the context of migration, currently, renegotiations over time and space have become a new way to understand the concept of home (Chattoraj and Gerharz 2019b). Displaced persons, while on move, experience continuous loss of home, yet reconstruct them (Jansen and Löfving 2011; Taylor 2015). Home experience, for them, entails both 'uprootings' and 'regroundings' (Ahmed et al. 2003). Indeed, when locating their homes, they usually ascribe a sense of belongingness, be it attachment or detachment, to both their former and present homes (Chattoraj and Gerharz 2019a). While some experience a perceived loss of a sense of home and only view their former homes to be their 'homes' (Chattoraj 2021a), others carry home within themselves and experience it as a 'journey' (Mallett 2004). Thus, the term 'home' denotes not only a physical space for sheltering and satisfying biological needs but also a social, cultural, political, and affective space where individuals give meaning to their everyday life experiences (Blunt and Dowling 2006; Taylor 2015).

Within the context of internally displaced persons' (IDPs) sense of belonging in Colombo, this chapter offers the way displacement has transformed their sense of belonging and cultivated a new kind of meaning to home. Thus, I delve into their integration stories (providing new opportunities and a scope for personal fulfillment) with Colombo.

Methodology

This research is qualitative in nature and has used primary and secondary data for the analysis. Interviews and personal communications were the major sources of primary data which were collected in Colombo between January-March 2013. The findings discussed in the empirical sections are based on a total number of 24 interviews with IDPs in Colombo, who fled during the civil war of 1983. For security reasons, I have used pseudonyms for all the respondents.

All the mentioned cases demonstrate the strategies of recreating home in Colombo followed by the reasons why they are unwilling to return to their places of origin in the northern provinces. Memory, as well as future perspectives and aspirations determine the ways in which people relate to their homes. This material shows that, for the displaced, integrating in Colombo is a necessary step in order to develop the capacity to formulate perspectives and aspirations and to envision the future.

Home and the Sense of Belonging

This section develops a conceptual and analytical framework to analyze the respondents' narratives of how conflict and displacement shape their concept of home that has been extensively discussed in the empirical sections of the chapter. Interdisciplinary research on home and migration has often assumed that home, identity, and belonging are attached to a single, site-specific geographical place. Home, in that regard, can be understood 'as a particularly significant kind of place with which, and within which, we experience strong social, psychological, and emotive attachments' (Easthope 2004, 135). When people are forced to leave that place, it is often that they lose their homes and become homeless (Perez-Murcia 2019a). Therefore, for them, returning home closes the so-called 'refugee/displacement cycle'. However, ambiguity does exist. There have been several cases where one spends one's entire life in a single place without experiencing any kind of belonging or any sense of cultural identity to home. In cases of refugees and IDPs, often, the idea of home challenges the idea of 'return' as a prevailing 'durable solution' (Chattoraj 2021a; Chattoraj 2018a). Because returning home, for them, is neither desirable nor viable (Chattoraj 2018b). Those escaping from conflict areas (homes) may not desire to return due to appalling crimes, such as rape and torture. For others, home does not exist any longer as they have been destroyed by the conflict. As Jansen and Löfving (2011, 1) state, 'people's "place in the world" after war and repatriation continues to be violently challenged'. And after experiencing such violence and displacement, both the former homes and the people change. Thus, I show that IDPs can remake home regardless of the place in which they are settled. Return might be the most desirable and viable possibility for some, but this is not true for all of them. When people are forced to flee their homes against their will, their desire to return becomes 'invariably powerful' (Kibreab 1999, 404). As Turner (2013, 486) stresses, home 'can be both dynamic and moored – a location, or a set of relationships that shape identities and feelings of belonging'. While some experience the sense of being neither fully separated from their (former) homes nor fully integrated into the new locale, others may form manifold attachments to several places they came across throughout their migratory journeys.

Having said this, I tend to demonstrate the sense of belongingness to understand how individuals and collectives construct and experience their position within a society (Chattoraj and Gerharz 2019b). A shattered sense of belonging, however, increases the risk for psychological and physical dysfunction (Ullah et al. 2021). In this regard, it is important to highlight integration and assimilation, which are considered to overlap with the sense of belonging.

A sense of belonging to a particular place or places is created through several traces that results in enjoyment of the place – these traces may include material things, non-material attitudes, performative practices, and groups of people – their languages, way of life, actions, and activities may be welcomed by the host or excluded by the host (Ullah et al. 2021). Within the host destination, there is a social order placed by the locals (e.g., signs, laws, warnings, policies, and regulations) that is ascribed to migrants if accepted. Therefore, when accepted or agreeable to the migrant – which can activate a sense of belonging by the locals – this order opens up the process for migrants to feel a sense of belonging – if not, therefore social, cultural, and even geographical bordering may occur. Thus, we may see the development of 'China town', 'Little Manila', 'Little India', or 'Little Jaffna', where people with similar cultural and social backgrounds may have a magnet to stick to each other due to similarities.

Why Colombo?

Located on the West coast of the island, Colombo comprises the majority of Sinhalese people in Sri Lanka (around 41 percent of the total population), several Tamil-speaking persons from the north and east, along with other minorities like Malays, Borahs, Burghers, and a large number of foreigners (Chattoraj 2017). Since the 1950s, Colombo, on one hand, kept witnessing riots, bombs, and violence; on the other hand, it was a relative safe place from the fear of the Liberation Tigers of Tamil Eelam (LTTE) and exploitation by other Tamils. Thus, Colombo became 'home' for several Tamils who fled the protracted war regions.

Wellawatte, a neighborhood in Colombo, also popularly known as Little Jaffna, has been known for its multi-ethnic locales, with a mix of both affluent as well as lower-end neighborhoods (Chattoraj 2021b). And the Tamils chose Wellawatte because of safety, as well as to maintain distance from the Sinhalese community.

Recreating the Sense of Home is Colombo

The foremost concern for the displaced persons revolves around 'where to go' and 'where to stay' in physical terms. Thus, 'materiality' plays a pivotal role when it displaced persons reflect upon their 'displacement journeys' and 'experiences of home' (Perez-Murcia, 2019b). This section argues that home is conceptualized by the IDPs as a 'material space' where ideas of socioeconomic, physical, and emotional stability interplay over time and space. Therefore, they view home as a place where they can become self-sufficient in regard to socioeconomic aspects, as well as physically and emotionally stable. The material structure, in this regard, evokes a domestic space in which ideas of comfort, everyday routines, and social practices interact.

'The last couple of decades have changed my style of living. Thanks to Colombo'. This quote hints at the present living style of Pahni, who migrated to Colombo from Naina Thivu (in Jaffna) to escape war, violence, and trauma. He is socioeconomically well-settled in Colombo and living a life that is completely different to his (past) home. The capital city has brought transformations in his life. His personal definition of 'a decent survival' is 'to earn a lot of money and live a life where there is air conditioner, refrigerator, television, washing-machine, computer, and several other electronic gadgets. Without them you can live but not survive!' Colombo is the only place in the whole country where he can earn a satisfying salary so that he can afford to lead a 'decent life'. To maintain this 'decent' life-style, he needs to maximize his income, which is only possible in the capital city. Vani, another IDP near Jaffna, showed that displacement has helped her to experience 'home while moving' because home is a family nest and all the experiences of living in different places move with her wherever she goes. 'This city (Colombo) has brought me refuge and helped me to achieve my goals. Thus, here is home'. Navya, who migrated from Killinochi, also stressed the centrality of the sense of family and friends to experience home as a 'mobile space'. She was with her family all the time (pre- and post-displacement), and thus experienced the sense that she moved her home from one place to another. She stated that 'home can be both rooted and mobile as far it satisfies the emotional and material needs of the individual'.

The narratives of Lina and Fiza suggested that they have succeeded in overcoming the sense of 'being in limbo' because of their abilities to identify opportunities in Colombo where they could refashion a life project on the move and adapt to change. Post-displacement, Nairita and Shikhar enrolled in higher education (a goal they said would be difficult to achieve in Mullaitivu) and joined social organizations that fight for the rights of the displaced. This helped them progress and move ahead in their lives. Amnah, a 60-year-old woman does not let displacement act as any kind of barrier in her life: 'displacement doesn't define who I am. What defines who I am is what I used to be before displacement. So, I decided not to see myself as a displaced person but simply as Amnah. I'll never forget I was brutally uprooted from my home [Jaffna], but I decided to see displacement as an opportunity to enrich my skills and move forward.'

'Displacement has become a blessing to me.' To this end, Sourya commented that he feels extremely lucky and blessed to have been displaced to Colombo. If he would have been in Velanai (his hometown), he would have never experienced this luxury, and 'would have died being unemployed or have either become a farmer or a primary school teacher at the most'. His uncertainty comes from the fact that, in the post-war northern part of Sri Lanka, lack of youth employment is one of the most alarming issues. This is because, during the years of warfare and isolation, the area's significant manufacturing and education industries shuttered. Moreover, the continuing confiscation of land by the military, even today, since 2009, has acted as a significant barrier to the rebuilding of livelihoods and employment opportunities in a region with limited natural resources.

Shiba, whose life has been affected by conflict and displacement since he was 8 years old, illustrates best the complexities of finding a safe place to call home within national boundaries: 'Return isn't an option for me or for my mother... The place we used to call home no longer exists. I was there [Mannar] recently and I found only destruction and devastation: the sweet memories of home have gone. The shelter is destroyed and the happy memories with my siblings is only memories... I used to see Mannar as a paradise, but now I hate it. I have experienced enough of violence; now I am 37 and I live in a place [Colombo] where families can stay together without any kind of fear.'

However, 'In the 90s, I really wanted to return to my home': Alka, at the time of her displacement, was so fond of her hometown (Mullativu) that she wanted to return. Her childhood memories were filled with a feeling of contentment: 'I really loved to be in Jaffna... I fell in love with the quietness... I used to ride bicycles and roam around without any fear. Our 'home' was the best thing we had. We felt like staying so close to nature there'. Having freedom and living close to nature are important aspects that she had in her childhood.

'[B]ut as days passed my feelings also changed'.

With the passage of time, the sense of belonging and the kind of attachment, that each of the respondents had to their places of origin changed. Their accounts highlight that, during their initial days, they not only had to cope with the pain of leaving their homelands, but also had to confront the resentments of a hostile Sinhalese population in many cases in the 1990s. Nevertheless, they kept on trying to adjust to the new cultural setting (language, food, religion, way of life, belief, dress, etc.). And in doing so, they also suffered a conflict between individuals and cultures based on cultural factors. Embracing all the hardships, each one respondent succeeded in making an identity of their own in the (new) Colombo society. Their struggles helped the fond memories of their past lives fade. Therefore, they have had the strong feeling that 'to what we were attached in the 1990s have become detachment now'. Attachment to their places of origin has become 'past'; as it failed to create any impact on individuals' lives in the formation of their present identity. Also, their rural homes, with the onset of globalization and mobility, have lost their importance. People in today's world are more inclined to adopt urban lifestyles, which greatly influence their self-image and identity and have distanced them from their rural lifestyles. Their childhood memories, no doubt, were entirely positive, but as soon they distanced themselves from their homes, things changed. The distance in time and space has enabled them to differentiate the positive and negative experiences from childhood by cultivating feelings of belonging to their homes represented by people and nature. Furthermore, the relationship between rural and urban lifestyles forms a point of departure for investigating social distinctions (Chattoraj 2018a).

The value of having a rural background in an urban context can be analyzed in the context of a cultural hierarchy where the urban displays a hegemonic position, even if the countryside retains an important position as a basis for central cultural values. This echoes the story of Veerat, where the stability of today's life restricts them from returning and thus inviting uncertainties. Furthermore, several other narratives disclose that attitudes toward return vary over time. Priti and Firoz stressed that return was not an option for remaking home. Either being threatened by the Sri Lankan army or compelled to move again was for them an overarching source of concern. Rather than a homecoming, they are afraid that return might lead to 'new uprooting' and the 'beginning of a new uncertainty'. Those who fled because of the forced recruitment in the LTTE consistently reject the idea of return as an opportunity for remaking home. Pilani demonstrated that her former home in Jaffna is not a home anymore: 'I was forcibly recruited in the LTTE from where, luckily, managed to run away. I cannot see that place as home. That place only evokes sadness, anguish, sorrow, kidnapping, and prison. I hope never to return there'.

Azam went to visit his birthplace Mannar: 'In 2009, I drove to Mannar alone for the first time after 1990 and the first question I encountered was, 'Who are you? Why are you here?' I was really astonished hearing this as Mannar is my hometown, my birthplace, I have the right to come… I have lost my identity in Mannar, now I am a stranger to them so they ask me all kinds of rubbish questions'. His arrival in his hometown in Mannar left him in a doubt about his own identity. His family used to be well-known in the region, so he was taken aback to know that he is a stranger to everyone who now stays in his area. This sounds annoying, but true. During the war, like his family, most of his neighborhood had shifted either to Colombo or to other parts of the country. Subsequently, most of their homes have been occupied by Tamils, displaced from the north in 1995. Therefore, his identity is at stake as no one he knew was there. This identity problem strongly influenced his idea of and feelings towards his home. It also played a pivotal role in his decision whether to return or not to return to Mannar. To him, all his former relationships in and of the town, magnified in his imagination, had changed over time and were unmatched by the experience of his visit. He was disappointed that relation-ships were 'not what they used to be'. This also means that he would not be enjoying his family's former status, as they are 'new' to the present occupants of the town. Therefore, his first visit, which was supposed to be the first physical and emotional connection with his place of origin, a meeting of past and present, of imaginations about his (past) home and the reality of the present, turned out to be disappointing and painful. A complexity of feelings arose for him when he faced comments on entering the town: 'you are a stranger to us'. His dissatisfied first visit shattered his perception of 'home', and he continues to view Colombo as his home.

All these experiences made a strong impression in terms of the way the respondents view their former homes; they also shape their hopes of finding a safe place to call home within the national borders. Return is just 'impossible'. They believe that it is their responsibility to look after their past homes, as they are the last symbol of their parents. They are willing to renovate and rebuild the broken structures and are also looking forward to spending a day or two during holidays to feel at ease. But at no point in time will they return to settle there. Thus, I argue, the meaning of home changes for IDPs as they are affected in subtle ways due to displacement. No matter where the location is, they understand home as 'a dynamic space', a space which cannot only be made, lost, and remade on the move, but which is also in permanent transformation.

Concluding Remarks

The contribution of this chapter is to unravel how the IDPs in Colombo strategize to recreate their sense of home. This chapter has shown that conflict and displacement contribute a lot in shaping their sense of home along with their aspirations to return. Those who locate home in the northern parts see themselves as outsiders in Colombo and believe return to be the only way to recover a sense of home. Conversely, those who locate home in Colombo experience a mobile sense of home. Second-generation IDPs are more attached to Colombo. I observed that they have given up some of their traditional norms and values in order to integrate and, thus, the value and importance of their 'past homes' has gradually decreased with time. They have recreated their 'past' home culture, which is influenced by norms and values from Colombo. They identify displacement as a blessing in disguise and believe integrating into Colombo paved their way to aspire for a better future. This has also led them to reconsider and renegotiate their attachment to their 'homes'. This brings in the argument that the 'attachment to home' implies a 'positive affective bond' where an individual must maintain closeness to a specific place alters with time, place, and priority. The discussed respondents have their own tales to tell regarding their displacement; nevertheless, when it comes to their decision of return, all of them share the commonality of 'no-return'. They have adapted themselves to the city and have asserted their own individual attachments. Also, they fear an uncertain future at their places of origin.

This chapter shows that the IDPs are reproducing their privilege in the landscape of Colombo. Besides, it also demonstrates a contrasting view of the notion of 'return'. Return, for some, has been perceived as 'the only opportunity to remake home' and 'close the cycle of life', while others perceive it as an 'uncertain beginning' and 'new uprooting'. It is not only in terms of the material challenges and opportunities to remake their former homes, but also about how to deal with painful memories of violence attached to those places. The IDPs are happily settled in Colombo and are unlikely to return to the rural life where livelihood opportunities are confined to either agriculture, labor work, or fishing. Moreover, if they return, they might have to experience 'social exclusion' from the rural locals who stayed back and suffered immensely due to the war.

References

Ahmed, Sara, Fortier, Anne-Marie, Sara Claudia Castañeda, and Mimi Sheller. 2003. 'Introduction. Uprootings/ Regroundings: Questions of Home and Migration', in *Uprootings/Regroundings: Questions of Home and Migration*. Oxford: Berg, 1–23.

Bakewell, Oliver. 2004. 'Repatriation: Angolan Refugees or Migrating Villagers?', in P. Essed, G. Frerks, and Schrijvers, J. (eds.) *Refugees and the Transformation of Societies, Studies in Forced Migration*. New York: Berghahn Books, 31–41.

Blunt, Alison. and Dowling, Robyn. 2006. *Home*. London: Routledge.

Chattoraj, Diotima. 2017. *Ambivalent attachments: shifting notions of home among displaced Sri Lankan Tamils,* Doctoral dissertation, Ruhr-Universität Bochum.

Chattoraj, Diotima. (2018a) 'Experiences of Sri Lankan Tamils Displaced to Colombo: Three Narratives'. *eTropic: Electronic Journal of Studies in the Tropics* 17(1): 137–148.

Chattoraj, Diotima. (2018b) 'Narratives of Sri Lankan Displaced Tamils Living in Welfare Centers in Jaffna, Sri Lanka'. *Journal of Maritime Studies and National Integration* 2(2): 67–74.

Chattoraj, Diotima (2021a). Displacement Among Sri Lankan Tamil Migrants: The Diasporic Search for Home in the Aftermath of War. Vol. 11. Springer Nature: Singapore.

Chattoraj, Diotima. (2021b). 'Mobilities and Home: the notion of becoming insiders among the Sri Lankan Northern Tamil IDPs in Colombo'. Accepted by Mobilities.

Chattoraj, Diotima, and Gerharz, Eva. 2019a. 'Difficult Return: Muslims' Ambivalent Attachments to Jaffna in Post-Conflict Sri Lanka,' Working Paper Series 46, Institute of Asian Studies, Universiti Brunei Darussalam: Gadong, Brunei.

Chattoraj, Diotima, and Gerharz, Eva. 2019b. 'Strangers at home: narratives of northern Muslim returnees in postwar Sri Lanka'. *Sri Lanka Journal of Social Sciences* 42(2): 113–126.

Collyer, M. 2011. 'When Does Mobility Matter for Migrants in Colombo?', in Koser and Martin, (eds.) *The Migration-Displacement Nexus: Patterns, Processes and Policies*. New York and Oxford: Berghahn Books, 61–78.

Easthope, H. 2004. 'A Place Called Home.' *Housing, Theory and Society* 21: 128–138.

Gureyeva-Aliyeva, Yulia, and Tabib Huseynov. 2011. Can You Be an IDP for Twenty Years? A Comparative Field Study on the Protection Needs and Attitudes Towards Displacement Among IDPs and Host Communities in Azerbaijan. Brookings Institution – LSE, Project on Internal Displacement. Baku.

Jansen, Stef. and Lofving, Staffan. 2011. 'Towards an Anthropology of Violence, Hope and the Movement of People', in Jansen, S. and Löfving, S. (eds.) *Struggles for Home: Violence, Hope and the Movement of People*. New York: Berghahn Books, 1–23.

Kibreab, Gaim. 1999. 'Revisiting the Debate on People, Place, Identity and Displacement.' *Journal of Refugee Studies* 12: 384–410.

Malkki, Lisa. 1995. *Purity and Exile: Violence, Memory, and National Cosmology among Hutu Refugees in Tanzania*. Chicago: University of Chicago Press.

Mallett, Shelley. 2004. 'Understanding Home: A Critical Review of the Literature.' *The Sociological Review* 52: 62–89.

Maunaguru, Siddharthan. 2010. *Brokering Trasnational Tamil Marriages: Displacements, Circulations, Futures*. PhD thesis, John Hopkins University.

Perez Murcia, Luis Eduardo. 2019a. 'The sweet memories of home have gone': Displaced people searching for home in a liminal space', *Journal of Ethnic and Migration Studies*, 45(9): 1515–1531.

Perez Murcia, Luis Eduardo. 2019b. 'Where the Heart Is and Where It Hurts: Conceptions of Home for People Fleeing Conflict', *Refugee Survey Quarterly*, 38(2): 139–158.

Taylor, Helen. 2015. *Refugees and the Meaning of Home, Migration, Diasporas and Citizenship.* London: Palgrave Macmillan.

Thurairajah, Tanuja, Pia Hollenbach, and Rina Alluri. 2020. 'Vertical living: transnational urbanisation and diasporic returns to Wellawatte/Colombo, Sri Lanka', *South Asian Diaspora* 12(1): 73–91.

Turner, Jennifer. 2013. 'Re-"homing" the Ex-Offender: Constructing a "Prisoner Dyspora"'. *Area* 45: 485–492.

Ullah, AKM Ahsan, Noor Hasharina Hasan, Siti Mazidah Mohamad, and Chattoraj, Diotima. 2020a. 'Migration and security: Implications for minority migrant groups', *India Quarterly,* 76(1): 136–153.

Ullah, AKM Ahsan, Noor Hasharina Hasan, Siti Mazidah Mohamad, and Chattoraj, Diotima. 2021. 'Privileged migrants and their sense of belonging: Insider or Outsider?'. (Accepted by *Asian Journal of Social Science*).

Ullah, AKM Ahsan and Nawaz, Farah. 2020. 'The culture of migration in Southeast Asia: Acculturation, Enculturation or Deculturation?' (unpublished).

Walicki, Nadine. 2011. *Part Protracted, Part Progress: Durable Solutions for IDPs Through Local Integration*. Washington, DC: Brookings Institution, 61–81.

8

The Cruelty of Kafala

LORCÁN OWENS

The heat. The humidity. My first reaction when I arrived in the Middle East was the absolutely unbearable intensity of heat and humidity. 'It's 1 o'clock in the morning. How is it so hot'? My newfound Irish friend who I had met at the airport in Dublin laughed. 'Didn't I tell you? You'll get used to it though. It'll be grand (fine) by mid-October'. We soon had to part ways as she was getting a flight to Doha while I had to wait another two hours for my flight to Kuwait, my final destination and where I would be for the next 10 months.

I moved to Kuwait in August 2014 with absolutely no idea what was ahead of me. I was armed with minimal knowledge of Kuwaiti, Arab and Islamic society and, for all intents and purposes, was moving blindly to the Middle East. I had been offered a job teaching in a school in Salmiya, Kuwait. I was put in touch with one of the current teachers, who told me about school life and so on. Even though I had months to prepare, I focused on the logistics of posting my passport to the Kuwaiti embassy in London, as there is none in Ireland. I had to get documents legalized, and then they had to be attested. I needed vaccines, the Kuwaiti embassy was a nightmare to deal with on the phone and everything just seemed to take ages. I never thought to research Kuwait bars coming to terms with the fact it was (and remains) a dry state. No alcohol. No pubs. No nightclubs.

> Oh, you can get drink in the compounds. I had a friend who worked on the oil rigs in Saudi years ago and they used to drink in their compound on the QT …
>
> … No, there's no alcohol in Kuwait. It is completely illegal. I have researched this.

And on it went in the months prior to my moving, with self-appointed experts who had never set foot in Kuwait and could not believe it bordered Iraq, telling me I would definitely get drink in this non-existent compound in which I was being told I would live. Oh, and that I was daft to be moving to a country bordering Iraq. It was only at the airport in Dublin where I met the girl who warned me about the heat that I got my first insight into Kafala. I was warned about 'the locals'. 'If your school is all locals, they'll be wild. They all have nannies at home and they do the homework for them, they do everything to be honest. They haven't the heed of the dog on them'.

I was stunned. I had not heard anything about this. How do they afford nannies? They all have one, not just princes and royalty? 'They all have one, some have more. They bring them over from The Philippines and Sri Lanka mainly. They have them working all hours to be honest. It's shocking really'. I was starting to wonder what I was doing. I had been nervous the night before my flight, which was the first time I had felt anxious about the move. Now, I felt mild panic. How bad will it be? Are they going to be hard to teach if their behavior is this bad? They must be so spoiled if they all have nannies. I was reassured. Behavior is an issue in all schools but it was not always that bad. 'You just accept it and live for the weekend and the salary'. Once we parted ways, I was on my own waiting for the last leg of my flight from Abu Dhabi to Kuwait. There was no going back.

I landed in Kuwait at 4 am, hours later than scheduled, as I had been delayed in both Dublin and Abu Dhabi. I had informed Human Resources (HR) that I would be arriving late into the night as I was told a member of staff would be there to meet me at the airport and bring me to my accommodation. After a tedious and tetchy encounter with border security, I was in Kuwait. Everyone was wearing a *dishdasha* or *thobe*. Everyone, that is, except the odd westerner and the airport staff who were scurrying around in their blue uniforms, heads down, no eye contact, silent. I made my way through the arrivals gates and scanned the signs held aloft by weary taxi drivers. I spotted my name. A small, dumpy woman seemed to know who I was before I approached her. She looked absolutely jaded.

'I'm sorry about the delay; at least you didn't have to wait here for hours waiting for me'.

'I've been here for six hours, sir'.

'Six hours?! I emailed HR and told them I was going to be hours late. Did they not tell you'?

'No, sir'.

I was stunned. Stunned that this woman, who was Filipina, was kept waiting for six hours when I had told HR not to have anyone waiting for me until 3 am at the earliest. Why does she keep calling me sir?

As we approached my new home, I looked outside and got a huge shock. I expected grand, arabesque houses along pristine avenues lined with palm trees and exotic flowers. Kuwait looked anything but. There were huge bins plonked intermittently on what should have been footpaths but were de facto parking spaces. Often, there was no footpath at all. The buildings were a ramshackle mess of aging apartment blocks with grimy windows. And the cats. There were cats everywhere. When we finally reached the apartment, I was relieved that it was in a relatively modern building. I was on the 18th floor.

'I'm really sorry you had to wait that long. Will you get to lie in tomorrow for a while'?

'No sir, I'm working again in two hours'.

A wave of guilt, pity and shock hit me. I thought back to my earlier chat in the airport, which seemed an age ago: 'They have them working all hours to be honest. It's shocking really'.

The next day when I met my new housemates, I told them about what had happened. One of them was 'fresh off the boat' like myself, while the other was starting his second year. 'I'm not one bit surprised to hear that', said the latter. 'They have her working flat out'. We went to school to get our classrooms organized. There were women in blue uniforms running around everywhere. They were all South Asian and Filipina, armed with brushes, scissors, display paper and dustpans. I was shown my classroom and set about organizing display charts. Suddenly, three of the women entered. 'Good morning sir', they chimed. 'Oh, hello my name is Lorcán, I'm new here, what're your names? Where are you from'? They seemed taken aback, almost embarrassed. I cannot even remember if they answered because they proceeded to take the scissors, tape and paper from my hands and methodically covered the display boards. I was mortified.

'I can do it myself; it is fine, I'm sure you're busy elsewhere'.

'It is ok sir, we'll do it all'.

I felt somewhat emasculated and useless. I was later told these were 'the helpers', a group of maybe 20 women who cleaned the school, escorted the smaller children to the bathroom, prepared the lunches and assisted at arrival and dismissal of pupils. There was a hierarchy within this group, led by the oldest, known as 'Momma', who spoke to us with confidence and assertiveness. She was the de facto mediator for the group. After a few weeks, I stopped trying to make conversation with 'the helpers', as it never went past pleasantries. Some had very limited English, but it became apparent that they were not used to interacting with teachers. We would often chat and joke with Momma, who held the unique position of liaising seamlessly with everyone in the school. The woman who greeted me at the airport was also held in high esteem, and had no problem letting people know if she was in a bad mood.

However, I became uncomfortably aware that the school was deeply stratified. I learnt that the helpers earned a pittance and lived together in shared accommodation, sending home as much as possible to their families via Western Union. They were from impoverished backgrounds with little to no education. Momma seemed to like Kuwait. She had been there for several years, had learnt English and held a position of authority within the school. She preferred being a helper than being a nanny.

I noticed how dismissive some of the children were towards their nannies. One day, when we were gathered in the hall for dismissal, one of the boys in my class threw his school bag at the feet of his nanny to pick up while he skipped off out the door. I gave the class a stern lecture the next day about respect. 'How many of you say thank you to your nanny? Do you ever ask her about her family and if she misses them'? The class fell silent. I was lucky in that I had a generally well-behaved class, and some students were evidently fond of their nannies. They often compensated for distant parents, many of whom I learnt had marital problems, a common problem in Kuwait. However, there was this sense that the children had no concept of a common humanity. There was no education in civic values, racism, tolerance and general decency. I often felt the children were good to be as good as they were. There were parents who cared deeply about their children and would talk to me weekly, sometimes even daily, about their children's behavior and progress. Others had no interest, and it was left to the nannies to rear, educate and discipline them.

Kafala: The Epiphany

As time progressed and I slowly settled into life in Kuwait, I saw evidence of a stratified and unequal society all around me. There was an unwritten and unspoken 'pecking order' of Gulf Cooperation Council (GCC) Arabs on the top, with Kuwaitis, Emiratis, Qataris and Saudis occupying first place. Omanis and Bahrainis were perceived as holding a lesser social status, reflecting their smaller economies. Westerners were next, Americans and British in highest esteem, followed by Canadians, Australians and Irish, other Europeans and white South Africans on the bottom of this subcategory. Lebanese were held in high esteem, as they dominated the social and cultural life of the Arab world, but this was not reflected in their salaries. Egyptians were not 'real' Arabs, as they are African. Palestinians held a contradictory position in Kuwait, being admired, pitied and despised simultaneously; admired for their resilience, pitied because many were officially refugees and despised because they sided with Saddam Hussein during the Gulf War. Jordanians and Syrians were somewhat neutral in Kuwait, though some Syrian children were taunted as being with 'DAESH' on the schoolyard, given that the Islamic State (ISIS) had just occupied vast swathes of the country.

Beyond these upper echelons, there was everyone else. They were the people who formed a majority of the population not only in Kuwait, but the entire GCC region. They were the ones who slaved on building sites in the searing heat, who drove taxis, who cleaned, who cooked, who served us in the vast malls, who served us in restaurants, who packed our shopping for us and carried it out to the awaiting taxi. These were the people who actually worked and kept Kuwaiti oil rigs pumping, who transported the oil to refineries, who built the refineries and rigs in the first place and who ensured the petro-economy functioned.

Within this enormous cohort, there was again a pecking order. The Filipina maid earned more than a Nepali or Bangladeshi maid, as she spoke fluent English and was considered less likely to be homesick or complain. The Pakistani taxi driver earned more than a Bangladeshi. And as it happened, an English teacher earned more than an Irish teacher, as they were British and had a desirable accent. Kuwait was like a much bigger and more complex version of the Titanic, only instead of A Deck to E Deck, there was A1, A2, E1, E2 and so on.

I soon learnt the only way to really learn about what was going on was to chat to the people affected. This was difficult. You could not strike up a conversation with your waiter about whether she lived 10 to a room. The helpers did not engage in conversation. The only people who could talk openly without being overheard were taxi drivers. I always sat in the front of a taxi in Kuwait, as I would do in Ireland. It was always the same format: haggle about the price of the fare (there were no taxi meters), explain I am not British and no, I am not married and I have no intention of marrying in the near future. The horror.

However, the conversation would often become very deep. It was universally clear that these taxi drivers were not happy to be in Kuwait. The sense of homesickness was palpable. They had families back in Pakistan or India or Bangladesh who were relying on the remittances sent from Kuwait to pay for their education. They were sacrificing their mental, emotional and sexual wellbeing to live in a country that had neither comprehension nor interest in the lengths these migrant workers were willing to go to raise their families. Kuwait was, for them, a means to an end; stay for a few years, save and leave. The same objective as the rest of us, only they suffered the receiving end of Kuwait's endemic racism and classism.

'How many of you share a room'?

'Nine, sir'.

Sometimes there were more. Then there was the confiscation of passports in case they absconded. They would arrive, get their permits, and their passport would then be confiscated for a year. They would travel home once a year for two weeks or perhaps a month. They worked long hours. They did not have a guaranteed salary, as the fares were negotiated. One dinar was the going rate, but they always asked westerners for three dinars. They always seemed weary or despondent or a combination of both. Some would become upset when they would talk about home. None of them ever said, 'I'm happy to be in Kuwait'.

Kuwait was not a happy place. People were there to make money, and money seemed to be the only priority in life. Kuwait was an Islamic state in name only. The religion of Kuwait was oil, and oil was money. There was nothing to do socially except shop, eat, sunbathe or play sport, that is if you were happy to train in 40 degrees at nine o'clock on a Friday morning. We had private house parties where we drank ethanol mixed with Fanta or Pepsi, which we would buy, often still warm, from a 'dealer'. It was a big occasion to be invited to a chalet party in the desert. You would pay 10 or 20 dinars for the privilege of dancing in a shed not unlike a dance hall in 1930s rural Ireland. These parties were the only time it felt like I was in a normal country, where you could actually enjoy yourself and be surrounded by people who cared about life other than work or money or buying things.

The chalet and house parties gave a false sense of equality and normality to an otherwise deeply hierarchical and classist society. We were the lucky ones who had the freedom to socialize, but at least there was diversity. There were Arabs from Lebanon, Egypt and beyond. Many Kuwaitis would join too, eager to escape the omnipresent watch of their families. There might be staff from the French embassy mingling with Sri Lankans on a business trip. It was an engineered microcosm of normality in a country where people were classified and categorised according to their race, status and passport.

Back at school, we were told that we would be getting teaching assistants in November or early December. We were delighted, as we needed the support, given the lack of provision for special educational needs and the misbehavior that was a problem in the senior classes. There would be one assistant per class in the junior classes, and Year Three and upwards would have one per year group. We were delighted when they arrived. In Year Three, we were joined by Ms. Lopez (names have been changed to protect identity). She and the others had arrived from the Philippines, and we later learnt that they were all qualified teachers. It was late November when they arrived, so I knew they would not be able to travel home for Christmas, as it had taken us over a month to get our permits and residency before we got our passports back.

In the meantime, we went to Dubai for the Dubai Sevens rugby tournament. I was gob smacked. I had already visited Bahrain at this point and was jealous of the nightlife and laissez-faire social scene I witnessed there. Dubai was like stepping from the 19th century to the 21st compared to Kuwait. The scale of the opulence, no open skips by the side of the road, no cats scavenging, the taxis had meters, the bus stops were enclosed and air conditioned, the Burj Khalifa, Barasti, the partying… It was everything Kuwait was not.

On the flight back to Kuwait, I was downbeat. What am I doing in this sandpit where you cannot even drink? I moaned all the way back in the taxi until one of my Irish friends said, 'Lorcán, you do realize Dubai is just a cleaner version of Kuwait with alcohol? They still have the same set up in their schools, the salary is not as good and they treat migrants as badly as they do here, or worse. At least they don't hide it here like they do in Dubai'.

She was right. I had got so caught up in the glamor and frenzy of the weekend that I had not noticed that the bars had a team of workers in uniform sweeping and washing, the children had their nannies in pink or blue uniforms chasing after them in Dubai Mall, the taxi drivers seemed as tired and wan and the many building sites were operating all through the night with minimal health and safety precautions in place.

I went home that Christmas and just forgot about Kuwait until I had to return. When we landed back in school, I spoke to Ms. Lopez. I had not actually gotten to know her before Christmas between her late arrival and exams. 'It must have been hard to miss Christmas, but at least you can go home next year'.

'No sir, I can't'.

'Why can't you? You'll get your passport back soon enough, and you can go where you want then'.

'No, we can't. We will not get our passports back. They took them off us and we can't leave for two years'.

I was absolutely stunned. I learnt that the school had confiscated the teaching assistants' passports and that they were being locked into their accommodation at night in case they escaped. This was the moment that I truly realized the ugly and cruel reality of the Kafala system. I still did not know this was the name of it, but it did not matter. None of the teaching assistants had been told this would happen when they signed their contracts. They had not consented to having their passports confiscated, they were told they would go home in summer, that they were free to do as they wished after work and during the weekends. None of this materialized. I spoke to other teaching assistants and suggested they complain to their embassy, but they said there was no point, nothing would happen and they needed the money. Besides, the embassy was already inundated with case after case of domestic workers who had fled their employer, been abused, had not received their salary in months and felt their lives were under threat.

I spoke to the vice principal about it. She was close to the teaching assistants and had already learnt of what was going on. She was equally appalled and had tried to speak to the owner, but the owner scoffed at her concerns. She told me the fire alarm went off one night and they panicked as they were locked in and could not escape. They had to wait for the woman who had the keys, the woman who met me at the airport, before they could escape. I spoke to my housemates about what I had learnt and one of them, the one who had joined in August, got angry. 'I'm bringing this up with HR. This is slavery. We can't let this go on'. True to his word, he did bring it up. The HR manager, who was British, was clearly uncomfortable that the issue was being highlighted. 'We can speak about this at another time if that's ok'.

If that's ok?

Locking women into their already crowded accommodation, confiscating their passports and controlling their movements down to allowing them to attend mass and go shopping while supervised on Fridays, and she wanted us to move on to discuss some inspection we needed to start preparing for. It was January at this point, and I finally realized what kind of country Kuwait, and the countries surrounding it, were really like: sandpits of greed, gross exploitation, modern-day indentured servitude at best and outright slavery at worst in all but name. I had already said I would only do a year here due to the boredom, but I had another more valid reason to leave now.

The children knew no better. 'I have had six nannies since I was born and they all leave', chimed one Egyptian boy in my class, with his Arabized English and blissful innocence highlighting how normal he seemed to think this was. I wondered why they all left, given I knew his father was difficult to deal with at the best of times. I saw how other westerners had normalized Kafala. They even had a term to distinguish and otherize the 'lesser', even though we were all subject to a *kafeel* (sponsor): we are expats, they are migrants. They became so entitled. Some of the teachers would pay one of the helpers to clean their apartment on Friday. Saying please and thank you steadily dropped the longer you lived there. People would complain about a slow taxi driver or slow service in a restaurant, with no empathy that maybe they were exhausted having worked for hours on end.

I witnessed a Kuwaiti go ballistic with a driver for failing to park his car correctly. He started roaring at him, throwing insults in Arabic at the man who was so shocked he had not time to process it. Then he proceeded to hit him on the head with his newspaper. I had had enough. I shouted at him to stop. They say your accent is most acute when you are angry, and this was true with me.

'Cop yourself on, he parked your car, if you don't like it get up and do it yourself'.

I froze. Had I crossed the line? I was told never to challenge 'the locals' way back that late August in Dublin Airport when I was wondering should I get on the plane at all. In the end, he walked away and complained to the guard on duty in the car park. This could be a sacking offense, as they would accept the flimsiest excuse or complaint to sack a migrant, thereby rendering their visa null and void and, suddenly, they are illegal and either leave the country or become undocumented laborers.

By the time I left Kuwait in June 2015, I understood how abnormal and obscene Kuwaiti society was. I was starting to normalize what was going on after only 10 months and knew the longer I remained, the more likely it was that I would lose my sense of morality and decency. It is not normal for whole races to be castigated as servile, docile and placid subservient workers, who do all the hard labor, all the menial tasks, build everything, do everything that allows society to function at a basic level and yet get no recognition or consideration for their human dignity.

This is the cruelty of Kafala. The Kafala system in Kuwait, the wider Gulf and Lebanon is a system entrenched in the belief that certain races exist to serve a supposed superior race. It is manifest and blatant racism coupled with arrogant classism that has become so normalized in these societies that even seemingly enlightened, educated and otherwise decent people find ways to rationalize the savagery that is tolerated and encouraged around them. The list of excuses is tiring and endless.

'They're better off here than they would be at home'.

'They need the money'.

'Nobody made them move here'.

'Think of how this is helping their families back at home'.

'I do not hear/see them complaining'.

'That's just the way it is'.

And on it goes. This is how Arab societies and many westerners who live in the region excuse something that would be intolerable and unspeakable in a liberal democracy. Children grow up thinking it is perfectly acceptable that their nanny sleeps in a room not the size of a bathroom, works anywhere from 12 to 20 hours a day and never expresses personal opinions, thoughts or emotions. In Lebanon, two domestic workers die a day and some Lebanese put this down to being emotionally unstable and incapable of adapting to 'a modern society' (Su 2017). This is perhaps the most pathetic and laughable trait of these societies: laughable if it were not so tragic. These countries really believe that they not only blend the best of old and new, they are doing these people a favor by giving them a job. In their twisted logic of trickle-down economics, the Saudis assert that they are assisting the global Ummah by allowing Bangladeshi, Pakistani and other Muslim migrants to share in the wealth and opportunity of the Land of the Two Holy Mosques. Indeed, they even allow Christian Ethiopian and Filipino migrants a chance to elevate their lot. The Emiratis give agrarian Afghan and Nepalese laborers a glimpse of western life, where Islamic tradition and western capitalism merge in a tacky display of ostentatiousness, gluttony and grotesque inequality.

In Lebanon, despite its own economic catastrophe with over 50 percent of the population facing poverty by the end of this year, many still think it is perfectly normal, indeed necessary, to have an Ethiopian domestic servant available minute and hour to tend to their every need (Su, 2017). Except now many cannot afford this status symbol, so they dump them at the Ethiopian, Filipino or relevant embassy in Beirut, emotionally destroyed, physically scarred and psychologically traumatized after years of de facto slavery. Qatar, eager to clean up its image as the world questions allegations of alarming mortality rates at World Cup building sites, has just announced an end to its Kafala system, increasing the minimum wage and allowing workers to switch jobs after six months with no penalty. Whether this will actually be implemented remains to be seen. In my experience in Kuwait, the United Arab Emirates and Lebanon, withholding salaries, confiscating passports and working without adequate rest are endemic in the region, and I do not foresee a change of law changing a mentality that views certain races and classes as perpetual servants for a supposed superior race. Back in Lebanon, in tandem with the Qatari announcement, social media activists who have campaigned for years to abolish Kafala were excited to learn that Lebanon would finally abolish its own Kafala structure, potentially ending the misery inflicted on hundreds of thousands daily.

But I wonder if the long-term damage caused by the normalization of Kafala will undo the social stigma, racism and classism that facilitates Kafala in the first place. Yes, Saudi Arabia is a theocratic dictatorship, but the Saudi government never forced anyone to hire a maid. The Emirati government does not force or officially allow its citizens to confiscate their domestic servants' passports. The Kuwaiti government did not force my former employer to lock in some 60 teaching assistants, drivers, cleaners and administrative staff into their accommodation at night. The western engineers working on building the stadia of the World Cup could insist on minimal personal protective equipment, a safe work environment and dignified accommodation for laborers, but choose to pass a blind eye. The Lebanese have a semblance of a democracy, and yet, while there is a growing and vibrant civil society movement advocating for the rights of migrants, the fact remains that Lebanese society, as a whole, prizes having a live-in maid as a status symbol, a visible yet docile and silent demonstration of belonging somewhere in the fast-shrinking Lebanese bourgeoisie. Having a live-in house cleaner in the Middle East is a commodity that tells your neighbors and society where you are in the pecking order, with the nationality and number of domestic workers a demonstration of wealth and prestige.

Abolishing Kafala in Qatar and potentially Lebanon is an important and significant step, but educating children and society that exploitation is immoral, that there is no pecking order, demonstrating real tolerance, equality and human dignity is the only way to ultimately end this mentality that has been allowed to persist for far too long. It is now well past time for the citizens and western residents of the GCC, Lebanon and beyond to seriously question the social structures that have allowed de facto modern-day slavery to persist so pervasively into the 21st century.

Abolishing Kafala on paper is a start, changing the mentality of normalized exploitation is going to take a lot longer.

Reference

Su, Alice. 2017. 'Slave labour? Death rate doubles for migrant domestic workers in Lebanon'. *The New Humanitarian.* May 15. Accessed April 17, 2021. https://www.thenewhumanitarian.org/2017/05/15/slave-labour-death-rate-doubles-migrant-domestic-workers-lebanon

9

English with a Non-Native Accent as a Basis for Stigma and Discrimination in the United States

MELTEM YILMAZ SENER

Although it is hard to argue that there is now awareness about, and protection against all kinds of discriminatory practices, some forms of discrimination have become more easily identified, and there are currently more widespread institutional protections against them. In many different country contexts, there are increasingly more recognized definitions of discrimination based on, for instance, class, gender or race. However, discrimination based on non-native accent is not one of those widely accepted categories of discrimination. In fact, accent is considered something that a person can change almost effortlessly if s/he has the will to do so, and thus, it is seen as different from other characteristics, such as race or gender, which admittedly cannot be changed. According to this rationale, the fact that you speak another language with an accent signals incompetence and lack of effort. If you are not changing, an aspect about you (accented speech) that you are capable of changing, differential treatment against you cannot be discrimination, the logic goes. Therefore, it gives employers, public officials, teachers and native speakers reason to treat you differently from those who speak 'without an accent'.

Accent refers to the phonological characteristics of speech. In that sense, everyone has an accent (Matsuda 1991). There are accents that are geographically or class-determined, and other accents are caused by the transfer of the phonological features of the native language to a second language. This second one is called an L2 accent (Derwing et al. 2014, 65), while L1 accent refers to the native variety of a language. This paper is about the non-native accent or L2 accent, which is an issue that has so far been especially discussed by linguists and researchers of education. While this chapter benefits from the contributions of these two groups of researchers on the subject, it mainly aims to make a sociological contribution to debates on accent by focusing on discrimination based on non-native accent. Although discrimination has been a well-researched sociological subject in general, it has especially been studied with reference to such categories as class, race and gender. Discrimination based on non-native accent remains a largely under-researched area for sociologists.

This chapter will start with a linguistic discussion on accent and non-native/L2 accent, and will then tie these discussions to a more sociological debate on how non-native accent can be a basis for stigma, how people make judgements about others based on non-native accent and what non-native accent discrimination implies especially in the context of the United States. The following section will first give information about the empirical research, where we conducted semi-structured interviews with 40 highly skilled Turkish migrants who left Turkey as adults with at least undergraduate degrees to have further degrees or professional careers in the US and returned back to Turkey after living in the US for at least five years. In this section, there will also be a discussion of the experiences of our respondents as non-native speakers of English during their stay in the US. This section will emphasize that, although they had left Turkey with certified proficiency in English, their everyday life in the US was largely shaped by the fact that they had non-native accents. Although the respondents did not name their difficulties related to accent as discrimination, depending on their accounts, I argue that their non-native accent functioned as a marker of their foreignness and became a basis for negative differential treatment in different spheres of life in the US. In the conclusion, I discuss the ways non-native accent can become a basis for discrimination in the context of the US and why migrants who experience discriminatory treatment do not call it discrimination.

Stigma and Discrimination Based on Non-Native/ L2 Accent

Lipi-Green (2011) argues that, like any other group of scholars, linguists do not form a homogeneous club; there are several differences of opinion among them. However, there are also certain points about which all linguists agree. She identifies five 'linguistic facts of life', where, she argues, most linguists would come together (Lipi-Green 2011 6–7).

– All spoken language changes over time.
– All spoken languages are equal in terms of linguistic potential.
– Grammaticality and communicative effectiveness are distinct and

independent issues.
- Written language and spoken language are historically, structurally and functionally fundamentally different creatures.
- Variation is intrinsic to all spoken language at every level, and much of that variation serves an emblematic purpose.

By stating the last point, Lipi-Green (2011, 20) points out the fact that spoken language varies for every speaker. If the language in question is English, this is 'true even for those who believe themselves to speak an educated, elevated, supra-regional English' (Lipi-Green 2011, 20–21). There are three major sources of variation in spoken language: language internal pressures, external influences on language and variation arising from language as a creative vehicle on free expression (Lipi-Green 2011, 21). Considering the variation in spoken language, she talks about *standard language* and *non-accent* as myths, reminding readers that 'myths are used to justify social order, and to encourage or coerce consensual participation in that order' (Lipi-Green 2011, 44). Following this line of argument, it will be appropriate to approach the notion of non-accent as a myth that justifies existing hierarchies between the individuals who have the 'right' accent and those who do not.

Goffman (1963, 12), in his classic work, defines stigma as 'an attribute that is deeply discrediting'. However, after giving this definition, he also emphasizes that we need a language of relationships, not a language of attributes while we are talking about stigma. It means that there may be certain attributes that will be discrediting in one context, while confirming the usualness in another context. In that sense, it may be more appropriate to think of stigma as 'a special kind of relationship between attribute and stereotype' (Goffman 1963,13). He discusses three different types of stigma based on various physical deformities, character traits and race, nation and religion, commonly interpreted as group identity (Goffman 1963, 13). The person who has a stigma possesses an undesired differentness from what others expect, and those others who conform to expectations are 'normals', as Goffman (1963, 14) identifies them. These 'normals' then exercise various types of discrimination against those with stigma and reduce their life chances (Goffman 1963, 15).

According to this framework, can non-native accent function as a basis for stigma? Being an indicator that one was born and raised in another country, non-native accent can be a basis for the third type of stigma that Goffman discusses. 'Normals' are the ones who speak the language with native accents, while those who have non-native accents are stigmatized. Although everybody has an accent and not having an accent is a myth, people use accent to make judgements about others, both in their official capacities and in everyday life encounters. In everyday usage, people say 'a person has an accent' to point out the difference from an assumed norm of non-accent, as if only foreigners have accent (Matsuda 1991). A non-native accent is one of the most noticeable characteristics of those individuals who are originally from other countries, and marks and potentially stigmatizes them as not being native born (Gluszek and Dovidio 2010). Research shows that native speakers/listeners are highly sensitive to the presence of foreign accents (Atagi and Bent 2017; Derwing and Munro 2009). Accent is certainly not the only factor that people use to evaluate others. There are many other categories, such as gender, skin color, other physical features, etc. However, as Derwing et al. (2014, 66) emphasize, society has become more aware of prejudices based on these categories and is more prepared to guard vulnerable groups against them compared to accent prejudices. Especially regarding the US context, researchers argue that following increasingly tighter anti-discrimination laws in the US, more subtle ways for exclusion have been created, and language and accent have become an acceptable excuse to discriminate (Gluszek and Dovidio 2010). As Zuidema (2005, 666) argues, linguistic prejudice is an 'acceptable' American prejudice; assumptions are made about the others' intelligence, competence, morality, etc. based on how they speak. Teachers, employers and landlords assume that a person whose first language is English might be a better student, employee or tenant than another person who speaks English with a non-native accent. Accordingly, these assumptions do not remain inconsequential thoughts, but turn into active discrimination.

As Lipi-Green (2011, 67) states,

> When an individual is asked to reject their own language, we are asking them to drop allegiances to the people and places that define them. We do not, cannot under our laws, ask a person to change the color of her skin, her religion, her gender, her sexual identity, but we regularly demand of people that they suppress or deny the most effective way they have of situating themselves socially in the world.

In other words, native speakers very often demand too easily that foreigners shift from their own language to another one, ignoring the complex and deeply rooted meanings of native language for individuals. In addition to discussing the desirability of an immediate language and accent shift, we can also question how doable it is. Researchers often refer to a *critical period* for second language acquisition (Vanhove, 2013). According to the critical period hypothesis, there is a critical period for attainment of second language and, beyond the critical period, people cannot achieve native-like competence in their second language.[1] Researchers argue that there is enough evidence to support the argument that there is an age-based limitation on the attainment of proficiency in a second language (Patkowski 1990). Therefore, if we consider the widely accepted notion that learning a second language after early childhood almost inevitably leads to non-native accent and speech that is different from the speech of native speakers (Tahta et al. 1981; Scovel 1988; Flege et al. 1995; Munro et al. 2006), expecting people to drop their L2 accent is almost like expecting them to change the color of their skin. It is unrealistic to expect a person who learned English as an adult to speak like a native speaker of English (Ingram 2009). However, it is rarely recognized as such, and differential treatment based on L2 accent is not considered as discrimination by many. As Akomolafe (2013) argues, of the major types of discrimination, accent discrimination is the one that gets the least attention.

Munro (2003) discusses the probable reasons behind negative reactions to foreign accents. The first possibility he discusses is *accent stereotyping*, where one's prejudice against a certain group is triggered when that person hears speech patterns associated with that group. The second possibility is that some people find accented speech unintelligible or difficult to comprehend. While he evaluates this second argument, he stresses that there is, in fact, no reason to think that accented language is typically difficult to understand, since 'an objection to accents on the grounds that they are unintelligible may sometimes have more to do with an unwillingness to accommodate differences in one's interlocutors than with a genuine concern about comprehension' (Munro 2003, 40). Munro (2003) looks at human rights cases that involve language-related issues in Canada and argues that, in most of those cases, the notion of accent was crucial. In his study, he identifies three types of accent discrimination: discrimination in hiring decisions, discrimination in employment and tenancy and harassment based on accented speech (Munro 2003).

What forms can non-native accent discrimination take in the context of the US? In the US, a person's intellectual ability is often evaluated based on his/her ability to speak 'standard English', and people who speak with foreign accents can be subject to negative evaluation and discrimination (Ingram 2009). Nguyen (1993), with reference to the US context, also argues that employers use claims of 'unintelligible English' to not hire accented but qualified applicants. She also reminds the fact that courts have recognized how discrimination against accent may function as the equivalent of discrimination against national origin, a violation of Title VII of the Civil Rights

---

[1]   For debates on the critical period hypothesis, see Penfield and Roberts (1959), Lenneberg (1967), Singleton and Lengyel (1995), Birdsong (1999), Scovel (2000), Bailey et al. (2001), Hakuta et al. (2003) and Singleton (2005).

Act of 1964 (Nguyen 1993, 1327). Some studies focus on the effects of non-native accents on employment-related decisions in the US (Hosoda and Romero 2010; Deprez-Sims and Morris 2010), which demonstrate that accent can have an impact on evaluations of an applicant's suitability for a job. What do we know about the extent of accent-focused discrimination in the US? Lippi-Green (1997, 153) mentions a statistical study of a stratified random sample of employers nationwide where 10 percent of the sample, or 461,000 companies, that employ millions of people openly disclosed that they 'discriminated on the basis of a person's foreign appearance or accent'. Although there is a need for further large-scale studies on the subject, this gives an idea about the extent of accent discrimination in the US.

Some researchers also argue that there is *differential accent discrimination* in the US (Holmes 1992; Quinn and Petrick 1993). This means that, in the evaluation of the accent, speaker's non-native status is not the only applicable issue; perceptions about the speaker's particular group or nationality can also be pertinent (Lindemann 2003). While the stigmatized identifier of using 'broken' English is used for non-native accents, this category may not necessarily apply to Western European accents (Lindemann 2005). Some non-native accents are considered high-status, whereas others are regarded as low-status. Low-status accents are usually thought of as difficult to comprehend and signaling incompetence, while high-status accents are evaluated as easy to understand and indicative of competence (Quinn and Petrick 1993; Matsuda 1991; Goto 2008). In the context of the US, a person with a high-status British accent will be regarded as well educated and upper class (Quinn and Petrick 1993) while French accents will be considered 'cute' (Lippi-Green 1997). In contrast, Hispanic, African and Eastern European accents will be considered negatively (Valles 2015). Individuals who speak English with a low-status foreign accent are more prone to accent discrimination (Akomolafe 2013; Valles 2015).

Turkish Highly-Skilled Migrants in the US

This chapter highlights some findings of a broader research project about return migration of highly skilled Turkish migrants who lived in either the US or Germany, and then returned back to Turkey. In a previous paper (Yilmaz Sener 2019), I discussed the findings of this research project with respect to discrimination perceptions of these two groups of returnees. According to these findings, returnees from Germany thought they experienced ethnic discrimination, and discrimination was a major reason behind their return, while returnees from the US did not mention discrimination, and discrimination was not a reason for return for them. To explain the difference between these two contexts, I used Alba's (2005) distinction between bright and blurry boundaries. I described Germany as a context that has bright ethnic boundaries for Turkish migrants even when we focus on a highly skilled group, whereas the US had blurry ethnic boundaries for this group. Many of the highly skilled Turkish migrants who lived in the US argued that they faced difficulties because of the fact that they speak English with a foreign accent. However, they did not consider those difficulties as discrimination.

In this chapter, I focus on interviews with the respondents who lived in the US and, contrary to what they claimed, I argue that what they experienced can in fact be considered accent discrimination. By analyzing their responses to questions not only about language and accent, but also about their experiences in the US, I aim to demonstrate how and why the instances that they described as the challenges of being a foreigner can be thought of as examples of accent discrimination. In parallel with the previous discussion of the literature on accent discrimination, I argue that the reason they do not think of these negative experiences as discrimination has to do with the fact that negative differential treatment based on foreign accent is rarely recognized as discrimination. Although they shared their negative experiences related to foreign accent as events that made their life more difficult and made them unhappy, they either blamed themselves individually for those experiences, as they were 'unsuccessful' in dropping their accent, or they thought of it as a part of the 'inevitable burden' attached to being a foreigner.

As mentioned previously, this research concerns highly skilled migrants. We interviewed people who emigrated from Turkey with at least an undergraduate degree (in three cases as university exchange students), had further degrees and/or professional experience in the host country and stayed there for at least five years and then returned back to Turkey. We conducted the interviews in Turkey after their return. Most of the interviews were conducted face-to-face, although in a few cases, they were conducted on Skype. They were semi-structured, in-depth interviews in Turkish, which lasted 1.5 hours on average. The interviews were recorded, transcribed and translated into English by the author. We interviewed 40 returnees from the US. (We also interviewed 40 returnees from Germany. However, this chapter only focuses on the returnees from the US.) Our respondents were all over 20 years old at the time of their migration. The majority completed their secondary and high school education at institutions where the language of instruction was English, including private schools or competitive public schools, which accept students based on central, countrywide examinations. They also completed their university education at prestigious public or private universities, which instruct in English. Although, in many cases, interviewees demonstrated their proficiency in written English, through their Test of English as a Foreign Language (TOEFL), Graduate Record Examinations (GRE) or Graduate Management Admission Test (GMAT) scores, they had all learned English after early childhood or after the *critical period*, and most had few experiences speaking English in daily life before migrating. In general, they had few international experiences before migrating. Consequently, most interviewees expressed difficulties speaking English, especially during their first years in the US. Rather than the academic language with which they were familiar thanks to their education in Turkey, they found the language of everyday life more challenging during this initial period. Below are three responses about the challenge of using English in everyday life during the initial stage.

> My English was good. I received my education at *Kadikoy Anadolu Lisesi*[2] and *Bogazici University*[3] afterwards... I was pretty good at writing and reading, but I was not that good at speaking. During the first two years, I can say, I had some problems related to speaking. In terms of both expressing myself and also making myself understood by others... It was challenging for me because we were not practicing English in Turkey. Especially after the first three years, I started feeling more confident... I had never gone abroad before this experience.

> My business English was good. But to be more fluent in the language of everyday life, you need to know those simple words... Like tweezers... It was a word that I had never used in English previously. After living there, you learn the name for it when you need to buy tweezers. Do you know when I realized that I became fluent in English? The TV was on in the living room and I was cooking in the kitchen. But I could follow the conversations on TV easily, as if they were in Turkish.

> Before going to the US, the level of my English was in fact advanced. I had an internet-based TOEFL score of 113 out of 120. But, you know, as is common for many Turks, I did not find myself so good when it came to speaking. There were times when I had issues in everyday conversations, especially during the first years. Sometimes because of the idioms that they use, other times because of the accent... But except that, for instance in writing, I did not have problems.

According to the accounts of our interviewees, although it created problems during the first period of their stay, the challenge of becoming familiar with

---

[2]   A prestigious public high school in Istanbul that gives education in English. Students are placed at the school according to their scores from a central nationwide exam.

[3]   A major research university in Istanbul. It was founded in 1863 as Robert College and was the first American higher education institution founded outside the US.

everyday language and becoming fluent in using it was something that they could overcome. It was a problem that they could work on and solve. There was a need to gain more information about the cultural context, but for a person who was open to learning, it was possible to eventually get familiar with new ways of doing things. However, as some of them discussed during the interviews, 'the problem of accent' was not something that they could solve. After a while, they realized that how they were perceived when they spoke with a non-native accent was important in terms of positioning them, but they had little control over their accent even if they wanted to change it.

> When I first went to the US, there were some very simple idioms or sayings that I did not know. However, I think that was a problem only at the very beginning. In a pretty short period, it is possible to overcome the challenges related to understanding what others are saying. Another dimension is about the pace of your speech. That can also be solved relatively fast. If you have a tendency to speak a lot, or if you are brave enough, you can also solve that quickly. But you cannot solve the problem of accent. You cannot change it. That is, in fact, what it means to be American or to speak like an American... If you speak with the same accent, with the same pace as an American, then you can be accepted... The critical distinction was not about being Turkish or being something else, but it was mostly about whether or not you can have those conversations with the same accent, with the same pace. That is what we cannot do.

This person feels that as a foreigner, he can only feel accepted in the US if he can speak English without a foreign accent. However, he also came to the realization that one cannot change his/her accent easily. In this context, while changing one's accent or solving the 'problem of accent' becomes the condition of being accepted, it is also unachievable. Defined as such, it is easy to see how it can be the source of a lot of frustration. In another example, many years after her return, one interviewee still blamed herself for not having been able to drop her accent. She was still reflecting on what she could have done to 'solve that problem'.

> I had many problems related to my accent, yes... As I had an accent, there was the problem of incomprehensibility. I wish I could have taken some courses... Courses on accent reduction for instance... Maybe it would have been useful for being understood.

The accent came to be understood as the main sign of foreignness.

According to these respondents, their foreignness was not necessarily something that others could immediately recognize based on their physical appearance. It became identifiable when they started speaking:

> The level of my English was advanced when I went to the US. I knew the language pretty well, I think... In Turkey, I'd had all my classes in English up to the completion of my Master's degree. [In the US,] I did not find the academic life challenging. However, when it came to the language of everyday life... Even to have a conversation at a restaurant... You need to get used to it. And the biggest challenge about speaking was the accent. When they look at you from the outside, they don't necessarily understand that you are a foreigner. However, at the moment you open your mouth and say something... You are a foreigner; you have an accent. I didn't like the fact that I could never be ordinary. It is not like racism or hostility to foreigners but... They lump you in another category. In that sense, after that point, you can never be ordinary. It's like, in terms of appearance, you are one of them. But when you start speaking, it becomes obvious that you are not one of them.

This quotation is important in many ways. First, it tells us how this respondent perceives the distinctions between 'us' and 'them' in the context of the US. He thinks that his physical appearance does not necessarily mark him as different from the members of mainstream society. According to his understanding, for American people, the distinction is especially based on whether or not one speaks English with a foreign accent. If we rephrase this using Goffman's (1963) vocabulary, non-native accent was the aspect that stigmatized them. Accent was what made it impossible for them to be 'normal'. Once native speakers hear the accent, the person was identified as the Other, which from then on made it impossible to be an 'ordinary person'; one is put into that other category of 'the foreigner'.

Respondents who lived in smaller towns or cities, which were less cosmopolitan, talked about having experienced even bigger problems in social life because of speaking English with a foreign accent. As the locals had limited experience interacting with people from other countries, their foreign accent became a significant barrier in everyday communication. However, according to the perception of our respondents, this barrier was not necessarily related to comprehension. Many of them talked about how they could successfully communicate with other international people in English during their stay in the US. They all spoke English as a second (or third or fourth) language, and they all had their different, peculiar accents. However, using English as a medium, they were able to communicate with each other effectively. According to some of our respondents, the problem about communicating with Americans in English was related to the fact that Americans 'did not want to understand' people who spoke English with non-native accents. This is in parallel with Munro's (2003) argument about the intelligibility and comprehensibility of accented speech, which I discussed in the previous sections: The objection to accented speech on the grounds that 'it is unintelligible seems to have more to do with an unwillingness to accommodate differences'. It seems to have less to do with a genuine concern about comprehension.

> Accent was a problem. With international friends, it was not an issue. But with Americans, it was a totally different story... This is the thing about Americans: they see it as their right not to understand you if you are speaking with an accent. They claim that they don't understand you. This really annoyed me both at the university and also outside. At the university, we were teaching, we were interacting with students. At the end of each semester, I got the same comment on evaluations: 'He has a very strong accent. We don't understand people who have accents, why do we have them as instructors' and such... Always the same kinds of comments... Economics is not like, for instance, philosophy. I don't need to lecture for hours. I solve problems, and then I explain the solutions with simple terminology. If you catch the terms, you will easily understand. But still, we always used to get the same types of comments.

He believes that in the case of the students who complained about his accent, there was not a sincere interest in communicating or a sincere effort to understand what he was explaining. How the students phrased their comments on the evaluation forms, putting it as 'he has a strong accent' also provides a hint that the students saw it as their right to criticize accented English. They mentioned a fact almost as a defect. This respondent was not the only one who got the comment that 'he has an accent' on student evaluation forms. As mentioned earlier, many of our respondents went to the US for graduate degrees and worked as teaching assistants, instructors or professors during their studies and afterwards. Depending on their accounts, getting the comment that one has an accent as a criticism from students seems to be a common experience.

Discussion and Conclusion

In this paper, I focused on non-native accent discrimination in the US, a type of discrimination that is not usually considered discrimination by the public and that has been a rather neglected subject in the sociological literature.

Benefiting from the works of especially linguists, I argued that the notion of not having an accent is a myth, and for those people who learn a second language after the critical period, it is almost impossible not to have an L2 accent and to speak that language in the same way as a native speaker. Next, depending on Goffman's (1963) arguments on stigma, I discussed how non-native accent can function as a basis for stigma. Moreover, depending on the literature, I also discussed how non-native accent can be a basis for discrimination, especially in the context of the US. Next, depending on our empirical research with highly skilled Turkish return migrants from the US, I tried to demonstrate what kind of difficulties or problems they had in the US related to speaking English as a second language and speaking it with an L2-accent. Our respondents had certified proficiency in English before their migration. However, having learned English during later years, not when they were kids, and not having spoken it in everyday life before their migration to the US as adults, they did not have native-level fluency and had a non-native accent. Referring to their narratives, I discussed the ways their non-native accent functioned as a marker of their difference, and what kind of problems it created for them.

One important question to ask at this point is whether the problems related to non-native accent narrated by our respondents can be considered examples of discrimination. As Altman (2011) discusses, although there are some disagreements about the definition of discrimination, it is possible to say that 'discrimination consists of acts, practices or policies that impose a relative disadvantage on persons based on their membership in a salient social group.' With its emphasis on *salience*, this definition suggests that groups based on, for instance, race, gender and religion can be potential grounds of discrimination, while groups based on, for instance, 'length of toe nails' would not count. Additionally, the definition of discriminatory conduct also indicates that it creates some kind of disadvantage or harm for those at whom it is directed. This disadvantage or harm is determined relative to a comparison group.

According to this definition, I argue that the accent-related problems that our respondents mentioned during the interviews can be considered examples of discrimination, although most respondents did not think of them as discriminatory conduct. Their non-native accent positioned them in this salient social category of the *foreigner* (or maybe a foreigner with a low-status foreign accent) which put them in a disadvantaged position relative to those who speak with native accents or high-status foreign accents. As highly skilled migrants who left Turkey with at least undergraduate degrees, they were accepted to graduate programs or professional jobs based on both their subject-area competence and certified proficiency in English. However, even after getting used to speaking English in everyday life, they were treated differently relative to the comparison group of native speakers because of an aspect that they cannot in fact change, as the critical period argument suggests. This differential treatment led to disadvantages in their lives. Consequently, the experiences they mentioned count as discrimination based on non-native accent.

How can we explain the fact that our respondents did not name these negative experiences as discrimination? First, like many other people, our respondents did not think that negative differential treatment based on accent would count as discrimination. They were thinking of discrimination as related to more well-known categories, such as race or gender. Additionally, when they noticed that they were assessed or treated negatively because of the kind of accent they had, they blamed themselves for 'not having been able to' drop their accent and speak 'without accent'. Some of them eventually came to the realization that it is not achievable to speak in the same way as a native speaker if one migrates after a certain age. However, they had mixed feelings, and this realization seemed to exist together with self-blame. Furthermore, in general, it is very hard to be sure about or prove discrimination if it does not take the form of direct confrontation, and in many instances, it does not take that form. Therefore, in most other cases, people just 'have a feeling' that they are treated negatively. Based on such vague feelings, people hesitate to call those experiences discrimination. The fact that one is being discriminated against can position that person as a victim, and many people do not prefer to be seen as victims. Consequently, while responding to the questions of a researcher about whether they were discriminated against during their time in the US, they may not necessarily want to reconstruct their past as a painful one and name their experiences as discrimination. I also argue that being highly educated people who are used to perceiving themselves as having a high status, they do not want to situate themselves as having been in a disadvantaged position as migrants in the US, based on their own perception of situations.[4] While considering their negative experiences as 'problems' that happened once in a while is easier, naming them as 'discrimination' means attributing to them a more structural, permanent nature. Many of our respondents seemed to be unwilling to position themselves as having been exposed to such continuous negative treatment. Further studies that reflect on why migrants (as well as other groups of people) avoid naming differential treatment directed at them as discrimination can help us better understand the dynamics of this phenomenon.

---

[4]   Although the findings of interviews with the highly skilled returnees from Germany are not discussed in this paper, it is important to stress that the responses of those respondents were strikingly different. Most of them stated that they were discriminated against in several different spheres. When the negative encounters take the form of direct confrontation and one has a large number of such experiences repeatedly, which seems to be the case for Turkish migrants in Germany, the person more readily accepts them as discrimination.

* This research was supported by TUBITAK (The Scientific and Technological Research Council of Turkey) Grant 1001, Project No: 114K685. Meltem Yilmaz Sener was the Principle Investigator for the Project. The author would like to thank Gonca Türgen for her assistance and support throughout the research process.

References

Akomolafe, S. 2013. 'The invisible minority: Revisiting the debate on foreign-accented speakers and upward mobility in the workplace', *Journal of Cultural Diversity*, 20(1).

Alba, R. 2005. 'Bright vs. blurred boundaries: Second-generation assimilation and exclusion in France, Germany, and the United States', *Ethnic and racial studies*, *28*(1), 20–49.

Altman, A. 2011. 'Discrimination'. https://plato.stanford.edu/entries/discrimination/

Atagi, E., & Bent, T. 2017. Nonnative accent discrimination with words and sentences. *Phonetica*, *74*(3), 173–191.

Bailey Jr, D. B., Bruer, J. T., Symons, F. J., & Lichtman, J. W. 2001. *Critical thinking about critical periods*. Paul H Brookes Publishing.

Birdsong, D. (Ed.). 1999. *Second language acquisition and the critical period hypothesis*. Routledge.

Deprez-Sims, A. S., & Morris, S. B. 2010. 'Accents in the workplace: Their effects during a job interview', *International Journal of Psychology*, 45(6), 417–426.

Derwing, T. M., Fraser, H., Kang, O., & Thomson, R. I. 2014. 'L2 accent and ethics: Issues that merit attention' in *Englishes in multilingual contexts* (pp. 63–80). Springer: Dordrecht.

Derwing, T. M., & Munro, M. J. 2009. 'Putting accent in its place: Rethinking obstacles to communication', *Language teaching*, 42(4), 476–490.

Flege, J. E., Munro, M. J., & MacKay, I. R. 1995. 'Factors affecting strength of perceived foreign accent in a second language', *The Journal of the Acoustical Society of America*, 97(5), 3125–3134.

Gluszek, A., & Dovidio, J. F. (2010). 'The way they speak: A social psychological perspective on the stigma of nonnative accents in communication', *Personality and social psychology review*, 14(2), 214–237.

Goffman, E. 1963. *Stigma*. London: Penguin.

Goto, S. 2008. 'Issues Facing Asian Americans and Pacific Islanders in the Federal Workplace'. The US Equal Employment Opportunity Commission, Meeting of July 22. https://www.eeoc.gov/eeoc/meetings/archive/7-22-08/goto.html

Hakuta, K., Bialystok, E., & Wiley, E. 2003. 'Critical evidence: A test of the critical-period hypothesis for second-language acquisition', *Psychological science*, 14(1), 31–38.

Holmes, S. A. 1992. 'U.S. sues over dismissal for accent', *New York Times*, January 28. http://www.nytimes.com/1992/01/18/us/us-sues-over-dismissal-for-accent.html?scp=2&sq=Holmes,%20January%2018,%201992&st=cse

Hosoda, M., & Stone-Romero, E. 2010. 'The effects of foreign accents on employment-related decisions', *Journal of Managerial Psychology*, 25(2), 113–132.

Ingram, P. D. 2009. 'Are accents one of the last acceptable areas for discrimination?', *Journal of Extension*, 47(1), 1–5.

Lenneberg, E. H. (1967). The biological foundations of language. *Hospital Practice*, 2(12), 59–67.

Lindemann, S. 2005. 'Who speaks "broken English"? US undergraduates' perceptions of non-native English 1', *International Journal of Applied Linguistics*, 15(2), 187–212.

Lindemann, S. 2003. 'Koreans, Chinese or Indians? Attitudes and ideologies about non-native English speakers in the United States', *Journal of sociolinguistics*, 7(3), 348–364.

Lippi-Green, R. 2012. *English with an accent: Language, ideology and discrimination in the United States*. Abingdon: Routledge.

Matsuda, M. J. 1991. 'Voices of America: Accent, antidiscrimination law, and a jurisprudence for the last reconstruction', *Yale Law Journal*, 1329–1407.

Munro, M. J. 2003. 'A primer on accent discrimination in the Canadian context', *TESL Canada Journal*, 38–51.

Munro, M. J., Derwing, T. M., & Sato, K. 2006. 'Salient accents, covert attitudes: Consciousness-raising for pre-service second language teachers', *Prospect: An Australian journal of TESOL*, 21(1), 67–79.

Nguyen, B. B. D. 1993. 'Accent discrimination and the test of spoken English: A call for an objective assessment of the comprehensibility of nonnative speakers', *Calif. L. Rev.*, *81*, 1325.

Patkowski, M. S. 1990. 'Age and accent in a second language: A reply to James Emil Flege', *Applied linguistics*, 11(1), 73–89.

Penfield, W., & Roberts, L. 2014. *Speech and brain mechanisms*. Princeton University Press.

Quinn, J. F., & Petrick, J. A. 1993. Emerging strategic human resource challenges in managing accent discrimination and ethnic diversity. *Applied HRM Research*, 4(2), 79–93.

Scovel, T. 1988. *A time to speak: A psycholinguistic inquiry into the critical period for human speech*. Newbury House Publishers.

Scovel, T. 2000. 'A critical review of the critical period research', *Annual Review of Applied Linguistics*, 20, 213–223.

Singleton, D. 2005. 'The critical period hypothesis: A coat of many colours', *International review of applied linguistics in language teaching*, 43(4), 269–285.

Singleton, D. M., & Lengyel, Z. (Eds.). 1995. *The age factor in second language acquisition: A critical look at the critical period hypothesis*. Multilingual Matters.

Tahta, S., Wood, M., & Loewenthal, K. 1981. 'Foreign accents: Factors relating to transfer of accent from the first language to a second language', *Language and Speech*, 24(3), 265–272.

Valles, B. 2015. The impact of accented English on speech comprehension. *ETD Collection for University of Texas, El Paso*. https://scholarworks.utep.edu/dissertations/AAI3708574

Vanhove, Jan. 2013. 'The Critical Period Hypothesis in Second Language Acquisition: A Statistical Critique and a Reanalysis'. *PLoS One*, 9(7): 1–15.

Yilmaz Sener, M. 2019. 'Perceived discrimination as a major factor behind return migration? The return of Turkish qualified migrants from the USA and Germany', *Journal of Ethnic and Migration Studies*, 45(15), 2801–2819.

Zuidema, L. A. 2005. 'Myth education: Rationale and strategies for teaching against linguistic prejudice', *Journal of Adolescent & Adult Literacy*, 48(8), 666–675.

10

Unaccompanied Children on the Move: From Central America to the United States via Mexico

MONICA TRIGOS PADILLA

In the 2014 fiscal year, United States immigration authorities at the US-Mexico border apprehended 68,541 unaccompanied minors (Lind 2014). This garnered the attention of different stakeholders at regional and international levels. Following policy amendments, the number of unaccompanied minors decreased for a short period. However, in the 2019 fiscal year, the number reached its highest peak, increasing to 76,873 and representing a 58 per cent increase from 2018 (CRS 2019). According to the US government, 'an unaccompanied minor is an immigrant who is under the age of 18 and not in the care of a parent or legal guardian at the time of entry, who is left unacc-ompanied after entry, and who does not have a family member or legal guardian willing or able to care for them in the arrival country' (CRS 2019). It is important to mention that, while some travel completely alone, others may cross with their families and then become separated from them or may be left behind by smugglers or other people on the move.

In 2019, around 85 percent of apprehended unaccompanied minors traveled to the US from Honduras, El Salvador and Guatemala (CRS 2019). Many of them fled domestic abuse and gang violence. Others attempted to cross the border to escape poverty, while others to reunite with their families. The journey to remain in the US gets harder as immigration policies get more rigid over time. This chapter will explore, through a storytelling and facts-based approach, the lives of the unaccompanied minors on the move. From their experiences in their countries of origin to what drives them to leave to the challenges they face throughout their travels and the unexpected hurdles along the way. Additionally, it will cover the current change in policies that concern them in Mexico and the US. Finally, it will conclude with recommendations amid the ongoing COVID-19 pandemic and its effects on their livelihoods.

'The Black Hole'

F is from Honduras; he is 14 years old. F knew his dad was being extorted by MS-13 for a long time. During an economic crisis, his dad lost his job, so he was not able to pay the extortion rate. One day, F was coming from the supermarket with his dad and witnessed his dad shot to death by two gang members. F was 10 when this happened. After this, he was continuously persecuted by gang members on his way to school every day. He left school. They waited for him outside his house. The options MS-13 gave him were to become part of the gang or die. It was the year 2014 and he decided to leave (live). He had an uncle that had already escaped up north in the United States. He joined a group of people that were leaving and also fleeing from violence and lack of opportunities. He didn't tell his mother he was leaving; he couldn't say goodbye. One day, very early, he left and started his journey.

S is from El Salvador; she is 16 years old. S lives with her mother and her mother's boyfriend. Her mother's boyfriend sexually assaults her. He is very violent with her and her mother. She is not safe at home, but neither is she safe on the streets. Gang members also sexually harass her in the streets, and every day is worse than the one before. She couldn't leave her house, but she couldn't live in her house either. After one night, while her mother was asleep, her boyfriend's mother tried to rape S. She fought back and was able to escape, but she knew she couldn't go back, so she went to her cousin's even though she knew she wouldn't be able to stay there for long. Her sister lived in the US. They had been planning S's trip for a long time; they had some money. S didn't have anywhere else to go. She had a few contacts and some money, so she was able to pay a smuggler. She had been advised that the journey to the US was going to be harder than life. She believed she couldn't go through something harder than what she was already experiencing. She took a contraceptive injection that protected her for three months. It was the late summer of 2019.

Although treated as such, the countries from the Northern Triangle – Guatemala, Honduras and El Salvador –are not the same. Each of them has its characteristics and particularities. In structural factors for migration, however, they do share some similarities in push factors and all have communities that have networks of people already living in the US (Mexa Institute 2019, 2).

Guatemala faces high levels of poverty and inequality (World Bank 2020). It has a population of 17.1 million, of which 53 percent is less than 24 years old. Guatemala has one of the highest teenage pregnancy rates in Latin America (Wilson, 2019). In 2018, Guatemala had a homicide rate of 39.9 homicides per 100,000 residents (UNODC 2018), though Guatemala's City homicide rate was 42.5 homicides per 100,000 residents, above the national average (Asmann and O'Reilly 2020).

Honduras is a low-income country, with high poverty and inequality levels (World Bank 2020). It has a population of 9.2 million, of which 51 percent is less than 24 years old (CIA 2020). One in four teenagers has become mothers at least once (Tejeda 2019). In 2018, Honduras had a homicide rate of 39.9 homicides per 100,000 residents, the third highest in Latin America (UNODC 2018).

El Salvador has low levels of growth and poverty reduction is moderate (World Bank 2020). It has a population of 6.4 million, of which around 45 percent is less than 24 years old (CIA 2020). One-fourth of teenagers have become pregnant (O'toole 2018). In 2018, Honduras had a homicide rate of 52 homicides per 100,000 residents, the highest in Latin America (UNODC 2018).

Gang violence, criminal organizations, and human trafficking

The Northern Triangle is one of the most violent regions of the world. Violence is not something recent, and has become more targeted towards children and youth in recent years. They have to decide between joining the gangs or criminal organizations and leaving. Hence, it becomes one of the main reasons of why they decide to flee with their families or as unaccompanied migrants (Acuna 2018).

Guatemala went through a civil war from 1954 to 1996, which caused a lot of structural, organized and political violence that continues in the democratic and post-conflict periods. Additionally, gangs, such as MS-13 and Barrio 18, have wide control in Guatemala City. Extortion is one of the ways they exert this control (Asmann and O'Reilly 2020). Drug trafficking from organized crime has become very powerful in the country. This has repercussions not only on criminal activities, but also fluctuations in politics, security and the economy. Additionally, human trafficking networks have gained power and increased their presence and connections globally (Gutiérrez 2018, 13).

Between the 1970s and 1990s, while Guatemala, El Salvador and Nicaragua were facing civil wars, Honduras was relatively stable. However, its poverty levels and surroundings made it vulnerable to corruption and crime. Since the

1980s, it has been used as a trafficking route of drugs and weapons, becoming a strategic point for drug trafficking through to the US. Also, it was used by the US as an anti-communist 'hub' and became severely militarized (Insight Crime 2018). Additionally, there has been political turmoil and protests against the government, which have been repressed by security forces (Amnesty International 2018, 2). Poverty and the lack of solid institutions and social services provide perfect opportunities for gangs and criminal organizations to operate. It is estimated that there are between 12,000 and 40,000 active gang members throughout Honduras, especially in urban areas (as in Guatemala, MS-13 and Barrio 18 have a presence). Eighty percent of homicide cases are not investigated and 96 percent are never resolved (Davis, Jensen and Kitchens 2012). Additionally, institutions tend to collaborate with gangs and criminal organizations, and this well-known corruption and impunity decreases the trust, reliability and protection of the population (AJS 2018).

During El Salvador's civil war, many had to seek refuge in the US. Hence, some of these gangs initially formed in the 1980s in Los Angeles. Later, many of them were deported to El Salvador, 'exporting the violence' (O'toole 2018). MS-13 and Barrio 18 are two of the most important gangs that, over time, started controlling the country and gaining power due to the poverty and unequal conditions in El Salvador. Additionally, it is a country that has been regularly used as a route for drug trafficking (Clavel 2017, 1–2). It is believed that, currently, around 60,000 gang members are present in at least 247 of the 262 municipalities, controlling the streets and public spaces. Gangs use violence and extortion in public places and, with this, have increased their territorial control, which has expanded from urban to rural areas. The police and government security institutions have not been able to protect the population and there have been allegations of collaboration between them and the gangs (HRW 2020).

These particular conditions in these three countries push children and youth to look for sources of income and protection and to search for their identities in the only alternatives they are given: to become part of a gang or flee for survival. Gangs and criminal organizations use violence, extortion, threats, drug trafficking, sexual and gender-based violence, disappearances, child recruitment (supposedly as young as 10 years old, though there is documentation of children between five to seven years old) and murder with impunity (AJS 2018). The main homicide victims from these gangs are young men from low-income areas. Additionally, children and youth are harassed on their way to schools, which leads them to drop out of school and end up with no access to education. Finally, those who decide to leave the gangs are potential victims of persecution (IRB 2018). Gangs have big networks not only inside each country, but also in the region, including in Mexico.

Sexual and gender-based violence

These three countries are extremely unsafe for women. In Guatemala, the homicide rate for women is more than three times higher than the global average. Honduras is almost 12 times more than the global average. Finally, in El Salvador, it is around six times higher than the global average (Ahmed 2019).

Sexual and gender-based violence has a great impact on the lives of many women, girls and lesbian, gay, bisexual and trans (LGBT) persons in these three countries. 'Gender based violence can take many forms including rape, slavery, forced impregnation/miscarriages, kidnapping/trafficking, forced nudity, and disease transmission, with rape and sexual abuse being among the most common' (Manjoo and McRaith, 2011). It becomes one of the reasons that force individuals to flee. As mentioned before, this type of violence is perpetrated by gangs and criminal organizations, but also by family members, the police and other authorities. As with other crimes, these also face high levels of impunity, and a very low percentage of crimes end in convictions. The ones that do are not prosecuted forcefully. So, they are not given an alternative between being victims of this violence and leaving (living).

Guatemala ranks among the countries with the highest rate of violent deaths among women (9.7 in 100,000) (OCDE 2019). Eighty-eight percent of cases reported by women go unpunished. A total of 89 extortion-related homicides were reported in the second half of 2020 (OSAC 2020, 2). In Guatemala, three in every ten women who are murdered had reported being victims of violence or had restraining orders issued for their protection (Dotson 2018).

In Honduras, young teenagers and girls are victims of gangs and criminal organizations. Women's homicide rate is 10.9 out of 100,000, of which 96 percent remain unpunished. On the other hand, 60 percent of cases of violence against women are committed by a close family member (IMUMI 2020, 32–34). Girls not only suffer domestic physical violence, but also an unequal distribution of food, education and household workload. Also, the access that they have to sexual and reproductive health information and services in restricted. More than one-third of teenagers marry or get together (IMUMI 2020, 23–31). Women have no incentives to file a complaint, since they know that they will not receive protection and, additionally, are discouraged from filing complaints by the police.

Women in El Salvador go through similar circumstances, as violence targeting girls and teenagers is found in the houses and on the streets. In

2017, 67 in 100 women have experienced a certain type of domestic violence. Of those, 34 have gone to the police to report it. In 2018, El Salvador was rated as the 'most femicidal country in Latin America' by the Economic Commission for Latin America and the Caribbean (CEPAL 2018). 'More than 60% of the 4,304 cases of sexual violence recorded in 2018 involved 12- to 17-year-olds, according to a report published the Organization of Salvadoran Women for Peace' (Nóchez and Guzmán 2020).

'The Death Corridor'

F walked, took rides and slept on the streets from Honduras to Guatemala, all his way to Mexico. He spoke with others, got informed about places, routes, food sources, dangers and safe places. Upon his arrival in Mexico, he crossed the Suchiate River in a raft, meeting other kids and adults that were doing the same. He wanted to be invisible because he knew he shouldn't be seen. He knew that he could be persecuted, that he could be abducted or assaulted by criminal organizations or even the police. He didn't want to be seen or heard. He followed the others, all of them mentioned that they had to find the beast (the train) and climb onto it. So, when they arrived, they did. He jumped on to continue his journey. He was told that he couldn't fall asleep, because if he did, he would fall and be run over by the train and die or lose a leg. He also faced criminal organizations and policemen that tried to hurt him and robbed all his money. Though he was able to continue, he didn't have anything to eat or drink. During his journey he tried to some shelter, sometimes finding a place to sleep indoors, sometimes just sleeping on the streets. Every night, he thought about his father and his family. Every night, he thought that his decision was a mistake, that he'd rather be dead, but he was too far now, and he had traveled for too long to give up. Finally, he arrived in Tijuana.

S met with the smuggler who was already gathered with a group of people. They crossed through different places she couldn't recognize. After some days, they crossed into Mexico. S kept receiving messages from her mother's boyfriend threatening her. She was tired, but she knew she couldn't go back. When reaching the highway, there was a container truck, the 'guide' opened the door and it was already full of people. They all managed to squeeze in as best they could. She felt there wasn't even space for her to breathe. She couldn't count how many days had passed before the first stop. That day, they were passing the night in a 'safe house'. After that, they had to continue. She lost track of time and space. She did as she was told. She jumped from one container to another through the journey. In the first part of the journey, she was always starving, but at some point, she completely lost her appetite. Some days, 'they' gave them some food, and sometimes they didn't. She just wanted to get out, breathe and walk. She knew it was not safe. People from the group told stories of their past journeys. It was not the first time. Most women just said it was better inside than outside. After a long journey, S arrived at a border town in Mexico called Reynosa. There, they were all taken to a safe house.

Mexico is a country that, over the past years, has faced a lot of internal violence. Organized crime has affected most of the country through the drug cartel's criminal activities and the fight against them. Besides drug trafficking, these organizations also perpetuate homicides, kidnapping, extortion, human trafficking, etc. Currently, there has been a high increase in 'murders committed with a firearm in public space against young people' (Data Cívica 2019). In addition to this, and similar to the countries of Central America, there is impunity in which these activities, especially homicides never get solved and there is no justice (Grillo 2020).

Additionally, violence against women has always been a problem in Mexico. Ten women are killed every day on average. Considering the effects of the 'start on the war on drugs', murders of women went from 1,089 per year in 2007 (two women per 100,000) to 3,824 in 2019 (almost six women per 100,000). Additionally, according to the National Survey on Discrimination, trans people are perceived as the group that faces the most discrimination in the country (ENADIS, 2017).

In this sense, the journey through Mexico is a very difficult one for all people on the move. Unaccompanied minors face different challenges, such as being exposed to criminal organizations or human trafficking, detention, violence, death, exploitation, lack of protection and discrimination. Additionally, it is difficult for them to find basic services like water, food and medicine (UNICEF). Although this is a journey made by many people that can encounter different groups, when traveling alone, unaccompanied minors face loneliness and despair, which affects their mental health. It becomes an uncertain journey, a combination of fear and courage.

The Mexican Migration Law of 2011 obliges the National Institute on Migration (INM) to allocate unaccompanied minors to shelters of the National System for Integral Family Development (DIF), which is in charge of providing necessary services to minors. Additionally, according to this law and the General Law on the Rights of Boys, Girls, and Adolescents, minors cannot be detained, and their well-being has to be considered all the time. As in many countries, unfortunately, this does not happen in most of the cases. Minors end up being deported to their countries of origin without the authorities following proper immigration procedures and with a lack of protection (IMUMI 2020, 42).

With the 'surge' of unaccompanied minors in 2014 in the US, Mexico was encouraged to implement enforcement measures to decrease the number of crossings. Hence, the *Programa Frontera Sur* was implemented. This program's objectives were to increase security at different points in Mexico's southern border and in popular routes throughout the country. In 2014, 21,514 minors were detained. Later, in 2016, this enforcement included controlling the railroad systems and 'reclaiming ownership' of *La Bestia* (Castillo 2016). This year, 31,991 minors were apprehended. Finally, from January to November of 2019, Mexican authorities reported the highest number of minors entering a migratory station: 50,621, of which, 67 percent were deported to their country of origin. In addition to this, the number of children of less than 11 years old increased by 188 percent from 2018 (Manu Ureste 2019).

In addition to facing all the dangers mentioned before, there is another risk of confronting gender-based violence. It is estimated that 60 percent of women and girls will be sexually or physically assaulted, or both, in their journey to the US (Acuna 2018). This violence may come from *coyotes* (smugglers), criminal organizations, authorities or travel companions. Although many take contraceptives knowing what their fate could be, this does not protect them from sexually transmitted diseases and other health risks. Additionally, many of them do not have access to or look for medical care in these situations (Fleury 2016). Additionally, when unaccompanied minors suffer from gender-based violence, they rarely report it to the Mexican authorities. This is because they do not trust them or are afraid of being detained or deported back to their countries (KIND 2017, 3).

'The American Nightmare'

F arrived in Tijuana and knew that he had to cross the border, that behind that wall he would alone, but safe. He stayed in Tijuana for some days, keeping a low profile because he wanted to be invisible. He was. After a couple of days in a shelter, he met a group of people that had decided to cross. They walked towards the border and found a hole and crossed. There was a second wall, and they found an open door. Immediately, some agents surrendered them (the border patrol). He told them that he was afraid of going back to Honduras. He was kept in the hielera (cold box). Detained there, he lost track of time, but it felt like an eternity. He didn't imagine that arriving was going to be this way. He was not able to bathe; he didn't have a place to sleep. He heard the guards mocking the kids, telling them they were going to send them back. He felt unsafe again. After that, he was transferred to a shelter, and things were a bit better. He was able to speak with his uncle. After months of interviews and speaking with a lot of people, he was transferred to live with his uncle in Maryland and continue there with his asylum case.

S went with a group; the coyote explained the procedure to cross. They encountered Mexican authorities and were detained. She told them that she was fearful of going back home to El Salvador. They didn't listen. They told her that they were taking her back home. She shouted and cried. She tried to explain that she couldn't go back, that they were going to kill her if she went back. After some days, she was sent back to the place she feared the most.

The process that unaccompanied minors go through when arriving in the US is not easy and can last longer than expected. Amelia Cheatham (2020) explains what an unaccompanied minor has to go through and with which institutions they have to face upon their entry. When arriving, they encounter agents from Customs and Border Patrol (CBP) of the Department of Homeland Security (DHS), who are in charge of apprehending, identifying, processing, detaining and, in some cases, deporting the minors. At the beginning of 2020, about 75 percent of unaccompanied minors in federal care were 15 years or older, though younger kids have also been detained. Since September 2018, six children have died in the care of immigration authorities (Cheatham 2020).

Before, depending on the children's nationality, DHS had different protocols. For example, with Mexicans and Canadians, they could be returned to their home countries if it was considered safe. Nevertheless, with other national-ities, like Central Americans, the Trafficking Victims Protection Reauthoriz-ation Act (TVPRA) mandates that those 'identified' as unaccompanied minors have to be transferred to the Department of Health and Human Services (HHS) within 72 hours. This is to always look for the best interest of the child and to be sure that their asylum claims are well processed (not ending up deporting the children to the dangerous places or situations they are coming from) and properly evaluated for trafficking (Immigration Forum 2018).

Once they are in the custody of HHS, the Office of Refugee Resettlement (ORR), is in charge of placing the children in their national network of around 170 state-licensed and federally funded independent facilities that respond to kids' necessities and basic needs. Children can also be placed in unlicensed temporary shelters, though with the objective that they are transferred from those shelters in less than 90 days. Once the children are placed in these facilities, ORR has the objective to look for the kids' sponsors within the country; this means parents or close relatives who can prove that can be in charge of the child. In one out of three cases, the agency is not able to find sponsors. Sometimes ORR took care of the children until they were 18 years old, releasing or transferring them to Immigration and Customs Enforcement (ICE) facilities, with some decide to leave the country and most others being deported. In 2019, on average, minors stayed with HHS for around 50 days before their release (Cheatham 2020).

Being transferred to their sponsors does not mean that their asylum cases are over. They have to continue with their processes with immigration courts of the Department of Justice's Executive Office of Immigration Review. The TVPRA inclines the government to provide legal justice for the minors, though this is not definite. In 2015, just seven percent of the children that appeared in an immigration court by themselves had a chance of winning their cases. If they were represented, their chances increased to 70 percent (Phippen 2015). In the last quarter of 2018, US Citizenship and Immigration Services (USCIS), part of DHS, granted just over 28 percent of child applicants' asylum. If they are not given asylum, they could be given another type of legal relief. Finally, in 2019, 71 percent of cases that involved unaccompanied minors ended in deportations. Deportees face violence when they are deported to their home countries, and most do not have a safe place to hide (Cheatham 2020).

Currently, the Mexican government has a tougher enforcement strategy. Together with the US government, both have deported more than 32,000 minors from January to August 2019 to Central America, two times more than the same period for 2018. The Migrant Protection Protocols (MPP), or Remain, in Mexico have also affected thousands of people, including minors. This has left thousands stranded at border towns waiting for their asylum claims in poor conditions (UNICEF USA). As mentioned before, unaccompanied minors that presented themselves at the border alone were supposed to be admitted into the United States. Because of these conditions, some of the parents have been willing to send their children alone.

Currently, with COVID-19 challenges for unaccompanied minors have gotten worse. While in Mexico, shelters have become over-crowded, increasing the probability of contagion. Some are still being targeted by criminal organizations, kidnapped or sexually abused (Kriel 2020). Since March 21, 2020, the CBP has deported around 1,000 unaccompanied minors to Mexico. Some have been placed in hotels in the US, waiting to be sent to deportation. Around 460 minors were sent back by Mexico to their countries of origin in Central America. Many others have been apprehended by Mexican authorities in the northern border and sent to shelters (UN News 2020).

Conclusions

The social, economic and political environment that surrounds unaccompanied minors determines their decision to leave looking for survival, for a better future far from their countries of origin, though these same factors and contexts in transit and destination countries also affect their lives. We cannot fail to see that the region is intertwined and that the policies or programs that aim to improve these minors' lives cannot be made unilaterally. To restrain their right to seek asylum will only have worse consequences on their lives.

As we have seen, unaccompanied minors have different vulnerabilities and needs, which does not end with them arriving in the US, if they do. With COVID-19, these have become more urgent and severe. Many of them do not have equal access to services as national children and live in precarious conditions. In the context of COVID-19, for example, they do not have access to public health care (testing, treatment, medicine and mental health resources) or essential or preventive services. This can have negative effects not only on their safety, but also on their chances of having a dignified and good quality of life and in their future.

We have to take into account that childhood, adolescence and youth are crucial phases of human development in which there is a transition between dependency in childhood and independence in adulthood. Hence, it is a very important period for a person's development and can have long-term effects on someone's life.

Successful protection and inclusion policies during this period of their lives help minors and lead them on a path in which they can fully develop in a place that is safe for them. To accomplish this, there need to be actions to protect them, secure access to all basic services and create conditions for a comprehensive development and integration in society. Complete approaches will allow them to develop while safeguarding their human rights, with the positive effect of shaping prosperous, diverse, inclusive and cohesive societies. These policies should be considered, but fundamentally, they have to be applied in Honduras, El Salvador, Guatemala, Mexico and the US to always maintain the best interest of the child.

It is imperative to create the conditions in which children and youth can live free of violence and in which they do not have to choose between living under others' conditions and having to flee for their lives. It is fundamental that they have access to services to fully develop. Likewise, it is imperative that their right to seek asylum is protected and treated carefully and in detail.

Bibliography

Ahmed, Azam. 2019. 'Women Are Fleeing Death at Home. The US Wants to Keep Them Out', *The New York Times*, August 18. https://www.nytimes. com/2019/08/18/world/americas/guatemala-violence-women-asylum.html

Alejandra Castillo. 2016. 'Programa Frontera Sur: The Mexican Government's Faulty Immigration Policy', *Council on Hemispheric Affairs,* October 26. https://www.coha.org/programa-frontera-sur-the-mexican-governments-faulty-immigration-policy

Amnesty International. 2018. 'Honduras 2017/2018'. https://www.amnesty.org/en/countries/americas/honduras/report-h/

Asmann Parker and Eimhin O'Reilly. 2020. 'InSight Crime's 2019 Homicide Round-Up', *Insight Crime,* January 28.

https://www.insightcrime.org/news/analysis/insight-crime-2019-homicide-round-up/

Association for a More Just Society. 2018. 'Violence in Honduras'. https://www.ajs-us.org/learn/honduras-violence/

Bonello, Deborah. 2019. 'Women in Guatemala: The New Faces of Extortion?', *Insight Crime*, April 26. https://www.insightcrime.org/investigations/women-guatemala-new-faces-extortion-2/

Central Intelligence Agency. 2020. *The World Factbook: El Salvador.* https://www.cia.gov/library/publications/the-world-factbook/geos/es.html

Central Intelligence Agency. 2020. *The World Factbook: Guatemala.* https://www.cia.gov/library/publications/the-world-factbook/geos/gt.html

Central Intelligence Agency. 2020. *The World Factbook: Honduras.* https://www.cia.gov/library/publications/the-world-factbook/geos/ho.html

Cheatham, Amelia. 2019. 'U.S. Detention of Child Migrants', *Council on Foreign Relations*, February 10. https://www.cfr.org/backgrounder/us-detention-child-migrants

Clavel, Tristan. 2017. '540 Children were Murdered Last Year in El Salvador: Report', *Insight Crime*. January 31. https://www.insightcrime.org/news/brief/540-children-murdered-last-year-el-salvador-report/

Congressional Research Service. 2019. 'Unaccompanied Alien Children: An Overview'.https://fas.org/sgp/crs/homesec/R43599.pdf

Davis, Robert, Carl Jensen, and Karin Kitchens. 2011. 'Cold-Case Investigations: An Analysis of Current Practices and Factors Associated with Successful Outcomes', Technical Report, CA, Santa Monica: RAND Corporation.

Gutiérrez, Edgar. 2016. 'Guatemala Elites and Organized Crime', *Insight Crime*, September 1. https://www.insightcrime.org/investigations/guatemala-elites-and-organized-crime-introduction/

Human Rights Watch. 2020. 'El Salvador: Events of 2020'. https://www.hrw.org/world-report/2020/country-chapters/el-salvador

INEGI. 2017. 'Encuesta Nacional sobre Discriminación (ENADIS) 2017'. https://www.inegi.org.mx/programas/enadis/2017/

IMUMI. 2020. 'Adolescentes y jóvenes hondureñas en México: una mirada exploratoria sobre sus necesidades y acceso a derechos'. https://imumi.org/2019/06/19/https-imumi-org-wp-content-uploads-2020-07-adolescentes-y-jovenes-hondurenas-en-mexico-una-mirada-exploratoria-sobre-sus-necesidades-y-acceso-a-derechos-pdf/

Insight Crime. 2018. 'Honduras Profile'. https://www.insightcrime.org/honduras-organized-crime-news/honduras/

Immigration and Refugee Board of Canada. 2018. 'Honduras: Information Gathering Mission Report'. https://irb-cisr.gc.ca/en/country-information/ndp/Pages/Honduras-2018P1.aspx#h1131

KIND (Kids in Need of Defense). 2017. 'Neither Security nor Justice: Sexual and Gender-based Violence and Gang Violence in El Salvador, Honduras, and Guatemala'. https://supportkind.org/wp-content/uploads/2017/05/Neither-Security-nor-Justice_SGBV-Gang-Report-FINAL.pdf

Kriel, Lomi. 2020. 'The Trump Administration Is Rushing Deportations of Migrant Children During Coronavirus', *Texas Tribune*, May 19. https://www.houstonpublicmedia.org/articles/news/politics/immigration/2020/05/19/370097/the-trump-administration-is-rushing-deportations-of-migrant-children-during-coronavirus/

Lind, Dara. 2014. 'The 2014 Central American migrant crisis'. October 10. https://www.vox.com/2014/10/10/18088638/child-migrant-crisis-unaccompanied-alien-children-rio-grande-valley-obama-immigration

Manjoo, Rashida and Calleigh McRaith. 2011. 'Gender-Based Violence and Justice in Conflict and Post-Conflict Areas', *Cornell Law School*. https://www.lawschool.cornell.edu/research/ILJ/upload/Manjoo-McRaith-final.pdf

Mexa Institute. 2019. Por qué los centroamericanos emigran y por qué no dejarán de hacerlo pronto. http://mexainstitute.org/wp-content/uploads/2019/09/Boletin-ESP-Centroamerica.pdf

Nóchez, María Luz y Valeria Guzmán. 2020. 'Violence against women has not slowed during the pandemic', *El Faro*, May 22. https://elfaro.net/en/202005/el_salvador/24460/Violence-against-women-has-not-slowed-during-the-pandemic.htm

O'Toole, Molly. 2018. 'El Salvador's Gangs Are Targeting Young Girls and the Trump administration's immigration policies are certain to make it worse'. *The Atlantic*, March 4. https://www.theatlantic.com/international/archive/2018/03/el-salvador-women-gangs-ms-13-trump-violence/554804/

Observatorio Género y Covid-19 en México, Feminicidios, 2020. https://genero-covid19.gire.org.mx/

OCDE. 2019. 'Gender, Institutions and Development Database'. https://stats.oecd.org/Index.aspx?DataSetCode=GIDDB2019

OSAC. 2020. 'Guatemala 2020 Crime & Safety Report' https://www.osac.gov/Country/Guatemala/Content/Detail/Report/d8c492ad-b604-457b-bd8f-18550eec1ff2

Phippen, J. Weston. 2015. 'Young, Illegal, and Alone', *The Atlantic*, October 15. https://www.theatlantic.com/politics/archive/2015/10/unaccompanied-minors-immigrants/410404/

Rosenblum, Marc and Isabel Ball. 2016. 'Trends in Unaccompanied Child and Family Migration from Central America', Migration Policy Institute. https://www.migrationpolicy.org/research/trends-unaccompanied-child-and-family-migration-central-america?gclid=CjwKCAjwm_P5BRAhEiwAwRzSO03dfGIucYiO0bRZxnbQ3T5DyNf3ppq0aedwubpthyFrBzxD8gq3VRoCQocQAvD_BwE

Tejeda, Mildred. 2019. 'Haciendo Camino al Andar', UNFPA Honduras. http://legacy.flacso.org.ar/newsletter/intercambieis/06/haciendo-camino-adolescentes-suenan-familias-apoyan.html

UN News. 2020. 'Danger awaits migrant children returned to Mexico and Central America during pandemic'. https://news.un.org/en/ story/2020/05/1064652

UNHCR. 2015. 'Women on the Run: First-hand Accounts of Refugees Fleeing El Salvador, Guatemala, Honduras, and Mexico'. https://www.unhcr.org/en-us/publications/operations/5630f24c6/women-run. html

UNICEF USA. 2019. 'Child Migrants in Central America, Mexico and the U.S.'. https://www.unicefusa.org/mission/emergencies/child-refugees-and-migrants/child-migrants-central-america-mexico-and-us

Ureste, Manu. 2019. 'En 2019, detenciones de menores migrantes y de niños no acompañados batieron todos los récords en México', *Animal Político*, December 31. https://www.animalpolitico.com/2019/12/2019-detenciones-menores-migrantes-ninos-batieron-records-mexico/

Wilson, Lynette. 2019. 'Episcopal-supported NGO empowers Guatemalan teenagers to take charge of their sexual and reproductive health', *Episcopal News Services*. July 18. https://www.episcopalnewsservice.org/2019/07/18/episcopal-supported-ngo-empowers-guatemalan-teenagers-to-take-charge-of-their-sexual-and-reproductive-health/

World Bank. 2020. *The World Bank in El Salvador.* https://www.worldbank. org/en/country/elsalvador

World Bank. 2020. *The World Bank in Guatemala.* https://www.worldbank.org/en/country/guatemala

World Bank. 2020. *The World Bank in Honduras.* https://www.worldbank.org/en/country/honduras

11

Migration Management and Safe Migration along the Indonesia-Malaysia Corridor

OANH K. NGUYEN

This Global Compact expresses our collective commitment to improving cooperation on international migration. Migration has been part of the human experience throughout history, and we recognize that it is a source of prosperity, innovation and sustainable development in our globalized world, and that these positive impacts can be optimized by improving migration governance. The majority of migrants around the world today travel, live and work in a safe, orderly and regular manner.

– 2018 Global Compact for Safe, Orderly and Regular Migration.

Since the 1970s, the international movement of people and their labor have become an integral component of labor markets within the developing world. Unsurprisingly, policymakers increasingly view international labor migration as a powerful tool for global development. Both the 2015 Addis Ababa Action Agenda and the 2030 Agenda for Sustainable Development make the argument that international labor migration is a 'win-win-win' situation not only for the labor-sending and destination countries, but also for the migrant worker her/himself (OECD and ILO 2018). For example, the rapid develop-ment of the Gulf states was owed in part to an infusion of foreign workers who made up more than 60 percent of region's population in 2015 (Rajan 2018). On the other end of the labor corridor, labor emigration is a critical part of the Philippine economy, where remittances make up 10 percent of annual GDP

(World Bank 2017b). In addition, for the migrant worker, working in a higher-income country is said to provide a potential pathway for upward mobility for foreign workers and their families.

Despite this optimism, there is an open acknowledgement among policymakers that the uneven power dynamic between the migrant worker and the governments that regulate their movement and labor creates a context ripe for exploitation. Conventional wisdom says that the best way to protect migrant workers against these the potentials for exploitation is through effective migration management. While what constitutes an 'effective' migration management regime might be debated, a principle that often goes uncontested is that the best way to pursue safe migration is to encourage migrant workers to travel through regular channels (i.e., state-sanctioned or state-controlled channels). Encouraging regular migration, the logic argues, better enables states to track and reduce the possibilities of discrimination in terms of wages, working conditions, and housing rights.

But who are the actors that make up the regular migration channel? Or, to ask this a different way, who manages migration? Undoubtedly, the image that comes to mind for most is the immigration official or border protection officers who line both sides of the border. While it is true that the state is the final arbiter regarding who gets to cross or stay within their borders, a focus on the state belies the fact that the global labor market is an industry and the cogs that allow it to function are private, for-profit agencies (Ernst Spaan and Hillmann 2013; Surak 2018). These actors occupy a wide variety of roles that enable the global labor market to function. For migrant workers, they are recruiters and guides starting from the first set of paperwork all the way through to immigration in the destination country. Similarly, employers rely on these labor recruitment agencies to not only help them locate potential workers, but also to navigate what is often a complicated labor-recruitment bureaucracy.

The purpose of this chapter is to highlight how the increased presence of these for-profit agencies have impacted the migratory experiences of migrant workers. I do so through a comparison of two generations of Indonesian migrant workers along the Indonesia-Malaysia corridor: Bimo, who came to Malaysia in the early 1990s through informal channels, and Gadis, who came in the mid-2000s using state-sanctioned labor agents. Through their stories and based on nine months of fieldwork in Malaysia, this chapter aims to complicate the relationship between regular migration and safe migration by moving away from a state-centric approach to migration management and instead focusing on how migrant workers themselves navigate the regime.

The Migration Industry: Migration Management and Postcolonial Economics

International Relations' study of migration management in the twenty-first century draws heavily on James Hollifield's (2004) concept of the *migration state*, which pushed the field to recognize the mass movement of people as an integral component of a globalized world. In this increasingly interconnected world, states must be prepared to manage larger flows of migration if they want to continue benefiting from other aspects of globalization, such as freer trade and investment (Hollifield 2004). The studies that followed Hollifield's seminal work have often privileged the state as the primary actor in migration management (e.g., Adamson 2006; Martin 2014; Peters 2015; 2017; de Haas, Natter, and Vezzoli 2018). These analyses treat different regimes of migration management – be they unilateral (e.g., United States nationalization laws), bilateral (e.g., US-Mexico labor programs) or multilateral (e.g., the Global Compact) – as a function of state interests. In brief, we can better understand the form, content and impact of migration management regimes if we study how state interests are expressed through the bargaining process or as a routinized compliance through the implementation process (Betts 2017).

While these studies have expanded our understand of migration management in international relations, I echo a newer generation of scholarship to argue that these dominant approaches have been derived from the historical and political experiences of the advanced industrialized economies in Europe and North America (Adamson, Triadafilopoulos, and Zolberg 2011; Shin 2017; Adamson and Tsourapas 2020). This chapter, instead, shifts the politico-historical focus to a postcolonial context where states' migration management regimes must work alongside an economic development plan centered on playing 'catch up' in the global economy. In these contexts, development not only means an overhaul of the colonial economy, but also often entails creating a labor force that is flexible and inefficient to remain competitive in the face of turbulent global market conditions. This development goal created the context allowing for the infiltration of market-driven logic into the domains of the political and the social, including matters as sensitive to sovereignty as migration management.

Fitting with this logic, the day-to-day work of managing migration corridors in post-colonial contexts are often outsourced to what Hernandez-Leon (2008) calls the migration industry, the 'ensemble of entrepreneurs, businesses and service... motivated by the pursuit of financial gain' (Hernández-León 2008, 154). Although they are meant to be agents of the state, their primary motivation is neither to protect state sovereignty nor protect migrant safety; their primary goals is to earn a profit by increasing the overall number of people moving across borders. As a result, these labor agencies often have a fraught relationship with the state (Xiang 2012).

The Migration Industry along the Indonesia-Malaysia Corridor

The presence of a migration industry has deep roots in the Indonesia-Malaysia corridor. Its origins can be found in late 19th century when *hajj* became a lucrative business with an intricate network of recruiters, agents, guides, financiers and facilitators operating out of key ports on the islands of Java, Sumatra and the Malaya peninsula (Amrith 2011). Decades later, when the British colonial government encouraged immigration from the Dutch Indies (modern day Indonesia) to grow British Malaya's labor force (Kaur 2010), Malayan employers relied on recruitment firms that hired Indo-European and Javanese labor agents (*werfagenten*, *ronselaars*) to recruit potential emigrants (E. Spaan 1994). A result of this deep history of migration is an extensive communal network built on kinship and hometown ties extending across the Malacca Strait. It is this network that allowed a small stream of Indonesian immigrants to continue trickling into the peninsula long after open migration ended (Wong 2006). The majority of these workers were Muslim and were perceived as *bangsa serempun* (of the same racial stock) by the Malay majority and, as a result, were seen as a preferred labor source compared to other traditional but more controversial sources, namely Chinese or Indian laborers (Liow 2003).

Bimo's Story: The Regularity of Irregularity

The first major shift in the management of Indonesia-Malaysia migration came in the 1970s when Malaysia sustained massive economic growth and undertook large-scale infrastructural and urban development projects (Narayanan and Lai 2005; Kaur 2010). This growth resulted in considerable labor shortages in agriculture, construction, domestic service and – by the 1990s – manufacturing sectors. The earliest (and still the largest) group of foreign workers who filled this labor shortage came from Indonesia, which struggled with high poverty and youth unemployment rates throughout 1970–1990s (World Bank 1981; 1983; Hugo 1993). During this era, Indonesian workers came to the peninsula using networks of kinship and village-level ties, which operated alongside a system of brokers and middlemen to create a chain from the villages in Indonesia to the worksites in Malaysia. This system often began with a *calo tenaga kerja* (employment broker) who recruited potential workers. Their passage was moderated by *taikong laut* (sea middlemen), who brought workers to the peninsula by boat, and *taikong darat* (land middlemen), who had connections with contractors on plantations helping to deliver workers from their landing point to their worksites. For some, this last part of the journey ended when they were handed over to a *kepala* – an Indonesian group leader appointed by the contractor – who might have been the person started this process by recruiting a trustworthy workforce from his own hometown (E. Spaan 1994).

This growth in the number and scope of Indonesian labor to Malaysia pushed the two governments to play a more active role in migration management. For Malaysia, the unregulated inflow of labor had become a 'problem' in the eyes of both the Malaysian government and public despite the business community welcoming the infusion of workers coming to meet labor demands. For Indonesia, a controlled outflow of emigration would have enabled the country to alleviate youth unemployment and create a new stream of foreign exchange (Palmer 2016). Negotiations between the two governments resulted in the 1984 Medan Agreement, a bilateral agreement that promoted and legalized labor migration. The agreement, however, was largely ignored by workers and employers alike allowing the number of undocumented workers to grow. When undocumented migration continued to be a 'problem', Malaysia, with the help of the Indonesian embassy, began use a combination of amnesty programs and deportation campaigns to control the number of undocumented workers in the country.

It was in this first era of migration management, where undocumented migration was the norm and regular migration the exception, that Bimo began his journey.

In the early 1990s, Bimo left his home in Central Java at dawn to avoid the Indonesian police, who had started monitoring undocumented labor emigrants. Years later, when he would return to visit over the holidays, the police, knowing that he had left without registering with the local government, would harass him for money (*duit rokok*). After leaving his home, he and others from his hometown (*teman sekampung*) caught a bus to Surabaya where a *taikong laut* was waiting with a boat to take them to Dumai (Sumatra) and then onto the western coast of Malaysia. The journey by boat took one week and cost 800,000 rupiah (437 USD), which he and his family paid by selling off livestock. Others who did not have livestock borrowed money.

They were not the first wave of migrant workers from his hometown. Before embarking on his own journey, Bimo knew a multitude of people – friends, neighbor and family members – who had left for Malaysia through unsanctioned channels. In fact, Bimo's decision to emigrate was based on the recommendation of these early movers. Bimo explained that, for a new migrant worker, it was necessary to have these connections in order to find a good and safe job.

When Bimo first arrived, he followed a relative (*saudara*) to work on a construction site. During the day, he stayed in the *kongsi* (makeshift housing located on construction sites), but at night he and others slept in the forest to avoid police raids. He explained that they were paid not hourly but upon completion of a project. The person who oversaw his work and who paid him was not the contractor who ran the construction site, but the *kepala*. Because of this structure, if a *kepala* ran away with the money, he would not get paid. This is one of the reasons why it was important to have good connections.

A few years into his stay, labor agents came to his *kongsi* announcing that, for a fee, they could help him get papers through the Malaysian government's amnesty program. When telling me this story, Bimo laughed, likening them to contemporary labor agents who travel to Indonesian villages 'looking for customers'. Unlike today, however, Bimo thinks that the smaller number of agents in the 1990s made it easier for foreign workers to figure out who was trying to deceive them and who was being honest. Bimo signed up and received temporary travel papers from the Indonesian embassy. Although he never actually got his employment pass, the temporary travel documents gave Bimo the confidence to move more freely around the country and change employers when he wanted to do so.

Gadis's Story: Regular Migration and the Migration Industry

The second major shift to the management of Indonesia-Malaysia migration came with the after-effects of the 1997 Asian Financial Crisis. The crisis contributed to historic socio-political transformations of both Malaysia and Indonesia that created the institutional conditions for sweeping changes to migration management of the corridor. In Indonesia, the crisis catalyzed the pro-democracy movement, putting an end to Suharto's New Order regime, which had ruled the country for more than three decades. The end of the New Order regime also launched a massive decentralization program where political power were increasingly reallocated to provincial and local governments (Caraway, Ford, and Nguyen 2019). In Malaysia, the financial crisis exacerbated the political turmoil within the United Malays National Organization, the political party that has ruled the country since independence. To project an image of strength and capability, the government began a heavy crackdown of 'illegal immigration', most notably amending its Immigration Act, to make unsanctioned work by foreign nationals a criminal offense (Ford 2006). The accumulation of these political changes laid the groundwork for the state to bring the migration industry under the control of its sanctioned agencies and away from the *taikong* and *calo*. A side effect of state intervention, however, was a maze-like bureaucracy regulating both emigration and immigration.

To meet their labor demands, Malaysian employers must confront a complex process where private agencies are built into the system. The process starts at the Ministry of Human Resources, which sets a quota of how many foreign workers employers are permitted to hire. During this part of the process, employers must demonstrate that they have a need for more labor and have done their due diligence attempting to hire local Malaysians. The rest of the process unfolds under the purview of the Ministry of Home Affairs, which approves the quota and issues the Temporary Employment Pass. Working under the Ministry of Home Affairs are also a set of private agencies contracted by the government to issue insurance, security bonds and medical examinations. This is a costly process; most employers cannot navigate this complex bureaucracy without the assistance of a labor recruitment agent. As a former labor agent explained to me: 'If an employer tries to go directly to Immigration, the officer will say, 'Why do you do this by yourself? Why don't you hire an agent?'.[1] He further explained that, because hiring freezes are so commonplace in Malaysia, employers are incentivized to over-ask for foreign workers; if their supply of workers exceeds demand, the employer could then outsource these workers.

On the other side of the border, migration management *policies* in Indonesia became more centralized as Indonesia's Department of Manpower passed regulations to determine the specific procedures of emigration (recruitment, training, document processing, etc.) (Ford 2006). The massive decentraliz-ation of the government in 2002 and the continued pressure from labor recruiters, however, meant that the *practice* of migration management often lacked coordination across different levels of government (Palmer 2016; Ernst Spaan and van Naerssen 2018). Since 2006, the formal labor emigration market has been controlled by private, for-profit labor recruitment agencies called PT (*Perusahaan Jasa Tenaga Kerja Indonesia*) that form partnerships with recruitment agencies in host countries (Hernandez-Coss et al. 2008). Although it had become illegal to use a *calo,* each of these agencies has relied on an army of informal brokers called *petugas lapangan* who often occupy a wide variety of positions within a community (e.g., teacher, tour guide, salesperson, etc.) to reach out to potential migrant workers (Lindquist 2012; 2015). The PT and the *pertugas lapangan* are instrumental in the emigration process. Just like it is for employers to hire through regular chan-nels, the current process to migrating through regular channels is costly and burdensome, with 22 separate administrative steps (World Bank 2017a). The *petugas lapangan* not only help foreign workers navigate this complicated process, but can help them find the money to emigrate. As a result, the vast majority of workers go into debt emigrating, which gets deducted from their wages.

---

[1]   Author's Fieldnotes, February 2019.

Gadis came to Malaysia during the decade following the Asian Financial Crisis when regular migration along the corridor became increasingly common. Gadis was one of the first people from her village (*desa*) in Central Java to travel abroad for work. During her last year of high school, a teacher gave Gadis a leaflet describing a manufacturing job in Shah Alam (near Kuala Lumpur). The teacher promised her many things – the job would offer a higher wage, free accommodation and the opportunity for her to go to university. Gadis had four younger siblings; her parents were poor and had no formal education. She saw this as an opportunity to improve life for her and her family. Moreover, because this information came from her teacher, she felt that she could trust it.

Gadis and a small group of girls from her school decided to sign up. The same teacher helped them fill out the application and gather their first set of documents – parental permission, proof of education and a *kartu kuning,* which indicated that she was searching for an overseas job. All of this cost her 250,000 rupiah (26 USD). After this, a labor agency came to their school to explain the next steps in the process – they had to make a passport, get their medical screening and so forth. It was still the teacher, however, who continued to help them get through this next stage and accompanied them to Yogyakarta to for their initial medical screening. When Gadis failed her first medical check, the agency gave her specific instructions on how to improve her health.

When they all passed their medical exam, Gadis and group of 50 girls from her area were sent to the labor agency's office in Yogyakarta. They stayed there for three days sharing a single room and two bathrooms sleeping on the floor next to each other 'like fish'. On the second day, National Agency for the Placement and Protection of Indonesian Migration Workers (BNP2TKI), the Indonesian agency tasked with protecting overseas workers, came and told them that, if anything happened to them, they should go to the embassy. On the third night, at around 10:00 pm, the labor agency called them up one by one to sign their contract. When they signed the contract, they agreed to owe the agency a debt of 2,400 ringgit (716 USD). The amount of the payment was for what Gadis called the 'package' that included document processing and travel. Until they paid back this debt, the agency kept their national identity card (*kartu tanda penduduk*) as collateral. After they signed the contract, they gave their passports and other documents. Gadis remembered that it was only then that many of the girls realized that their documents had false information, mainly to make them older and eligible to work abroad. But they had already signed the contract. If they were to back out now, they would still owe the debt. At 5:00 am the next morning, they all left for Kuala Lumpur. The whole process took two months.

Gadis's employer picked them up from the airport and took them to their company-provided dormitories. She worked 12 hours a day, five days a week assembling computer parts for a wage of 450 ringgit (134 USD) per month plus over-time pay for work above eight hours. Every month for the first 10 months, the labor agency came to the dormitory to collect 240 ringgit (71 USD) to pay off the debt she owed. The company warned the girls that if they went too far from the manufacturing compound, they would be arrested. During her time in Malaysia, Gadis left the manufacturing compound only once to go to Kuala Lumpur City Centre – a popular tourist destination in Kuala Lumpur. While there, she was stopped by the police who asked if she was Indonesian. When she said yes, they asked to see her papers.

After working there 10 months, the managers called the girls in for a meeting. They told the girls that the company was experiencing issues and had to cut over-time hours. After 13 months, Gadis was down to working only two weeks per month. By the 15th month, the company called the girls in again and gave them two letters. The first explained that the company has decided to terminate their contract and would be giving them one month's compensation; the second was an airline ticket back to Indonesia. She was then deported.

The Limits of Documents

Reading these two migration stories side-by-side highlights that maintaining a documented status can sit in tension with pursuing safety. Gadis began her migration journey through an informal broker (*petugas lapangan*) who led her through the bureaucratic processes that made her a documented worker. Yet, with each step of the process, she became more precarious as she fell further into debt. Besides the few girls from her school, the only relationships she had in Malaysia were made through the company that hired her and the labor agency that sent her to Malaysia. This lack of a social safety net and knowledge of the Malaysian context further skewed the power dynamics between her and her employer. Although she was documented, she had no recourse to voice her grievances when her contract was terminated and she was deported. While Gadis went back to Indonesia after her contract was terminated, it was common for others in her position that remained behind, consequently becoming undocumented, to work and pay the debt incurred through the migration process.

In contrast, Bimo relied on communal networks not just to cross the border, but also to find employment in Malaysia. Owing to his status as an undocumented migrant worker, Bimo feared the police, suffered poor working conditions and was a cheated by employers and fellow countrymen. However, unlike documented workers, who must remain with the employer who sponsored them in order to maintain their documented status, Bimo felt no obligation to stay with an employer who mistreated him. Instead, Bimo used this same communal network to leave and find better employment opportunities. When I asked him to reflect on his experience in comparison to the current system controlled by labor agents, Bimo told me:

> Back then, everything was more open and not so complicated. Before, it was easier to earn money… I felt safer back then. Even though I had no documents, it was just that. Now, even with documents, we are afraid of the agents – they control everything. You have documents, but it is the agents who provide them. You never know if there is something wrong.[2]

Implications for the Pursuit of Safe Migration

There is a consensus across development institutions and policymakers that the pursuit of safe migration necessitates the advocacy of regular migration. This is exactly what Malaysia and Indonesia did. In response to both the demand for labor and the need to portray themselves as protective states, Malaysia and Indonesia have worked to create institutions and mechanisms aimed at ensuring that foreign workers travel through regular channels. Bimo and Gadis's stories, however, brings our attention to the identities and interests of the actors who line the migration corridors and perform the day-to-day work of migration management. As their stories show, the increasing complexity of the systems, alongside the drive to maintain economic growth, opened the pathway for the entrenchment of the migration industry into the migration process.

The intricate relationship between the migration industry, the states' drive for economic development, and long history of migration between the two countries creates a complex relationship between regular migration and safe migration. To be clear, I am not advocating for nor am I romanticizing undocumented migration. Instead, I want to highlight the drawbacks of regular migration in a context where the migration industry plays a critical role in migration management. Previous studies have shown that simply bringing workers under the purview of the state, particularly one interested in curtailing migrant rights for the sake of economic development, does not necessarily produce safety (Campbell 2018; Bylander 2019). Moreover, the development of a network based on kinship, ethnicity or nationality is a critical component of safe migration as they provide knowledge, care and economic resources to new generations of migrants (e.g., Hagan 1998; Sanders, Nee, and Sernau 2002). Yet, as we saw in Bimo's and Gadis's stories, the migration industry

---

[2]   Author's Fieldnotes, March 2019

can hamper the creation of these networks by making the foreign worker reliant on the labor agents for information on how to survive in a new, strange land. By decoupling safe migration from regular migration, we are able to further discuss alternative notions of safety that not only acknowledge the role of the migration industry, but also foregrounds how migrant workers navigate this landscape.

References

Adamson, Fiona B. 2006. 'Crossing Borders: International Migration and National Security', *International Security* 31(1): 165–99.

Adamson, Fiona B., Triadafilos Triadafilopoulos, and Aristide R. Zolberg. 2011. 'The Limits of the Liberal State: Migration, Identity and Belonging in Europe', *Journal of Ethnic and Migration Studies* 37(6): 843–859.

Adamson, Fiona B., and Gerasimos Tsourapas. 2020. 'The Migration State in the Global South: Nationalizing, Developmental, and Neoliberal Models of Migration Management', *International Migration Review* 54(3): 853–82.

Amrith, Sunil S. 2011. *Migration and Diaspora in Modern Asia*. Vol. 7. Cambridge University Press.

Betts, Alexander. 2017. *Protection by Persuasion: International Cooperation in the Refugee Regime*. Cornell University Press.

Bylander, Maryann. 2019. 'Is Regular Migration Safer Migration? Insights from Thailand', *Journal on Migration and Human Security* 7(1): 1–18.

Campbell, Stephen. 2018. *Border Capitalism, Disrupted: Precarity and Struggle in a Southeast Asian Industrial Zone*. Ithaca: ILR Press, an imprint of Cornell University Press.

Caraway, Teri L., Michele Ford, and Oanh K. Nguyen. 2019. 'Politicizing the Minimum Wage: Wage Councils, Worker Mobilization, and Local Elections in Indonesia', *Politics & Society* 47(2): 251–76.

Ford, Michele. 2006. 'After Nunukan: The Regulation of Indonesian Migration to Malaysia', in *Mobility, Labour Migration and Border Controls in Asia*, edited by Amarjit Kaur and Ian Metcalfe, 228–47. London: Palgrave Macmillan UK.

Haas, Hein de, Katharina Natter, and Simona Vezzoli. 2018. 'Growing Restrictiveness or Changing Selection? The Nature and Evolution of Migration Policies', *International Migration Review* 52(2): 324–367.

Hagan, Jacqueline Maria. 1998. 'Social Networks, Gender, and Immigrant Incorporation: Resources and Constraints', *American Sociological Review* 63 (1): 55–67.

Hernandez-Coss, Raul, Gillian Brown, Chitrawati Buchori, Isaku Endo, Emiko Todoroki, Tita Naovalitha, Wameek Noor, and Cynthia Mar. 2008. 'The Malaysia-Indonesia Remittance Corridor: Making Formal Transfers the Best Option for Women and Undocumented Migrants', World Bank Working Papers. The World Bank.

Hernández-León, Ruben. 2008. *Metropolitan Migrants: The Migration of Urban Mexicans to the United States*. Berkeley: University of California Press.

Hollifield, James F. 2004. 'The Emerging Migration State', *The International Migration Review* 38(3): 885–912.

Hugo, Graeme. 1993. 'Indonesian Labour Migration to Malaysia: Trends and Policy Implications', *Southeast Asian Journal of Social Science* 21(1): 36–70.

Kaur, Amarjit. 2010. 'Labour Migration in Southeast Asia: Migration Policies, Labour Exploitation and Regulation', *Journal of the Asia Pacific Economy* 15(1): 6–19.

Lindquist, Johan. 2012. 'The Elementary School Teacher, the Thug and His Grandmother: Informal Brokers and Transnational Migration from Indonesia', *Pacific Affairs* 85(1): 69–89.

———. 2015. 'Of Figures and Types: Brokering Knowledge and Migration in Indonesia and Beyond', *Journal of the Royal Anthropological Institute* 21(S1): 162–77.

Liow, Joseph. 2003. 'Malaysia's Illegal Indonesian Migrant Labour Problem: In Search of Solutions', *Contemporary Southeast Asia: A Journal of International and Strategic Affairs* 25(1): 44–64.

Martin, Susan F. 2014. *International Migration: Evolving Trends from the Early Twentieth Century to the Present*. Cambridge University Press.

Narayanan, Suresh, and Yew-Wah Lai. 2005. 'The Causes and Consequences of Immigrant Labour in the Construction Sector in Malaysia', *International Migration* 43 (5): 31–57.

OECD, and ILO. 2018. *How Immigrants Contribute to Developing Countries' Economies*. OECD.

Palmer, Wayne. 2016. *Indonesia's Overseas Labour Migration Programme, 1969-2010*. Verhandelingen van Het Koninklijk Instituut Voor Taal-, Land- En Volkenkunde 307. Leiden: Brill.

Peters, Margaret E. 2015. 'Open Trade, Closed Borders Immigration in the Era of Globalization', *World Politics* 67(1): 114–54.

———. 2017. *Trading Barriers: Immigration and the Remaking of Globalization*. Princeton University Press.

Rajan, S. Irudaya. 2018. 'The Crisis of Gulf Migration', in *The Oxford Handbook of Migration Crises*, edited by Cecilia Menjívar, Marie Ruiz, and Immanuel Ness. Oxford Handbooks Online. New York: Oxford University Press.

Sanders, Jimy, Victor Nee, and Scott Sernau. 2002. 'Asian Immigrants' Reliance on Social Ties in a Multiethnic Labor Market', *Social Forces* 81(1): 281–314.

Shin, Adrian J. 2017. 'Tyrants and Migrants: Authoritarian Immigration Policy', *Comparative Political Studies* 50(1): 14–40.

Spaan, E. 1994. 'Taikongs and Calos: The Role of Middlemen and Brokers in Javanese International Migration', *The International Migration Review* 28(1): 93–113.

Spaan, Ernst, and Felicitas Hillmann. 2013. 'Migration Trajectories and the Migration Industry: Theoretical Reflections and Empirical Examples from Asia', in *The Migration Industry and the Commercialization of International Migration*, edited by Thomas Gammeltoft-Hansen and Ninna Nyberg Sørensen. Global Institutions Series 69. Abingdon: Routledge.

Spaan, Ernst, and Ton van Naerssen. 2018. 'Migration Decision-Making and Migration Industry in the Indonesia-Malaysia Corridor', *Journal of Ethnic and Migration Studies* 44(4): 680–695.

Surak, Kristin. 2018. 'Migration Industries and the State: Guestwork Programs in East Asia', *International Migration Review* 52 (2): 487–523.

Wong, Diana. 2006. 'The Recruitment of Foreign Labour in Malaysia: From Migration System to Guest Worker Regime', in *Mobility, Labour Migration and Border Controls in Asia*, edited by Amarjit Kaur and Ian Metcalfe, 213–27. London: Palgrave Macmillan UK.

World Bank. 1981. 'Indonesia - Development Prospects and Policy Options', 3307. The World Bank. http://documents.worldbank.org/curated/en/697991468268788109/Indonesia-Development-prospects-and-policy-options.

———. 1983. 'Indonesia – Wages and Employment', 3586. http://documents.worldbank.org/curated/en/844111468050336277/Indonesia-Wages-and-employment.

———. 2017a. 'Indonesia's Global Workers: Juggling Opportunities and Risks'. http://pubdocs.worldbank.org/en/357131511778676366/Indonesias-Global-Workers-Juggling-Opportunities-Risks.pdf.

———. 2017b. 'Migrating to Opportunity: Overcoming Barriers to Labor Mobility in Southeast Asia'. https://www.worldbank.org/en/region/eap/publication/migrating-to-opportunity-overcoming-barriers-to-labor-mobility-in-southeast-asia

Xiang, Biao. 2012. 'Predatory Princes and Princely Peddlers: The State and International Labour Migration Intermediaries in China', *Pacific Affairs* 85(1): 47–68.

12

Governing Movement in Displacement: The Case of North Jordan

HANNAH OWENS

The landscape and demographics of northern Jordan have undergone immense change since the start of the Syrian Civil War in 2011. Mafraq and Irbid, two large cities in the north, have been overwhelmed by international non-governmental organizations (INGOs), aid workers and refugees. Zaatari camp, created in 2012, currently hosts 80,000 Syrian refugees, and is located 34 kilometers from the Nassib-Jaber international border (UNHCR 2020). A kilometer away from the camp is Zaatari village, which now hosts an equal number of Syrians as it had Jordanians before the crisis (AFCI 2019). Despite this and its proximity to refugee hotspots, the small community has received relatively little attention from INGOs. The Syrians living in the village make up just some of the 79 percent of refugees in Jordan living outside of formal camps (AFCI 2019). This chapter argues that, within the context of conflict-induced mass displacement, refugee-hosting spaces – for instance, rural non-camp settlements – are not constituted by the state, the border-crossing or international humanitarianism alone. Despite the movements of refugees and forced migrants being continuously stifled and obfuscated, these sites are further enacted by the movements of refugees, connecting regional social histories, economic patterns and the decision-making strategies that constitute lives within protracted displacement.

I conceptualize movement as a form of creative communication deeply embedded in socio-historical links and relations. Movement is both an individual and a collective pursuit. Taken as a practice, it connects temporal roots and lineages, but is also explicitly bound to wider geopolitical and economic forms of power. By conceptualizing understandings of movement and its enduring implications as deeply tied to the local histories and spaces it inhabits, I propose an analysis of movement to understand how it is articulated and experienced in the present context of mass displacement. By prioritizing notions of movement based within a local, historical context, it provides a counterpoint to looking at displacement and displacement governance that starts with and centres those most affected.

I argue that a politics of movement is constructed as distinct from a politics of governance, which is traced to particular forms of power as related to the state, the international border system and humanitarian governance. This viewpoint therefore focuses on what people do, rather than the (post)colonial borders or international humanitarian spaces built and maintained to control movement. Migrant spaces do not exist independently as spaces, but rather are enacted by the migrants embedded within them. For example, an international border works and is recognised by the mechanisms that make it a border – the requirement of a passport or visa, the checking of individuals or vehicles or the ability to close and stifle movement. However, they are enacted as borders only when one tries to cross them, putting in motion these requirements. Refugee camps work under similar logics. Within the Middle East and North Africa, only 9.6 percent of refugees live in camps (UN Global Report 2018), and therefore to study displacement within these narrow parameters, rather than starting with migrant movement itself, which co-creates and co-constitutes these sites, is to overlook vital trends in migration.

This chapter seeks to show how the movement of refugees works in tandem with wider governance polices to simultaneously constitute spaces and situations, facilitating new possibilities and opportunities for how we study protracted displacement. I evoke the concept of movement as creative comm-unication as a methodological exploration to analyze protracted displacement outside of the usual prisms of investigation: security, political economy or international politics and humanitarianism. Traditionally, in the study of forced migration, the sites through which migrants move – the border, the camp, the detention center or settlement – are constituted solely by the wider political, legal or geographical dynamics that work to control movement and define the migrant in specific ways. Such framing positions the migrant as an object to be governed, removing the autonomy of each migrant and their ability to co-constitute the situations or spaces within these wider dynamics. This conceptualization does not ignore state or humanitarian policies of refugee governance, but rather reveals the potential for understanding the alternative strategies and articulations used by migrants' movement to constitute their own situation while being deeply embedded in such rigid contexts. Hence, the study of displacement is shifted from the confines of the border crossing or the refugee camp.

Taking into consideration the material effects of structures of governance, how does a study focusing on migrant movements challenge existing understandings of protracted displacement? How do refugees and forced migrants move within the matrix of refugee governance to constitute their own migration experiences and enact the sites lived in during protracted displacement? What are the implications for studying displacement when the focus on institutions or borders is broadened to include how migrants themselves make these spaces what they are?

To answer these questions, I start with a brief examination of the literature on Syrian migration to Jordan, with a particular focus on how regional displacement is studied. I draw out some of the wider systems of governance to show how migrants work within these structures, both resisting and operating through them. Next, I consider how these spaces within displacement narratives are co-constituted by the migrants themselves. In doing so, I focus on Zaatari village, a dynamic hosting community close to refugee hotspots. This village was selected because it represents wider migration patterns in the Middle East of refugees self-settling in urban environments, rather than in formal camps. This site is constituted by kinship, historical, social and labor movements that have lived consequences in the present. It represents a space that has worked within the wider confines of refugee governance, yet has simultaneously been enacted by the movement and communicative practices of the migrant.

The Study of Regional Displacement and Syrian Migration

Since 2011, there has been an immense canon of scholarly work completed on the Syrian crisis and the subsequent mass displacement of Syrians. Such work has included studies on international humanitarian responses, the effect of the crisis on Europe, the internally displaced within Syria and the regional responses to the mass movement of Syrians across its neighboring borders into Turkey, Lebanon and Jordan.

Specifically, the studies focused on Turkey, Lebanon and Jordan have produced rich insights into the experiences of Syrians in cross-border protracted displacement, drawing on the political, legal, economic and tribal systems of care and control pertaining to refugee governance (Pallister-Wilkins 2016). Previously, the literature has analyzed refugee governing strategies of (non) encampment (Turner 2015; Gatter 2017), hosting communities (Fiddian-Qasmiyeh 2016b, 2018), social networks amongst urban refugees (Fiddian-Qasmiyeh 2018; Betts et al. 2017; Chatty 2013; Stevens 2016), faith-based NGOs (Wagner 2018), the political economy of hosting states (Turner 2015), the histories of previous refugee populations (Chatty 2017), pre-existing labor routes (Oesch 2014; Wagner 2017) and state policies of integration, protection, border control and security (Şahin Mencütek 2019; Achilli 2015; Achilli et al. 2017), to name but a few.

Such studies, however, predominantly frame the regional cross-border mass movement of refugee populations within wider narratives of security, political economy or international politics. For example, Zeynep Şahin Mencütek's (2019) comparative study of refugee governance in Turkey, Lebanon and Jordan focuses primarily on state policies and their motivations, seeking to find potential patterns of governance and policy shifts over time. Similarly, Lewis Turner's (2015) study of (non)encampment policies in Lebanon and Jordan centers around an excavation of the economic and labor markets to analyze the reasons behind the differing policies of governance put forth onto refugee populations. Dawn Chatty (2017) and Ann-Christin Wagner (2020) utilize a historical framework in their studies of Syrian displacement, drawing out the kinship and tribal connections that 'continue to characterize community and individual relations across modern state borders' (Chatty 2017, 26). In doing so, the histories of regional displacement in both colonial and postcolonial contexts are analyzed, alongside pre-war labor patterns and previous nomadic experiences as drivers of movement. Matthew Stevens (2016) pushes this analysis further to discuss these social networks and subsequent social capital between Syrians and Jordanians to suggest that social networks between Syrians and Jordanians, although once strong, have dwindled and fatigued due to a lack of support from international aid organizations as the situation turned to one of protracted displacement.

While important dynamics to consider under the guise of protracted displacement, these studies focus on the experience of refugees through dynamics far removed from the refugees themselves, often with attention given to the motivations behind policies or the experiences of the migrant in relation to such governance policies, after the fact. Such processes risk de-historicizing the migrant, disconnecting them from a multiplicity of experiences and survival mechanisms. In doing so, these studies risk overlooking how refugees themselves enact their own situation within displacement and how they articulate their displacement experiences through their own movements. This involves careful consideration of the reasons behind movement and how movement itself constitutes the situation of the refugee and the sites within which refugees work. Put differently, by centralizing the movements, which take place within the context of displacement, as a form of communicative practice, such movement cannot be understood as simply border crossing, fleeing from violence or refuge seeking. Movement conceptualized in such terms connects refugee governance because of displacement, while incorporating the particular and contextual relationship of movement in the creation of a site.

Drawing on critical human geography, I argue that sites and situations are not only created from the borders drawn, the policies produced or the apparatus built to contain and control, but also through human activity; by what migrants do to enact the space for themselves. As critical geographer and border historian Matthew Ellis (2015, 415) contends, the practices of cartography do not erase the imagined meaning or 'human activity "inscribed" upon space'. Space is given meaning through the social processes of those who live in the space, alongside the wider geopolitical power dynamics at play. Therefore, it is not the borders or boundaries created by imperial powers, state actors or international aid organizations that should be the sole focus in studies of protracted displacement. Rather, it should incorporate how the territory itself is made in the imagination of those who use the space: the 'patterns of usage and histories of settlement' (Ellis 2015, 415).

Constructing Displacement Differently: Labor, Law and Hosting Histories

The practices of governance discussed in this section, I argue, obfuscate diverse articulations and experiences of space that divulge alternative strategies and possibilities for the politics of movement. Practices of movement, from economic labor patterns, to family and kinship bonds, to accessing goods and other resources, are an important part of connected local histories.

Prior to the Syrian Revolution, Levantine neighbors would travel and work freely across the borders. The Syrian middle classes found business opportunities in Damascus, Beirut and Amman, creating circulatory patterns of labor. These 'mobile strategies' were far from linear, as Syrians – both the rural low-skilled laborers and the urban middle-classes – travelled back and forth between sites for professional reasons (Oesch 2014). Crucially, those who travelled for work – for example, teachers, actors, artists – justified their movement not within a displacement narrative, but rather as an inability to do their job (Oesch 2014). As the violence increased and people were forced to leave Syria, many continued these circulatory patterns, showing how mobility cannot be understood in isolation from its history: it is 'not a new phenomenon but rather an extension of their movements before the crisis' (Oesch 2014).

Similarly, many males sought work in northern Jordan prior to the war. Syrians partook in low-skilled, manual labor revealing important 'translocal mobilities' beyond the framework of 'conflict-induced displacement' (Wagner 2020, 184). When the war began, Syrians with a history of working in the agricultural sector in north Jordan 'capitaliz[ed] on old employment networks' to make a living (Wagner 2017, 110). These cross-border economic patterns reflect why many Syrians did not register on arrival in Jordan or Lebanon, as many did not consider themselves refugees (Oesch 2014). Recognizing and incorporating such circulatory border patterns as the economic, social and desired norms that existed prior to the conflict has been lost in practices of refugee governance. Cross-border kinship and labor connections existed long before the civil war, yet this crisis placed immense pressure on these employment, family and tribal links.

In the wider context of refugee governance in the Levant since 2011, neither Jordan nor Lebanon has signed the 1951 United Nations Refugee Convention. Historically, Chatty (2017, 26) contends, 'the Arab and Syrian institution of hospitality and refuge' created space for the movement of peoples across vast areas of land, throughout the past century as brother Arabs. Such people were often well looked after by both the state and society, through integration programs, the granting of citizenship and the offer of land and other provisions to encourage self-sufficiency as soon as possible (Chatty 2017, 25–26).

When Syrians in large numbers began to cross these borders, Lebanon and Jordan took significantly different approaches to the influx of Syrians. Dating back to the Ottoman Empire, refugee resolutions in the region had been based on traditional understandings of personhood, grounded in Arab, Islamic or tribal notions of brotherhood, refugee or guest. International or 'Western' humanitarianism in the Levant had not played a significant role. Lebanon continued with these traditions, choosing to cope with their Syrian neighbors independently of international aid networks through 'civil society engagement' (Chatty 2017, 56).

Jordan, on the other hand, invited the UNHCR into its borders, creating the first Syrian refugee camp, Zaatari, in 2012 to dispel 'makeshift settlements' near cities and towns (Hoffman 2017, 103). Despite being praised during the initial influx of Syrians as 'generous and hospitable', access for certain people – 'unaccompanied male youths', for example – became increasingly difficult (Chatty 2017, 29). Security, rather than hosting, was replaced as the dominant narrative. In utilizing international humanitarian governance, the Jordanian government further reinforced the correlation between migrant and security, drawing on the colonial Syrian-Jordanian border to solidify who belongs and who represents the 'other'. Many of those from the Syrian governorates of Homs or Dara'a did not view themselves as refugees, but rather drew on their tribal histories for belonging. However, such policies constructed 'Syrian' Bedouins as refugees, and therefore distinctly as not belonging (Wagner 2020, 176). Extending this further, many Syrians in Jordan found the term refugee condescending and chose to ignore this label altogether (Simpson and Abo Zayed 2019, 6). Such linguistic preferences depict how familial connections far outweigh modern categorizations in governance.

Historically, prior to the crisis, Jordan welcomed migrants and refugees into its borders as a key hosting country in the region (Achilli et al. 2017). Identifying the wider histories of displacement in the Levant helps unravel the complexity of the paths taken by Lebanon and Jordan, and the contexts in which forced migrants were able to communicate strategies of movement in order to shape their new circumstances. Turner (2015) posits that Jordan's initial policies towards Syrians were prompted largely by their hosting history, namely that of Palestinians and Iraqis, and the saturation of these populations in the labor market. While camps were built in Jordan for Palestinian refugees after the 1967 Arab-Israeli War, these spaces were deemed 'a serious source of political instability' (Turner 2015, 392). However, governance policies changed dramatically as Iraqi refugees headed to Jordan not due to security dynamics, but rather due to the capital and resources of those arriving. Initially, Iraqis arriving in 2005 were 'overwhelmingly urban, educated and upper- and middle-class', and therefore were not labelled 'refugees' by the Jordanian regime (Turner 2015, 392). Iraqis were able to integrate them-selves into society due to their class status and economic potential. Given their position, camps were not built and Jordan did not seek international aid until late 2006 (Turner 2015, 393). However, in initially choosing a policy of non-encampment for Iraqi refugees, Jordan was unable to later gain the adequate recognition required for international funding.

Subsequently, when Syrians began arriving in large numbers, Jordan constructed policies of encampment and severe economic restrictions to both control movement and justify international funding. Turner (2015) argues that security concerns were only partially responsible for such policies. Economic considerations were fundamental to displacement decision-making. Governance strategies had to balance the domestic impact of those crossing the border from lower socioeconomic classes who had limited resources, while considering the demands of the Jordanian workforce which had already begun to show discontent at the arrival of Syrians, simultaneously highlighting the need for international support and finance (Turner 2015, 394–396).

Zaatari Village under North Jordan's Displacement Narrative

Zaatari village is one such place that has been co-constituted by Syrians and Jordanians who enact their own situations in displacement through moving, working and communicating, thereby utilizing the site as an effective space to live, despite the policies of governance permeating throughout. The village has been reshaped and reconstituted by displacement since 2011. As a hosting community, both Syrians and Jordanians living here have suffered from immense economic hardship and social pressure due to gaps in aid provision (AFCI 2019). Jordanians and Syrians share access to resources and space, often relying on pre-existing and re-activated social, economic and historical networks. This site represents a multiplicity of communicative movements characterized by labor and local historical geographies, wider patterns of community movement between the Syrian areas of Dara'a and Homs and its proximity to the border and refugee hotspots.

Within the settlement, land was provided by relatives for free, allowing refugees to build their own homes at a fraction of the cost compared to other areas (Wagner 2020, 182). Those who have the financial means have been allowed to build concrete houses and other infrastructure, such as shops, in order to make a living (Omari 2014). At the heart of the village lies a 'makeshift tent city' – around 50 percent of refugees living in the village live in tents (Wagner 2020, 180). Some tents have electricity, and homes often consist of multiple tents to accommodate larger families. Many newly arrived Syrians provide cheap labor as tilers, field workers or bakers in exchange for a site to live on or access to electricity (Wagner 2020).

In the study of displacement, the reasons behind why and where one seeks refuge are often minimized. The role of transnational connections has been understudied, both in the context of the Syrian uprising and in its aftermath of mass displacement. Currently, '80 percent of the Syrian refugee flow across international borders is self-settling in cities, towns and villages where they have social and economic networks' (Chatty 2017, 26). Such decision-making strategies help piece together a dynamic puzzle of local social histories and imaginaries of space and identity, while having profound implications for the analysis of refugee governance.

Since 2014, the governance policies imposed on Syrians in Jordan have become significantly harsher. For those living in urban spaces, it is increasingly difficult to access basic services, such as food programs, health care provision and education. Syrians who work without appropriate docu-mentation risk exploitation through longer hours and lower wages than their Jordanian counterparts. However, contrary to popular belief, Syrians who are working in Jordan's labor markets have predominantly replaced other migrant workers in specific sectors, rather than replace Jordanians themselves (Turner 2015, 396). Urban refugees living in severe poverty are at risk of 'arrest [and] exploitation' and are forced to decide between moving to a formal camp or being deported back to Syria should they seek informal employment opportunities (Achilli 2015, 7). As the situation progressed to one of protracted displacement by 2014, Syrians who entered Jordan were encouraged to stay in designated areas controlled by international humanitarianism in an attempt to curtail Syrians from urban spaces. These strategies of tightening opportunities and services for refugees are a direct attempt to control movement.

Chatty (2017, 26) argues that, in order to understand the nature of Syrian displacement and Jordanian hosting in the present, the historical networks and 'ethno-religious communities' must be extrapolated. Many of those who fled to northern Jordan came predominantly from Homs and Dara'a and share with north Jordanians a belonging to the Beni Khaled Bedouin (Wagner 2020, 181). Within Syria, although many of the rural populations – from Homs to Aleppo to Palmyra in the west – moved into the cities and towns for education and employment, 'kinship ties through tribe, clan and family still matter' (Chatty 2015). These kinship ties are fundamental for understanding how relationships and routines have shaped villages and towns in northern Jordan and the present movements during war and displacement. In a sub-national study of the Jordanian response to Syrian migration, Mafraq, the city closest to the Syrian border in the study, was shown to be more welcoming and accessible to Syrians than the cities of Sahab and Zarqa, precisely because of the 'extended cross-border kinship networks' (Betts et al. 2017, 12). Interesting to note, and disputed among academic scholars of the region, is how the economy was deemed less central than these tribal links. Still, the importance of the local context within this study cannot be denied given the proximity of this site to Syria and the subsequent kinship links.

Despite debate, it holds true that communication between these communities has been upheld through years of visits and marital ties, therefore allowing newly arrived Syrians to feel welcomed and connected by a 'common ancestry' – 'the same dialect and the same family' (Wagner 2020, 181). Although unable to verify, Ann-Christin Wagner (2020) recalls a story from an interlocutor who suggested 'Zaatari Village was founded by Syrians in the 1960s, and in return each had received Jordanian citizenship for their services to the town'. Although immense strain has been put on the economies of these rural towns and settlements, there is a 'passive acceptance… endured partly because of longstanding kingship ties that predate the conflict' (Betts et al. 2017, 12).

In a similar vein, Matthew Stevens (2016) asserts the desire and need for friends and family during emergencies, relaying the importance of identity and social networks during displacement. In doing so, he echoes Wagner's (2020, 182) statement that 'where Syrians seek refuge and how well they fare in exile depends on the type of pre-war transnational connections'. Many Syrians, in 'reactivating older notions of tribal identity… subvert[ed] state logics of containment' (Wagner 2020, 184).

One arrangement that illustrates the importance of these prior links was the bailout scheme, which allowed Jordanians to sponsor their Syrian relatives, helping them avoid refugee camps. As restrictions in 2014 became tighter, this scheme was one of the only ways in which Syrians could legally leave the camp and gain access to services provided by the United Nations High Commissioner for Refugees or the Jordanian government (Achilli 2015, 5–6). Sponsors had to be 'over 35 years of age, married, with a stable job, no police record and [in] a direct family relation' of the Syrian; yet even with these credentials, bailouts were not always approved (Achilli 2015, 5–6). Hence, Syrians found it increasingly difficult to move within urban spaces and legally leave the camp (Achilli 2015).

Although the official bailout scheme ended in 2015 at the request of Jordanian authorities, many of the Syrians who were granted refuge did so through 'host families related either by blood or marriage, particularly those fleeing from Der'a and its surrounding villages' (Chatty 2017, 31). Having such 'transnational kinship networks' provided Syrian refugees with more security in the form of a 'legal status, material resources and livelihoods' (Wagner, cited in Lenhard and Samanani 2020, 181). Navigating through systems of governance together, many Syrians were able to avoid the harsh conditions of the camp, favoring instead local integration.

Wagner (2020, 181) describes the story of Abu Mohammed, whose movements represented a specific form of communication dictated by strong 'transnational kinship networks'. Abu Mohammed phoned relatives before his journey from Homs began, informing his family of his plans. On arrival in Jordan, his extended Jordanian family were waiting for him to finalize his papers and return to Zaatari village with him, rather than the formal camp (Wagner 2020). For Abu Mohammed, seeking passage over the border reflected an ancestry of movement, a historic understanding that held solidarity with kinsmen (relatives) far above regulations of displacement governance. This extended family navigated their way through governing apparatus drawing on entangled histories of movement – associated with labor, family and land – which threw into contention the categories used to govern displacement.

However, while these kinship ties and complex geographic social histories should not be ignored, drawing on these links alone does not capture the complexity of dynamics within protracted displacement. North Jordan's encampment policies in 2012 were driven by both government officials and by tribal leaders, who were concerned about the strain on rural northern villages given the volume of Syrians crossing the border (Turner 2015, 392, 395). The northern governorate of Mafraq comprises many communities of 5,000 persons or fewer, and with the influx of Syrians – estimated between 70,000 and 200,000 – these settlements were forced to change dramatically (Turner

2015, 396). Turner, in analyzing displacement within an economic framework, draws out two important aspects relating to movement within displacement: the class and resources of the refugee – what they bring with them – and how these elements fit into the sites to and within which they move.

With '58 percent of out-of-camp Syrians' from rural backgrounds and less well-educated than their Jordanian counterparts, many of the Syrians from the poorer regions of Dara'a and Homs are more likely to settle in towns and villages in the north that have a cheaper cost of living than the larger cities or the capital (Turner 2015, 396). While the previous refugee population, comprising wealthy Iraqis, moved to Amman, poorer Syrians did not have the financial ability to settle in such spaces. Furthermore, this population is comprised of many unskilled laborers, who work in the agricultural sectors based outside of cities. These smaller towns and villages already experience high unemployment, and Syrians – many of whom accept lower wages than Jordanians – exacerbate the hardship experienced by hosting communities (Turner 2015). This shows us that, within the study of displacement, capacity for movement must be explored alongside the contextual decisions of how and where to move.

Wagner (2017) exposes the survival mechanisms of many of the younger generations from rural families in Mafraq, a city close to Zaatari village. These strategies work beyond displacement narratives or humanitarian governance understandings, rather relying on 'translocal mobility schemes' that existed long before 2011 (Wagner 2017, 113). Prior to the crisis, rural communities, often from lower socioeconomic classes, relied on 'the contribution of all family members', including the involvement of minors in agricultural labor and early marriage (Wagner 2017, 112). Syrians from lower socio-economic backgrounds had an in-depth experience of 'short-term seasonal migration', crossing the border in order to make ends meet for their families (Wagner 2017, 113). Not only did these economic ties link to kinship experiences, but they also supported Jordan's agricultural land needs (Betts et al. 2017,12). Therefore, in the specific context of northern Jordan, the socioeconomic dynamics and movement norms prior to the crisis are fundamental to understanding the patterns of communication, which take place within the refugee governance rubric.

Conclusion

Analyzing experiences of displacement through the conceptualization of movement as creative communication, draws on a multiplicity of motivations, histories, relations, needs, requirements and forces. Combined, they co-constitute the situations and sites in experiences of displacement. In prioritizing the movements of forced migrants as the object of study, and how this movement interacts with the power structures governing border cross-ings, urban settlements or camps, such sites can be theorized as spaces of communication whereby refugees enact their own situations in spite of oppressive forces. Evoking such a framework allows for the inclusion of an analysis of the political, economic, legal and social, but it does so through an understanding that the migrants themselves – working within these categories and policies – simultaneously enact these spaces by their very presence and movement.

Within the context of protracted displacement, movement is often stifled by the state, national borders or through interactions with humanitarian apparatuses. Framing movement as creative communication does not deny this, but rather facilitates a discussion on the highly contextual need to study displacement, focusing on migrant movement not as a linear practice, but as belonging to wider circulatory, translocal patterns. The movements of people are explicit iterations made to constitute their own situations.

Centralizing movement reveals the power migrants have to enact their own spaces and situations, where usually the conditions of the spaces projected upon them through domestic or international governing policies are the focus. I identify an interconnected web of communication strategies and histories often ignored within the traditional study of displacement. Such a methodo-logy presents the refugee or forced migrant not as a subject to be governed, but rather a dynamic and complex individual, entangled in power dynamics often beyond their control. The case of Zaatari village shows how migrants hold a capacity to enact sites and situations through their very presence and relationship to structured governance.

References

Abboud, Samer, Omar S. Dahi, Waleed Hazbun, Nicole Sunday Grove, Coralie Pison Hindawi, Jamil Mouawad and Sami Hermez. 2018. 'Towards a Beirut School of critical security studies', *Critical Studies on Security* 6(3): 273–295.

Achilli, Luigi. 2015. 'Syrian Refugees in Jordan: A Reality Check', Migration Policy Centre, EUI.

Achilli, Luigi, Nasser Yassin and M. Murat Erdogan. 2017. 'Neighbouring Host-Countries' Policies for Syrian Refugees: The cases of Jordan, Lebanon, and Turkey', *European Institute of the Mediterranean* (January).

Acting for Change International. 2019. 'Projects'. https://www.
actingforchangeinternational.org/projects

Betts, Alexander, Ali Ali & Fulya Memisoglu. 2017. 'Local Politics and the
Syrian Refugee Crisis: Exploring Responses in Turkey, Lebanon, and Jordan',
Oxford Department of International Development.

Chatty, Dawn. 2013. 'Syria's Bedouin Enter the Fray', *Foreign Affairs*, 13
November.

Chatty, Dawn & Aron Lund. 2015. 'Syria's Bedouin Tribes: An Interview with
Dawn Chatty', Carnegie Middle East Centre, 2 July. https://carnegie-mec.org/
diwan/60264

Chatty, Dawn. 2017. 'The Syrian Humanitarian Disaster: Understanding
Perceptions and Aspirations in Jordan, Lebanon and Turkey' *Global Policy*
8(1): 25–32.

Del Sarto, Raffaella A. 2017. 'Contentious borders in the Middle East and
North Africa: Context and concepts', *International Affairs* 93(4): 767–787.

Ellis, Matthew. 2015. 'Over the Borderline? Rethinking Territoriality at the
Margins of Empire and Nation in the Modern Middle East (Part I)', *History
Compass* 13(8): 411–422.

Fiddian-Qasmiyeh, Elena. 2016a. 'Rerpessentations of displacement from the
Middle East and North Africa', *Public Culture* 28(3): 457–473.

Fiddian-Qasmiyeh, Elena. 2016b. 'Refugees hosting refugees', *Forced
Migration Review* (53), https://www.fmreview.org/community-protection/
fiddianqasmiyeh

Fiddian-Qasmiyeh, Elena. 2018. 'Refugee-Refugee relations in contexts of
overlapping displacement', *International Journal of Urban and Regional
Research* 42(2).

Gatter, Melissa. 2017. 'Restoring childhood: humanitarianism and growing up
Syrian in Za'tari refugee camp', *Contemporary Levant* 2(2): 89–102.

Hoffmann, Sophia. 2017. 'Humanitarian security in Jordan's Azraq Camp',
Security Dialogue 48(2): 97–112.

Hourani, Albert. 2013. *A History of the Arab Peoples*. London: Faber & Faber.

Human Rights Watch. 2017. '"I have no Idea Why They Sent us Back" Jordanian Deportations and Expulsions of Syrian Refugees'. 2 October. https://www.hrw.org/report/2017/10/02/i-have-no-idea-why-they-sent-us-back/jordanian-deportations-and-expulsions-syrian

Mencütek, Zeynep Şahin. 2019. *Refugee governance, state and politics in the Middle East*. London: Routledge.

Munif, Yasser. 2020. *The Syrian Revolution: Between the Politics of Life and the Geopolitics of Death*. London: Pluto Press.

Neep, Daniel. 2015. 'Focus: The Middle East, Hallucination, and the Cartographic imagination', *Discover Society* (16). https://discoversociety.org/2015/01/03/focus-the-middle-east-hallucination-and-the-cartographic-imagination/

Oesch, Lucas. 2014. 'Mobility as a solution', Forced Migration Review: The Syrian crisis, displacement and protection (47). https://www.fmreview.org/syria/oesch

Omari, Raed. 2014. 'Syrians build houses on donated land in Zaatari Village', *The Jordan Times*, 21 August, http://www.jordantimes.com/news/local/syrians-build-houses-donated-land-zaatari-village

Pallister-Wilkins, Polly. 2016. 'Hotspots and the geographies of humanitarianism', *Environment and Planning D: Society and Space* 1–18.

Simpson, Charles and Agyead Abo Zayed. 2019. 'New Faces, Less Water, and a Changing Economy in a Growing City: A Case Study of Refugees in Towns. Irbid, Jordan', Feinstein International Centre (July), refugeesintowns.org

Stevens, Matthew R. 2016. 'The collapse of social networks among Syrian refugees in urban Jordan', *Contemporary Levant* 1(1): 51–63.

Tejel, Jordi and Ramazan Hakki Oztan. 2020. 'The Special Issue "Forced Migration and Refugeedom in the Modern Middle East" Towards Connected Histories of Refugeedom in the Middle East', *Journal of Migration History* 6: 1–15.

Turner, Lewis. 2015. 'Explaining the (Non-)Encampment of Syrian Refugees: Secuirty, Class and the Labour Market in Lebanon and Jordan' *Mediterranean Politics* 20(3): 386–404.

UNHCR. 2018. 'North Africa and Middle East', Global Report 2018. https://www.unhcr.org/uk/publications/fundraising/5e4ffaec7/unhcr-global-report-2018-middle-east-north-africa-mena-regional-summary.html

UNHCR. 2020. Syria Regional Response Plan: Operations Portal. https://data2.unhcr.org/en/situations/syria/location/53

UNICEF/ REACH. 2014. 'Syrian Refugees Staying in Informal Tented Settlement in Jordan: Multi-Sector Assessment Report' (August). https://reliefweb.int/sites/reliefweb.int/files/resources/REACH_UNICEF_ITS_MS_AUGUST2014_FINAL.PDF

Wagner, Ann-Christin. 2017. 'Frantic Waiting: NGO Anti-Politics and "Timepass" for Young Syrian Refugees in Jordan', *Focus* (9): 107–121.

Wagner, Ann-Christin. 2018. 'Giving Aid Inside the Home', *Migration and Society: Advances in Research* (1): 36–50.

Wagner, Ann-Christin. 2020. 'Acts of 'homing' in the Eastern Desert – How Syrian refugees make temporary homes in a village outside Zaatari Camp, Jordan', in Johannes Lenhard and Farhan Samanani (Eds.) *Home: Ethnographic Encounters*. London: Bloomsbury Publishing.

13

When Social Reproduction Becomes Political: How London's Latin American Women Make their Families, Communities and Rights Visible

DOMIZIANA TURCATTI

Latin American migrants constitute an important part of London. Yet they remain institutionally unrecognized. Despite the campaigns for visibility carried out by advocacy groups, such as the Coalition of Latin Americans in the United Kingdom (CLAUK), the British government has still not included the Latin American category in the British Ethnic Recognition Scheme used by institutions, such as the Office for National Statistics (ONS), to collect census data (CLAUK 2020). The absence of a demographic category means that the contributions of Latin Americans to British society and the everyday challenges they confront go unnoticed. Institutional invisibility has obscured the stories of how Latin American women nurture their families and communities. These stories have also remained untold by the limited scholarship on this community. Despite documenting the inequalities Latin Americans face in London, scholars have paid little attention to how these inequalities affect the families and communities of Latin American migrants and the role women play in coping with these inequalities.

This chapter attempts to bring to light the experiences of London's Latin American migrant women by presenting the practices through which they maintain and make their families, communities and rights visible. Specifically, this study focuses on the strategies London's Latin American migrant women deploy to carry out social reproductive work, the 'array of activities and relationships involved in maintaining people both on a daily basis and intergenerationally' (Nakano Glenn 1992, 1). As such, social reproductive work refers to activities like domestic work, childcare and the intergenerational transmission of culture, but also the maintenance of community ties. This study is based on 203 hours of ethnographic fieldwork conducted between October 2018 and July 2019, which took place mostly within a London-based non-governmental organization (NGO) supporting Latin American migrants. During the fieldwork, the narratives of 17 Latin American women and 14 Latin American men were collected through semi-structured interviews. In this study, the category Latin American refers to people originally from South America, Central America and the Caribbean whose inhabitants speak Spanish, Portuguese or French (Kittleson et al. 2017). However, most of the people I met and interviewed during the fieldwork were middle-aged Colombians, Ecuadorians and Peruvians working in low-income jobs.

After problematizing the lack of attention on the social reproductive work of London's Latin American migrant women, I present the literature conceptualizing social reproduction from a feminist perspective and the methodology used to conduct this study. I then describe the social reproduction work through which Latin American women ensure the survival of their families and communities. I will demonstrate how Latin American women's social reproductive work acquires a political dimension, as it becomes key to the survival not only of their families but also of NGOs advocating for the rights and visibility of Latin American migrants in the UK. I conclude by calling for the recognition of the political nature of migrant women's everyday social reproduction practices.

Latin American Migrants in London

The lived experiences of social reproduction among London's Latin American migrant women have largely remained unaddressed. In what seems an effort to begin understanding the experiences of a relatively new and unrecognized migrant group in the UK, scholars have focused mostly on the reasons behind Latin Americans' migration to the UK, their experiences in the labor market, in dealing with 'illegality' and in accessing support.

Research shows that Latin American migration to the UK began increasing in the 1970s as an outcome of the socioeconomic instability in Latin America (McIlwaine et al. 2011). Latin American migration to the UK increased further with the tightening of immigration policies in the United States during the 1990s and after 9/11, which forced Latin Americans to look for alternative destinations to find job, safety and study opportunities (Pellegrino 2004). Following the 2008 global economic crisis, Latin Americans began migrating to the UK also from Southern Europe using the European passports acquired while living there (McIlwaine and Bunge 2016). Having been negatively affected by the crisis, Latin Americans living in Southern Europe decided to look for better opportunities in London (McIlwaine and Bunge 2016). In 2019, the ONS estimated that there were 255,000 people born in Central and South America in London.

Much of the literature on the adaption experiences of London's Latin Americans has focused on their experiences in the labor market. Research shows that a considerable size of London's Latin American community earns salaries below the London Living Wage, the threshold for lifting people out of poverty in London (McIlwaine and Bunge 2016). Latin American migrants are overwhelmingly concentrated in low-paid jobs in the cleaning, care and construction sectors for which they are overqualified (McIlwaine and Bunge 2016; McIlwaine and Bunge 2018). Scholars attribute such downward mobility to limited English language skills and employers' reluctance in recognizing their educational titles (McIlwaine and Bunge 2016).

Other studies have addressed the experiences of London's Latin Americans in dealing with 'illegality'. McIlwaine et al. (2011) demonstrate the difficulties Latin Americans have had to enter and remain in the UK, since many were denied asylum and work permits. Dias's (2017) study on the way Brazilians deal with being undocumented reveals how 'illegality' meant constantly moving between houses and odd jobs to avoid being identified. Gutierrez Garza (2018) introduced the expression 'temporality of illegality' to indicate how some Latin Americans in London would move in and out of 'illegality' due to changes in migration laws and expiring visas.

Scholars have also highlighted the challenges facing London's Latin American migrants to access social protection. In 2011, only one-fifth of London's Latin American community received some kind of state assistance (McIlwaine and Bulge 2016). These numbers have been explained in terms of insufficient English language skills and lack of information available in Spanish and Portuguese (Turcatti and Assaraf 2020; Mas Giralt and Granada 2015). In this respect, scholars have shown the vital role played by the NGOs established and run by Latin Americans in supporting Latin American migrants to access health care and welfare benefits (Mas Giralt and Granada 2015; Turcatti and Assaraf 2019; Turcatti and Assaraf 2020).

This scholarship has raised awareness about the inequalities facing Latin American migrants in London. However, researchers have paid relatively little attention to the practices through which London's Latin American women maintain their families and communities. The literature we do have is sparse. Some studies have shown how social reproductive labor, such as domestic work, childcare and the transmission of heritage culture, is often carried out by women (Souza 2015; McIlwaine 2008; McIlwaine 2010). Other scholars have explored how Latin American migrant women care for their left-behind families from distance through remittances and by providing emotional support through visits and everyday communication (Passarelli Tonhati 2017).

While demonstrating the key role Latin American women play in their families, these studies tend to confine women to the familial sphere, preventing us from fully appreciating how they contribute to their communities. In order to build on and expand this literature, this study presents the strategies Latin American migrant women living in London deploy to carry out social reproductive work not only to nurture families, but also to maintain their communities. The next section defines in more detail what social reproduction and social reproductive work is from a feminist perspective.

Social Reproduction from a Feminist Perspective

From a feminist perspective, social reproduction is a term that refers to 'maintaining and sustaining human beings throughout their life cycle' (Troung 1996, 32). As such, social reproductive work includes the activities needed to maintain and sustain human beings, which range from domestic work and the care of children, the elderly and the ill to the intergenerational transmission of culture (Kofman 2014). The maintenance of kin and communities has also been considered a form of social reproductive labor (Nakano Glenn 1992; Gedalof 2009).

Since the seventies, feminists have highlighted the gendered nature of social reproductive work. Scholars such as Benston (1969) attributed the fact that it is often women who are held responsible for social reproductive work to gender ideologies constructing women as the 'natural' carers and men as the 'natural' breadwinners. Since the 1970s, feminists have placed reproductive labor at the center of women's oppression due to its undervalued character and because reproductive responsibilities make climbing the social ladder harder for women (Benston 1969; Nakano Glenn 1992).

While exposing the gendered nature of social reproductive labor, feminist scholars explain that the family is not the only site of social reproduction (Razavi 2013). Families can outsource reproductive tasks to other families (e.g., ask relatives or friends to care for their children) or use markets to arrange the provision of food (e.g., restaurants) or childcare (e.g., paid care workers) (Kofman 2014). The welfare state and NGOs also assume social reproductive functions. The welfare state provides households with benefits and health care, which may be vital for the social reproduction of low-income families, while NGOs can act as bridges to help families access welfare support (Razavi 2007). Put another way, the market, NGOs and the welfare state become resources that can be used to secure one's family's social reproduction.

Yet access to such resources is uneven. Colen (1995, 78) coined the term 'stratified social reproduction' to indicate that social reproductive labor is 'differentially experienced, valued and rewarded according to inequalities of access to material and social resources in particular historical and cultural contexts'. Colen (1995) developed this concept from her investigation of the parenting practices of West Indian childcarers and of their employers in New York. Colen found that the migration of West Indian middle-class mothers allowed their employers in New York to secure two salaries *and* their children's care. This meant, however, that West Indian carers could not provide the same level of security to their children, as they would struggle with both bringing their children to the US and providing them with adequate childcare, due to fragmented local networks, low wages, low-quality housing and insecure legal status.

Framed by this literature, this study investigates the kind of social reproductive work London's Latin American women do to sustain their families and communities and the meaning such work acquires in a context of institutional invisibility. The next section describes the methodology used to understand the lived experiences of social reproduction of London's Latin American women.

Understanding Social Reproduction through Ethnography

The everyday social reproduction practices of Latin American women were documented through 203 hours of ethnographic fieldwork mostly conducted between October 2018 and May 2019 in a London-based NGO. Run by Latin Americans, this NGO helps Spanish- and Portuguese-speaking migrants access welfare support, health care and their employment rights through one-on-one advice sessions. The NGO also provides English classes, social events and workshops on topics that interest the NGO's clients.

The fieldwork started by collecting data through participant observation at the NGO. I participated in 68 advisor-client one-on-one sessions and in various social activities and workshops. Conducting participant observation at the NGO allowed me to become more familiar with the kind of everyday challenges Latin American migrants and their families face and for which they seek support, while also observing the role women play in the NGO.

Apart from participant observation, I collected the narratives of 17 Latin

American women and 14 Latin American men through semi-structured interviews aimed at understanding the ways in which Latin American migrants make sense of their lived experiences of social reproduction. I interviewed both men and women in order to better understand the role that women play in their families and communities by comparing what men and women said about their social reproductive labor. Most of the interviewees were accessed through the NGO and were Colombians, Ecuadorians and Peruvians, middle-aged, documented and working in low-paid jobs, mostly in the cleaning sector. The interviews lasted between 45 and 90 minutes, were recorded and were conducted in Spanish.

While transcribing field notes and interviews, I assigned pseudonymous to participants and removed potential identifiers in order to protect anonymity and confidentiality. Field notes and interview transcripts were then analyzed through thematic analysis, defined by Braun and Clarke (2006, 79) as 'a method for identifying, analyzing and reporting patterns (themes) within data'. This analytical method was chosen as this study aimed to identify 'themes', such as the types of family and community responsibilities participants may have.

The findings are presented in the next two sections. First, I present the social reproductive practices through which Latin American women ensure the survival of their families. I then discuss Latin American women's social reproductive labor in their communities and how these are fundamental to making their families, communities and rights visible.

From Ensuring the Survival of their Families...

Through a variety of everyday practices, Latin American women nurture and ensure the survival of their families in economic, social and cultural terms. First, the Latin American women I met while conducting participant observation at the NGO and whom I interviewed played important breadwinning roles in their families. They would often work along their partners to provide for their children, while single mothers were often the only breadwinners in their families. Women's salaries, regardless of whether they had children or partners, were often meant to enhance the lives of family members living in other countries. If in some cases remittances were meant to raise their families' living standards, they often secured everyday necessities.

In order to provide for their families, women would often work long hours in more than one company. Working in the cleaning and domestic sector meant that their salary was often below the London Living Wage, the wage required to lift people out of poverty in London. While both women and men worked long hours, it was mostly women who would queue at the NGO waiting to be attended by one of the advisors to inquire about the welfare benefits to which their families were entitled and to seek help filling out the application forms for welfare benefits and social housing.

Apart from playing a key role in securing their families' everyday necessities, women were often responsible for domestic work, childcare and the care of the elderly living in the UK. Unable to afford nurseries or residential homes and in absence of family members living in London who could help them with childcare and the care of the elderly, parents reported sharing some of these tasks. Single mothers, on the other hand, had to be both 'fathers and mothers'. As Annamaria, a Colombian single mother with three children put it:

> Sometimes I rest to find the strength to cook... clean... do laundry... talk with my daughter... feed my children... meet their teacher, check how they do at school... ask them how they are doing these days... make sure I have the money to buy them shoes to go to school.

Yet it is important to highlight that having a partner does not necessarily mean help with domestic work and childcare, as Rosana, a Peruvian mother with a two-year-old son, repeatedly emphasized during the interview. Rosana explained how her ex-partner would not help her at nights when their baby was just born. Instead, he expected her to do his laundry, cook and keep their baby quiet so that he could rest.

Many women would also care for family members living elsewhere. For instance, some of the Latin American women I met while conducting participant observation at the NGO and who I interviewed were or had been at some point in their life transnational mothers. For seven years, Hadi could not bring her two children, who remained in Venezuela with their grandmother, to the UK. Being a transnational mother meant sending remittances back home to ensure her children had access to food, a roof and education. Furthermore, through 'chats all the time, video calls day and night', Hadi would do her best to provide her children with the guidance and emotional support they need to deal with issues ranging from how to deal with discussions with friends to making sense of why she has been away so long.

For some Latin American women I interviewed, securing the survival of their families meant helping them cross borders and settle in London. Daniela, a Colombian woman who came to London during the 1980s, explained how she helped her siblings escape the violence they experienced in Colombia:

They [her siblings] didn't suffer here. They stayed with me [at her house], they found jobs [she found work for them], they got their documents [she instructed them on how to get them]. Step by step, they organized themselves.

According to Daniela, had she not shared her resources with her siblings, her family members would either be in danger or scattered around the world by now.

Latin American women's social reproductive work included organizing family gatherings in order to maintain the strength of familial bonds. It was women who would often organize visits to their left-behind families, when they could afford them and when their legal status allowed them to travel. Gathering the family also means getting together with loved ones who live in London. Romina, a Bolivian mother, provides an example:

When my husband comes home from work… we have a family moment. We sit on the bed and play with our baby… But to have that moment, the baby needs to be cleaned and the food ready.

The importance of creating the conditions that allow families to enjoy 'family moments', as Romina calls them, can be best appreciated when considering the fact that, for many of the people I interviewed and met at the NGO, free time is a luxury. Working long hours often limits the time available to families to be together.

For many of the women I interviewed and met at the NGO, nurturing their families also meant maintaining their heritage languages. For instance, women wanted their children to be able to communicate with them and their family members. Women, more often than men, reported spending time teaching their children Spanish and planning activities that would foster the learning of Spanish. This was made evident during the interview with Xiomara, a Colombian woman I interviewed whose children are now in their twenties. Xiomara explained that, apart from talking to them in Spanish, she would take them to the free Spanish classes offered by an NGO in London and test their Spanish after class. She used to tell her children: 'when you learn it well [Spanish], you will be able to speak the language you want [Spanish or English]'.

Furthermore, for the women I interviewed, nurturing their families also meant teaching their children about their heritage cultures. Mothers and parents would often mention during the interviews how they feared their children becoming 'too British' and not appreciating their heritage culture, which would lead to familial misunderstandings. This is why mothers would cook heritage food and take them to so-called Latin shops and Latin organizations to meet other Latin Americans and participate in their cultural activities.

The women I interviewed tended to be proud of the efforts they make every day to nurture their families. Yet the fact that some of the women would burst out into tears during the interview is a testament to how ensuring the social reproduction of their families is not always easy when lacking support and socioeconomic resources. As Sofia, an Ecuadorian woman, put it: 'you have to find the strength even if you don't have it'. What motivates women to find such strength can be appreciated through the words a young Colombian woman used to console Annamaria, a single mother who was crying in the hall of the NGO where I conducted fieldwork:

> In a few years, your children will recognize your fights and they
> will keep you as a queen. They will have a diploma and will
> become someone.

It is clear that what keeps many women going is the hope that their efforts will bring a better future to their families.

...to Making their Families, Communities and Rights Visible

Latin American women are key not only to the social reproduction of their families, but also of their communities. Some volunteer for their communities where Latin American migrants receive help and support. Other women contribute to the maintenance of a shared 'Latin American' identity on the basis of which Latin American migrants created and keep developing NGOs advocating for the rights and institutional recognition of London's Latin American migrants. There are also women who become leaders in their own communities in order to enhance the quality of life of London's Latin American migrants and claim for their recognition and visibility.

At the NGO where I conducted participant observation, the majority of volunteers were Latin American women who would help at the organization by answering calls at the reception, helping to clean the office or cooking lunch for the advisors. Some women would also help advisors address the NGO clients' questions when they had the skills and the time to do so. For example, having studied law in Spain and being more fluent in English, Fernanda, a Colombian woman who came to the UK from Spain, decided to volunteer at the NGO and help advisors with minor tasks, such as helping clients figure out whether their driving license is valid in the UK and what to do if it is not. These women's volunteer work should not be underestimated. As one of the community workers explained, there are not funds specifically allocated for the Latin American community, precisely because Latin Americans are still not institutionally recognized. This means that the NGO is severely understaffed and overworked. To attend the clients that queue at the NGO every day, advisors had little time to have lunch and take breaks. This is why the volunteer work of Latin American women in the NGO is crucial.

Latin American women are also key to the maintenance of a shared 'Latin American' identity on the basis of which Latin American migrants create and keep developing NGOs advocating for the rights and institutional recognition of London's Latin American migrants. At the NGO where I conducted fieldwork, women were often responsible for organizing activities and social events such as monthly gatherings and parties. In these events, women would often cook heritage food. For major events, such as the Christmas party and the anniversary party of the NGO, they would invite professional dancers to perform choreographies based on salsa, cumbia and bachata music. By doing so, Latin American women create spaces where their heritage cultures can be celebrated and enacted. As one of the advisors of the NGO emphasized, these social and cultural activities play an important function in making Latin Americans feel they belong to the same community despite their diverse cultural backgrounds, histories and migratory trajectories. The sense of belonging to a Latin American community instils an obligation to help each other, which is the rationale and the motor of many of the NGOs in London funded by Latin Americans, including the one where I conducted fieldwork, whose objective is to enhance the quality of life and claim the recognition of Latin American migrants in the UK.

Here it is important to emphasize that the Latin American women I interviewed contribute to the social reproduction of their communities even when not directly volunteering in their communities. In the previous section, I highlighted the social reproductive work women do to maintain and reproduce their heritage cultures and languages inter-generationally. These practices contribute to their children's development and the maintenance of a Latin American identity. Feeling Latin American, the second generations may decide to contribute to enhance the quality of life of other Latin Americans living in London once they grow up. At the NGO where I conducted fieldwork, one of the advisors was a young woman in her twenties who was the daughter of a Colombian woman who came to the UK as an asylum seeker. Claudia studied at university and decided first to volunteer and then work for the NGO where I conducted fieldwork as she wanted to use the knowledge and skills that she acquired in school to support London's Latin American migrants. The case of Claudia is only one example of how Latin American women play a crucial role in the social reproduction of their communities even when not directly involved in volunteer or community work merely by virtue of transmitting their heritage culture to their children.

Finally, I met and interviewed women who had become leaders in their own communities and contribute more proactively to enhance the quality of life of London's Latin American migrants. The case of Valeria, a Colombian mother, illustrates this. Valeria approached the NGO where I conducted fieldwork a few years ago when she was diagnosed with a chronic illness that prevented her from working and supporting her two children. At the NGO, the advisors helped her access health care and the welfare benefits she needed until she could return to work. Since then, Valeria started participating in various activities of the NGO and volunteering, as it was a space for her to not feel alone. When her health got better, Valeria decided to start a course to become an advisor specialized in social housing and began volunteering for the NGO by assisting advisors helping migrants access social housing. While she was still training at the time of my research, she started to handle some social housing cases at the NGO on her own. She also became the president of the board of trustee of the NGO, where key decisions about the kind of services that the NGO provides to the Latin American community are made.

There are many reasons why women participated in their communities more or less actively. Some of the women I met volunteered at the NGO where I conducted fieldwork because they wanted to 'give back'. Having been helped by the NGO to access health care and the welfare benefits to which they are entitled; volunteering was a way of expressing their gratitude to the advisors of the organization. At the same time, volunteering was a way of socializing and making friends with people who understood them by virtue of coming from the same culture, speaking the same language or having shared similar challenges. There were also women who more explicitly stated that their community involvement stemmed from being aware of the lack of support available to Latin American migrants in London. 'We are invisible', Valeria said, 'and I want to support my community, the same way they supported me'. Yet, regardless of the reasons why and the extent to which women become involved in their communities, Latin American women play a crucial role for the social reproduction and therefore survival of these communities.

Conclusion

In order to bring to light the experiences of London's Latin American migrant women, this chapter presented the practices through which London's Latin American women maintain and make their families, communities and rights visible. Specifically, this study focused on the strategies London's Latin American migrant women deploy to carry out social reproductive work for their families and their communities and the function that such work acquires in a context of invisibility.

This chapter showed that Latin American women play a crucial role in the social reproduction of their families. While at times men and women shared domestic and childcare tasks, women were often responsible for these. Women were also breadwinners in addition to being responsible for keeping families together by organizing family gatherings, helping their family members migrate to London and transmitting their heritage cultures to the next generation.

Apart from securing the survival of their families in economic, social and cultural terms, there were women who would volunteer for NGOs and communities supporting Latin American migrants in London. Fieldwork allowed me to appreciate the journey some women undertake to become leaders in their own communities, where the objective is to enhance the quality of life of London's Latin American migrants and claim for their recognition and visibility.

In a context of institutional invisibility, the social reproductive work Latin American women do to nurture their families and communities acquires a political dimension. By volunteering and becoming leaders in their communities, women ensure that the NGOs enhancing the quality of life and visibility of Latin American migrants in London continue to operate. By passing along their cultures to the next generations, women are keeping up the hope that these Latin American communities and organizations will be supported by the next generations and continue to claim for the rights and visibility of London's Latin American migrants.

Not only does this chapter make visible the experiences of London's Latin American migrant women, it also clearly demonstrates how confining migrant women's social reproductive work to the *private* realm of domesticity prevents us from appreciating its political and *public* dimensions. Only when considering the social reproductive work migrant women do both within their families and for their communities can we appreciate and recognize the political nature of migrant women's everyday social reproduction practices within and beyond the boundaries of domesticity.

References

CLAUK. 2020. 'CLAUK Wrote to Public Health England about COVID-19 and the Latin American Community'. http://www.clauk.org.uk/clauk-wrote-to-public-health-england-about-covid-19-and-the-latin-american-community/

Benston, Margaret. 1969. 'The Political Economy of Women's Liberation', *Monthly Review, 21,* no. 4 (September): 31–44.

Braun, Virginia, and Clarke, Victoria. 2006. 'Using Thematic Analysis in Psychology', *Qualitative Research in Psychology, 3,* no. 2 (July): 77–101.

Colen, Shellee. 1995. '"Like a Mother to Them": Stratified Reproduction and West Indian Childcare Workers and Employers in New York', in *Conceiving the New World Order: The Global Politics of Reproduction* by Faye. D. Ginsburg and Rayna Rapp, 78–102. Berkeley: University of California Press.

Dias, Gustavo. 2017. 'Dealing with the UK Inner Borders: A Study of Brazilians and Their Temporary Dwellings in London', *Migrações Internacionais Contemporâneas, 22,* no. 1 (June): 156–182. http://www.uel.br/revistas/uel/index.php/mediacoes/article/viewFile/28784/pdf

Gedalof, Irene. 2009. 'Birth, Belonging and Migrant Mothers: Narratives of Reproduction in Feminist Migration Studies', *Feminist Review, 93,* (November): 81–100.

Gutiérrez Garza, Ana. 2018. 'The Temporality of Illegality: Experiences of Undocumented Latin American Migrants in London', *Journal of Global and Historical Anthropology, 81* (June): 86–98.

Kofman, Eleonore. 2014. 'Gendered Migrations, Social Reproduction and the Household in Europe', *Dialect Anthropology*, 38 (February): 81–94.

Kittleson, Roger A., Bushnell, David, and Lockhart, James. 2017. 'History of Latin America'. https://www.britannica.com/place/Latin-America

Mas Giralt, Rosa, and Granada, Lucila. 2015. 'Latin American Migrating from Europe to the UK: Barriers to Accessing Public Services and Welfare', *LAWRS.* http://www.lawrs.org.uk/wp-content/uploads/2015/11/Latin-Americans-migrating-from-Europe-to-the-UK.pdf

McIlwaine, Cathy. 2008. 'Subversion or Subjugation: Transforming Gender Ideologies among Latin American Migrants in London', *Queen Mary University of London.* http://citeseerx.ist.psu.edu/viewdoc/download?doi=10.1.1.473.3526&rep=rep1&type=pdf

McIlwaine, Cathy. 2010. 'Migrant Machismos: Exploring Gender Ideologies and Practices among Latin American Migrants in London from a Multi-Scalar Perspective', *Gender, Place, Society*, 17, no. 3 (May): 281–300.

McIlwaine, Cathy, and Bunge, Diego. 2016. 'Towards Visibility: The Latin American Community in London', *Trust for London*. https://www. trustforlondon.org.uk/publications/towards-visibility-latin-americancommunity-london/

McIlwaine, Cathy, and Bunge, Diego. 2018. 'Onward Precarity, Mobility, and Migration among Latin Americans in London', *Antipode*, 0, no. 0 (November): 1–19.

McIlwaine, Cathy., Cock, Juan Camilo, and Linneker, Brian. 2011. 'No Longer Invisible: The Latin American Community in London', *Queen Mary University of London.* https://www.qmul.ac.uk/geog/media/geography/docs/research/ latinamerican/No-Longer-Invisible-report.pdf

Nakano Glenn, Evelyn. 1992. 'From Servitude to Service Work: Historical Continuities in the Racial Division of Paid Reproductive Labour', *Signs*, 18, no. 1 (Autumn): 1–43.

ONS. 2020. 'Population of the UK by Country of Birth and Nationality'. https:// www.ons.gov.uk/peoplepopulationandcommunity/populationandmigration/ internationalmigration/datasets/ populationoftheunitedkingdombycountryofbirthandnationality

Passarelli Tonhati, Taria Maria. 2017. 'The Transnational Family: Migration, Family and Rituals among Brazilian Migrant Women in the UK'. PhD Diss., Goldsmiths University of London.

Pellegrino, Adela. 2004. 'Migration from Latin America to Europe: Trends and Policy Challenge', *International Organization for Migration, Migration Research Series*, 16 (May): 1–76. https://publications.iom.int/books/mrs-ndeg16-migration-latin-america-europe-trends-and-policy-challenges

Razavi, Shahra. 2007. 'The Political and Social Economy of Care in a Development Context: Conceptual Issues, Research Questions and Policy Options', *United Nations Research Institute for Social Development*. http://www.unrisd.org/80256B3C005BCCF9/ (httpAuxPages)/2DBE6A93350A7783C12573240036D5A0/$file/Razavi-paper. pdf

Razavi, Shahra. 2013. 'Households, Families, and Social Reproduction', in *The Oxford Handbook of Gender and Politics* by Georgina Waylen, Karen Celis, Johanna Kantola, and S. Laurel Weldon. Oxford: Oxford Handbooks Online.

Souza, Ana. 2015. 'Motherhood in Migration: A Focus on Family Language Planning', *Women's Studies International Forum,* 52 (September – October): 92–98.

Troung, Thanh-Dam. 1996. 'Gender, International Migration and Social Reproduction: Implications for Theory, Policy, Research and Networking'. *Asian and Pacific Migration Journal*, 5, no. 1 (March): 27–52.

Turcatti, Domiziana, and Assaraf, Kiara. 2019. 'The Experiences of the Latin American Clients of LADPP: Identifying What Works and the Interventions Needed to Enhance the Wellbeing and Quality of Life of LADPP's Clients', *Latin American Disabled People's Project.* http://www.ladpp.org.uk/news.html

Turcatti, Domiziana, and Assaraf, Kiara. 2020. 'Lessons Gained from a Case Study of a Latin American NGO in London: The Role Intercultural Competence Plays in the Delivery of Services to Migrant Communities', *Proceedings of the International Association for Intercultural Education (IAIE) Conference: Another Brick in the Wall*, 113–133. Amsterdam: The Netherlands.

14

Between Oppressions and Resistance: A Decolonial Feminist Analysis of Narratives from Nicaraguan Caregiving Grandmothers and Women Returnees from El Salvador

FIORE BRAN ARAGÓN

Since the last decade of the 20th century, globalization has stimulated different and varied forms of mobility: while it favors the transnationalization of capital, it restricts human mobility, especially for vulnerable populations. In addition, First World countries have created discriminatory narratives and policies that shape migration (Donato and Massey 2016). This paradox of contemporary mobility has favored the emergence of research paradigms that seek to respond to the challenges posed by such dissimilarity. In this context, scholars of Latin America have devoted themselves to the study of migration from different disciplines to understand causes and propose solutions to mass migration in the region.

Among those intellectuals, feminist scholars have raised debates about the importance of qualitative methodologies that listen to and analyze the narratives of migrants, disrupting the dominant logic that makes the right to have a face and a voice a privilege of a few. In an era when mass migration is portrayed by the media with agglomerated and anonymous bodies, research methodologies that present migrants' stories are essential to avoid dehumanization, denormalize oppressions, and make their resistance visible (Cacopardo 2018).

To listen to and understand migrant women stories, I take the epistemological approach of decolonial feminism according to María Lugones. She proposes decolonial feminism as a theoretical framework to circulate counter-hegemonic narratives about the mobilities of women of color, to highlight the multiple oppressions they experience, but also their resistance and possibilities of creating coalitions to overcome inequality and exclusion. This approach makes visible these aspects of the stories of Nicaraguan migrant women.

According to the International Organization for Migration (IOM), by 2012, Nicaragua had experienced three waves of emigration, but only in the last one, which started in the 2000s, have women represented 50 percent of the migration flow (IOM 2013). This third wave was mostly formed by economic migrants who had diverse destinations: the traditional destinations like Costa Rica and the United States, but also new countries, such as Panama, Spain and El Salvador. Most of the migrant women started working as caregivers and domestic workers (González 2012). By 2016, Nicaragua was the country that expelled more migrant women to other Central American nations (González 2016), while El Salvador became a preferred destination for migrants, especially for women from the border state of Chinandega.

Chinandega is the northernmost state in Nicaragua that borders El Salvador, a country in which the main labor market for migrants is in caregiving and domestic work. As a result, in the last few years, many women have migrated seasonally because it is nearer and cheaper to come and go between both countries. It is also easier in logistical terms, as no passport is required, and because Chinandegan women have extensive networks of transnational communities in the states of Usulután and San Miguel in southwestern El Salvador (Ramos 2009). Finally, migrating to El Salvador is a relatively safe option for women, who can avoid the dangers of the road taken by many Central American migrants to the United States (González 2016). All of this has favored the continuity of the flow of migrant women from Chinandega, Nicaragua to El Salvador, and with this, large regional care chains have been formed that involve both migrant women, as well as substitute caregivers – generally grandmothers – who stay in the communities of origin.

These regional care chains tend to bolster the oppression of migrant women and of caregivers who remain in the communities of origin, because the contemporary 'caregiving system' reproduces an 'intrinsic contradiction between the actual needs of care for a good quality of life and the capital reproduction needs' (Orozco and Gil 2011, 23). Namely, the 'caregiving system' and the logic of globalization of capital prioritize revenues obtained from migrants' lives over their well-being (Sassen 2003). This tends to perpetuate inequalities suffered by migrant women and based on gender, race, ethnicity, socioeconomic status and citizenship. In the case of

Nicaragua, the perpetuation of these care chains is favored by the absence of the state in providing care and by the increase in single-parent families (Espinoza, Gamboa, Gutiérrez and Centeno 2012).

Therefore, the maternal grandmothers generally take care of the grandchildren, household duties and sometimes get a job to provide children, even if they do not have the age or energy to do so (Yarris 2017). On the other hand, migrant women, who are generally heads of family, frequently receive low wages and do not have social security. This does not allow them access to better living conditions for themselves and their families and exposes them to labor exploitation. Moreover, because of the generalized violence in El Salvador, Nicaraguan migrant women are also exposed to being victims of organized crime. In this chapter, I map some of the instances of oppressions as well as the resistance strategies articulated by migrant women in this context.

On Narrative Inquiry as Methodology

The research question that has led this work is: In which ways do the infra-political and political resistances articulated by migrant women and caregiver grandmothers contribute to the reconfiguration of their identities? How do these resistances redraw maps of power and create new possibilities for a dignified life in the face of an unjust care regime?

These questions arose from my fieldwork with migrant women in the border area between Nicaragua, Honduras and El Salvador, between 2016 and 2017. The project aimed to identify needs for psychosocial and legal attention and support for migrant women who returned and their families. In the initial dialogues with migrant women and their mothers, I found that they defined themselves as resistant women in the face of a socioeconomic and care system that they considered unfair. Hence, I realized I needed to seek a methodological approach that would adapt to their narratives, and so I used the framework of narrative research methodology and decolonial feminism.

Narrative inquiry emphasizes the value of life stories as a 'journey' rather than a 'destination' (Ellis and Bochner quoted in Trahar 2009). This methodological approach highlights the relevance of being 'sensitive to the different worldviews of the interlocutors', and to recognize one's own positionality – in terms of intersectionality – that could favor unequal power relations. In addition, narrative inquiry considers that understanding the text as a journey implies the encounter of 'three common places': 'temporality, sociality and place' as specific dimensions that serve as a conceptual framework to interpret stories and approach the narrator's gaze. This is a process of learning to 'think narratively' (Clandinin and Huber cited in McGaw, Baker and Peterson 2010, 9).

Based on these considerations, I conducted open interviews with six women from Chinandega, Nicaragua: three caregiver grandmothers and three returned migrants from six different communities in the border area. The interview process consisted of multiple conversations and participant observation in community activities. To select these women, I used snowball sampling. At the time of the interviews, all the caregiver grandmothers were between 57 and 65 years old and were full-time caregivers of grandchildren who are children of migrant women. All the returned migrants were between 30 and 40 years old and were the heads of families, who had migrated to El Salvador between 2010 and 2018 and had left their children in the care of their mothers.

The interview guide consisted of a list of key topics with guiding questions. I also asked some questions directly to guide the dialogue. The key themes were childhood and youth memories in relation to caregiving, gender and migration; adult life, including motherhood, mobility, work and caregiving; personal and/or daughter's migratory experience; and return, including notions of care, a dignified life and resistances.

Mapping Oppressions: Caregiving, Migration, Violence

The grandmothers I interviewed are Flora, Emilia and Pilar (names may have been altered). Flora and Emilia live in a peri-urban neighborhood in the central area of Chinandega. Pilar lives in a rural community near the maritime border with El Salvador. All of them have been intraregional migrants. The returned migrants are Deborah, Marisa and Carla. Deborah lives in a rural community near the maritime border, while Marisa and Carla live near the land border with Honduras.

In the six narratives, there are common socio-historical events that women interpret in different ways, but which are essential for understanding their views of the world and of themselves. In order to find the 'three common places' of narrative research, these events are presented:

The economy of the banana and cotton enclaves in Chinandega during the Somoza dictatorship (1960s and 1970s)

The grandmothers remember the economy of the banana enclave as the only source of local employment and as a place where they suffered labor exploitation. It was also a place to gain some freedom from home and family:

there, they spent time away from home doing non-domestic tasks and were able to manage their income partially or fully. The banana plantations were also sites of solidarity between women who resisted discrimination against community members for being farm workers. For Flora and Pilar, it was also the place where they got involved in civil groups associated with the Sandinista Front (FSLN).

Meanwhile, for the returned migrants, the memories of relative economic prosperity and women independence associated with the plantations were only inherited by their mothers. By 1980, as a consequence of the Nicaraguan Revolution and the war, the banana and cotton plantations had disappeared and most of the local jobs with them. In the narratives of the returnees, the banana plantations are associated with economic precariousness, the migration of relatives to urban centers and an undesirable place to work due to the abuses to which women were subjected.

The Sandinista Popular Revolution and the war between Contras and Sandinistas (1980s): Memories of solidarity, grief and exile

Flora and Pilar were involved in the insurrection of 1979. For them, these processes were an opportunity to strengthen solidarity ties and carry out tasks that, before the armed struggle, were only designated for men: sending messages, supplies transportation and logistical work with the local guerrilla. Pilar's political participation allowed her to get a better job in the public sector once the FSLN triumphed. Flora's employment situation became more precarious after 1979, while Emilia, who was already a mother, returned to her native Honduras with her children, waiting to obtain her permanent residence in Nicaragua.

For the returned migrants, the Revolution is a heroic past that they did not live, but of which they have ideas and feelings derived from family stories. Both in their narratives and in those of the grandmothers, the Revolution is an event remembered with sadness and anger because it did not bring the expected change but, on the contrary, war. In addition, the war between the Contras and Sandinistas caused an increase in impoverishment, hunger and exile.

Neoliberal Economic Reforms (1990s): Peace and 'ghost towns'

After the signing of peace accords in 1990, some refugees in Honduras returned to Chinandega. However, peace did not bring jobs, as was supposed to happen. On the contrary, because of economic reforms that prioritized capital over people's lives (Martínez and Voorend 2012), impoverishment and lack of access to services in rural and peri-urban areas increased. In some communities, the few remaining agricultural farms closed, while in others the war devastated everything.

Deborah refers to this period as marked by 'ghost towns', because refugees who returned from Honduras and repopulated communities soon left for Costa Rica and El Salvador in search of jobs, leaving entire communities abandoned. According to Deborah and Carla, the population flow that left the towns was mixed: it was no longer just men fleeing forced recruitment into the army or entire families fleeing the war, but young women migrating alone or in groups of friends looking for jobs.

'After being a mother, one is a grandmother and goes back to playing the role of mother. But I no longer had the same force': Interconnected oppressions in the narratives of caregiving grandmothers

Some 'interconnected oppressions' in the grandmothers' narratives marked their lives and the ways they saw themselves and the world. Among the oppressions that were intertwined in their narratives were gender violence, motherhood/being a grandmother, caregiving and migration.

For all of them, gender violence that manifests itself in physical, verbal, psychological, sexual and patrimonial violence has been a constant in their lives. All this violence has marked the way they see their relationships with men of power and with the state. Emilia told me:

> At home, we had to be quiet. Whether you were a girl or an adult, women had to be quiet. We had to do all the housework, and if we worked outside in the banana plantations, we had to give the money to our father. But my dad and then my husband spent everything on liquor... Who was going to look after me? Now they tell me that the government has protection programs for women, but I have never seen it here. We are like abandoned.

That feeling of being 'abandoned' and unprotected from those who exerted gender violence against her is repeated in the stories of the other grandmothers. When they mentioned reasons why they tolerated gender violence, they generally referred to their children. They described motherhood and parenting as a rewarding process, but one that was not undertaken fully voluntarily, but rather considered a part of the process of becoming an adult. All three grandmothers had children when they were teenagers. Flora said:

Nobody ever explained anything to me about menstruation or how to have children. I only remember that my boyfriend told me that I had to have a child, and I did not know, and when I looked, I was already pregnant. Later my grandmother told me, 'Well, my little girl. Now you have to look for a stable job and learn to take care of the baby'.

Early motherhood was also a cause of migration for the grandmothers seeking a better life for themselves and their children. Usually, they left their children in the care of their mothers. Although, historically, this social organization of caregiving based on extended families led by grandmothers has been fundamental for sustaining life in rural Nicaragua, caregivers do not necessarily think of it as the best option. On the other hand, they all recognize that both fathers and the state should play an equally responsible role in caregiving and in the redistribution of paid and unpaid labor. They also admit that this organization of care is exhausting and that a change is necessary that involves a shared responsibility for the family, especially for fathers. Pilar commented:

My grandmother and my aunt took care of me. My mom also took care of my cousins. It has always been like this. I also left my children to my grandmother when I migrated, and I thank her, but I know it is exhausting. And it should be otherwise. When my daughter left, I also stayed looking after my grandchildren... I do believe that women and men have the same ability to work, both outside and inside home. What divides us is gender, but we must all assume everything evenly.

The grandmothers consider that the state should also assume part of the care needs; however, their experiences with government care programs has been negative. According to Emilia:

I once went to the hospital with my two grandchildren. As the girl had a mark on her foot because she fell while playing, an official from the Ministry of the Family told me in a threatening way that if I did not take good care of these children, they would take them away from me. I was enraged, and I told him, 'Tell the Ministry that I want to set my rules too. If they are going to demand something of me, give me something for these children: a little help for their education, for their clothes. But you demand and you don't give us anything'.

'There, it is Not Like in Nicaragua. One Has to Learn the Law of The Neighborhood: See, Hear and Be Silent': Interconnected Oppressions in the Narratives of Returned Migrants

The returnees' narratives have common oppressions with those of the grandmothers, but they also differ in the particularities of their migratory condition. Among the most common oppressions are gender violence and the impact of generalized violence in migrant women's lives. For example, both Deborah and Marisa migrated to El Salvador due to intra-family violence. However, as Deborah relates, migration did not end gender violence:

> When my partner threatened me with a gun in front of my children... I left the country. I was terrified. I only had $20 and felt bad about leaving my children. I believed that after arriving there, there was going to be a change, but no... I met some men who called me 'whore', 'thief', just for being Nicaraguan. And that is why I got involved with my husband, the other one who tried to kill me, so that they would not attack me any more in the street... I think I have a bad fate.

For Carla, the immigration experience was different. Her mother migrated to El Salvador when she was a child and left her with her grandmother. When she was 13 years old, her mother decided to take her to work with her. Carla returned to Nicaragua a couple of months later because gangs threatened her. At 18 years old, she had returned to El Salvador looking for a job and, since she was undocumented, she only had access to precarious jobs where her safety was at risk.

> I told my mom that I wanted to come because a gang member wanted to make me his girlfriend. And I did not want to [be his girlfriend] because that is how they makes girls prostitutes and 'mules'[1]. And I went back without telling her... But after [a few] years, I had to leave again because there were no jobs. And that is when I started at the bar as a waitress. But that was a dangerous place too. The gangs were the VIP clients, and they scared the waitresses with their guns.

Marisa also worked in a bar, but left to work as a domestic worker: '[A]lthough I earned less, it was safer for me'. However, her safety was threatened due to an error in compliance with what she calls 'the law of the neighborhood'.

---

[1]   *Mulas* in Spanish is a slang term that refers to people, usually women, who carry and transport drugs, with or without their consent.

I worked and lived with my employers and had a day off every two weeks. I washed, ironed clothes, cooked, [and] looked after their children and my son. I also did the shopping, cooked and served as a waitress at the patrons' restaurant. They paid me $75 a month without insurance. But sometimes they gave me milk and clothes for my son. Everything was going well, but when I went to live alone, it changed.

I went to a neighborhood with several Nicaraguans, but there were some gang members who were neighbors, and one day I saw them doing something, and they looked at me. I did not speak. There it is not like in Nicaragua. One has to learn the law of the neighborhood: see, hear and be silent. And since they thought I was going to say something, they threw me to the police. They gave a false lead and I was accused of being a drug 'mule'.

The police entered the house, put a gun on me in front of my children, yelled and beat me. Although they found nothing, I got imprisoned. Because there, a migrant woman without money, who was going to look after me? Being in jail away from my children and my country was the saddest thing.

Mapping Everyday Resistances: Infra-politics and Coalitions

In all the narratives, multiple and sometimes fused oppressions persist. Therefore, the possibility of resistance or emancipation seems insignificant. According to Lugones (2008), the modern/colonial gender system sustains these oppressions. This system categorizes, separates and subtracts agency from individuals by placing them in a 'fractured locus' in the margins of power. But against this 'logic of oppression, there is a 'logic of resistance' that implies the recognition of interconnected oppressions and the possibilities of concrete coalitions in everyday life to overcome it. Women of color, situated at the 'margins' – geographically and of power – have an 'epistemological advantage' to learn the logics of oppression from experience and, at the same time, articulate resistance in the liminal space they inhabit.

These resistances are infra-political, anonymous, intersubjective and collective. That is why 'they include the affirmation of life above profit, comm-unalism' (Lugones 2011, 116). These conscious and shared practices can lead to the beginning of a major political struggle. Some of the 'infra-political resistances' are 'adaptation, rejection, non-adoption, not taking into account', the silences and the celebration of life (Lugones 2011, 116). All of them shape the way in which women understand themselves, and their world, and facilitate the reconfiguration of their identities, which are historical and situated processes, open to change based on new experiences. In the narratives of the grandmothers and returnees, the process of 'oppressing → ← resisting' and its impact on their discourses and practices regarding identity are remarkable.

'But When I Talked About it with Other Women in the Community... I Felt Accompanied': Dialogues and Silences As Resistance

In the interviews and community activities I witnessed, the grandmothers and returned migrants emphasized the importance of recognizing and naming oppressions in order to confront them. This implies denormalizing oppressions that are culturally accepted as parts of life. For Emilia, the experience of self-organized mutual support groups, formed by grandmothers, allowed her to speak of experiences of sexual abuse in childhood. An essential part of her healing process was feeling heard:

> That is why I suffered a lot when I was a child. I had a hard time seeing how that was related to me accepting violence from other men as normal. But when I talked about it with other women in the community, and they listened to me, I felt accompanied... It was also accepting the anger I felt. I also saw that there were beautiful things in life for me and my granddaughters.

During her time in jail, Marisa talked to a psychologist about her experiences and emotions. That was essential to feel healthier and planning for the future.

> She told me that I was going to get out of jail and that I had to be ready for that. She talked to me about my self-esteem and self-care. She helped me write a plan for life after jail. So, I started going to workshops on baking, and I managed to get the best position in the bakery. There, I earned money to buy my things, and it felt good... But with my children, I chose to shut up. Maybe one day I will tell them all about the jail, but now my silence is better for them.

'When you have your own house and earn money, no one will stop you': Economic independence as resistance

One of the fundamental resistances in the narratives is the pursuit of economic independence. Pilar believes that this facilitated a life free of violence and certain stability for her and her children.

After I came back to the country, I bought my land. Only with my land I felt fulfilled. When you have your own house and earn your money, no one will stop you. This way, you will be free and will not have to endure *machismo*... Before it was not common for a separated woman to buy a house to live alone with her children, but I managed it, [and] there are more of us. Now, we hope that our daughters will achieve the same, even if it is by migrating.

'I like to Dance and Laugh to Feel Free': Playfulness as Resistance

Playfulness, despite oppression, is also a common resistance for the narrators. Sometimes, even laughter and jokes about politics and the situation of their communities are used to simplify the difficult and find the good in the adverse.

> Carla: 'I like to dance and laugh to feel free. Even if they tell me, "Do not dance and sing, that is crazy", it makes me feel good in the face of adversity'.

> Deborah: 'And sometimes we just make jokes about this country, the corrupt ones and that. Well, we have to laugh so as not to cry'.

'I Cry Out to God to Give me Peace and do me Justice': Spirituality as Resistance

In the grandmothers' narratives, the Christian God is a source of spiritual strength to overcome adversity. They see God as a close friend fighting injustice. Also, some grandmothers combine Christian spirituality with the indigenous religious traditions of their communities. Flora and Pilar commented:

> Flora: 'Every day, I cry out to God for peace and justice for the death of my son. I cannot do justice against the gang members, but God can. I forgive them, because God is merciful to me, and he will know how to do it. Talking with God gives me a lot of relief and strength'.

> Pilar: 'For me, it is my San Roque Indio and the people's Santeria. I ask him for miracles, and he does them for me. I remember that a *curandero* from Guatemala said that hard things were going to happen, but that everything would be fine. And now I see it that way'.

'Even if I am Not in My Country, I Have the Right to Know What My Rights Are in the Other Country': Knowledge as Resistance

In addition to personal resistance processes, grandmothers and returnees articulated forms of collective resistance and organization to support themselves emotionally, demand rights and organize projects for community well-being. The grandmothers organized mutual support groups to discuss strategies for balancing caring for grandchildren with self-care and other issues of their emotional and physical health. Returned migrants worked together in both Nicaragua and El Salvador to organize human rights workshops in their communities and raise funds for projects to support migrants in El Salvador. According to Carla, all these projects have been inspired by knowledge: 'That process of organizing ourselves has been good and is a result of us learning about rights. I am happy to be here and to do something'.

Deborah is now a facilitator in the group of returned migrants. She shares her immigration experience and knowledge of human rights. For her, the solidarity networks that she managed to establish with other women in El Salvador were key to learning about and overcoming oppression:

> I went to Ciudad Mujer[2], to a support program for migrant women. There, they taught me about my rights and my self-esteem, and I shared with other migrant women from other countries. I made friends, and one of them who later went to the United States was the one who sent me money for my son's food when I didn't have any... Now I know that, even if I am not in my country, I have the right to know what my rights are in the other country. It does not matter if I am a citizen or not. I have rights.

Conclusion

The narratives analyzed from the perspective of decolonial feminism show that the grandmothers and returned migrant women are agents of their own change in complex processes of 'oppressing → ← resisting' that take place in everyday life. These infra-political resistances have favored the articulation of discourses and praxes that support the emancipation of women in contexts of multiple oppressions. In the case of these women, those oppressions arise from questions and complaints of the state and those with power in the

---

[2]   Ciudad Mujer (Women's City) is a Program of the Social Inclusion Secretariat of El Salvador. It supports the human rights of Salvadoran women and has some projects for migrant women.

socioeconomic order that sustain the care regime. Their discourses also question ideas of family loyalty and the suppression of female anger. In terms of practical resistances, these women have organized mutual support groups and community initiatives to assist migrants and returnees.

These are all valuable practices that should be considered and reproduced by the state when thinking about policies on care provision and integration for returned migrants. It is important for the Nicaraguan government to change its policy approach from one focused on welfare and short-term solutions to one that considers women's and communities' experiences, capabilities and worldviews to create long-term solutions grounded in the community. As Carla put it: 'Only with this support can we build a community where no one has to leave if it is not by will'.

References

Cacopardo, Ana. 2018. 'El testimonio como práctica de memoria y resistencia: apuntes conceptuales y metodológicos'. Seminario Memorias colectivas y Luchas políticas. *Diploma Superior en Memorias colectivas, Género y Migraciones*, Consejo Latinoamericano de Ciencias Sociales.

Clandinin, Jean. and Huber, Janice. (no date). 'Narrative inquiry' in *International encyclopedia of education*, edited by Barry McGaw, Eva Baker & Penelope Peterson. http://www.mofet.macam.ac.il/amitim/iun/ CollaborativeResearch/Documents/NarrativeInquiry.pdf

Donato, Katherine and Massey, Douglas. 2016. 'Twenty-First- Century Globalization and Illegal Migration', *The Annals of The American Academy,* no. 666: 7–26.

Espinoza, Ana, Gamboa, Marbel, Gutiérrez, Martha and Centeno, Rebeca. 2012. *La migración femenina nicaragüense en las cadenas globales de cuidados en Costa Rica.* Managua: ONU Mujeres.

González Briones, Heydi. 2012. *Perfil Migratorio de Nicaragua.* Managua: Organización Internacional para las Migraciones.

González Briones, Heydi. 2016. *Factores de riesgo y necesidades de atención para las Mujeres Migrantes en Centroamérica. Estudio de actualización sobre la situación de violencia contra las mujeres migrantes en la ruta migratoria en Centroamérica.* Managua: Secretaría General del Sistema de la Integración Centroamericana.

IOM. 2013. *IOM releases the Migration Profile for Nicaragua.* June 28. https://
www.iom.int/news/iom-releases-migration-profile-nicaragua

Lugones, María. 2008. 'Colonialidad y Género', *Tabula Rasa*, no. 9. (July–
December): 73–101. https://www.redalyc.org/articulo.oa?id=39600906

Lugones, María. 2011. 'Hacia un feminismo descolonial', *La manzana de la
discordia* 6, no. 2 (July–December): 105–119. http://manzanadiscordia.
univalle.edu.co/index.php/la_manzana_de_la_discordia/article/
view/1504/1611

Martínez, Juliana and Voorend, Koen. *25 años de cuidados en Nicaragua:
1980–2005. Poco Estado, poco mercado y mucho trabajo no remunerado.*
San José: Guayacán, 2012.

Orozco, Amaia and Gil, Silvia. 2016. *Desigualdades a flor de piel: Cadenas
globales de cuidados. Concreciones en el empleo de hogar y políticas
públicas.* ONU Mujeres.

Ramos, Elsa. 2009. 'Migración sur- sur: el caso de los nicaragüenses en El
Salvador', *Entorno,* no. 43: 42–45. http://biblioteca.utec.edu.sv/entorno/index.
php/entorno/article/view/122/121

Sassen, Saskia. 2003. 'Women´s Burden: Counter-geographies of
Globalization and the Feminization of Survival', *Journal of International Affairs*
53, no. 2: 503–524. https://www.researchgate.net/publication/233639034_
Women's_Burden_Counter-Geographies_of_Globalization_and_the_
Feminization_of_Survival

Trahar, Sheila. 2009. 'Beyond the Story Itself: Narrative Inquiry and
Autoethnography in Intercultural Research in Higher Education', *Forum
Qualitative Social Research* 10, no. 1: Art. 30. http://www.qualitative-research.
net/index.php/fqs/article/view/1218/2653

15

Women for Profit: Seeking Asylum in the United States – a Neocolonial Story

SARA RIVA

Paloma[1] had been in the immigration detention center for four days when I met her. While in confinement, she and her children had been given clothes and a room to share with other families. When I went to talk to her about her asylum interview, I asked her about her job in her native country. Taking her hand to the back of her neck and pulling the tag of her t-shirt to show me the brand's name, she said, 'I used to work in a maquiladora for this company. I made these t-shirts!'[2]

Each year, thousands of hetero-nuclear families cross the United States-Mexico border fleeing from the violence in their countries of origin and seeking asylum in the US. Even though locking up people who seek asylum goes against guidelines from the United Nations High Commissioner for Refugees (UNHCR), many of these women and their underage children often end up confined in one of the family immigration detention centers that exist in the US. They are held at the immigration centers until they pass their credible fear interview with an asylum officer. This interview will determine whether they can enter the US or be deported. Two things are important to note here. First, migration regimes today are based on deterrence rather than human rights (Gammeltoft-Hansen and Tan 2017, 28), and the confinement of refugees has become a common practice across the world. The second

---

[1]   All names have been changed to protect interviewees' identities.
[2]   This epigraph is based on a story that was told to me during an interview I conducted with a member of the NGO staff working at the immigration detention center at the US-Mexico border.

issue, also a global practice, is the inclusion of private actors in the migration management arena, from Australia paying private companies to confine asylum-seekers in nation-states like Nauru and Papua New Guinea, to the United States, which locks refugees in privatized detention centers at the border. In this way, corporations profit from the confinement of populations fleeing violence.

This chapter explores the relationship between the state and the refugee by investigating one element of contemporary border control: privatized confine-ment. In particular, I look at the detention experience that women like Paloma have to face when seeking asylum. Third World women are subject to an endless cycle of exploitation, first in their countries of origin and then once they reach the global north[3] looking for asylum. The inclusion of private actors in the migration management regime has been key for its expansion around the globe. Neoliberalism has enabled the outsourcing of border practices to private companies, and now the border has become an assemblage of different practices that countries exercise beyond the limits of their territories. These assemblage of parts and discourses that impede those who seek asylum reach countries in the global north are called bordering mechanisms and can range from border externalization measures to dehumanizing discourses about refugees. Migrant detention, visa processing, border surv-eillance, transportation of detained migrants, offshore processing and so on have all been privatized and are managed by corporations. Like in Paloma's case, these companies receive money from the government for each person they keep confined. In this way, states cooperate with private actors to carry out their work. These public-private agreements increase restrictive migration control policies, resulting in the creation of a transnational assemblage that extends beyond individual countries and impedes refugees from reaching safe shores.

While I focus on the United States, I refer to other examples in the Anglo-sphere, as practices travel through big corporations. This chapter has four parts. First, I detail how I combine a transnational feminist framework with ethnographic work conducted in a detention center at the US-Mexico border. A transnational feminist lens allows us to connect global economic structures and their on-the-ground effects. Second, I detail how private detention became a relevant course of action in the migration management regime and the neoliberal entanglements that connect private interests to public matters.

---

[3]   I use 'Global South' mainly to describe former colonies. Similarly, I use 'Global North' or Western countries, to refer to former colonial powers, in particular, Australia, the European Union and the US. I understand these terms are broad and contested. For a full discussion on the meaning of Global South, see *The Global South Journal* Vol. 11 No 2. 2017 special issue: 'The Global South as Subversive Practice'.

Third, I argue that, today, women's bodies are both exploited in their countries of origin and through confinement practices. Additionally, I claim that discourses are essential for maintaining practices, such as the confinement of women and children looking for asylum. There is a history of dehumanizing discourses from people in the global north that legitimize practices such as migration confinement. In closing, I argue that the inclusion of private actors is paramount to the creation of a transnational assemblage that contains people in the global south, while it transforms states into profit-making apparatuses that follow a neoliberal logic.

Transnational Feminism and Ethnographic Work at the Border

Through an engagement with transnational feminism, I seek to add ethnographic evidence to the ways in which borders are constructed as violent spaces that reinforce racialized neocolonial ideologies. A transnational feminist lens draws attention to the long lineage of violence that people from the global south have historically experienced. My particular focus on how these practices affect displaced women both challenges the idea of borders as spaces of protection and evidences the 'present-day neocolonial global hierarchy' (Herr 2014, 8).

Transnational feminism is a tool for anti-colonial struggle and takes into account how dimensions of identity – such as race, class, sexuality or ability – travel across borders (Briggs, McCormick, and Way 2008; Sudbury 2005). Drawing on the insights of Third World women and women-of-color feminism and activism, transnational feminism is based on intersectionality and the pluralization of feminist politics that contests the essentializing idea of a global sisterhood. It is a framework that has been very productive in exploring political solidarity movements across the globe (Parikh 2017), as well as cross-border organizing (Desai 2005). In this chapter, I want to extend its use from the study of different scales of activism to the exploration of the neocolonial structure of the migration management system that rules the global north. I analyze how the bodies of women who seek asylum end up exploited by the neoliberal structures of privatized immigration detention centers.

Since a transnational feminist framework illustrates a matrix of relationships between people, discourses, nations, economies and practices (Herr 2014), it is particularly well suited to make connections between colonial and neocolonial relations (see, for instance, Lemberg-Pedersen 2019). This methodology pays attention to particular historical and political contexts and how the inter-relations of each of these regions enable updated forms of racialized stereotyping of certain groups – for instance, in the United States,

Central Americans are viewed as criminals, smugglers, drug dealers and gang members (Riva 2017). These stereotypes are built upon years of militarism, imperialism and geopolitical intervention shaped by neocolonial racialized ideologies and become visible at the border. These dehumanizing discourses legitimize practices, such as the confinement of refugees. A transnational feminist lens illuminates how the particular racial formations that we encounter today are a result of years of colonialism and neoliberalism that have historically exploited people of color. However, neoliberalism does not only exploit women in their countries of origin – through labor processes – but also, the system profits from those who seek asylum once they reach the United States. This is done through confining them in privatized detention centers. Neoliberalism has given place and space to the privatization of many structures and processes across the planet, including migration management practices that take place around the world. A transnational feminist analysis takes into account global economic structures, legal-juridical oppression (Grewal and Kaplan 1994) and their on-the-ground effects.

This chapter is the result of critical engagement with secondary literature, academic writing, analysis of news accounts, laws and reports and ethnographic work. The empirical research for this study was conducted in 2016 at an immigration detention center located in south Texas where I interviewed legal advocates working for a non-profit organization while I worked as a volunteer myself. The detention facility is owned and managed by a private prison corporation – CoreCivic (formerly Corrections Corporations of America) – that has contracted with the federal government. Legal advocates in this facility offer their services on a volunteer basis and are not contractually engaged or obliged by the government or other authorities to aid detainees. In addition to conducting interviews with the legal advocates and volunteering in the center to aid detainees, my research involved participant observation research methods and a critical engagement with secondary literature. Such methodologies aid in understanding the everyday realities of those who seek asylum while in detention.

Neoliberal Entanglements

'For each woman detained here, the company that runs the prison receives money from the government', says Dana, one of the legal advocates that works in the detention center as a volunteer. As in many detention centers in the US, the one where I did my fieldwork had been privatized. Before the 1980s, detention as a governing immigration practice was 'largely an ad hoc tool employed mainly by wealthy states in exigent circumstances that typically made use of prisons, warehouses, hotel rooms or other "off-the-shelf" facilities' (Flynn 2014, 167). Thus, the commodification of migrant detention took place mostly after the 1980s. Within border securitization, confinement today has become one of the key elements in detention and thus in the management of migrant and refugee populations. The origins of confinement as a common practice in immigration governance are connected to the securitization of migration (Bigo 2002; Huysmans 2006; Mountz 2011). After 9/11, border security merged and became the center of national security (Golash-Boza 2016; Longo 2018, 3). The securitization rhetoric is based on the idea that migrants are potential threats – to security, culture, the economy – and justifies the confinement of any foreign population. Immigration detention centers, such as Campsfield in Oxford, United Kingdom; the South Texas Family Residential Center, in Texas, US; and the Curtin Immigration Reception and Processing Centre in Australia, are run by private corporations. Extreme cases of offshore, privately run processing centers are the ones Australia has contracted with Papua New Guinea and Nauru; or the one the United States has in Guantánamo Bay, Cuba (Frenzen 2010, 392). One of the elements that facilitates the homogenizing of detention regimes in the world is the fact that many of the same big, for-profit corporations run most of the private prisons in most countries of the global north. This is one means through which techniques of confinement are diffused in different countries. The global security firms that lobby and bid for contracts to develop the new technologies and infrastructures of border enforcement (Gammeltoft-Hansen 2013; Hernández-León 2013; Lemberg-Pedersen 2013; Menz 2013), intentionally or not, homogenize the regimes of border control. During the 2018 fiscal year, a daily average of 42,188 migrants were held by US Immigration and Customs Enforcement (ICE) (US Immigration and Customs Enforcement 2019). 'I feel like each month, the number of people [detained] keeps growing', says Flora, another legal advocate that works as a pro bono lawyer in the center. Several examples offer a broad overview of how neoliberalism has reached different places through the privatization of detention centers: in the UK, seven out of the nine immigrant detention centers – and all of the short-term holding facilities – are run by multinational, for-profit companies; in the US, for-profit companies control more than half of all detention bed spaces (Sinha 2016, 83); and in Australia, all immigration detention centers are run by private companies (Bacon 2005, 3; Simonds and Wright 2017).

Neoliberalism has been a key feature in the expansion of the immigration and refugee detention system (Doty and Wheatley 2013, 434). Private and non-state actors have gradually entered the border control arena, including through detention and removal (Abbott and Snidal 2009; Menz 2011). Within immigration and refugee management, many logistical services, such as transportation of migrants and asylum-seekers, clothing and food provision and telephone service in detention centers, airborne deportation operations, processing of visa applications, security, prison management, drone vigilance and so on, have been privatized. 'When they arrive here, they take away their belongings and they give them those horrible clothes', says Flora, pointing at the t-shirts the women wear, 'This [the company who makes the clothes] is yet another company profiting from the confinement of this people'. Similarly, other companies profit from the private management of the prison, such as the company in charge of food services, maintenance, education, health services, the bail industry and so on (Austin and Coventry 2001; Henderson 2015; Requarth 2019). There has been work done on how the privatization of prisons has led to understaffed centers, with less training, fewer benefits, high rates of employee turnover, more accidents and discouragement from organizing in trade unions (Binder 2017; Clark 2016; Eisen 2017; Sudbury 2005; Wrenn 2016).

In the United States, confining migrants and asylum-seekers in detention centers costs taxpayers approximately $2 billion each year (Sinha 2016, 85; Williams 2015, 12). 'If people were aware of how much it costs them to have these women and their children detained, they would probably be against it', says Rosa, another legal advocate that has been working in the center for over two years. Today in the US, nine out of the 10 biggest ICE immigration detention centers are privately managed, making 62 percent of all ICE immigration beds operated by private corporations. Of this amount, the GEO Group and CoreCivic operate a combined 72 percent of the privately contracted ICE immigration beds (Flynn 2016a, 184). Occasionally, counties charge ICE above daily cost, effectively using immigration detainees to fund jails and other county services (Martin 2019, 246). In addition, a *Washington Post* investigation found that CoreCivic receives $20 million per month to detain women and children at the South Texas Family Detention Center, regardless of how many women and children are actually held (Detention Watch Network 2015a). Dana points out: 'It shouldn't be an economic issue, but one directly related to human rights. It is not right to confine women and children that are fleeing from violence'. Yet the reasons for confining them are purely economic. CoreCivic and GEO are two very profitable companies that have expanded their share of the private immigrant detention industry from 37 to 45 percent in just 2014. CoreCivic's profits increased from $133,373,000 in 2007 to $195,022,000 in 2014, and the company has obtained a $1 billion contract with the US Department of Homeland Security (Garbus 2019). Similarly, GEO's profits increased by 244 percent during this same period (2007–2014) (Sinha 2016, 92). In addition, CoreCivic owns a subsidiary called TransCor America, LLC, which is the largest prisoner transportation company in the United States. TransCor generated $4.4 million in 2014 and $2.6 million in 2016. This shows that the trend to privatize detention centers and its services, combined with the increase in immigrant and asylum-seeking detention serves the interests of private corporations (Conlon and Hiemstra 2014). Despite the fact that these companies have generated profit over the years, some of them have other activities that are not exclusively related to immigrant and refugee detention such as cleaning, information technology and parking management services. Thus, it is hard to know how much profit they earned from each area of business. In any case, if prison management were not a profitable business, these companies would most certainly not be investing in that sector. In addition, data shows that, in the United States, alternatives to detention would save the federal government a lot of money, as some alternatives cost between 70 cents and $17 per person per day in comparison to the $159 that ICE currently spends (National Immigrant Justice Center 2017).

Does privatizing migrant detention centers actually increase the number of detainees? In 2009, the Obama administration established a mandatory detention bed quota that required the Department of Homeland Security to have up to 34,000 beds available daily for immigration detention. Anita Sinha (2016, 82) argues that 'quotas generally have demonstratively compelled action', and in this case, it has proven to be true, as the mandatory bed quota resulted in an increase in the number of detainees (Flynn 2016b; García Hernández 2015). The way this quota contributes to the increase of migrant detention is through the guaranteed minimums that ICE is required to pay contractors, regardless of how many people are detained. Contractors receive a set payment from ICE independent of the number of beds that are filled. Because ICE's interests are not the same as the private detention centers' – which would probably save money with fewer people confined as long as they received their guaranteed minimums – ICE is motivated to detain as many people as possible in facilities with guaranteed minimums to avoid the appearance of inefficiency. These guaranteed minimums influence ICE's decisions as to how many people to confine, where to confine them and for how long (Detention Watch Network 2015b).

Our current neoliberal system encourages public-private partnerships that financially incentivize increases in refugee detention. In the United States, for instance, corporations try to make profits through collaborating with political actors who favor transferring immigration functions from the federal to the state level. In that vein, Tania Golash-Boza (2009) has linked corporations that profit from the incarceration of migrants to conservative commentators and politicians as part of a large complex of increasingly privatized control. An example of this direct connection can be seen on the attempt to pass Arizona's Senate Bill 1070, also know as the 'show me your papers law', which allows police officers to check the immigration status of people they suspect are undocumented immigrants. With this law passed in 2010, the number of detained people, and thus the number of detained people in private immigration detention centers, increased (Hernández-León 2013, 39). CoreCivic/CCA, GEO, prison lobbyists and companies gave financial backing to many of the politicians campaigning for its legislative approval – the 1070 bill was co-sponsored by 36 people, and 30 of those received campaign contributions from private prison corporations (Doty and Wheatley 2013, 429; Feltz and Baksh 2012). Lobbying for incarceration laws becomes part of the profit-maximizing strategy for these private firms (Hall and Coyne 2013; Wrenn 2016). Prior to the last election, GEO gave $225,000 to a Trump political action committee. Additionally, CoreCivic and GEO both contributed $250,000 to President Trump's inauguration (Garbus 2019).

A transnational feminist framework illuminates how private actors produce new power structures that echo colonialism. The inclusion of these actors also influences, shapes and even hardens detention techniques, to the extent that profit is extracted from every marginal migrant who goes to detention. In this way, the market logic transforms sovereign regimes through, for instance, the incentive to confine people. Economic and legal incentives – such as the mandatory bed quotas – to lock up people have resulted into higher confinement rates. Authors such as Alison Mountz argue that detention and deportation are interlocking industries in the migration assemblage that generate profit through the privatization of services (Mountz et al. 2013). Thus, when both detention and deportation increase, the 'output', as well as the profits of migration control, increase. In this way, private actors influence the state through the incentive to confine people, and thus corporations profit from detained populations. In addition, the confinement of non-citizens reinforces the image of asylum-seekers as criminals that deserve to be punished and whose eligibility for citizenship should be questioned (Conlon and Gill 2013; Skodo 2017).

Neoliberalism and Neocolonialism

'Many of these women worked in *maquiladoras* [clothing factories] before they came here. They worked more than 12 hours a day for us to wear the clothes we wear', says Rosa. Very much like in franchise colonialism, women in the global south are exploited for their labor and positioned in an interdependent economic relationship of uneven development (Baker 2017, 146). These ongoing structures of domination take place today. The failure to acknowledge the constitutive role of colonial exploitation in contemporary neoliberalism leads to weak representations of what is happening today in regard to the confinement of asylum-seekers. The Western world has a long history of confining and exploiting the bodies of women and people of color. It is not only through the exploitative form of labor and resource extraction that characterized colonialism – echoed by Paloma's example of making t-shirts in a *maquiladora* in her country – that Western states profit from postcolonial subjects; here profit emerges from the technologies of exclusion themselves, where passive, confined bodies produce profit from being 'out of place' rather than through their labor. The demonized asylum-seeker is confined, and profit is generated from the physical care of her body (housing, feeding, clothing and transporting it). This is how corporations extract wealth from asylum-seekers' bodies (Mavhunga 2011, 152). Even though there are alternatives to immigrant detention (Sampson 2019), confining refugees in private facilities is a more lucrative business than having people in the communities.

These material practices of confinement are supported by discourses and technologies that conceptualize the refugee as the 'invasive other' (Ticktin 2017), what Martinican thinker Aimé Césaire (2000) referred to as (colonial) 'thingification'. This dehumanizing vision of asylum-seekers can lead to practices that consider them as things, such as the agreement President Obama – later honored by President Trump – made with Prime Minister Turnbull to exchange refugees who had arrived in Australia with refugees who had arrived in the US, commonly known as the 'refugee swap'. Refugees and migrants fall into neocolonial systems of representation where they are either victims to be saved, usually by humanitarian organizations, or demonized by the media and politicians (Holohan 2019). The current rhetoric presents an image of refugees as invaders that threaten the status quo. There is a long colonial history of concepts and words like invasion, pollution, dirtiness, insects and infestation being used metaphorically in connection with 'undesirable' populations, which are now reappearing with reference to asylum-seekers. Clapperton Mavhunga (2011) writes about the African colonial context and how the use of metaphors that linked the colonized to pests leads to treating people as plagues threatening to destroy everything and thus justifying the confinement and isolation of certain groups.

Those previously dehumanized bodies thus become commodities for exchange – or for keeping – in order to make a profit. Locking up people who seek asylum illuminates how global confinement systems work. As most refugees come from countries from the global south, confinement is highly racialized and can therefore be seen as a part of the larger racist system of mass incarceration (Cisneros 2016; Davis 1988; Davis 2011; Gilmore 2007). Punishment regimes are shaped by neoliberalism and are substantively enforced by transnational corporations controlling the detention, transportation and visa processing (among other things) of migrants and refugees, tasks that were formerly performed by the state. The locking up of people who seek asylum and belong to the global south perpetuates a system that has colonial overtones while illuminating and enforcing racialized ideologies (Sudbury 2005, xiii).

Conclusion

Over recent years, neoliberalism has enabled private actors to enter the refugee management regime. This has resulted in public-private partnerships, such as the privatization of migration detention centers. By privatizing these facilities, the state creates an economic incentive to confine people who seek asylum. In this way, the privatization of migration management highlights how the private and public spheres cooperate with each other. Not only does it allow the state's arm to reach further, it also allows the state to be subject to less accountability (Gammeltoft-Hansen 2015).

Using a transnational feminist lens, I have analyzed how, through neoliberal processes, women who seek asylum are subject to exploitation both in their countries of origin and once they reach their destinations. Through the confinement of the refugee population, private detention centers are profiting out of the bodies of people of color in continuity with their operations overseas where they are exploited through labor processes. This process is seamlessly integrated with the public's perception that refugees are a threat that requires efficient management rather than subjects whose treatment deserves accountability.

The inclusion of private actors on the one hand is paramount for the creation of a transnational assemblage that contains people in the global south, and on the other hand, shapes sovereign regimes by transforming them into profit-making apparatuses that follow a neoliberal logic.

References

Abbott, Kenneth W, and Duncan Snidal. 2009. 'The governance triangle: regulatory standards institutions and the shadow of the state', in *The politics of global regulation*, edited by Walter Mattli and Ngaire Woods, 44–88. Princeton, NJ: Princeton University Press.

Austin, James, and Garry Coventry. 2001. *Emerging Issues on Privatized Prisons*. edited by U.S. Department of Justice. Washington DC: Bureau of Justice Assistance.

Bacon, Christine. 2005. *The evolution of immigration detention in the UK: the involvement of private prison companies.* Oxford: Refugee Studies Centre Oxford.

Baker, W Oliver. 2017. 'Democracy, class, and white settler colonialism', *Public* 28(55): 144–153.

Bigo, Didier. 2002. 'Security and immigration: toward a critique of the governmentality of unease', *Alternatives* 27(1): 63–92.

Binder, Sue. 2017. *Bodies in Beds: Why Business Should Out of Prisons.* New York: Algora Publishing.

Briggs, Laura, Gladys McCormick, and JT Way. 2008. 'Transnationalism: A category of analysis', *American Quarterly* 60(3): 625–648.

Cisneros, Natalie. 2016. 'Resisting "Massive Elimination": Foucault, Immigration, and the GIP', in *Active Intolerance. Michel Foucault, the Prisons Information Group, and the Future of Abolition*, edited by Perry Zurn and Andrew Dilts, 241–257. London, New York: Palgrave Macmillan.

Clark, Kelsey. 2016. 'Prisons for Profit: Neoliberal Rationality's Transformation of America's Prisons.' Bachelor thesis. https://openworks.wooster.edu/independentstudy/7242/

Conlon, Deirdre, and Nick Gill. 2013. 'Gagging orders: asylum seekers and paradoxes of freedom and protest in liberal society', *Citizenship Studies* 17 (2): 241–259.

Conlon, Deirdre, and Nancy Hiemstra. 2014. 'Examining the everyday micro-economies of migrant detention in the United States', Geographica Helvetica 69(5): 335–344.

Davis, Angela Y. 1988. 'Racialized punishment and prison abolition', in *A Companion to African-American Philosophy*, edited by Tommy L. Lott and John P. Pitman, 360–369. Oxford: Blackwell Publishing.

Davis, Angela Y. 2011. *Women, race, and class*. New York: Vintage.

Desai, Manisha. 2005. 'Transnationalism: the face of feminist politics post-Beijing', *International Social Science Journal*, 57 (184): 319–330.

Detention Watch Network. 2015a. 'Banking on Detention: Local Lockup Quotas and the Immigrant Dragnet'. Detention Watch Network and Center for Constitutional Rights.

Detention Watch Network. 2015b. 'Ending the Use of Immigration Detention to Deter Migration'. Detention Watch Network.

Doty, Roxanne Lynne, and Elizabeth Shannon Wheatley. 2013. 'Private detention and the immigration industrial complex'. *International Political Sociology,* 7(4): 426–443.

Eisen, Lauren-Brooke. 2017. *Inside private prisons: An American dilemma in the age of mass incarceration*. Columbia University Press.

Feltz, Renee, and Stokely Baksh. 2012. 'Business of Detention', in *Beyond Walls and Cages: Prisons, Borders and Global Crisis*, edited by Jenna Loyd, Matt Mitchelson and Andrew Burridge, 143–151. Athens and London: University of Georgia Press.

Flynn, Matthew. 2016a. 'Capitalism and Immigration Control: What Political Economy Reveals about the Growth of Detention Systems', in *Global Detention Project Working Paper*: Global Detention Project

Flynn, Michael. 2014. 'There and Back Again: On the Diffusion of Immigration Detention', *Journal on Migration and Human Security*, 2(3): 165–197.

Flynn, Michael. 2016b. 'Detained beyond the sovereign: Conceptualising non-state actor involvement in immigration detention', in *Intimate Economies of Immigration Detention: Critical Perspectives*, edited by Deirdre Conlon and Nancy Hiemstra, 15–31. New York: Routledge.

Frenzen, Niels. 2010. 'US Migrant Interdiction Practices In International And Territorial Waters', in *Extraterritorial Immigration Control (Immigration and Asylum Law and Policy in Europe)*, edited by Bernard Ryan and Valsamis Mitsilegas, 369–390. Leiden/Boston: Martinus Nijhoff Publishers.

Gammeltoft-Hansen, Thomas. 2013. 'The rise of the private border guard: Accountability and responsibility in the migration control industry', in *The Migration Industry and the Commercialization of International Migration*, edited by Thomas Gammeltoft-Hansen and Ninna Nyberg Sorensen, 128–151. London: Routledge.

Gammeltoft-Hansen, Thomas. 2015. 'Private security and the migration control industry', in *Routledge Handbook of Private Security Studies*, 207–215. London: Routledge.

Gammeltoft-Hansen, Thomas, and Nikolas F Tan. 2017. 'The end of the deterrence paradigm? Future directions for global refugee policy', *Journal on Migration and Human Security,* 5(1): 28–56.

Garbus, Martin. 2019. 'What I Saw at the Dilley, Texas, Immigrant Detention Center', the Nation. Accessed June 16, 2020. https://www.thenation.com/article/archive/dilley-texas-immigration-detention/

García Hernández, César Cuauhtémoc. 2015. 'Naturalizing Immigration Imprisonment' *California Law Review*, 103(6): 1449–1514.

Gilmore, Ruth Wilson. 2007. *Golden Gulag: Prisons, Surplus, Crisis, and Opposition in Globalizing California*. Berkely, CA: University of California Press.

Golash-Boza, Tanya. 2016. 'Racialized and Gendered Mass Deportation and the Crisis of Capitalism', *Journal of World-Systems Research* 22(1): 38–44.

Golash-Boza, Tanya. 2009. 'A confluence of interests in immigration enforcement: How politicians, the media, and corporations profit from immigration policies destined to fail', *Sociology Compass*, 3(2): 283–294.

Grewal, Inderpal, and Caren Kaplan. 1994. *Scattered hegemonies: Postmodernity and transnational feminist practices*. Minneapolis, MN: University of Minnesota Press.

Hall, A. R., and C. J. Coyne. 2013. 'The militarization of U.S. domestic policing', *The Independent Review*, 17(4): 485–504.

Henderson, Alex. 2015. '9 Surprising Industries Profiting Handsomely from America's Insane Prison System', *Justice Policy Institute*. http://www.justicepolicy.org/news/8751

Hernández-León, Rubén. 2013. 'Conceptualizing the Migration Industry', in *The Migration Industry and the Commercialization of International Migration*, edited by Thomas Gammeltoft-Hansen and Ninna Nyberg Sorensen, 24–44. New York: Routledge.

Herr, Ranjoo Seodu. 2014. 'Reclaiming third world feminism: Or why transnational feminism needs third world feminism', *Meridians* 12(1):1–30.

Holohan, Siobhan. 2019. 'Some human's rights: Neocolonial discourses of otherness in the Mediterranean refugee crisis', *Open Library of Humanities* 5(1).

Huysmans, Jef. 2006. *The Politics of Insecurity: Fear, Migration and Asylum in the EU*. London: Routledge.

Lemberg-Pedersen, Martin. 2013. 'Private security companies and the European borderscapes', in *The Migration Industry and the Commercialization of International Migration*, edited by Thomas Gammeltoft-Hansen and Ninna Nyberg Sorensen, 152–171. New York: Routledge.

Lemberg-Pedersen, Martin. 2019. 'Manufacturing displacement. Externalization and postcoloniality in European migration control', *Global Affairs* 5(3): 247–271.

Longo, Matthew. 2018. *The Politics of Borders: Sovereignty, Security, and the Citizen after 9/11*. Cambridge, UK: Cambridge University Press.

Loyd, Jenna M, Matt Mitchelson, and Andrew Burridge. 2013. *Beyond walls and cages: Prisons, borders, and global crisis. Vol. 14*. Athens, GA: University of Georgia Press.

Martin, Lauren. 2019. 'Carceral mobility and flexible territoriality in immigration enforcement', in *Handbook on Critical Geographies of Migration*. Cheltenham: Edward Elgar Publishing.

Mavhunga, Clapperton Chakanetsa. 2011. 'Vermin Beings On Pestiferous Animals and Human Game', *Social Text* 29(1[106]): 151–176.

Menz, Georg. 2011. 'Neo-liberalism, privatization and the outsourcing of migration management: a five-country comparison', *Competition & Change*. 15(2): 116–135.

Menz, Georg. 2013. 'The neoliberalized state and the growth of the migration industry', in *The Migration Industry and the Commercialization of International Migration*. London and New York: Routledge.

Mountz, Alison. 2011. 'The enforcement archipelago: Detention, haunting, and asylum on islands', *Political Geography*, 30(3): 118–128.

Mountz, Alison, Kate Coddington, R Tina Catania, and Jenna M Loyd. 2013. 'Conceptualizing detention: Mobility, containment, bordering, and exclusion', *Progress in Human Geography*, 37(4): 522–541.

National Immigrant Justice Center. 2017. Detention Bed Quota. National Immigrant Justice Center.

Parikh, Crystal. 2017. 'Transnational Feminism'. *The Cambridge Companion to Transnational American Literature*. 221–236.

Requarth, Tim. 2019. 'How Private Equity Is Turning Public Prisons into Big Profits', *The Nation*. https://www.thenation.com/article/archive/prison-privatization-private-equity-hig/

Riva, Sara. 2017. 'Across the border and into the cold: hieleras and the punishment of asylum-seeking Central American women in the United States', *Citizenship Studies*, 21(3): 309–326.

Sampson, Robyn. 2019. 'The biopolitics of alternatives to immigration detention', in *Handbook on Critical Geographies of Migration*. Edward Elgar Publishing.

Simonds, Raven, and Kevin A Wright. 2017. 'Private prisons'. *The Encyclopedia of Corrections*: 1–4.

Sinha, Anita. 2016. 'Arbitrary Detention: The Immigration Detention Bed Quota', *Duke Journal of Constitutional Law & Public Policy* 12(2): 77–121.

Skodo, Admir. 2017. 'How Immigration Detention Compares Around the World', *The Conversation*. https://theconversation.com/how-immigration-detention-compares-around-the-world-76067

Sudbury, Julia. 2005. *Global lockdown. Race, Gender and the Prison Industrial Complex*. New York: Routledge.

Ticktin, Miriam. 2017. 'Invasive Others: Toward a Contaminated World', *Social Research: An International Quarterly* 84(1): xxi-xxxiv.

U.S. Immigration and Customs Enforcement. 2019. 'U.S. Immigration and Customs Enforcement: Budget Overview', Department of Homeland Security. https://www.dhs.gov/sites/default/files/publications/19_0318_MGMT_CBJ-Immigration-Customs-Enforcement_0.pdf.

Williams, Jill M. 2015. 'From humanitarian exceptionalism to contingent care: Care and enforcement at the humanitarian border', *Political Geography* 47: 11–20.

Wrenn, Mary V. 2016. 'Immanent critique, enabling myths, and the neoliberal narrative', *Review of Radical Political Economics* 48(3): 452–466.

16

Rejected Asylum Claims and Children in International Human Rights Law: Changing the Narrative

ANNE-CECILE LEYVRAZ

Adopted in 1989, the International Convention on the Rights of the Child (CRC) is the most widely ratified international human rights instrument. The CRC applies to both citizen and non-citizen children. Yet, some Articles more specifically address situations experienced by non-citizens, such as deportation or being a refugee. Article 3 – the principle that the best interest of the child should be the prime consideration in all actions that affect the child – and Article 2 – which forbids discrimination based on the status of the child's parents or legal guardians – are considered key in the protection of immigrant children, including those who had their asylum-claim rejected. This being said, violations of the human rights of children and impairment of their dignity is widespread. Children in an irregular situation, namely whose 'presence on the territory of a State… does not fulfil, or no longer fulfils the conditions of entry, stay or residence in the State' (IOM 2019) suffer additional violations because of their lack of regular migration status. International reports and the United Nations have been documenting such cases for decades.

Policies that encourage rejected asylum-seekers to leave the territory of the receiving state include the suppression or limitations of rights and access to social services, such as housing or health care (European Migration Network 2016). Even when rights are not legally curtailed, their effective implemen-tation and enjoyment can be infringed by threats or fears of deportation, such as in countries where the education system and immigration authorities share information. The irregularity of the status, the right of states to control access to their territory, and the credibility of the asylum procedure are just but a few examples of justifications used by states to adopt such policies. They portray asylum-seekers whose claims have been rejected (RAS, CRAS for children) not only as irregular or illegal immigrants, but also as departing. Yet, available data is at odds with such a proposition: in Europe, only a few RAS are being deported. Most end up undocumented and destitute (Harlan 2019). This includes both children and adults.

Most international or regional human rights instruments have instituted a control mechanism – namely a tribunal or expert committee – that is accessible to individuals. International and regional procedures are available to RAS (Leyvraz 2018), not to review the asylum decision as such, but to evaluate an alleged violation of an international obligation. Should they feel a right enshrined in an international human rights convention has been violated, RAS can submit a complaint and have the situation reviewed by an international or regional (quasi-)judicial body. RAS are more active than other irregular migrants before judicial or quasi-judicial human rights bodies and have spurred an important jurisprudential development in international and regional arenas (Chetail 2013). The focus on this specific category adopted in this contribution is thus functional: they are a visible part of irregularity (De Bruycker and Apap 2000). Yet, as the situation experienced by CRAS often overlaps with that of other children unlawfully present on the territory of a state, this chapter will dwell on decisions and comments affecting both.

This chapter will discuss how international and regional (quasi-)judicial bodies handle cases that involve accompanied and unaccompanied CRAS in order to assess the relevance of national socio-legal categories in the international legal order. Drawing from quasi-judicial cases and observations adopted by expert bodies operating within the United Nations human rights system, I claim that such bodies oscillate between a status-centred approach, where the immigration status is decisive, and an experience-based approach, curbing the relevance of state-based categories. To this end, they appeal to different rationales. In the process of decision-making within the international legal order, international bodies construct a counter-narrative about migration that differs from state-centred discourses on irregularity. In the subsequent sections, I will begin by addressing the context of the emergence of the discourse framing asylum as a 'problem' at domestic level and present the different approach adopted within the international legal order. Then, discussing case law and observations of international expert bodies on situations pertaining to children, I will consider situations where such bodies adopted a status-centred approach or an experience-based approach. I claim that international institutions and movements should build upon experience-based approaches to influence discourse at domestic levels. Indeed, because of the performative capacities of discourse (Cherfas 2006; Crépeau, Nakache, and Atak 2007), experience-based approaches could alleviate the difficulty migrants face in trying to enjoy their fundamental rights. Access to human rights should not be addressed as a purely legal consideration, but also as context-dependant. The social environment, stigmatization, and criminalization of irregular migration play a non-negligible role in the difficulties of access and enjoyment of fundamental human rights (Cholewinski 2005).

Framing 'Irregularity' from a Domestic and International Perspective

For the last centuries, migration control has been regarded as an expression of sovereignty. Yet, its significance has changed over time, along with the social, historical, economic, and political environment (Plender 1988). Some authors claim that it was not until the 20th century that migration control became an essential attribute of state power (Chetail 2014; Dauvergne 2014). Nowadays, 'governing through migration control' is considered key by most states (Bosworth and Guild 2008).

State sovereignty is not just about power. It also entails responsibility, notably to respect and implement international obligations, such as human rights obligations. It has been described as both 'power' and 'duty' (Saroléa 2006). CRAS are thus situated at the intersection of two areas of law: on the one hand, they are subjected to the sovereign right of the state to control access to its territory and, on the other, they enjoy the protection of the international human rights corpus. In addition, they are subjected to both international and domestic legal orders. However, domestic and legal orders do not apprehend CRAS from the same perspective. The dominant logic governing each legal order expresses a different rationale, as will be discussed in the coming subsections.

Undeserving and Outgoing: Attributes of Irregularity at Domestic Level

Nowadays, the categorization and stratification of persons along such dividing lines as migrants/nationals, regular/irregular, refugee/rejected asylum-seeker is a common feature of national migration policies. This categorizing process occurs within the domestic legal order and then leads to a differentiated application of rights depending on the category the person belongs to.

> Contemporary migration management typically operates through various mechanisms (classification and selection, admission procedures, conditions and restrictions). As a result, contemporary migration management involves a proliferation, fragmentation and polarisation of different statuses and related

bundles of rights with regard to admission, residence, work, and social rights (Kraler 2009).

From a state's perspective, suppression or limitation of rights is meant to encourage the departure of migrants unlawfully present or deter potential immigration. Such a practice has become part of domestic immigration control. Within domestic orders, human rights are being turned into instruments of power and control (Morris 2010) over an unwanted population, a population expected to leave, and thus whose stay is contemplated as merely temporary.

In most countries, the rejection of an asylum claim is subjected to the obligation to leave the country. Yet individuals' departure proves difficult for states to enforce (Paoletti 2010). One of the direct consequences at the domestic level has been the adoption of coercive measures, such as harsh reception conditions, restrictive access to economic, social, and civil rights, and exclusion from society in order to 'encourage' the RAS to depart. Restricting rights has not proved necessarily efficient to ensure the departure of the RAS (Valenta and Thorshaug 2011). Yet, it affects those enduring restrictions, sometimes for years. The perception that RAS are 'on the go' or departing is misleading, as in some cases departure proves impossible (Legomsky 2014).

The irregularity of the presence starts when the asylum procedure ends with a negative decision. It is thus the result of national policies embedded in domestic legislation. However, the process is not merely a neutral administrative act of classification: it also triggers a socially constructed representation of the person as 'bogus claimants', 'abusers', and 'undeserving poor' (Da Lomba 2010). This discourse emerged during the 1980s, as states started to frame asylum as a problem. In other words, negative representations of RAS are not contemporary with the adoption of the 1951 Geneva Convention Relating to the Status of Refugees, but only developed decades later, when the economies contracted, the origin of asylum-seekers changed, and the return of RAS proved difficult to enforce (Stünzi and Miaz 2020).

Additionally, operating as a self-reinforcing prophecy, the discourse on the need to 'fight abuses' in the asylum system and 'deter bogus claims' has had a performative impact that led to further impairment of rights (Frei et al. 2014). Such discourses – and the resulting restrictions – are not only directed to adults. They also affect children, whether accompanied, separated, or unaccompanied (PICUM 2015). However, this is not a merely domestic matter: these measures affect the enjoyment of fundamental rights that are protected in international and regional human rights law instruments.

Emphasis on Jurisdiction and Humanity: The Key Elements at International Level

Among the nine core human rights conventions adopted within the international legal order,[1] none specifically addresses the rights of persons whose asylum claims have been rejected. Yet, this does not mean that international instruments are irrelevant. Nevertheless, their applicability is contingent, depending on the material and personal scope of the treaty. For example, the Convention on the Elimination of All Forms of Discriminations against Women will be relevant only in situations involving women RAS; the CRC will be applicable to CRAS. In other words, the entire international and regional human rights corpus is applicable, as long as personal or material criteria of the treaty are met.

The applicability of international norms also depends on the existence of a jurisdictional link. For the CRAS to fall under the jurisdiction of the state usually depends on the territorial presence. As Bosniak (2007, 390) points out, the 'rights and recognition enjoyed by immigrants are usually understood to derive from either their formal status under law or their territorial presence'. While at the domestic level, formal status is key, international human rights law is strongly rooted in jurisdiction and territoriality (Saroléa 2006).

However, this does not mean that the migration status becomes irrelevant to the applicability of human rights: 'international human rights law does not make immigration status irrelevant to one's treatment in the social sphere. What international human rights law does, however, is to carve out a zone of protected personhood' (Da Lomba 2010). The logic of international law is somehow pragmatic or binary: as long as the removal has not been implemented, one's presence in the territory of the rejecting state is sufficient to enable the relevant human rights standards to be applied. Labelling one's stay as irregular or describing a CRAS's presence as merely temporary thus has a lesser impact within the international legal order than at domestic level.

A Status-Centred Approach

Because of domestic laws, rejection of an asylum claim and irregularity often go hand in hand. Such legal status – or absence thereof – permeates the international legal order and influences the interpretation and adjudication of rights-based claims.The case discussed in this section adopts what I call a 'status-centred approach', namely meaning that status is considered a central element in the decision-making process. Yet, status is never the sole

---

[1]   The treaties are accessible at: https://www.ohchr.org/EN/ProfessionalInterest/ Pages/CoreInstruments.aspx

consideration: experts or judges have to balance personal characteristics with the rights of states to control access to the territory. Adjudicated by an expert committee monitoring the implementation of the European Social Charter, the following case is insightful as the instrument explicitly excludes migrants unlawfully present from its personal scope. Nonetheless, the European Committee of Social Rights (ECSR) extended the personal scope of the treaty to protect the dignity of all human beings and in particular the dignity of children.

Protecting Dignity, but Not Interfering with Departure: A Difficult Task

Defence for Children International (DCI) v. the Netherlands (ECSR 2009) is a case submitted to the ECSR by an organisation willing to prevent the deprivation of accommodation suffered by children in an irregular situation, particularly children of families whose asylum claims had been rejected. The claimant argued it was, amongst others, a violation of Article 31(1) and 31(2) of the European Social Charter protecting the right to housing. Although the European Social Charter explicitly excluded from its personal scope persons without a lawful right of presence, the ECSR did not rule out the case for lack of competence. Instead, it proceeded as follows: it first declared that the Netherlands was not required to guarantee access to housing for CRAS as per Article 31(1) because the ECSR had interpreted it as entailing a guarantee of continued residence (ECSR 2009, 43). It also recognised that the obligations arising from the European Social Charter should not undermine the objectives of domestic migration policy and stated that 'to require that a Party provide such lasting housing would run counter the State's aliens policy objective of encouraging persons unlawfully on its territory to return to their country of origin' (ECSR 2009, 44). For these reasons, it concluded that 'children unlawfully present on the territory of a State Party do not come within the personal scope of Article 31(1)' (ECSR 2009, 45), thus upholding the relevance of domestic laws and categories in the international legal order and acknowledging the legality of a differentiated treatment based on irregularity, including for children.

The ECSR went on to examine Article 31(2) on the prevention and reduction of homelessness. It interpreted it as relevant to protect the dignity of children, even those unlawfully present. To meet this obligation, the ECSR found that states should not proceed with the removal of children from their shelter: 'the Committee holds that, since in the case of unlawfully present persons no alternative accommodation may be required by States, eviction from shelter should be banned as it would place the persons concerned, particularly children, in a situation of extreme helplessness which is contrary to the respect for their human dignity' (ECSR 2009, 63).

Thus, the protection against hardship and the prevention of homelessness were not found to harm the objectives of domestic migration policies. Yet, the reasoning of the ECSR is complex and puzzling: it first excluded CRAS from the personal scope of Article 31(1) due to the guarantee of tenure, but then required states to provide shelter as long as the CRAS falls under its jurisdiction, mostly to prevent homelessness.

Building Acceptance to a Differentiated Treatment

The decision of the ECSR in *DCI* provides for a solution that seeks to balance the different interests at stake. Legal status is deemed relevant, yet considerations of dignity, humanity, and the obligation to tackle homelessness call for the establishment of a bottom line in the treatment of children. The ECSR agrees that children unlawfully present do not deserve to the same housing standards as other children, whether nationals or migrants lawfully present. In particular, accommodation does not have to meet the characteristics of security and permanence that would make it a home. Because of the status and the right of states to curb irregular immigration, some children can be treated differently in the eyes of the law.

This reasoning builds on the idea that a CRAS's presence in the territory of the state is temporary and on a long-term discourse of fight against abuses. As pointed out by Fox O'Mahony and Sweeney (2010), such discourses have overshadowed the personal experiences of children housed in shelters that do not meet such requirements as stability, permanency, and privacy. The effort to reconcile states' immigration policies with their protection of fundamental rights is common in the international legal order. By doing so, the result, as is the *DCI* case, invisibilize the experience of those directly affected and is questionable from a human rights perspective. Indeed, 'the provision of a house does not necessarily lead to a realisation of the right to housing if a house is provided absent attention to the rights, freedoms, and dignity we associate with claims to a house in the first place' (Hohmann 2014, 225).

How can the argument of the adequacy of temporary shelter, short of any requirement of privacy be upheld when empirical data show that removal is a long process, assuming it is possible at all? The Special Rapporteur on the Human Rights of Migrants addresses the issue and states that the right to housing, including for failed asylum seekers, must provide security of tenure (UNGA 2010, 41). The Special Rapporteur emphasizes the interdependence of rights and points out that children, as well as adults, can have their well-being affected by the lack of a place to call home (UNGA 2011, 39). In doing so, the Special Rapporteur not only underlines the necessity of considering the interdependence of rights, but also how curtailing one right necessarily has consequences for the enjoyment of other rights. It also makes way for adopting an experience-based approach.

An Experience-Based Approach

The experience of hardship is not restricted to persons with precarious immigration status. Citizens and migrants with a right to remain are also concerned. Yet, some categories – designated as 'vulnerable' or 'marginalized' – are more affected. Adopting what I call an 'experience-based approach', namely focusing primarily on the risk or experience of (future) hardship, international bodies have in some cases placed lesser emphasis on the relevance of the legal status of the individual within the international legal order. Considering some aspects of the right to health and education, in this section I discuss the approach followed by international bodies and point to the rationale they adopt.

Caring and Protecting Vulnerable Ones: Access to All Level of Health Care

The right to health is complex and embedded within several layers of medical care and other obligations (ECOSOC 2000). Access to preventive, primary, secondary, and emergency health care for CRAS, but also for other categories of migrants unlawfully present, is difficult to enjoy in practice. Yet, when emergency health care is at stake, treaty bodies have unequivocally found that access should be granted to all persons (ECOSOC 2008, 37), including children and adults unlawfully present. In other words, all persons within the jurisdiction of states must have access to emergency health care. Medical condition, not immigration status, must prevail. Such an obligation is not merely embedded in the right to health. It also affects the right to life, as emergency health care in most cases address life-threatening conditions.

For other levels of care, such as secondary health care, there is a distinction between adults and children: the latter are to be granted full access, while the former trigger a more complex answer. For example, addressing the situation of unaccompanied or separated children, the Committee on the Rights of the Child called on states-party to ensure that all have the same access to health care as national children, regardless of their migration status (Committee on the Rights of the Child 2005, 5–6). The Special Rapporteur on the Human Rights of Migrants stated:

> Regrettably, there were vast discrepancies between intern-
> ational human rights norms and their actual implementation in
> the field of health care for migrant children whether these

children are in regular or irregular situations, accompanied or unaccompanied. Inadequate care had long-lasting consequences on a child's development; for this reason, and in the light of the State duty to protect the most vulnerable, access to health care for migrant children should be an urgent priority (UNGA 2011, 40).

Contrary to the obligation to grant emergency health care, an obligation animated notably by the protection of life and addressing an immediate threat, other levels of health care lean on a different rationale. The development of the child, and thus her future, as well as the mitigation of her vulnerability are contemplated. The temporary presence in the territory of the state is not sufficient to deprive the CRAS from her right.

In the case *International Federation of Human Rights Leagues v. France*, the ECSR had to decide, among other things, whether France's policy to restrain a CRAS from accessing medical care was in compliance with Article 17 of the European Social Charter. Children would be admitted to a medical scheme only after three months, except for emergency health care. Referring to the CRC, the ECSR found it to be contrary to the European Social Charter (ECSR 2004, 36–37). Nevertheless, it did not come to the same conclusion for adults, who did not have to benefit from the same duty of 'care and assistance' (ECSR 2004, 36).

Protecting Present and Future Experiences

When international bodies apply an experience-based approach, they favor a protective stance over domestic policies. They consider children's immediate and future life experiences and seek to preserve the dignity of vulnerable children. To this end, they can draw on the interdependence of all rights. For example, health can only be achieved if housing is adequate. Using its own rationale, the international legal order is thus able to produce a counter-narrative to discourses produced within the domestic order. The right to education is but another example.

Schools play an important role in the process of integration within the host society. School creates an environment where relationships and attachments can be established (FRA 2010). As a consequence, education somehow obstructs state immigration policy: integration and relationships make removal more difficult and uncertain. Additionally, as stated by the UN Committee on Economic, Social and Cultural Rights, it is a way to raise the future prospect of the child. It is 'the foundation for lifelong learning and human development on which countries can systematically build other levels and types of education and training. It is also about providing children with tools for the future that will make them less vulnerable and exploitable' (ECOSOC 1999a). Immediate consideration of integration and that of the future of the child compete. Yet, the international order favors the latter.

Just as for the right to health, the right to education is stratified into different levels, primary education being one of them (ECOSOC 1999b). Treaty bodies have consistently interpreted relevant human rights norms as stating an obligation to provide free primary education for all children who fall under the jurisdiction of the state. This obligation was deemed valid not only for Western states, but also for countries in the 'global south', such as Ecuador (Committee on the Rights of the Child 2010), Egypt (Committee on the Rights of the Child 2011), and Ethiopia (Committee on the Rights of the Child 2015). Addressing the situation in Hong Kong, the UN Committee on Economic, Social and Cultural Rights explicitly urged the state 'to amend its legislation to provide for the right to education of all school-age children in its jurisdiction, including children of migrants without the legal right to remain in [Hong Kong]' (ECOSOC 2005, 101). However, as children move from primary school to higher education, how does it affect the obligations of states? Decisions or comments of international bodies fail to provide an unequivocal answer. However, the European Court of Human Rights did not rule out the possibility of limiting access through higher fees based on nationality or status for secondary education (European Court of Human Rights 2011).

This being said, considerations regarding the legal status of children or domestic immigration policies are always in the background. Moreover, as the rights get more complex, or specific, usually arguments on the rights of states to control immigration start to leak more compellingly into the decisions or observations of international bodies. The rights of states and human rights both belong to the international legal order and influence their decision-making processes. In practice, the status-based approach and the experience-based approach are almost like ideal types (Bosniak 2007). The approach they follow lies on a spectrum between these two extremes. Yet, conceptually, the experience-based approach is powerful: it offers an alternative way to portray children, emphasizing primarily the child, and less on domestically produced socio-legal categories.

Conclusion

The international legal order proceeds according to its own system and rationale and, by doing so, contributes to creating a discourse that differs from the discourse emanating from the domestic legal order. Yet, sometimes both discourses overlap. As discussed in this chapter, socio-legal categories created at state level can be relevant, and decisions taken within the international legal order may seek to protect domestic policies meant to encourage the departure of CRAS, even when such policies affect their human rights. Indeed, from the vantage point of the state, the irregular nature of the stay of CRAS predominates and entails that she should leave the territory. Her stay is viewed as temporary. When the international legal order espouses this view, it follows what I call a 'status-centered approach'.

However, in other cases, immigration status is not deemed relevant. Considerations of humanity, dignity, and/or interdependence of rights prevail. Indeed, encroaching or limiting a right will affect the enjoyment of other rights enshrined in international instruments. Protecting the dignity, life, and future of CRAS can demand a different approach that emphasizes one's experience. It thus departs from legal categories and construes the situation in terms of vulnerability and needs. When the international legal order espouses this view, it follows what I call an 'experience-based approach'.

In the process of decision-making, an international perspective thus creates as a counter-narrative on migration that stands out from state-centered discourses on irregularity and fights against abuses. While the international order is not fully impermeable to socio-legal categories created at the state level, the opposite is also true: the international legal order influences domestic legal orders and dominant state-centered narratives. And the narrative it has developed allows for a different stance towards CRAS and migrants unlawfully present on the territory of the state. The global pandemic bluntly reveals social inequalities and vulnerabilities of marginalized populations. Yet, at the same time, it also triggers an upsurge of solidarity that could allow alternative discourses to flourish. The time may thus be ripe for the international rationale to be seized as a performative counter-narrative.

References

Bosniak, Linda. 2007. 'Being Here: Ethical Territoriality and the Rights of Immigrants', *Theoretical Inquiries in Law,* 8(2).

Bosworth, Mary, and Mhairi Guild. 2008. 'Governing Through Migration Control. Security and Citizenship in Britain', *The British Journal of Criminology,* 48(6): 703–19.

Cherfas, Lina. 2006. 'Negotiating access and culture: organizational responses to the healthcare needs of refugees and asylum seekers living with HIV in the UK'. RSC Working Paper Series 33.

Chetail, Vincent. 2013. 'The Human Rights of Migrants in General International Law: From Minimum Standards to Fundamental Rights', *Georgetown Immigration Law Journal* 28(1): 225–55.

———. 2014. 'The transnational movement of persons under general international law – Mapping the customary law foundations of international migration law', in *Research handbook on international law and migration*, Vincent Chetail and Céline Bauloz (eds). Cheltenham: E. Elgar.

Cholewinski, Ryszard Ignacy. 2005. 'Study on Obstacles to Effective Access of Irregular Migrants to Minimum Social Rights'. Council of Europe.

Crépeau, François, Delphine Nakache, and Idil Atak. 2007. 'International Migration: Security Concerns and Human Rights Standards'. *Transcultural Psychiatry*, 44(3): 311–37.

Da Lomba, Sylvie. 2010. 'Immigration Status and Basic Social Human Rights: A Comparative Study of Irregular Migrants' Right to Health Care in France, the UK and Canada'. *Netherlands Quarterly of Human Rights* 28(1): 6–40.

Dauvergne, Catherine. 2014. 'Irregular migration, state sovereignty and the rule of law' in *Research handbook on international law and migration*, Vincent Chetail and Céline Bauloz (eds), 75–92. Cheltenham: E. Elgar.

De Bruycker, Philippe, and Joanna Apap (eds). 2000. Les régularisations des étrangers illégaux dans l'Union européenne. Collection de la Faculté de droit, Université Libre Bruxelles. Bruxelles: E. Bruylant.

European Migration Network. 2016. 'The Return of Rejected Asylum Seekers: Challenges and Good Practices, EMN Synthesis Report for the EMN Focused Study 2016, Migrapol EMN Doc 000', 3 November.

Fox O'Mahony, Lorna, and James A. Sweeney. 2010. 'The Exclusion of (Failed) Asylum Seekers from Housing and Home: Towards an Oppositional Discourse'. *Journal of Law and Society* 37 (2): 285–314.

FRA – European Union Agency for Fundamental Rights. 2011. 'Fundamental rights of migrants in an irregular situation in the European Union', Luxembourg, 21 November.

Frei, Nula, Teresia Gordzielik, Clément De Senarclens, Anne-Cécile Leyvraz, and Robin Stünzi. 2014. 'La lutte contre les abus dans le domaine de l'asile: émergence et développement d'un discours structurant le droit d'asile suisse'. Jusletter, mars.

Harlan, Chico. 2019. 'Denied Asylum, but Not Deported, Migrants in Europe Live in Limbo'. *Washington Post*, 7 August. https://www.washingtonpost.com/world/europe/denied-asylum-but-not-deported-migrants-in-europe-live-in-limbo/2019/08/07/1b9f3082-a4ad-11e9-a767-d7ab84aef3e9_story.html.

Hohmann, Jessie. 2014. *The right to housing: law, concepts, possibilities*. Repr. pbk. Oxford United Kingdom; Portland, Oregon: Hart Publishing.

International Organization for Migration – IOM. 2019. Glossary on Migration, Geneva.

Kraler, Albert. 2009. 'Regularization: A Misguided Option or Part and Parcel of a Comprehensive Policy Response to Irregular Migration?' IMISCOE Working Paper, 24: 1–39.

Legomsky, Stephen H. 2014. 'The removal of irregular migrants in Europe and America', in *Research handbook on international law and migration*, Vincent Chetail and Céline Bauloz (eds), 148–69. Cheltenham: E. Elgar.

Leyvraz, Anne-Cécile. 2018. 'Pourquoi les personnes requérantes d'asile déboutées sont-elles autorisées à saisir des instances internationales ?' *Des faits plutôt que des mythes*. 12 July.

Morris, Lydia. 2010. *Asylum, welfare and the cosmopolitan ideal: a sociology of rights*. Abingdon, Oxon; New York: Routledge.

Paoletti, Emanuela. 2010. 'Deportation, non-deportability and ideas of membership', *RSC Working Paper Series*, 65: 1–28.

PICUM – Platform for International Cooperation on Undocumented Migrants. 2015. 'Protecting undocumented children: Promising policies and practices from governments', Brussels, February.

Plender, Richard. 1988. *International Migration Law*. Rev. 2nd ed. Springer.

Saroléa, Sylvie. 2006. 'Droits de l'homme et migrations: de la protection du migrant aux droits de la personne migrante'. Collection du Centre des droits de l'homme de l'Université catholique de Louvain 3. Bruxelles: Bruylant.

Stünzi, Robin, and Jonathan Miaz. 2020. 'Le discours sur les abus dans le domaine de l'asile: contexte d'émergence dans une perspective historique et européenne', in *Asile et abus. Regards pluridisciplinaires sur un discours dominant*, Anne-Cécile Leyvraz, Raphaël Rey, Damian Rosset, and Robin Stünzi (eds), 27–66. Cohésion sociale et pluralisme culturel. Genève; Zürich: Seismo.

Valenta, Marko, & Kristin Thorshaug. 2011. 'Failed Asylum-Seekers' Responses to Arrangements Promoting Return: Experiences from Norway'. *Refugee Survey Quarterly* 30(2): 1–23.

17

Gendered Border Practices and Violence at the United States-Mexico Border

MITXY MENESES GUTIERREZ

The Mexico-United States border is the most crossed and busiest frontier in the world, with millions of documented border crossings per year (US Customs and Border Protection 2019). These characteristics, along with the political and economic asymmetries between both countries, make it a region of interest for border and migration studies. The complexity of the assemblages of dynamics compels scholars to adopt different approaches to (re)define and (re)understand this region. The socio-cultural and political intersections, paired with other community practices, have become defining conditions of this 'line of division'. As a result, the border has been de-territorialized and observed as a symbolic and metaphorical one. These approaches that include transnationalism furthered the understanding of the US-Mexico border, particularly regarding the adjacent communities that are conditioned by border practices and policies. However, the main focus of migration and border scholarship is placed on undocumented border crossers' practices and narratives. This falls under the traditional notion that vulner-ability is mainly linked to illegality in such a context. Even though the 'title' of the busiest and most crossed border in the world is based on documented border crossers, their narratives have not been of epistemological interest.

In particular, the experiences of transborder women at US ports of entry (POE) between Mexico and the US contribute to the thickening and understanding of this topical border. The unique dynamics of adjacent border communities have made female documented border crossers especially vulnerable with regards to gender violence. This chapter aims to show the prevalence of gender violence at US POEs since the 20th century mainly in the form of sexual violence. For this purpose, a discussion about the critical border approach and transborderism is first provided to set the line of departure. Then, the role of US Customs and Border Protection (CBP) in mediating border crossing experiences is necessary to show the context of power that border crossers frequently face. In the second part of this chapter, an account of women's experiences at US POEs will illustrate the violent practices of border law enforcers. In the early 1900s, women's bodies and imposed sexual identities played an essential role in the establishment of border policies, including the work of border protection and law enforcement agencies.

Furthermore, and based on the experiences of female former transborder pupils and students at the POEs of Mexicali, Baja California-Calexico, California, this chapter will discuss the reproduction of such gender violence between the past decades and the present. The information was gathered through in-depth semi-structured and open-ended interviews with a population of 15 transborder women that attended school during the 1990s or later. The visibility of the narratives by female transborder pupils and students contribute to a more complex understanding of this topical border and their aggressive, systemic practices toward women.

(De)bordering the US-Mexico 'line of division'

The US-Mexico border consists of 3,154 kilometers and was established between the years 1848 and 1854. This politico-administrative division was the aftermath of the Mexican-American War that began in 1846. Through the signing of the Guadalupe-Hidalgo Treaty and the Treaty of Mesilla, Mexico lost 55 percent of its northern territory (Ganster and Lorey 2016, 31–33). This historical episode is pivotal to understand part of the binational dynamics, including northbound Mexican migration that occupies a significant role in Mexico-US relations. The establishment of the border signified the beginning of new socio-cultural, political, economic, and state dynamics of sovereign insistence and resistance that could provide sense to this sudden dividing line.

There is a significant amount of literature concerning different approaches to the border. Such is the case for physical or metaphorical borders underscoring their polysignificance and heterogeneous essence (Balibar 2002, 75–86; Mezzadra and Neilson 2013, 4–7), a more contemporary approach as a state institution to manage and determine the included and excluded (Vila 2000, 1–20), and the purpose they serve for 'world-configuring' (Balibar 2002, 79).

Departing from a critical border studies (CBS) perspective, the border should be understood through the notion of bordering practices defined as:

> The activities which have the effect ... of constituting, sustaining, or modifying borders. Such practices can be both intentional and unintentional; carried out by state actors and non-state actors, including citizens, private security comp-anies, and others engaged in the conduct of what Chris Rumford has called 'borderwork'... emphasize attention to 'the everyday' – the processes through which controls over mobility are attempted and enacted – and the effects of those controls in people's lives in social relations more widely (Parker and Vaughan-Williams 2012, 3).

Bordering practices then make the border intersect with state border policies of control and management. Because of such an interaction, several conditions and dynamics are constructed. Such is the case for transborderism, defined by Norma Iglesias (2011, 43) as 'the frequency, intensity, directionality, and scale of crossing activities; the type of material and symbolic exchanges; and the social and cultural meanings attached to the interactions'. Transborders, including transborder pupils and students, have a complex and deep understanding of border practices (Iglesias 2018, 43–62) and policies of human mobility management, including border-crossing protocols at POEs. Transborder students and pupils in this chapter, who are Mexican or binational, live on the Mexican side of the border and cross it even twice daily to attend school on the US side. Their high levels of interaction with border policies, practices, and mediators make this population relevant for in-depth analysis and understanding of the US-Mexico border. Unfortunately, this demographic group has been mostly understudied in border and migration scholarship (Castañeda 2020, 2), including the experiences of female transborder students that would contribute to the developing of a gender border approach.

Mediating the Border: The Role of CBP

The narratives and experiences of transborder people contribute to the understanding of the border beyond a 'line of division'. They endure the assemblages of power and state policies crystallized in quotidian dynamics. Transborder populations, including pupils and students, live on the Mexican side, but cross the border often or daily to attend to work or school in the US. In this sense, they have to go through US POEs, where their trustworthiness to access to the US will be granted or denied. Currently, there are 48 POEs along the US-Mexico border (GSA 2018). The POE is also a space of contestation, resistance, oppression, and power asymmetry. It is essential to look at these POEs and their implementation of state policies to fully grasp border-crossing dynamics that are mainly mediated by interactions with US CBP.

The infrastructure of US POEs varies throughout the US-Mexico border stripe. These POEs have different ecologies depending on the city and if crossing by car or foot. Although the process of any type of crossing begins before getting in line to cross the border, the main focus in this chapter is on the gendered practices endured by female transborder students and pupils at the Mexicali, Baja California-Calexico, California POE. In general, land-based POEs have been evolving from symbolic demarcations to the techno-structure in place today (Vukov and Sheller 2013, 233–237). POEs serve different purposes, such as human mobility management rendered by CBP officers. Hence, CBP law enforcers become the primary mediators between border crossers and US state politics. Carl Schmitt defines the sovereign as 'he who decides on the exception' (Schmitt 2005, 5). In a Schmittian way, CBP officers are the temporal sovereigns deciding over exception and inclusion of transborder people. Such law enforcement practices crystallize the absorption of documented border crossing and migration into the national security continuum that characterizes contemporary US politics and their War on Terror.

CBP was created in 2003 and has since become one of the largest law enforcement organizations in the world, with approximately 60,000 active officers. After the terrorist attack on the World Trade Center in New York City in September 2001, the Department of Homeland Security consolidated various law enforcement groups, such as the Border Patrol, Immigration Inspectors, US Customs Service, Agricultural Inspectors, and Texas Rangers, among others. Each year, CBP officers process 390 million people through all their POEs (land, air, and sea), apprehend approximately 416,000 persons at POEs, arrest 8,000 wanted criminals, and identify 320,000 persons of national security concern (US Customs and Border Protection 2019). Based on these statistics, the US government is continuously increasing the number of CBP officers to 'safeguard the sovereignty' of the United States from aliens and their inherent dangers. Even though the attack to the Twin Towers happened hundreds of miles away from the US-Mexico border, overall documented border crossers but specially transborder commuters, have suffered the consequences of harsh US migration policies.

Racism and racial profiling have historically been a characteristic of US Border Patrol and CBP (Castañeda 2020, 3), which is justified by the existence of a 'reasonable suspicion' especially in relation to immigration. In 1974, in the case of the *United States v. Brignoni-Ponce*, the US Supreme Court (1974, 885) ruled that a 'characteristic appearance of persons who live in Mexico' is a valid element for reasonable suspicion. Thus, the court's decision in the Brignoni-Ponce case made the US Border Patrol an essentially racist law enforcement organization regardless of their comprehensive advertised approach to their work and the border community.

This decision is especially critical at the US-Mexico border and for documented border crossers who cross northbound and have 'Mexican features'.

In addition to the already precarious and vulnerable situation of transborder students when transiting the border, gender violence worsens their daily dynamic. Female transborder students endure mainly sexual harassment from Mexicans and CBP agents at the POEs while waiting in line to cross the border. Specifically, female documented border crossers are subjects experiencing assemblages of different types of power and violence, such as political and gender-related practices of oppression. Unfortunately, migration scholarship has been mostly interested in the narratives of undocumented women and their transit.

Women and the Construction of the US-Mexico Border

A gender perspective was introduced during the 1980s in migration studies related mostly to undocumented international mobility (Donato et al. 2006, 8–10). This needed approach crystallized the complexity and diversity of experiences in the immigration phenomenon. It is in this sense that the inclusion of the narratives of documented female border crossers is pivotal to the understanding of the border as a space for legal human mobility management.

Gender and sexuality are essential elements on the construction of identity, along with race and class. This entanglement is particularly crucial in a border context where international crossers are continually negotiating their identity with regards to the state (Medrano 2013, 235). Joane Nagel (2003, 14) coined the term 'ethnosexual frontiers', referring to 'territories that lie at the intersections of racial, ethnic, or national boundaries-erotic locations and exotic destinations that are surveilled and supervised, patrolled and policed, regulated and restricted, but that are constantly penetrated by individuals forging sexual links with ethnic Others across ethnic border'. Nagel's definition assertively shows the relation between the state and the construction of identities particularly in a border context.

Part of the identity of the US-Mexico border and thus of its borderlands was constructed throughout the 20th century. The 'vice' and therefore 'dirty' element of the Mexican identity appointed by the US government and its policies had its peak in the 1920s. The era of prohibition in the US (1920–1933) contributed to the explosion of 'vice tourism' in the Mexican borderlands. Mexican bars and cabarets experienced a boom in international customers. US citizens crossed the border southbound to consume alcohol and adult entertainment (Medrano 2013, 236). In the case of the Mexican border city of Mexicali, Eric Schantz (2009) writes about the importance of the Owl Café and Theatre with regards to the local economy and the binational relations with the US, based on the negotiations of contrasting domestic policies concerning the local reality. At that time, US reformers warned about the dangers of Mexicans and their 'vice essence' that represented a direct threat to US moral identity. People from different backgrounds aligned with this conception affecting domestic policies. Law enforcers at the border needed to protect the US population from the 'contaminated' Mexican border crossers, especially women, as they comprised the majority of sex workers (Schantz 2004, 9–14). In words of Medrano (2013, 235) in particular, state actors, including law enforcement agencies, immigration inspectors, border patrol agents, and military personnel racialized and sexualized Mexican women's bodies, emphasizing their 'dangerous femininity' and their perceived threat to the body politic'. Mexican women's bodies and their sexual identity and 'immorality' helped shaped border policies as they became victims of gender violence.

At US POEs, women have suffered sexual violence historically. One of the most discriminatory, racist, and sexually violent episodes at this border is known as the 'Bath Riots'. On January 28th, 1917, Carmelita Torres, a 17-year-old border commuter working as a housekeeper in El Paso, Texas, initiated a riot against the delousing practices implemented at the US POE. She refused to undergo the delousing process, which consisted of transiting through different chambers as part of the 'sanitary process' established to contain the spread of typhus. US authorities believed the disease was prevalent in Mexican revolutionary groups. The first step of the delousing process was to force children, women, and men to remove their clothes to have their body inspected by customs inspectors. Those who had lice were shaved immediately. Their clothes were steam dried and fumigated in a separate chamber that could cause damage. Border commuters that passed the body inspection were directed to a gas chamber to be fumigated with Zyklon B. Then, their disinfected clothes were returned and granted a pass to the US for only eight days. After this period, documented border crossers needed to undergo the process again. This episode had a profound impact on international events. Dorado (2013) found a German pest science journal called *Anzeiger fur Schadlinskundle* written by Dr. Gerhard Peters demonstrating the effectiveness of Zyklon-B on killing pests and referring to the delousing chambers at the Texas border. This doctor then became one of the leading suppliers of such a chemical, which was used in Nazi gas chambers. Peters was convicted during the Nuremberg trials but found not guilty of charges (Dorado 2013, 153–173). Dorado (2013, 165) states that 'the events in Germany did not take place in a historical vacuum. There were important connections between the discourse of eugenics, immigration control, and the racialized politics of public health underlying the disinfection chambers in both parts of the world'.

This humiliating process not only crystallized the systemic discrimination of Mexicans in the US, but also reflected gender violence practices by customs and border officers. One of the reasons that made Carmelita Torres refuse to go through the delousing process was the fact that the border officers in charge of the process took pictures of the naked women and posted them on the wall of a local bar in El Paso, Texas. Carmelita and many other women working in El Paso, but living in the Mexican city of Juárez, Chihuahua were victims of sexual harassment (Dorado 2013, 153–173).

Today, discriminatory, sexual harassment and gender violence are still present in US CBP practices. CBP agents do not post pictures of Mexican or binational women on the walls of local bars, but rather their harassment is made public through Facebook groups. In 2016, a group of attorneys from Philadelphia, Pennsylvania made public several Facebook posts from local authorities with explicitly violent, sexist, and bigoted content (The Plain View Project 2017). In 2019, a Facebook group of CBP officers called 'I am 10-15' was made public. '10-15' is an allusion to a code used by CBP officers for 'aliens in custody' (Thompson 2019). At least 70 officers were identified, out of which 62 were active law enforcers at that time. The alarming content of such posts included sexually explicit comments attacking immigrant women, especially those of Latin American descent. Later that same year, a second Facebook group of CBP officers of the exact nature was disclosed. CBP authorities only expressed that their investigation was still in process (Sands and Valencia 2019).

This systemic gender violence and abuse of power throughout border law enforcement agencies are part of the fabric that transborder students and pupils have to navigate daily. In addition, they experience sexual violence while lining up at POEs on their way to school. It is in this sense that their experiences and narratives of gender violence in such spaces reflect the assemblages of power from both countries crystallizing the Mexican *macho* culture and sexual harassment by US CBP officers. When this 'gender violent combo' is part of one's daily routine, it is easy for victims to normalize it and not feel as transgressed as they would in a different context. Currently, there is no mechanism in place to generate information with regards to gender violence suffered specifically by documented border crossers at US POEs. The lack of indicators and data, unfortunately, perpetuates the invisibility of their condition.

Female Former Transborder Pupils and Students at the Mexicali-Calexico Port of Entry

The word Mexicali is a composition of the words Mexico and California. The name of the city on the other side, *el otro lado*, is Calexico, which is a composition of the words California and Mexico. The city deal of Mexicali includes a dotted line in the name representing the border with the US. As for the city deal of Calexico, the Mexican flag is included along with the motto, 'Where California and Mexico Meet'. In a way, the conception of these twin cities, a term regularly given to urban duos (Gildersleeve 1979, 1–5; Kearney and Knopp 1995, 2; Alegría 2012, 148–174) was strongly linked with each other. The historical link between Calexico and Mexicali contributes to the development of border dynamics, such as transborderism.

Mexicali has two land POEs in the area, Calexico and Calexico East. The latter was constructed in 1996 (General Services Administration 2010, 1) to help with heavy traffic and crossings to Calexico. With data from 1996 to 2020, the Calexico POE reports a total of 129,056,999 of personal vehicles, 278,482,108 of passenger vehicles and 132,667,217 of pedestrians (Bureau of Transportation Statistics, 2020). However, during the same period, the number of pedestrian border crossers decreased at the Calexico POE with an average of 5,300,000 per year (US Custom and Border Protection 2020). These numbers reflect the regular crossing dynamics of this border city with a population of just 988,417 (INEGI 2020). The transborder community represents an essential part of this circular border motion, as stated previously.

The invisibility of the transborder phenomenon renders a lack of updated statistical information preventing us from having an accurate picture of this dynamic. With numbers from 2015, the *Prontuario sobre Movilidad y Migración Internacional: Dimensiones del Fenómeno en México*, published by the Mexican government, estimated a total of approximately 124,000 transborder migrants, out of which 43,918 (35.2 percent) were women (Government of Mexico 2015). This publication showed that 36,470 people crossed the border daily to study, and an additional 3,129 crossed to study and work in the US. A total of 39,599 transborder students represent 31.8 percent of all transborder migrants. The Mexican border city of Tijuana, Baja California, holds approximately 37.2 percent of all transborder population, which means a total of 46,337 migrants. Out of which, the female population was of 14,808. The border city of Mexicali has a transborder population of 18,329, and the female population consists of 6,209 migrants. With regard to specifically transborder students and pupils, Tijuana has a population of approximately 9,221 (19.9 percent) and Mexicali has a population of roughly 4,472 (24.4 percent). These numbers show that at least 13,696 transborder students and pupils crossed the border daily to attend school in the US. (CONAPO 2017). However, that number could be potentially higher now as not all transborder pupils and students are open about their daily dynamic. One of the requirements for accessing US public education is their place of residence since the budget for education relies heavily on property taxation (Kenyon 2007, 4). Under this rule, US students living on the Mexican side of the US-Mexico border should not have access to US public schools. These students or the parents of the pupils use different mechanisms to meet the requirements.

If analyzed by city, these students do not represent half of the population commuting daily. However, if interpreted by states, they do represent 44.3 percent of the commuters in the Baja California-California region. In other words, in Mexicali, approximately 4,780 students attended school daily in the US and, in the case of Tijuana, we are referring to about 10,464 students with the same characteristics. In the case of Mexicali, and taking into consideration all levels of education, including postgraduate students, transborder students represented 1.65 percent of all students in Calexico. In the case of Tijuana, they represented the 2.23 percent of all students in San Diego, California (Rocha and Orraca 2018, 109–111). Unfortunately, there is no statistical information disaggregated by gender. The lack of data furthers the invisibility of women's experiences and their epistemological value to the understanding of the US-Mexico border.

As stated previously, the transborder dynamic is a complex process of state policies and socio-cultural intersections. This practice renders a deep understanding of the methods that constitute the US-Mexico border. The day for these students can begin as early as 3 a.m. They need to get ready and prepare to line up at the POE, which could take up to several hours. Even if it seems to be a regular day, anything can happen at the border. They cross the border by car or foot. If driving, they would sleep or have breakfast while waiting in line. If they cross the border by foot, they would mostly do homework or eat something. These are not the only border hacks these students developed but are amongst the most common.

Those crossing by foot were more likely to be by themselves, with siblings, or with friends. However, the absence of a parent or adult is typical. This means that those transborder pupils are documented unaccompanied children crossing one of the most policed and surveilled borders in the world. Nevertheless, they are not included in the traditional notion of unaccompanied children as it exclusively focuses on the undocumented population. This indicates that documented unaccompanied children border crossers are not likely to be considered vulnerable. In addition, this is a normalized border dynamic in the US-Mexico region but not well researched or documented. In this context, the absence of a guardian in their binational transit contributes to the struggles and violence endured by female transborder pupils and students.

The Mexicali-Calexico POE that was modified in 2020, had a unique ecology. This location was surrounded by shops or stands selling all kind of products, including Mexican indigenous handcrafts. The Hotel del Norte is one of the most iconic buildings in the city and present in most of the stories of documented border crossers. There is also a Chinese Pagoda that reminds passers-by of the immigration history of the city and the close connection with the Chinese population. This POE is in a busy location where the heterogeneous population confluence on their entry or exit to the US. The designated path where the pedestrians line up to cross northbound is also surrounded by shops, currency exchange locales, and pharmacies. This area also attracts homeless people asking for money and peddlers. This border area is considered a dangerous zone by locals based on the amount of violent incidents that occur. This space of concern is part of the daily school trajectory of transborder students and pupils, which is experienced differently depending if people cross by car, by themselves or accompanied, and depending on one's gender. In general, it is in this area of the POE where female transborder students and pupils experience gender violence.

Gender violence in Mexico has been increasing exponentially in the last years. Now, Mexico is experiencing a critical phase of gender violence. In a study published in June 2020 by the Mexican National Institute for Women, the government reported that approximately 66 percent of women age 15 or older had experienced some type of violence in their lifetime (INEGI 2020). Furthermore, 10 women are victims of femicide daily. The Mexican state of Baja California is ranked as one of the most violent states for women, having 81 femicides between January and April 2020 (INMUJERES 2020). In addition to the risk these female pupils and students face when interacting with US CBP officers, they endure sexual harassment waiting in line or transiting the POE while still on the Mexican side. Unfortunately, the male population present in such a space shouts obscenities at these female students. Such conduct is normalized, as there are no repercussions for it and therefore, they are easily and continuously reproduced.

Specifically speaking of gender violence in the form of sexual harassment, which includes sexual offenses and comments directed at the body or gender, the National Institute for Statistics, Geography, and Computing (INEGI) reported that in the second semester of 2019, 13.6 percent of women age 18 or older had experienced sexual harassment in their city (INEGI 2020).

The former female transborder students and pupils in the Mexicali-Calexico context do have 'anecdotes' where they felt uncomfortable either in line or when crossing to the US. Most of them recalled that it was quotidian to be the target of sexual comments by the male population present at the POEs. Such offenses included comments about their bodies and uniforms. It is worth pointing out that these episodes happened when they were aged 13 or older and without parental supervision. Just a few of them said that their parents would accompany them the entire way. Hence, this population is not only vulnerable to the harsh methods of CBP but also because of their gender, as stated previously. When female former transborder pupils or students described the POE, they would commonly portray it as a dangerous place due to overall insecurity and sexual harassment. In contrast, male former transborder students or pupils only mentioned the levels of insecurity in Mexicali that would extend to the POE.

Concerning the encounters with CBP officers, one-third of this female population reported that they have felt uncomfortable or offended at least once. They recall being asked if they had a partner, what they do after school, or other types of insinuations. Since dealing with an authority with a historical lack of accountability, none of them filed a complaint. It was normal, and because nothing serious happened after the encounter, they did not feel the need to report it. Moreover, they felt that reporting it would only cause them troubles in their daily routine. A myriad of these type of cases by female transborder students goes unnoticed by the authorities and scholarship.

Without a doubt, these stories illustrate the pervasiveness of gendered border violence that, regardless the age or nationality, female transborder students and pupils still face today. Their bodily experiences contribute to the analysis of the US-Mexico border mostly seen through the undocumented migration lens and trade. Documented border crossers, especially women, hold a unique perspective of the border and of how their gender shapes transborder dynamics by showing the assemblages of violence they endured daily. Transborder women are not exempt from gender violence at the US-Mexico border; they experience it daily.

Conclusion

Aggressive gendered border practices and violence have been part of the construction of the US-Mexico border. Women's bodies and sexual identity shaped border policies that are still in place today. Through a critical border studies perspective, the border is conformed and built through everyday practices, such as transborderism. Female documented border crossers have been experiencing gender violence at POEs as the episode of the 'Bath Riots' illustrate. Carmelita Torres was the first transborder woman to rebel against gendered border violence and sexual harassment by border protection law enforcers at the El Paso POE. Today, similar practices by CBP are present on technological and social platforms. Such is the case with Facebook groups where active and former CBP officers post sexist and discriminatory comments towards immigrants. The experiences of female former transborder students or pupils provide a snapshot of the prevalence of gender violence suffered at the Mexicali-Calexico Port of Entry.

Until we take into consideration the narratives of documented women crossing the border, we will be unable to fully grasp what constitutes it, its essence, and all the levels of violence suffered by border crossers, especially when conditioned by their gender. These stories need to be further researched and, most importantly, to be told.

References

Alegría, Tito. 2012. 'The Transborder Metropolis in Question: The Case of Tijuana and San Diego', in *Tijuana Dreaming: Life and Art at the Global Border*, edited by Josh Kun and Fiamma Montezemolo, 148–174. Durham and London. Duke University Press.

Balibar, Etienne. 2002. *Politics and The Other Scene*. London. Verso.

Castañeda, Estefanía. 2020. 'Transborder (in)securities: transborder commuters' perceptions of U.S. Customs and Border Protection policing at the Mexico–U.S. border', *Politics, Groups, and Identities*, 1–20.

Comisión Nacional Nacional de Población y Unidad de Política Migratoria. 2016. *Prontuario sobre Movilidad y Migración Internacional: Dimensiones del fenómeno en México*. https://www.gob.mx/cms/uploads/attachment/file/192259/Prontuario_movilidad_y_migraci_n_internacional_Parte2.pdf.

Consejo Nacional de Población. 2017. Prontuario sobre movilidad y migración internacional. Gobierno de Mexico.

Donato, Katharine, Gabaccia, Donna, Holdaway, Jennifer, Manalansan, Martin, and Pessar, Patricia. 2006. 'A Glass Half Full? Gender in Migration Studies'. *International Migration Review,* 40(1): 3–26.

Dorado, David. 2013. 'Charting the legacy of the revolution: how the Mexican Revolution transformed El Paso's cultural and urban landscape', in *Open borders to a revolution: culture, politics, and migration*, edited by Jaime Marroquín, Adela Pineda, and Magdalena Mieri, M. 153–173. Washington, D.C.: Smithsonian Institution Scholarly Press.

Ganster, Paul with Lorey, David. 2016. *The U.S. Mexican Border Today: Conflict and Cooperation in Historical Perspective*. London. Rowman & Littlefield.

General Services Administration. 2017. *Fact Sheet – Construction Calexico West U.S. Land Port of Entry Phase II Calexico CA*. https://www.gsa.gov/cdnstatic/FY2017_Calexico_CA_Calexico_West_U_S_Land_Port_of_Entry_Phase_II.pdf.

General Services Administration. 2018. Land Ports of Entry Overview. https://www.gsa.gov/real-estate/gsa-properties/land-ports-of-entry-overview

Iglesias Prieto, Norma. 2011. 'El otro lado de la línea/The other side of the line', in *GeoHumanities: Art, History, text at the edge of place* edited by Michael Dear, Jim Ketchum, Sarah Luria, Doug Richardson. 143–153. New York. Routledge.

Iglesias Prieto, Norma. 2018. 'Creative Potential and Social Change. Independent Visual Arts Spaces in Tijuana', in *Cultural and Creative Industries. A Path to Entrepreneurship and Innovation* edited by Marta Peris-Ortiz, Mayer Cabrera-Flores, and Arturo Serrano-Santoyo. 43–62. New York. Springer.

Instituto Nacional de Estadística y Geografía. 2020. *Encuesta Nacional de Seguridad Pública Urbana*. https://www.inegi.org.mx/contenidos/saladeprensa/boletines/2020/ensu/ensu2020_01.pdf

Instituto Nacional de Estadística y Geografía. 2020. *Información de México para Niños*. http://cuentame.inegi.org.mx/monografias/informacion/bc/poblacion/

Instituto Nacional de Mujeres. 2020. *Violencia contra las mujeres: indicadores básicos en tiempos de pandemia*. https://www.gob.mx/cms/uploads/attachment/file/558770/vcm-indicadores911.pdf

Kearney, Milo, Knopp, Anthony.1995. *Border Cuates: A History of the U.S.-Mexican Twin Cities*. Austin, Texas. Eakin Press Eakin Press.

Kenyon, Daphne. 2007. *The Property Tax-School Funding Dilemma*. Cambridge, Massachusetts. Lincoln Institute of Land Policy. https://www.lincolninst.edu/sites/default/files/pubfiles/the-property-tax-school-funding-dilemma-full_0.pdf

Medrano, Marlene. 2013. 'Sexuality, Migration, and Tourism in the 20th Century U.S.-Mexico Borderlands', *History Compass 11/13.* 235–246. Minnesota University. https://onlinelibrary.wiley.com/doi/epdf/10.1111/hic3.12039?saml_referrer

Mezzadra, Sandro and Neilson, Brett. 2013. *Border as a Method, or the multiplication of labor.* Durham, North Carolina. Duke University Press.

Nagel, Joane. 2003. Race, Ethnicity, and Sexuality: Intimate Intersections, Forbidden Frontiers. Oxford. Oxford University Press.

Parker, Noel., Vaughan-Williams, Nick. 2012. 'Critical Border Studies: Broadening and Deepening the "Lines in the Sand" Agenda', *Geopolitics* 17(4): 727–733.

Plan View Project. 2017. https://www.plainviewproject.org/about

Rocha, David, Orraca, Pedro. 2018. 'Estudiantes de educación superior transfronterizos: Residir en México y estudiar en Estados Unidos', *Frontera norte*, 30(59): 103–128.

Schantz, Eric. 2001. 'All Night at the Owl: The Social and Political Relations of Mexicali's Red Light District, 1909–1925', *Journal of the Southwest,* 43(4): 91–44.

Schmitt, Carl. 2005. *Political Theology: Four Chapters on the Concept of Sovereignty*, translated by George Schwab. Chicago and London: The University of Chicago Press.

Supreme Court of the United States. 1974. *U.S. Reports: United States v. Brignoni-Ponce.* https://www.loc.gov/item/usrep422873/

U.S. Custom and Border Protection. 2019. *On a Typical Day in Fiscal Year 2019, CBP.* Accessed 18 August 2020. https://www.cbp.gov/newsroom/stats/typical-day-fy2019

U.S. Custom and Border Protection. 2020. Border Crossing Entry Data. https://explore.dot.gov/views/BorderCrossingData/Annual?:isGuestRedirectFromVizportal=y&:embed=y

Vila, Pablo. 2000. *Crossing Borders, Reinforcing Borders Social Categories, Metaphors, and Narrative Identities on the U.S.-Mexico Frontier.* Austin. University of Texas Press.

Vukov, Tamara and Sheller, Mimi. 2013. 'Border work: surveillant assemblages, virtual fences, and tactical counter-media', *Social Semiotics*, 23(2): 225–24.

18

European Union Readmission Agreements: Deportation as a Gateway to Displacement?

MANUELA DA ROSA JORGE

In 2015, the European Union (EU) adopted measures to tackle the perceived 'refugee crisis'. Among them were the elaboration of the European Agenda on Migration in May 2015 by the European Commission, which developed a strategy to tackle 'irregular' migration into Europe (European Commission 2015a, 2), alongside a specific 'return' strategy called the EU Action Plan on Return in September 2015. The Action Plan set out that the 'return' of 'irregular migrants who do not have a right to stay in the EU to their home countries, in full respect of the principle of *non-refoulement*, is an essential part of EU's comprehensive efforts to address migration and in particular to reduce irregular migration' (European Commission 2015b, 2).

By the end of 2015, one of the EU's key priorities in addressing migration – as stipulated in the Agenda and in the Action Plan – was to accelerate the 'removal' of 'irregular' migrants and 'failed' asylum-seekers through readmission agreements with non-EU countries (Carrera and Allsopp 2017, 70, 73). Hence, the EU reinforced and/or edited its existing EU readmission agreements (EURAs) with non-EU countries, and agreed new ones, thus including EURAs among the main tools of the EU's migration 'policy-toolbox' (Zaiotti 2016, 8) focused on the 'removal' of 'illegal' individuals from EU territory, including 'rejected' asylum-seekers (Cassarino 2015, 219; Giuffré 2016, 263; Trauner 2017, 252). Essentially, readmission agreements are policy instruments (Wolff and Trauner 2014, 11) that 'stipulate the obligation to readmit nationals of the country with which the EU has signed the agreement' (European Commission 2005, 2).

A considerable body of literature has been developed on EURAs, focusing largely on the EU and its institutions (Carrera 2016), the relationships between EU member states and institutions (Trauner 2017), the efficiency of agreements for the EU (Carrera 2016; Carrera and Allsopp 2017; Emiliani 2016; Giuffré 2016), and the increasing numbers of informalized agreements rather than legally binding ones (Carrera 2016; Cassarino 2007, 2017; Trauner and Slominsky 2020). However, the serious consequences for people subjected to these agreements have been largely neglected in the prior research and are rarely analyzed within the EURAs framework – with the exception of studies focusing on their legal implications for deportees' human rights (Carrera 2016, Giuffré 2020). In contrast, studies focused on the practice of deportation more broadly (i.e., not within the EURAs framework) have investigated the violent implications for those who are deported and what happens post-deportation, demonstrating that deportees live in a permanent state of marginalization and precarity (De Genova 2017, 2018; De Genova and Peutz 2010; Khosravi 2017, 2018; Majidi, 2017; Schuster and Majidi 2013, 2019).

Therefore, by combining an analysis of EURAs with a focus on deportation, this chapter discusses the practices of 'readmission' and 'return' as stipulated in EURAs as de facto deportations by showcasing the implications of this policy for those subjected to it as an example of the EU's regulatory power on mobility, which subjugates some populations by exposing them to yet another re-displacement through deportation. Theoretically, I employ Gibney's (2013) conceptualization of deportation as a form of forced migration and related literatures, while empirically, I utilize the 2016 Joint Way Forward Declaration (JWF) between the EU and the Islamic Republic of Afghanistan as a case study. The JWF is particularly revealing, not least because it was signed when the situation in Afghanistan was deteriorating: between January and August 2016 alone, almost 250,000 Afghans became internally displaced, bringing the total number of internally displaced individuals there to 1.2 million (UNHCR 2016).

Consequently, through a critical analysis of international organizations' reports, official statements, and academic works, I discuss the JWF's negotiation and implementation in order to showcase the normalization of deportation as 'return' and 'removal' and the enforcement of this policy through pressure and conditionalities on the part of the EU. I also demonstrate how, despite acknowledging the worsening situation in Afghanistan and denying the financial conditionality attached to the readmission of Afghans, the EU used discourses of partnership, cooperation, and development to justify and legitimize deportations. I conclude by arguing that despite this rhetoric, the forcible removal of individuals from Europe to Afghanistan disguises the violent outcomes of such policies for deportees, namely marginalization, abandonment, and for many, another displacement and re-departure. Accordingly, this chapter is divided into three parts. The first part briefly illustrates the theoretical background underpinning our argument, the second part discusses the case study, and the final part concludes.

Deportation as Forced Migration: A Gateway to Further Displacement?

There is no definition for the term 'deportation' in the European Commission – Asylum and Migration Glossary; instead, it is synonymous with 'removal' (EU Glossary 2018, 320). In the EU context, 'removal' is described as 'the enforcement of the obligation to return, namely the physical transportation out of the EU Member State' (EU Glossary 2018, 320) as stipulated in Article 3(5) of Directive 2008/115/EC (Return Directive). It also establishes that:

> Under EU legislation, removal is a specific form of forced return. While deportation and removal often are understood as synonyms, deportation is not used as a legal term in all EU Member States (only DE, FI, IE and UK define 'deportation' in their legislation) and is only applicable as a general concept by the public, sometimes with a negative connotation. Because of this variation, 'removal' is the preferred term to use (EU Glossary 2018, 320).

In contrast, 'return' is defined as 'the movement of a person going from a host country back to a country of origin, country of nationality or habitual residence usually after spending a significant period of time in the host country whether voluntary or forced, assisted or spontaneous' (EU Glossary 2018, 329).

In this context, according to some scholars, deportation is a form of forced migration that 'has been made fit for the modern liberal State' (Dunn, quoted in Gibney 2013, 123) as it is legitimate for a sovereign state to deport 'aliens' from its territory if they have breached immigration laws (Gibney 2008). Similarly, De Genova (2017, 9) illustrates what the deportation of 'unwanted' individuals means to the deporting state: 'Here today, gone tomorrow. Out of sight, out of mind. Case closed. Thus, at least from the perspective of the deporting state power, deportation appears to be the final act, the proverbial last word'. Yet, it should be highlighted that despite the 'legitimate' and legal aspects involved in the expulsion of those considered by a 'destination state' as 'aliens', the act of removing an individual from a territory 'is one of the most severe forms of exclusions from a society and community' (Trauner 2017, 251), particularly since many deportees are 'returned' to conflict areas, 'converting their deportations into de facto acts of refoulement, whereby return may subject them to persecution, extortion, rape, torture, and death' (De Genova 2018, 254).

Due to the legitimization of deportation, in recent decades, this practice has become somewhat normalized (Schuster and Majidi 2019, 90–91) within migration policies in Western states, which regard it as a natural outcome in the state's instrumentalization process of governing mobility (De Genova and Peutz 2010, 1, 3; Khosravi 2018, 4). Thus, calling deportation 'return' naturalizes the process, since people are returned to where they are said to belong (Schuster and Majidi 2019, 92). Consequently, the use of terms like 'return' or 'readmission' deflect attention away from the act of expulsion and its devastating implications for deportees by implying a one-fits-all approach via the constructed and imagined natural order of going back home (Khosravi 2018, 11; Schuster and Majidi 2019, 92).

Further, this language conflates varied going-back-home dynamics wherein some individuals are forcibly expelled (e.g., deported 'failed' asylum-seekers and 'illegal' migrants), while others freely choose to go back (e.g., the end of a 'migration cycle', especially regarding labor) (Cassarino 2015, 220; Khosravi 2018, 11). Yet, since deportation is rarely voluntary (Andrijasevic and Walters 2010, 993; Collyer 2018, 106), to 'return' means to be forcibly removed from a 'destination state' to a place assumed to be 'home'. Nevertheless, the place considered 'home' by the deporting state might not be home for the deportee; instead, it usually means being sent back into a conflict situation, and therefore a higher risk of further displacement (Khosravi 2018, 12; Schuster and Majidi 2019, 100).

Picozza (2017, 235) asserts that consideration of the different trajectories followed by people on the move, regardless of the decisions of the 'destination state', is key to understanding the heterogeneity of such trajectories, which defy any linear and static order in migrating from a 'home' country to a 'destination country'. The heterogeneity involved is far more complex and less linear than orthodox approaches to the study of deportation have assumed. Consequently, if we analyze migration as a multidirectional process (Schuster and Majidi 2013, 2019) comprising multiple cycles instead of a pre-determined cycle of emigration-immigration-return (Cassarino 2015, 217), or as a unidirectional movement between departure and arrival, we can see that deportation is not the end of a migration cycle, but a rupture in a complex process that affects and disrupts the lives of both those being deported and those whose lives depend on that emigrant (Collyer 2018, 108; De Genova and Peutz 2010, 2; Khosravi 2018, 2; Schuster and Majidi 2013, 222–223).

In this context, I argue that, despite employing a language of 'return' and 'readmission', deportation is at the heart of EURAs and similar expulsion policy mechanisms, as in practice, they systematize international agreements and similar declarations with third countries to deport third-country nationals (Trauner 2017, 251). In such policies, 'return merely refers to the act of removing unauthorised migrants and rejected asylum-seekers from European territory. Moreover, it does not take into account migrants' post-return conditions' (Cassarino 2015, 219), as the language is carefully politically constructed to legitimize deportation. In this regard, Cassarino (2015, 220) brilliantly argues that 'as long as no distinction is made [between return and deportation], current "return" policies are not return policies' – they are deportation policies that forcibly displace individuals. I concur with De Genova's observation (2018, 255) that:

> While deportations are plainly debasing and destructive for individual deportees, their loved ones, and their wider communities, the bureaucratic rationality that coldly executes such severely punitive measures as "standard operating procedure," and the consequently heartless disregard for the veritable cruelty of deportation for those whose lives are thereby derailed, convert a systemic violence into the simple and banal functionality of a presumptively efficient governmental apparatus.

Therefore, I understand the act of an individual's 'removal' from a given territory (i.e., their deportation) as a form of forced migration (Gibney 2013) with serious implications for deportees, including re-displacement.

The Joint Way Forward Declaration

At the beginning of 2016, an EU memo was leaked showing that while they acknowledged the deteriorating situation in Afghanistan 'with record levels of terrorist attacks and civilian casualties', both the European Commission and the European External Action Service (EEAS) also saw this situation as a driving factor for Afghans to migrate to Europe, so they called 'for a strengthening of interventions to maintain asylum space in the region' (StateWatch 2016, 3). The memo emphasized that 'more than 80,000 [Afghans] persons could potentially need to be returned in the near future' (StateWatch 2016, 2). Similarly, the EU Action Plan on Return prioritized Afghanistan among those countries requiring high-level dialogues on 'readmission' (European Commission 2015b, 12).

Against this backdrop, in recent years, different EU member states, including Denmark, Finland, the Netherlands, Sweden and the United Kingdom (prior to Brexit), have concluded informal readmission agreements with Afghanistan (StateWatch 2016, 5; Trauner and Slominsky 2020, 13). Authors have argued that, due to the difficulty of conducting negotiations with third countries and the bureaucratic nature of legally binding agreements, informal arrangements such as declarations, bilateral deals, exchanges of letters, and memorandums of understanding are increasingly seen by the EU as alternatives to legally binding readmission agreements (Carrera 2016, 10; Cassarino 2007, 2017; Giuffré 2016, 272; Trauner 2017, 253–254; Trauner and Slominski 2020, 2). These informalized agreements reduce bureaucracy and usually bypass parliamentary scrutiny and debate in both the EU and the non-EU country, raising the risk that fundamental protection mechanisms such as human rights norms might be ignored (Cassarino 2017, 94; Trauner 2017, 256). Yet, importantly, Giuffré (2020, 8–9) recently argued that legally binding agreements and more flexible arrangements should be considered together when analyzing and studying EU 'readmission' policies, because despite their (important) legal differences, their aim is the same: to expel 'unwanted' third-country individuals from the EU to non-EU countries.

By the end of 2016, alongside an international conference in Brussels dedicated to issues related to Afghanistan, the EU and the Islamic Republic of Afghanistan signed the JWF Declaration. It aimed to deport 'refused' Afghan asylum-seekers and 'irregular' Afghan migrants from Europe to Afghanistan over four years (2016–2020) and to deter others from migrating to Europe, in return for the EU maintaining its current aid funding and offering additional financial support to deportees (Afghanistan Analysts 2016; EEAS 2016a; European Commission 2016a). Deportations were to take place through scheduled and non-scheduled flights from different EU member states in coordination with the European Border and Coast Guard Agency (Frontex), and there were plans to build a terminal at Kabul airport exclusively to receive deportees (EEAS 2016a, 4).

As an informalized agreement, the JWF did not create legal obligations; instead, it 'pave[d] the way for a structural dialogue and cooperation on migration issues' between the EU and Afghanistan, and it 'establish[ed] a rapid, effective, and manageable process for a smooth, dignified, and orderly return of Afghan nationals' to Afghanistan (EEAS 2016a, 1). However, it did create solid commitments between the two parties, similar to a formal readmission agreement (Trauner and Slominski 2020, 4–5).

Negotiations and Reactions

According to a report from the Afghanistan Analysts Network (AAN 2016), more than a year passed before the JWF was signed due to internal disagreements on the Afghan side. In contrast to Afghan President Ashraf Ghani, the Minister for Refugees and Repatriations, Sayed Alemi Balkhi, and the Minister for Foreign Affairs, Salahuddin Rabbani, did not agree to sign the JWF and suggested that it receive parliamentary scrutiny and voting, which caused internal friction, leaving EU diplomats worried about delays (AAN 2016), as this statement from the European Commission and EEAS shows:

> The dialogue with Afghan authorities is difficult and uneven. While President Ghani and parts of the Afghan Government are publicly committed to cooperate on readmission, other members of the Government do not appear to facilitate the return of irregular migrants, while attempting to re-negotiate conditions to restrict the acceptance of returnees (StateWatch 2016, 4).

After the impasse in the Afghan parliament, the Afghan Deputy Minister of Refugees and Repatriations, Alema Alema, together with Deputy Head of the EU Delegation to Afghanistan, George Cunningham, 'quietly signed the Joint Way Forward in a low-key event at the presidential palace on 2 October 2016' (AAN 2016). The next day, the EU released the following press statement:

> Yesterday, the European Union and Afghanistan reached an important political arrangement, 'The EU-Afghanistan Joint Way Forward on Migration issues', to effectively tackle the challenges in both the European Union and Afghanistan linked to irregular migration. This is the result of a constructive dialogue based on partnership and a willingness to enhance dialogue and bilateral cooperation in this area. (EEAS 2016c).

Upon the announcement, several international and European organizations, including Amnesty International, the European Council on Refugees and Exiles (ECRE), the European Association for the Defense of Human Rights (AEDH), PRO ASYL, Save the Children, Oxfam, and the International Federation for Human Rights (FIDH), jointly signed a letter to the members of the European Parliament (MEP) stressing their concerns (Relief Web 2016). The letter stressed that the JWF had been signed without proper parliamentary and civil society scrutiny, preventing 'any form of democratic accountability'; thus, it would instigate 'major risks of rights violations such as the principle of non-refoulement, protection against collective expulsions and the right to asylum' (Relief Web 2016, 1). Dimitris Christopoulos, FIDH President, argued that 'attempts by the EU to leverage its humanitarian and development aid to Afghanistan to secure the readmission of Afghan nationals in their country of origin represents a new low. This dubious deal negotiated behind closed doors opens the door to the deportation of an unlimited number of failed asylum-seekers' (FIDH 2016).

Moreover, some members of the European Parliament, such as Dutch MEP

Judith Sargentini, opposed the Declaration, arguing that the EU was breaking its own laws by sending people back to war zones, including violating the international legal principle of *non-refoulement* (Sargentini quoted in Schultz 2018). In 2017, the ECRE argued that an asymmetric European priority was placed on the number of Afghans being deported, on the speed of those deportations, and on short-term solutions to the EU's own perceived 'crisis, rather than on negotiating a sustainable solution that considers Afghanistan's interests and needs, the Afghan people's history of mobility, and their motives for fleeing their homeland in its current situation (ECRE 2017a, 13).

The Declaration: Reciprocity, Financial conditionalities, Human Rights, and Safe Areas

In theory, the obligations of the parties involved in readmission agreements and similar arrangements appear equal and reciprocal (Cassarino 2007, 182; Giuffré 2016, 268; Trauner 2017, 253). However, authors have argued that, although each side has its own agenda, the EU often has leverage to offer incentives to non-EU countries, such as development aid, financial packages, visa facilitation, and other so-called benefits to persuade third countries to sign readmission agreements (Cassarino 2007, 183; Giuffré 2016, 268; Trauner 2017, 253; Wolff and Hadj Abdou 2017, 387). For instance, both the Agenda and the Action Plan asserted that the EU should make use of all leverage available to return non-EU citizens residing irregularly in Europe back to their countries of origin, or to the transit countries through which they arrived in the EU (European Commission 2015a, 10; 2015b, 13–14; Trauner 2016, 319).

The language utilized throughout the JWF mentions 'partnership' and 'reciprocity' between the EU and Afghanistan. It stresses that both parties face migration challenges and that to tackle them, 'solidarity, determination, and collective efforts' are needed from both sides (EEAS 2016a, 1). It also contends that 'the return programmes and reintegration assistance are separate from and irrespective of the development assistance aid provided to Afghanistan' (EEAS 2016a, 6). Nevertheless, reports and interviews with members of the Afghan government revealed concern over the conditions of the EU's allocation of aid to Afghanistan.

To attempt to persuade ministers of Parliament (MPs) to support the Declaration's signing, the Afghan Minister of Finance, Eklil Hakimi, told the Afghan Parliament that 'if Afghanistan does not cooperate with EU countries on the refugee crisis, this will negatively impact the amount of aid allocated to Afghanistan' (AAN 2016). Salahuddin Rabbani, the Afghan Minister for Foreign Affairs, also stated in parliament that 'European countries told us: you should either receive our aid to Afghan refugees in our countries, or for development projects in Afghanistan; you can choose between these two options. They asserted very clearly that they could not help Afghanistan in both areas' (AAN 2016).

Similarly, at the time of signing of the Declaration, Rasmussen (2016) reported in the *Guardian* newspaper that 'the pressure on Afghanistan is part of a broader EU strategy of making aid to poor countries conditional on them accepting deported migrants'. Hence, because Afghanistan is highly dependent on humanitarian and foreign aid (StateWatch 2016, 5), the Afghan government had little choice but to sign (Quie and Hakimi 2018). In an interview in 2018, Hafiz Ahmad Miakhel, a spokesman for the Afghan Ministry of Refugees and Repatriations, stated that the Afghan government 'have 1.6 million refugees back from Pakistan and Iran... We [the Afghan government] have signed the deal [with the EU] and we are cooperating, but we have requested again and again that Europe review its Afghan policies' (Miakhel, 2018).

Yet, despite apparently making the EU's financial aid allocation dependent on the Afghan government receiving Afghan deportees from Europe, EU officials denied this connection, with the High Representative of the EU for Foreign Affairs and Vice-President of the European Commission, Federica Mogherini, claiming at the time of the Brussels Conference, 'There is never, never a link between our development aid and whatever we do with migration' (EEAS 2016b). Nevertheless, in a leaked memo, the Commission and EEAS stated that:

> The EU should stress that to reach the objective of the Brussels Conference to raise financial commitments 'at or near current levels' it is critical that substantial progress has been made in the negotiations with the Afghan Government on migration by early summer, giving the Member States and other donors the confidence that Afghanistan is a reliable partner able to deliver (StateWatch 2016, 8).

Although the Declaration references the 1951 United Nations Convention Relating to the Status of Refugees and its 1967 New York Protocol, the EU Charter on Fundamental Rights, and the Universal Declaration of Human Rights (EEAS 2016a, 2), it 'ignores both the inhumane upheaval and trauma caused by deportation and discredits the imminent danger facing asylum-seekers upon returning to their home country' (Wakil 2018). The leaked memo detailed that even though conflict was recognized as widespread in Afghan-istan, some areas of the country needed to be classified as 'safe' so that

Afghans could be deported (StateWatch 2016, 3). In legal terms, this 'safe areas' prerogative within a non-EU country can be found in Article 8 (1) of Council Directive 2004/83/EC (the Qualification Directive), which states that 'an applicant is not in need of international protection if in a part of the country of origin there is no well-founded fear of being persecuted or no real risk of suffering serious harm and the applicant can reasonably be expected to stay in that part of the country.'

Nonetheless, organizations such as the United Nations Assistance Mission in Afghanistan (UNAMA 2018), Oxfam (2018), and Amnesty International (2017a, 2018) have claimed that the EU and its member states made efforts to present parts of Afghanistan as 'safe' for Afghans to be deported to through the internal safe area prerogative, thus prioritizing the number of individuals being deported over the actual situation in the country (Relief Web 2016, 1). The policy classified Kabul as safe for Afghans to live in, and consequently to be deported to, despite it being among the least secure cities in the country (EASO 2018, 26–27; Oxfam 2018, 3; Schuster and Majidi 2019, 97–98; van Houte 2017; Trauner and Slominski 2020, 14; Warin and Zhekova 2017, 155).

Afghan Deportees: Forced back to displacement, hardship, and re-migration

A year after the Declaration was signed, in a parliamentary question to the European Commission (E-007189/2017), EU parliamentarians asked the age and gender of the deportees, the total amount of money spent on deport-ations, and who paid for them (European Parliament 2017). The Commission answered as follows: the flights were 'financed by the European Border and Coast Guard Agency (EBCGA)' with a total cost of €5,479,694.95 (European Parliament 2018b) – just over €15,000 per person. Moreover, the Commission stated that most deportees were male adults, 'with a small number of females (11) and minors (6), who have been returned as part of a family. The Commission and the EBCGA do not have information on the exact age of the returnees' (European Parliament 2018b).

These answers illustrate the concerns of Amnesty International (2017a, 2017b), the ECRE (2017a), and other international organizations regarding deportations from the EU to Afghanistan: despite the volatile situation in Afghanistan and the expense involved, there is an urgency on the EU's part to deport Afghans. Indeed, one year into the JWF, Abdul Ghafoor from the Afghanistan Migrants Advice and Support Organization said in an interview that 'it does not make any sense to deport people to Afghanistan right now. It is a loss on both sides. The European countries spent a lot of money to return people while people re-migrate again' (Ghafoor quoted in ECRE 2017b).

Similarly, Gerry Simpson from Human Rights Watch stated that although it is not unlawful for a state to deport 'aliens' from its territory, in the case of the JWF, 'it ma[de] no sense to do so if the EU wants to stabilize Afghanistan. By doing this, they are fueling the fames for the situation on the ground and for more Afghans to come [to Europe]' (Simpson, quoted in Birnbaum and Van den Berghe 2016).

To date, research investigating 'migrants' post-deportation lives in Afghanistan remains scarce, and little is known about their long-term experiences (Collyer 2018, 111; Schuster and Majidi 2019, 98). The few available studies and reports indicate that deportation is extremely harmful, especially to deportees' mental health and chances of reintegration into Afghan society, leading many to re-displacement or re-migration (Carrera and Allsopp 2017; Erdal and Oeppen 2017; Khosravi 2017, 2018; Kumar 2018; Majidi 2017; Schuster and Majidi 2013, 2019; van Houte 2017; van Houte et al. 2014).

These post-deportation challenges include stigma for different reasons, such as their 'failed' migration to Europe, lack of money to repay debts, belonging to an ethnic minority, Western 'contamination' (i.e., in the ways they speak, behave, and dress), and suspicions from local governments (Schuster and Majidi 2013, 230–231). These factors and the situation in Afghanistan mean that for many deportees, deportation is not the end of their migration journey, and they are likely to flee the country again (Kumar 2018; van Houte 2017). Moreover, many Afghans who migrate to Europe have never been to Afghanistan before; they are second or third generation undocumented Afghans born in Iran or Pakistan. Hence, when deported to Afghanistan, they are again displaced, having nowhere to go and no one with which to be reunited (Carrera and Allsopp 2017, 77; ECRE 2017b; Khosravi 2018, 2).

Khosravi (2017, 3) contends that although for the purposes of Afghanistan's commitment with the EU, deportees are considered Afghan nationals if they have lived their whole lives in either Iran or Pakistan, but upon arrival in Afghanistan they are denied Afghan national ID cards, which makes integration into society all but impossible. They eventually become 'denizens': 'The condition of social abandonment is experienced by being regarded as both "failed citizen" and "failed migrant" before and after deportation. Deportees in their country of citizenship are turned into denizens with limited access to their citizenship rights' (Khosravi 2018, 4). Consequently, such people are not only displaced again, with no connections to loved ones, but have no possibility of integration into society.

Those who do have relatives in Afghanistan face difficulties travelling to their hometowns due to widespread conflict, adding to their risk of being internally displaced (ECRE 2017b; Norwegian Refugee Council 2018, 10). For instance, the main road from Kabul leading to Hazarajat, in central Afghanistan, is called the 'Death Road' due to the dangers individuals face on it, leading some Afghans to stay in Kabul rather than doing crossing this road, at the cost of becoming internally displaced (Khosravi 2017, 2).

With the above in mind, I argue that by deporting individuals back to Afghanistan, a country experiencing widespread conflict and which has a deteriorating outlook, the EU becomes complicit in the forced displacement of Afghans in that country, so the urgency with which deportations are taking place should be scrutinized. Moreover, the EU claims that it is committed to the development and stability of Afghanistan (European Commission 2016), but studies (Khosravi 2017; Schuster and Majidi 2019; van Houte 2017) show that as the vast majority of deportees do not reintegrate into society but become internally displaced or decide to leave the country again. The more deportees that are sent back to Afghanistan, the more unsustainable the situation might become, both for deportees without support there, and also for the Afghan state.

Finally, by December 2019, the number of internally displaced persons in Afghanistan reached 4,191,000, of which 1,198,000 were displaced by natural disasters and 2,993,000 by conflict (Internal Displacement Monitoring Centre 2020). Thus, 'return' to Afghanistan does little for Afghan deportees, as Khosravi (2017, 2) brilliantly argues: 'opposite to what European states attempt to show, the [Afghan] deportees do not go back home, but they re-(join) a transnational space of expulsion, oscillating between re-departure and re-deportation'.

Conclusion

By utilizing the JWF Declaration as a case study alongside research and reports on Afghan deportees, this chapter has elaborated on the conceptualization of deportation as a form of forced migration (Gibney 2013) to demonstrate that despite using terms such as 'return', 'removal', and 'readmission' combined with the normalization of the practice of deportation, the EU subjugates individuals by enforcing them to another re-displacement through deportation. Hence, the violent outcomes of such policy are disguised, and Afghans' re-displacement and their 'return' to a place some of them have never been before are normalized, like deportation itself.

References

Afghanistan Analysts. 2016. 'EU and Afghanistan Get Deal on Migrants: Disagreements, Pressure and last-Minute Politics'. https://www.afghanistan-analysts.org/eu-and-afghanistan-get-deal-on-migrants-disagreements-pressure-and-last-minute-politics/

Amnesty International. 2017a. 'Afghanistan: Forced Back to Danger: Asylum-Seekers Returned from Europe to Afghanistan'. https://www.amnesty.org/en/documents/asa11/6866/2017/en/

Amnesty International. 2017b. 'European governments return nearly 10,000 Afghans to risk of death and torture'. https://www.amnesty.org/en/latest/news/2017/10/european-governments-return-nearly-10000-afghans-to-risk-of-death-and-torture/

Amnesty International. 2018. 'Afghanistan: Record high Civilian Casualties Make Returns Unjustifiable'. https://www.amnesty.org/en/latest/news/2018/07/afghanistan-record-civilian-casualties-returns-unjustifiable

Andrijasevic, Rutvica and William Walters. 2010. 'The International Organization for Migration and the International Government of Borders', *Environment and Planning D: Society and Space* 28 (6): 977–999.

Birnbaum, Michael, and Anabelle Van den Berghe. 2016. 'Europe Pressing Harder on Countries to Take Back Deported Migrants', *The Washington Post*, October 17. https://www.washingtonpost.com/world/europe/europepressing-harder-on-countries-to-take-back-deported-migrants/2016/10/12/c822453a-8fb4-11e6-bc00-1a9756d4111b_story.html

Carrera, Sergio. 2016. *Implementation of EU Readmission Agreements: Identity Determination Dilemmas and the Blurring of Rights*. Brussels: Springer International Publishing.

Carrera, Sergio and Jennifer Allsopp. 2017. 'The Irregular Immigration Policy Conundrum: Problematizing "effectiveness" as a frame for EU criminalization and expulsion policies', in *The Routledge Handbook of Justice and Home Affairs Research*, edited by Ripoll Servent, A. and Trauner, F., 70–82. London: Routledge.

Cassarino, Jean Pierre. 2007. 'Informalising Readmission Agreements in the EU Neighbourhood', *The International Spectator* 42 (2): 179–196.

Cassarino, Jean Pierre. 2015. 'Return Migration and Development: The significance of Migration Cycles', in *Routledge Handbook of Immigration and Refugee Studies*, edited by Triandafyllidou, A., 216–222. London: Routledge.

Cassarino, Jean Pierre. 2017. 'Informalizing EU Readmission Policy', in *The Routledge Handbook of Justice and Home Affairs Research*, edited by Ripoll Servent, A. and Trauner, F., 83–98. London: Routledge.

Collyer, Michael. 2018. 'Paying to Go: Deportability as Development', in *After Deportation: Ethnographic Perspectives*, edited by Khosravi, S., 105–125. Palgrave Macmillan.

Council of the European Union. 2016. 'Brussels Conference on Afghanistan, 4–5 October 2016'. Meeting Information, October 4. https://www.consilium.europa.eu/en/meetings/international-summit/2016/10/04-05/#:~:text=On%205%20October%2C%20the%20European,presented%20by%20the%20Afghan%20government

De Genova, Nicholas. 2017. 'The Autonomy of Deportation', Los Quaderno, 44: 8–12.

De Genova, Nicholas. 2018. 'Afterword – Deportation: The Last Word?', in *After Deportation: Ethnographic Perspectives*, edited by Khosravi, S., 253–266. Palgrave Macmillan.

De Genova, Nicholas and Nathalie Peutz. 2010. 'Introduction', in *The Deportation Regime: Sovereignty, Space and the Freedom of Movement*, edited by De Genova, N. and Peutz, N., 1–29. Durham and London: Duke University Press.

El Qadim, Nora. 2017. 'De-EUropeanising European Borders: EU-Morocco Negotiations on Migrations and the Decentring Agenda in EU Studies', in *Critical Epistemologies of Global Politics*, edited by Woons, M. and Weier S., 134–151. Bristol: E-International Relations.

Emiliani, Tommaso. 2016. '"Refugee Crisis" – "EU Crisis"? The Response to Inflows of Asylum-Seekers as a Battle for the European Soul', *College of Europe Policy Brief* 4(17).

Engelmann, Claudia. 2014. 'Convergence against the Odds: The Development of Safe Country of Origin Policies in EU Member States (1990–2013)'. *European Journal of Migration and Law* 16(2): 277–302.

Erdal, Marta Bivand and Ceri Oeppen. 2017. 'Forced to return? Agency and the role of post-return mobility for psychological wellbeing among returnees to Afghanistan, Pakistan and Poland', in *Return Migration and Psychosocial Wellbeing: Discourses, Policy-Making and Outcomes for Migrants and their Families*, edited by Vathi, Z. and King, R., 39–55. London: Routledge.

Erdal, Marta Bivand and Ceri Oeppen. 2018. 'Forced to leave? The discursive and analytical significance of describing migration as forced and voluntary', *Journal of Ethnic and Migration Studies* 44(6): 981–998.

European Asylum Support Office (EASO). 2018. 'EASO Country of Origin Report: Afghanistan Security Situation – Update'. https://coi.easo.europa.eu/ administration/easo/PLib/Afghanistan-security_situation_2018.pdf

European Commission. 2005. 'Readmission Agreements'. 5 October. MEMO/05/351. https://ec.europa.eu/commission/presscorner/detail/en/ MEMO_05_351

European Commission. 2015a. 'Communication from the Commission to the European Parliament, the Council, the European Economic and Social Committee and the Committee of the Regions: A European Agenda on Migration', 13 May 2015 COM 240 final. https://ec.europa.eu/home-affairs/ sites/homeaffairs/files/what-we-do/policies/european-agenda-migration/ background-information/docs/communication_on_the_european_agenda_on_ migration_en.pdf

European Commission. 2015b. 'Communication from the Commission to the European Parliament and to the Council: EU Action Plan on Return'. 9 September 2015 COM 453 final. https://ec.europa.eu/home-affairs/sites/ homeaffairs/files/what-we-do/policies/european-agenda-migration/proposal- implementation-package/docs/communication_from_the_ec_to_ep_and_ council_-_eu_action_plan_on_return_en.pdf

European Commission. 2016a. 'Commission Decision on the Signature on Behalf of the European Union of a Joint Way Forward on Migration Issues Between Afghanistan and the EU'. 19 September 2016 C 6023 final. http:// ec.europa.eu/transparency/ regdoc/?fuseaction=list&coteId=3&year=2016&number=6023&language=EN

European Commission. 2016b. 'Cooperation Agreement on Partnership and Development between the European Union and its Member States, of the one part, and the Islamic Republic of Afghanistan, of the other part'. 16 November 2016. http://data.consilium.europa.eu/doc/document/ST-12966-2016-INIT/en

European Council on Refugees and Exiles (ECRE). 2017a. 'EU migration policy and returns: Case study on Afghanistan' https://www.ecre.org/wp-content/uploads/2017/11/Returns-Case-Study-on-Afghanistan.pdf

European Council on Refugees and Exiles (ECRE). 2017b. 'Interview with Abdul Ghafoor, Afghanistan Migrants Advice & Support Organisation on one-year Joint Way Forward between EU & Afghanistan'. https://www.ecre.org/interview-with-abdul-ghafoor-afghanistan-migrants-advice-support-organisation-on-one-year-joint-way-forward-between-eu-afghanistan/

European Parliament. 2017. 'Question from Judith Sargentini (Verts/ALE), Bodil Valero (Verts/ALE), Jean Lambert (Verts/ALE), Malin Björk (GUE/NGL), Marie-Christine Vergiat (GUE/NGL), Barbara Spinelli (GUE/NGL), Elly Schlein (S&D) to the European Commission'. 22 November, E-007189/2017 (QWA). https://www.europarl.europa.eu/doceo/document/E-8-2017-007189_EN.html

European Parliament. 2018b. 'Answer of Commissioner Avramopoulos to the European Parliament'. 13 February, E-007189/2017(ASW). https://www.europarl.europa.eu/doceo/document/E-8-2017-007189-ASW_EN.html

European Union External Action (EEAS). 2016a. 'Joint Way Forward on Migration Issues Between Afghanistan and the EU'. https://eeas.europa.eu/sites/eeas/files/eu_afghanistan_joint_way_forward_on_migration_issues.pdf.

European Union External Action (EEAS). 2016b. 'Remarks by the High Representative/Vice-President Federica Mogherini upon arrival at the Brussels Conference on Afghanistan'. https://eeas.europa.eu/headquarters/headquarters-homepage/11122/remarks-by-the-high-representativevice-president-federica-mogherini-upon-arrival-at-the-brussels-conference-on-afghanistan_en.

European Union External Action (EEAS). 2016c. 'The European Union and Afghanistan reach an arrangement to tackle migration issues'. Press Release, October 3. https://eeas.europa.eu/headquarters/headquarters-homepage/10899/the-european-union-and-afghanistan-reach-an-arrangement-to-tackle-migration-issues_en

European Union Glossary. 2018. 'European Commission: Asylum and Migration Glossary 6.0'. https://ec.europa.eu/home-affairs/sites/homeaffairs/files/what-we-do/networks/european_migration_network/docs/interactive_glossary_6.0_final_version.pdf.

Gibney, Matthew. 2008. 'Deportation', in *The New Oxford Companion to Law*, edited by Cane, P. and Conaghan, J. Oxford University Press.

Gibney, Matthew. 2013. 'Is Deportation a Form of Forced Migration?' *Refugee Survey Quarterly* 32 (2): 116–129.

Giuffré, Mariagiulia. 2016. 'Obligation to Readmit? The Relationship Between Interstate and EU Readmission Agreements'. In Migration in the Mediterranean: Mechanisms of International Cooperation, edited by Ippolito, F. and Trevisanut, S., 263–287. Cambridge: Cambridge University Press.

Giuffré, Mariagiulia. 2020. The Readmission of Asylum-Seekers under International Law. Hart Publishing.

Green, Nile. 2008. 'Tribe, Diaspora, and Sainthood in Afghan History'. The Journal of Asian Studies 67 (1): 171–211.

Guild, Elspeth. 2014. 'Conflicting Identities and Securitisation in Refugee Law: Lessons from the EU', in Refugee Protection and the Rule of Law: Conflicting Identities, edited by Kneebone, S., Stevens, D., and Baldassar, L., 151–173. London: Routledge.

Hunt, Matthew. 2014. 'The Safe Country of Origin Concept in European Asylum Law: Past, Present and Future', *International Journal of Refugee Law* 26 (4): 500–535.

Internal Displacement Monitoring Centre. 2020. 'Afghanistan'. https://www. internal-displacement.org/countries/afghanistan

International Federation for Human Rights (FIDH). 2016. 'The EU-Afghanistan Joint Way Forward on Migration: a new low for the EU'. https://www.fidh.org/ en/issues/migrants-rights/the-eu-afghanistan-joint-way-forward-on-migration- a-new-low-for-the

International Organisation for Migration. 2017. 'Return of Undocumented Afghans from Pakistan and Iran: 2016 An Overview'. https://afghanistan.iom. int/sites/default/files/Reports/iom_afghanistan_-_return_of_undocumented_ afghans_from_pakistan_and_iran_-_2016_overview.pdf

Khosravi, Shahram. 2017. 'Why Deportation to Afghanistan is Wrong'. https:// allegralaboratory.net/deportation-afghanistan-wrong/

Khosravi, Shahram. 2018. 'Introduction'. In After Deportation: Ethnographic Perspectives, edited by Khosravi, S., 1–14. Palgrave Macmillan.

Kumar, Ruchi. 2018. 'Europe send Afghans back to Danger'. The New Humanitarian, January 4. https://www.thenewhumanitarian.org/news/2018/01/04/europe-sends-afghans-back-danger

Majidi, Nassim. 2017. 'Deportees lost at "home": Post-deportation outcomes in Afghanistan'. In After Deportation: Ethnographic Perspectives, edited by Khosravi, S., 127–148. Palgrave Macmillan.

Manchanda, Nivi. 2020. Imagining Afghanistan. Cambridge: Cambridge University Press.

Miakhel, Hafiz Ahmad. 2018. 'Europe is Rejecting Thousands of Afghan Asylum-Seekers a year but what Awaits Them Back Home?'. Interview by Pamela Constable and Andrew Quilty. *The Washington Post*, May 25. https://www.washingtonpost.com/news/world/wp/2018/05/25/feature/europe-is-rejecting-thousands-of-afghan-asylum-seekers-a-year-but-what-awaits-them-back-home/?noredirect=on

Norwegian Refugee Council. 2018. 'Escaping War: Where to Next? A Research Study on the Challenges of IDP Protection in Afghanistan'. https://static1.squarespace.com/static/5cfe2c8927234e0001688343/t/5d5d3b039af98c0001166adc/1566391069737/NRC-IDP_Afghanistan_FINAL.pdf

Oxfam. 2018. 'Returning to Fragility: Exploring the Link Between Conflict and Returnees in Afghanistan'. https://oxfamilibrary.openrepository.com/bitstream/handle/10546/620399/rr-returning-fragility-afghanistan-310118-en.pdf?sequence=4

Picozza, Fiorenza. 2017. 'Dubliners Unthinking Displacement, Illegality, and Refugeeness within Europe's Geographies of Asylum', in *The Borders of "Europe". Autonomy of Migration, Tactics of Bordering*, edited by De Genova, N., 233–254. Durham, NC: Duke University Press.

Quie, Marissa and Hameed Hakimi. 2018. 'EU Pays to stop Migrants'. Chatham House, December and January, 2017–18. https://www.chathamhouse.org/publications/twt/eu-pays-stop-migrants

Rasmussen, Sune Engel. 2016. 'EU's Secret Ultimatum to Afghanistan: Accept 80,000 Deportees or Lose Aid'. *The Guardian*, September 28. https://www.theguardian.com/global-development/2016/sep/28/eu-secret-ultimatum-afghanistan-accept-80000-deportees-lose-aid-brussels-summit-migration-sensitive

Relief Web. 2016. 'The European Parliament must immediately address the Joint Way Forward Agreement between the EU and Afghanistan'. https://reliefweb.int/sites/reliefweb.int/files/resources/joint_statement_eu-afghanistan_deal.pdf

Relief Web. 2017. '2017 Afghanistan Humanitarian Needs Overview'. https://reliefweb.int/report/afghanistan/2017-afghanistan-humanitarian-needs-overview

Schultz, Teri. 2018. 'EU States push ahead with Afghanistan Deportations, Despite Increasing Danger'. DW, October 20. https://www.dw.com/en/eu-states-push-ahead-with-afghanistan-deportations-despite-increased-danger/a-45835755

Schuster, Liza and Nassim Majidi. 2013. 'What happens post-deportation? The experience of deported Afghans', *Migration Studies* 1 (2): 221–240.

Schuster, Liza and Nassim Majidi. 2019. 'Deportation and Forced Return', in *Forced Migration: Current Issues and Debates*, edited by Bloch, A. and Dona, G., 88–105. London: Routledge.

StateWatch. 2016. 'Joint Commission-EEAS Non-paper on Enhancing Cooperation on Migration, Mobility and Readmission with Afghanistan'. http://statewatch.org/news/2016/mar/eu-council-afghanistan-6738-16.pdf

Trauner, Florian. 2016. 'Asylum policy: the EU's "crises" and the looming policy regime failure', *Journal of European Integration*, 38(3): 311–325.

Trauner, Florian. 2017. 'Return and Readmission Policy in Europe: Understanding Negotiation and Implementation Dynamics', in The Routledge Handbook of the Politics of Migration in Europe, edited by Weinar, A., Bonjour, S., and Zhyznomirska, L., 251–260. London: Routledge.

Trauner, Florian and Peter Slominski. 2020. 'Reforming me Softly – How Soft Law Has Changed EU Return Policy Since the Migration Crisis'. *West European Politics*.

United Nations Assistance Mission in Afghanistan (UNAMA). 2018. 'Midyear Update on the Protection of Civilians in Armed Conflict: 1 January to 30 June'. https://unama.unmissions.org/sites/default/files/unama_poc_midyear_ update_2018_15_julyenglish.pdf

United Nations High Commissioner for Refugees (UNHCR). 2016. 'Overview of UNHCR's Operations in Asia and the Pacific, 23 September 2016'. https:// www.refworld.org/docid/57f257454.html

van Houte, Marieke. 2017. 'Afghan Returns Built on False Policy Narrative'. News Deeply, 21 February. https://www.newsdeeply.com/refugees/ community/2017/02/21/afghan-returns-built-on-false-policy-narrative- researcher

van Houte, Marieke, et al. 2014. 'Return to Afghanistan: Migration as reinforcement of socio-economic stratification', *Population, Space and Place,* 21(8): 692–703.

Wakil, Mirwais. 2018. 'Never Again? Europe's False Human Rights Promise'. *The Diplomat*, June 29. https://thediplomat.com/2018/06/never-again- europes-false-human-rights-promise/

Warin, Catherine and Zheni Mitkova Zhekova. 2017. 'The Joint Way Forward on Migration Issues between Afghanistan and the EU: EU External Policy and the Recourse to Non-Binding Law'. *Cambridge International Law Journal,* 6 (2): 143–158.

Webber, Francis. 2011. 'How voluntary are voluntary returns?', *Institute of Race Relations*, 52(4): 98–107.

Wolff, Sarah. 2014. 'The Politics of Negotiating EU Readmission Agreements: Insights from Morocco and Turkey'. *European Journal of Migration and Law*, 16(1): 69–95.

Wolff, Sarah and Hadj-Abdou, Leila. 2017. 'Mediterranean Migration and Refugee Politics between Continuities and Discontinuities', in *Routledge Handbook of Mediterranean Politics*, edited by Volpi, F. and Gillespie, R., 382–393. London: Routledge.

Wolff, Sarah and Florian Trauner. 2014. 'The Negotiation and Contestation of EU Migration Policy Instruments: A Research Framework'. *European Journal of Migration and Law*, 16(1): 1–18.

Zaiotti, Ruben. 2016. 'Mapping remote control: the externalization of migration management in the 21st century', in *Externalizing Migration Management: Europe, North America and the spread of 'remote control' practices*, edited by Zaiotti, R., 1–30. London: Routledge.

19

On Collaboration and Cooperation: Transnational Governance as a Framework for Migration Control

ALMA STANKOVIC

It is one of the few undisputed matters in international law that there is no single international migration governance framework (Betts 2011, 2). And with little political impetus at the moment, the prospects to create a global governing regime appear bleak (Laessing and Rinke 2018). What this simplified statement misses, however, is that migration *is* governed internationally, only not through traditional international legal tools, such as treaties and conventions. Looking closer, there are plenty of formal and informal bilateral agreements governing migration, often with negative impacts on migrants (Partlow and Miroff 2018). Criticisms abound by both scholars and activists about these agreements, especially as they pertain to the human rights of migrants. What goes mostly unreviewed is the development of 'prevention' of migration movements as a policy.[1]

This development is in part due to transnational law, or transnationalism. Transnationalism was initially developed as a concept during the Cold War to describe the way the East-West divide caused states to be influenced by the domestic developments and presumed interests of other states. Once the Cold War was over, the theory was developed further, predicting that the rise of the 'regulatory state' along with its disaggregation into its individual

---

[1]   Cf. Hathaway and Gammeltoft-Hansen (2015). Nevertheless, even Hathaway and Gammeltoft-Hansen look at the issue from the perspective of human rights and refugee law, not from the perspective of migration governance.

components – executive, legislative, and judiciary – would allow for greater collaboration between different states.

The original view was that this type of cooperation would lead to a more 'just' world order (Slaughter 2005, 6–7); however, while these networks have become entrenched enough to create a system of governance, it is not as benevolent as initially envisaged. The current system allows immigrant receiving countries (core countries) to exert influence over changes to internal laws and policies of their neighboring, transit, and immigrant-sending countries (periphery countries). In doing so, core countries prevent not only immigration into their own territories, but the entirety of the migration movement. In a sense, they coopt the interests and policies of periphery countries, making them part of the core's regulatory system and converting them into a semi-periphery.

There is no international normative framework of irregular migration governance in the traditional sense of treaties and formal global covenants, but this chapter argues that transnationalism shows that a framework does exist, informal as it may be, and it is used to control migratory patterns. The structure of this chapter is as follows. The next section will briefly define the main premises of transnationalism and its relation to governance, along with their application to irregular migration. Then, it turns to the case study of the United States (US) and Mexico, which provides an example of how this framework actually works and the changes it has produced in migration governance and migratory patterns. Finally, the conclusion briefly summarizes the main points of the arguments made.

Transnational Migration Governance

Transnationalism is not a new concept. The most prominent advocate for it was Jessup (1956, 52–53), who saw that international norms were bleeding into the traditional *domain reservé* of states having absolute control over the laws created within their sovereign borders. Scholars of international law after the Cold War asserted that law itself would become *transnational*, meaning that states would start to harmonize their internal laws as they became more aware of how their own laws may effect cross-boundary interactions. This change would materialize thanks to the development of the regulatory state, where the power to shape internal laws is disaggregated and where policymakers in the executive are as inclined to share notes among their counterparts in other countries as to listen to the other branches of government (Slaughter 2005, 3–6).

A subsection of international relations (IR) scholars and policymakers came to the same conclusion: traditional international regimes built on multilateral covenants and treaties were no longer the norm. They attempted not only to understand, but also create new norms and principles underpinning the more regionalized and diverse set of interstate relations in the hopes of streamlining the management of the globalized world. Thus, the concept of global governance was born (Betts 2011, 4).

In combination, these two concepts became the underpinning of the current approach to managing a variety of transnational fields. Migration, being a cross-border phenomenon by nature, falls within the scope transnational governance, with bordering countries establishing rules not just on how to treat each other's citizens' movements across the border, but also those of other nations (The Schengen Acquis 2020). Indeed, the control of entry of those falling outside the 'desired' class of immigrants, so-called irregular migrants, has become the most predominant 'worry' of policymakers in core countries. As a result, they have turned to transnational governance tools to ensure that their neighbors stop irregular migrants long before they reach their borders.

Transnational Governance Defined

The first time transnational law was used to describe cross-border matters was in 1955 by Jessup, who coined the term. Jessup's (1956, 3) main position was that the traditional dichotomy of domestic and international law cannot hold in the realities of the Cold War world. The key issue was that the distinction was not necessary, as jurisdiction in the classical Westphalian sense of territorial sovereignty was no longer exclusive under 'modern' international law, since concepts such as human rights limit the exercise of state power even internally (Jessup 1956, 36, 39–41). For Jessup (1956, 30), this was proof that domestic law had developed beyond its traditional role, having 'taken account of the new social consciousness'.

Keohane and Nye (1974, 40–41) developed this idea further and posited that transnational interactions have become increasingly significant and as a result sensitize nations to each other. Specifically, as the world was becoming more interconnected, governments would have to start designing policies and rules that are sensitive to those of other states, since any attempts to regulate, encourage, or disrupt the private cross-border interactions within one nation's borders would have an impact on the citizenry of another state (Keohane and Nye 1974, 41–42). In their view, these sensibilities encourage more transgovernmental interaction among the bureaucracies of the respective states, causing potential for greater convergence between their laws and policies (Keohane and Nye 1974, 42).

This idea of harmonization was taken further after the end of the Cold War. Slaughter (2005, 10–11) argued in her seminal work, *A New World Order*, that states were no longer unitary actors who control the international sphere; rather, it is a web of formal and informal transnational networks of individual 'components' of a state that now determines interactions between states (Slaughter 2005, 10–11). For Slaughter, this was a positive development for two reasons. For one, it solves the legitimacy problems that would occur under a world government (Slaughter 2005, 7). The other benefit is that these networks would foster problem-solving through three main functions: (1) creating convergences by facilitating a 'regulatory exportation' of best practices and norms from one country to another (information networks), (2) improving compliance with international norms through information sharing and capacity building (enforcement networks), and (3) increasing international cooperation by transferring regulatory rules from the domestic to the international sphere (harmonization networks) (Slaughter 2005, 19–20, 23–24). This harmonization would foster cooperation on a global level, replacing traditional multilateral international laws.

Around this same time, IR theorists also sought to understand how the international order was changing, naming their studies global governance. The term eschews a fixed definition, with various scholars having similar yet differing views on what it actually means (Betts 2011, 3–4; Rosenau 1995, 14; Weiss 2009). Looking at their commonalities, one can understand global governance as the sum of all supra-national regulation, cooperation, and organization of the normally present 'anarchy' in the international sphere, these actions being pursued and achieved by a variety of actors forming and instituting rules, norms, and policies that govern behavior. In essence, governance is the result of the lack of an overarching world government structure and is nevertheless a means to achieve cooperation on matters that a single state cannot manage on its own due to territorial limitations.

The key concept for both governance and transnationalism is the drive towards multilateral cooperation in the international sphere (Rosenau 1995, 13). Governance theories argue that, to ensure effective governance, trans-national networks should be used to influence the results of global policies.[2] This idea is synonymous with the horizontal networks of transnationalism, where networks transport best-practices and enforcement of agreed-upon rules and laws across borders, which can assist in creating coherent systems of governance for cross-border concerns. Hence, transnational governance then can be defined as the summation of the two concepts. It is the conglomeration of regulations and cooperation across national borders (the

---

[2]   Slaughter (2005, 25) notes specifically that looking through the disaggregated state lens, states can be more effective in realizing global governance.

governance component) through horizontal networks, whose aim is to harmonize practices and laws to achieve a particular result (the transnational component).

Transnational Governance of Irregular Migration Reviewed

Human history has been marked by migration. However, the desire to systematically control migration, especially 'irregular migration', is relatively recent (Triandafyllidou 2016, 33). But who is an irregular migrant? There is no officially accepted definition of that term. Moreover, the definition has become muddled due to a variety of misuses. To really understand irregular migration, one must understand how it is formed. According to Crépeau (2013, 2; 2018), irregular migration results from a combination of three factors: (1) the un-recognized labor needs in destination countries, where there is an incentive to 'profit from [the irregular migrants'] vulnerability... [with] little political appetite to repress this, since this could cost jobs and taxes in low profit-margin sectors'; (2) the emigration needs in home countries, such as high unemployment rates or remittance dependence; and (3) the lack of legal avenues for migrants to enter destination countries.

This disconnect between the different economic needs of sending and receiving countries and restrictive immigration laws is crucial in creating the phenomenon of irregular migration. Most immigration laws and policies are designed with the alleged economic benefit an immigrant brings, with preference given to 'highly skilled' immigrants. However, the unacknowledged need for cheap, unskilled labor means there is an economic benefit of those immigrants as well. Moreover, the economic benefit to sending countries of unburdening themselves of a large unemployed or underemployed workforce is significant, but is rarely considered in the creation of immigration rules by the destination country. Essentially, without the means to enter legally, those who fill these economic needs are labeled irregular migrants.

Applying the transnational governance definition to irregular migration, such governance is the formal and informal collaborations and cooperation among core countries and their neighboring periphery countries with the goal of containing, diverting, or preventing migration movements to ensure that the above noted economic needs are still met. To do so, core countries have developed a variety of tools and methods, especially as regards the externalization of migration control. The European Union (EU) is one of the most prominent examples of such externalization. From the European Neighborhood Policy to readmission agreements, the EU actively seeks to control immigration into its territory by negotiating rules on what its neighboring countries do with migrants who transverse *their* countries (Triandafyllidou and

Dimitriadi 2014, 11). But more informal collaborations exist as well. For example, the EU Border and Coastal Guard Agency has cooperated with Moroccan authorities regularly on border surveillance and policing, which allows Morocco to stop certain migrants in transit, preventing their reaching the EU (Carrera 2016, 7–10; den Hertog 2017, 3–4, 9–10).

The key tools to effect these policies are deterrence and regionalization. Deterrence takes many forms, from making immigration and other domestic laws more restrictive and transgressions thereof punitive to increasing military/police presence on borders. Regionalization seems more benign in comparison, with development aid and repatriation assistance often used as tools to ensure such returns. Yet, there is also a darker side of regionalization, namely the argument that its true goal is not assistance, but containment (Crépeau 2018). Both of these tools contribute to the denial of human rights, which is why a significant amount of current literature reviewing irregular migration governance focuses on that issue (e.g., Gammeltoft-Hansen 2011; Mann 2016; Hesch 2018). Some, like Mann (2013, 316), argue directly that the existence of the transnational migration governance networks undermines the multilateral human rights regime. Nevertheless, in many cases, the boundaries of irregular migrants and refugees are blurred, and the academic focus tends to center on the latter and their situations in periphery countries (Gammeltoft-Hansen 2011).

Given its well-established externalization policies, the EU has been one of the most studied examples. Australia's harsh rules on dealing with asylum seekers by placing them in detention on an island outside its borders is another prominent example (e.g., Nethery, Rafferty-Brown, and Taylor 2013) Also, the US's detention of migrants and refugees has a long history of academic review from various perspectives (e.g., Motomura 1999). Though more recent projects have been developed that attempt to collect and study data on the impact of immigration regulations on migration movements in their entirety, few authors consider the effect on the movement as a whole or the changes within the periphery countries.[3] This is not a coincidence. Given the high level of informal collaborations, it is neither easy to collect the necessary data nor is it easy to make the connections.

The United States-Mexico Case Study

The US-Mexico migration patterns have traditionally moved from south to north, from Mexico to the US. Therefore, migration control, as well as scholarly and policy concern, has traditionally been an issue of US immigration control.

[3]   Cf. Nethery, Rafferty-Brown, and Taylor (2013, 94–98); Helbling and Leblang, (2019, 259–260).

Mexico, in contrast, had no formulated migration policy for most of the 20th century. Its main focus was on the emigration of its own citizens, which since World War II benefitted the country twofold: one, it relieved the economic pressure of having a large un- or underemployed workforce, and two, the remittances sent home allowed the Mexican economy to maintain some stability (Zong and Batalova 2018; Gillespie 2018).

Thanks in part to the 2008 financial crisis, this south-to-north emigration trend has slowed, (Zong and Batalova 2018); in the years immediately after the crisis, there was a net deficit of Mexicans arriving in the US (Gonzalez-Barrera, 2015). Nevertheless, the overall immigration rate into the US has continued rising in large part due to an increase of migrants of other nationalities (Passel and D'vera 2015). Hondurans, Salvadorans, and Guatemalans fleeing violence and poverty have entered and traversed Mexico since the 1960s and 1970s, but they started to do so in even greater numbers in the 1990s and 2000s. As the US increased its entry restriction, Mexico became more of an immigrant receiving country. Consequently, it started to develop its own migration policies and laws. Some of these changes had a positive effect, such as the decriminalization of irregular migrants and the adoption of a wide-reaching refugee definition. Others were much more concerned with allowing for greater migration control.

This latter development was not unaided by the US. Having a significant interest in stopping or at least containing migrants from the south, the US government has exercised a certain amount of influence over Mexico's policies. The most conspicuous type of influence has been the technical support provided by the US in terms of trainings and equipment to allow for greater cooperation on the US-Mexico border. However, financial assistance was also provided for increasing migration control on Mexico's southern border. As a result, much of Mexico's migration actions, especially those exercised on the southern border, appear to be almost identical to those the US uses on its border with Mexico, so extending the reach of the US migration control efforts.

A Brief History of Migration Control Measures by the US

For the most part, the relationship between Mexico and the US was marked by immigration control imposed by the US, and while there were certain positive (Ngai 2004, 138-139) and negative (Ngai 2004, 71-73; Koch 2006) policies throughout the 20th century, the general migratory pattern was a circular one, with mostly Mexican labor moving to the US as needed and leaving or being deported when not (Blakemore 2018). With public perception growing increasingly negative towards immigrants, the US instituted rigorous immigration controls starting in the 1980s, which had a lasting effect. In 1986, the US Congress passed the Immigration Reform and Control Act (IRCA), which imposed, *inter alia*, high requirements for future immigrants.

These effects were entrenched in the 1990s, when Congress passed the Illegal Immigration Reform and Immigrant Responsibility Act (IIRIRA). The IIRIRA was responsible for creating a more structured set of rules to increase the efficiency of border patrol efforts and immigration court proceedings. It also introduced the concept of unlawful presence and criminal penalties for it, along with an expansion of who would be deportable (Lundstrom 2013, 389, 395; Abrego, Coleman, Martínez, Menjívar, and Slack 2017, 697). Most importantly, it also provided the US government with two main methods by which persons are apprehended for deportation: 'employment raids and cooperation with local law enforcement' (Stankovic 2018). The latter practice has particularly increased since 9/11 (Juárez, Gómez-Aguiñaga, Bettez 2018, 75–77); the former took on a particularly aggressive form under the Trump administration (Mazzei 2018; Sacchetti 2018). Together with a proliferation of security measures at ports of entry and the increased militarization of the southern US border and the increased detention migrants in the US, these new rules allowed the US to better achieve its main migration control goal: deterrence (Brown 2018).

The militarization of the border has not only increased the presence of border officials but has – thanks to technological advances, internal support by the military, and external capacity building networks – increased their functional capabilities. With immigration seen a threat to national security, the power of US Customs and Border Protection (CBP) has also been extended in the legal sphere. Through such concepts as 'expedited removal', CBP agents can turn away persons 'within 100 miles of the boundary, [with] the discretion to remove unauthorized persons from the country without any formal legal or administrative process at all, in some cases with a record of formal deportation' (Heyman and Campbell 2012, 88).

The Trump administration increased the use of expedited removals and instituted harsh new rules, such as family separation and the Remain in Mexico policy, in its attempt to further stifle immigration.[4] All these developments had a domino effect, with Mexico needing to adapt new rules for its own territory as a result.

---

[4]   Designating Aliens for Expedited Removal, Fed Reg 35,409 (23 July 2019) (making any alien less than two years in the US removable via expedited procedures regardless of where apprehended).

US-Mexico Migration Governance

Collaborations between the US and Mexico and their Influences on Mexican Border Control Measures

For Mexico, migration control has not traditionally been a major concern, (Alba and Castillo 2012, 3) as it saw itself primarily as an emigrant country (Fitzgerald 2009, 55–56). Emigration was a benefit, as it provided a means of lowering economic pressures by having a good portion of the workforce emigrate instead of being present in the depressed labor market (Fitzgerald 2009, 55–56; Alba 2013). In addition, remittance funds sent back home also alleviated pressures on the social system (Alba 2013; Gillespie 2018). Consequently, Mexico had little to no official migration policies in place during the early- and mid-20th century. Change came once the US started restricting its immigration policies in the 1980s and 1990s. Suddenly, Mexico did become interested in migration control – though initially mostly concerned with its citizens' free movement (Baker 2011, 8–11; O'Neil 2003). Efforts to establish some formal multilateral agreements on this issue (Schmitt 2001), however, failed to take off after the US abandoned immigration reform in the immediate aftermath of 9/11 (Waslin 2003, 2; Bueno Pedraza 2005, 600–601; Gutiérrez 2007, 71–72).

This does not mean that no collaborations were made on migration post-9/11. One such attempt was the so-called Smart Border Agreement (Sullivan 2002). The agreement was ostensibly geared towards regulating and securing the movement of people across the US-Mexico border (Silva Quiroz 2014, 48) with a particular goal being the development of more coordinated information-sharing. But there was already an external aspect to the agreement: it called for increased cooperation in identifying persons who could pose a threat *before* they entered either territory, for the development of technological systems at ports of entry to streamline (and monitor) entries and exists, and for the coordination of efforts to prevent the human trafficking of third-country nationals (Silva Quiroz 2014, 48–49). This combined approach implied that the US and Mexico both shared the same interest in keeping others out.

On the US side, the Smart Border Agreement meant a hefty increase in funding for personnel and technology for the relevant enforcement agencies; for Mexico, the agreement's objectives were imported into its *Plan Sur* (Silva Quiroz 2014, 48-49). *Plan Sur*'s purpose was essentially to increase control of the migratory movements from the Isthmus of Tehuantepec to the southern Mexican border, specifically by focusing on increased inspections of migrants' documentation and greater inter-institutional cooperation in halting smugglers (Silva Quiroz 2014, 49; Gonzalez-Murphy 2013, 60). To do so, the government established two lines of checkpoints, one covering the states of Chiapas and Tabasco and one covering the states of Veracruz and Oaxaca, increasing personnel and essentially starting a militarization of Mexico's southern border similar to what had taken place in the US a decade earlier (Gonzalez-Murphy 2013, 60).

The most prominent effort, however, was the Mérida Initiative. Intended to deal with the illegal weapons and drug trade between the two countries (Ribando Seelke and Finklea 2017, 9; Olson 2017, 3–4), the US provided equipment for purchase for the Mexican police and military in the amount of almost $600 million along with technical assistance and training for Mexican forces (Evolution of Mérida 2018).[5] Under President Obama, the initiative was expanded to include other concerns, such as migration. This expansion was one of the main US efforts to contain and deter Central American migration, and also the best means to export its immigration policies to and secure the collaboration of Mexico.

One way of doing so was to emphasize the concept of security (Beer 2015; Pope 2016). While Mexico changed its laws to allow for greater collaboration at the US-Mexico border (Ribando Seelke and Finklea 2017, 19–20), the US also spent significant funds under the Mérida Initiative on Mexico's southern border. During the Obama administration, over $2.6 billion was appropriated by Congress for Mexico's southern border (Ribando Seelke and Finklea 2017, 11–12; Knippen, Boggs, and Meyer 2015, 16). The measure remains popular in Congress, which continues to appropriate funds for the program (Sieff and Sheridan 2018).

But there were also less informal means of cooperation, under which US resources were appropriated to assist migration control on the territory of its southern neighbor. One set of such cooperations came directly from the US immigration authorities as early as the 1990s. Under 'Operation Global Reach', the US appropriated over $8 million for the opening of Immigration and Naturalization (INS) offices extraterritorially in Mexico and other Central American countries (Flynn 2002, 29–30; Koslowski 2011, 69). From these offices, INS agents trained host-country agents, participated in 'special operations to test various illegal migrant deterrence methods in source and transit countries', and accompanied 'local authorities to restaurants, hotels, border crossings, checkpoints, and airports to help identify suspicious travelers' (Flynn 2002, 30).

Another line of informal cooperation is military-to-military assistance (Olson 2017, 20–21). Similar to how civilian law enforcement in the US provided

---

[5]   Sum of funds appropriated through 2019.

equipment and training to their Mexican counterparts, the US Department of Defense (DOD) has provided the same services to the Mexican military, including training in the US (Olson 2017, 20–21). Officially, more than $9.8 million in assistance was given to Mexico between 2008 and 2016 (Olson 2017, 33).[6] Additional funding for DOD assistance to Mexico was funneled through the State Department's Foreign Military Financing program, where a total of $463 million was used in the same time period for similar activities (Olson 2017, 33).[7]

These more informal means are particularly valued by the relevant executive agents. From 2006 through 2012, Mexico's efforts to develop a common vision of responsibility between the two countries has resulted in more institutional and informal channels of dialogue and cooperation (Libro Blanco 2012, 5). Such dialogue and cooperation is evident in the plans and declarations made by the two countries. Between 2004 and 2012, 16 declarations were made by the governing executives of the two countries on issues of migration, mobility, and security, along with three relevant plans of actions (Libro Blanco 2012, 10–11). An additional 30 memoranda, agreements, declarations, and plans of actions were made between 2013 and 2018 (Libro Blanco 2018, 15).

Mexico's Changing Policies

The violent political upheavals of the 1960s and 1970s in Central America affected Mexico greatly (Castillo 2002, 40–41). Many refugees from the region found themselves on the Mexican side of the border because of the indiscriminate violence in their home countries (Castillo 2002, 40–41; Alba and Castillo 2012, 4–5). With the US increasingly trying to restrict entry into its own territory, Mexico suddenly found that it was no longer only an emigration country. For most of the 1980s and 1990s, however, Mexico's migration policy was rather incoherent (Castillo 2002, 42; Alba and Castillo 2012, 6). Nevertheless, there was a distinct strategy of containment and deportation of migrants crossing its southern border. This strategy was implemented by increasing requirements Mexico started putting on those seeking entry (Alba and Castillo 2012, 5), but it also developed because Mexico's immigration laws consisted of only the provisions in the 1974 *Ley General de Población*, which criminalized irregular immigration.[8] With the

---

[6]   Sum of funding in the given years deriving from the Foreign Military Financing and International Military and Eduction Training funds.

[7]   The funding amounts varied between $3 and $8 million; however, there were two spikes in funding in 2008 and 2010 of over $116 and over $260 million, respectively.

[8]   Ley General de Población, Diario Oficial de la Federación, 7 de enero de 1974 (Mexico), Art 103.

requirement that transiting passengers have an entry visa for their final destination – a requirement partially the result of US pressures (Alba and Castillo 2012, 5) – meant that virtually any migrant from Central America would be labeled a criminal.

Due to migrants increasingly entering clandestinely, Mexico's policy started taking greater shape in the 2000s. Two plans were initially developed to contain immigrant and transit migrant flows: the *Sellamiento de la Frontera Sur* program and the above-mentioned *Plan Sur* (Alvarado Fernandez 2006, 74). Both plans were seen as means to appease the US and to allow the favoring of Mexicans entering the US (Flynn 2002, 32; Galemba 2015). These plans resulted in a multitude of 'control operations and mechanisms [that] were implemented at strategic points… particularly along the highway routes migrants and their guides favor[ed]' (Castillo 2006). A complex web of immigration, law enforcement, and military officials engaged in verification and control activities at these checkpoints (Isaacson, Meyer, and Morales 2014, 27). These new developments were welcomed by the US, where it was noted that the Mexican government was *finally* doing something about the 'migrant problem' (Flynn 2002, 34).

Deportation, often euphemistically labeled repatriation, also became a more common tool. Under *Plan Sur*, Mexico deported Guatemalans back to their own country by bussing them directly to their home authorities; it also deported non-nationals to Guatemala if it determined that they entered Mexico through that country (Flynn 2002, 29). The costs for the deportations were covered in large part by the US (Flynn 2002, 29). In 2003, *Plan Sur* was superseded by the *Fortalecimiento de las Delegaciones Regionales de la Frontera Sur* program, whose aim was, *inter alia*, to increase control over migration movements and to establish repatriation agreements with Central American countries. One such agreement, akin to the EU's readmission agreements, had already been signed with Guatemala in 2002 and is renewed regularly (Alvarado Fernandez 2006, 74). Under that agreement, persons found to be in Mexico without permission would be deported to Guatemala; it was then left to Guatemala to further deport those persons who were not nationals (Castillo 2006). In 2006, a regional agreement was signed between Mexico and several of its southern neighbors with similar provisions.

On the legislative side, Mexico also became more active. As the US increased border controls, it created pressure on Mexican communities throughout the country. Interestingly, at least on paper, this pressure did not mean a greater restriction as it had in the US. Seeking a greater role in regional cooperation generally (Alba and Castillo 2012, 9–10), Mexico amended the *Ley General de Población* in 2008, to *decriminalize* irregular immigration into the country. Shortly thereafter, in 2011, an extensive new legal regime was adopted, dealing with refugee and subsidiary protections. In the same year, the legislature also passed a sweeping new immigration law, the *Ley de Migración*.

Several aspects of the immigration law seem to give migrants broad rights. For example, Article 7 notes that all persons have the freedom to transit Mexico without having to prove their nationality or migration status, save when requested by competent authorities as permitted by the law specifically. It is also especially insightful that the law makes provisions regarding transit migrants in minute detail. Some of these are quite revolutionary when compared to the laws in the US: in Mexico, transit migrants presented to the immigration authorities have a right to legal assistance and must be informed of the possibility to regularize their entry into Mexico.

Within the law, however, there are also provisions that create tension with this apparent human rights approach. Under Articles 66 through 68, the Mexican state reserves the right to detain and deport irregular migrants and to notify their own countries of their presence in Mexico to safeguard its own sovereignty. This tension is also evident in the practical application of the law. Critics were worried from the outset that in the heightened security atmosphere at the time, retraining the staff implementing the law could prove challenging. (Alba and Castillo 2012, 17–18). Also, the process has been burdened due to the overlapping deployment of different agencies together with the *Instituto Nacional de Migración* (INM) to enforce the law (Isaacson, Meyer, and Morales 2014, 10–11). Moreover, it has also been marred through corruption and criminality concerns (Isaacson, Meyer, and Morales 2014, 17; Knippen, Boggs, and Meyer 2015, 22; Nolen 2016).

Most importantly, the execution of the law was still influenced by US-desired policies. When an unprecedented number of unaccompanied minors made their way through Mexico and across the northern border in 2013 and 2014, Mexico, at the urging of the Obama administration, increased the presence of border control forces, checkpoints, and detentions along Mexico's border with Guatemala and Belize (Ribando Seelke and Finklea 2017, 21; Castillo 2016, 2). Part of the *Programa Frontera Sur*, these stronger controls were installed at 12 points of entry into the country and along three corridors stretching across 100 miles of Mexico's southern border, and more boots on the ground were put in place by including INM officials, making checks alongside federal and local police (Mexico Enforcement Efforts 2016, 1). This maneuver allowed the government to create over 100 mobile checkpoints (Mexico Enforcement Efforts 2016, 1). Little surprise that these increased control measures resulted in far higher numbers of apprehensions, detentions, and deportations, mirroring US policies (Castillo 2016, 3-4; Mexico Enforcement Efforts 2016, 1; Arriola Vega 2017, 16–17; Holman 2017).

These efforts could not have been done without US assistance. The details of US aid do not tend to be divulged too publicly (Matalon 2016; Olson 2017, 6–7; Arriola Vega 2017, 13). What *is* known is that the US appropriated $100 million for border security equipment and training alone (Ribando Seelke and Finklea 2017, 15). In addition, in 2015 the US invested $75 million 'to help Mexico develop an automated, interagency biometrics system to help agencies collect, store, and share information on criminals and migrants', and an additional $75 million was appropriated in 2016 'to improve secure communication capabilities among Mexican agencies working in eight southern states' (Ribando Seelke and Finklea 2017, 15). Even more crucially, the US has actively assisted Mexico in strengthening its documentation checks, allegedly sending its own officers to the southern border to help their Mexican colleagues in identifying migrants who had been previously deported (Matalon 2016). This assistance seems unsurprising given that some US officials at the time considered the Mexico-Guatemala border 'our southern border' (Miller 2014, 200).[9]

Far from being appalled at the Trump administration's treatment of immigrants in the US – and the anti-Mexican rhetoric tied to those policies – the Mexican government under the López Obrador administration has continued its collaboration with the US. Whether it was Mexico's agreement to the US's Remain in Mexico policy on its northern border or the deployment of the National Guard to stifle migration flows on both borders, the López Obrador administration seems to continue to apply strategies according to US pressures (Rivers 2020). Even its new human rights-oriented laws appear to be overlooked by authorities. Human rights non-governmental organizations argue that the López Obrador administration treats migrants as abhorrently as the Trump administration (Vivanco 2020). Further, most Central American migrants are shuffled into the Mexican immigration system via the so-called humanitarian visa. Ostensibly, the visa is a positive tool, as it gives immigrants the right to remain and even work in Mexico. However, the visa's duration only lasts one year, and its renewal is usually not assured (Vonk 2019). Moreover, the receipt of the humanitarian visa prevents qualified migrants from applying for any human rights-related statuses, such as refugee status (Vonk 2019).

Conclusion

There is no international normative framework for irregular migration – but that does not mean no one controls irregular migration. Core countries, those receiving immigrants, tend to be the ones setting the rules not just when it

---

[9]   Originally reported by Dave Gibson, 'DHS Official: Our Southern Border Is Now with Guatemala' Examiner.com (no longer accessible).

comes to their own *immigration* laws, but also when it comes to laws and policies affecting their neighbors. This influence is often transmitted through horizontal networks between state agencies by providing funding and capacity-building support. To be clear, the influence of core countries is not the sole reason why periphery countries change their national rules on migration. Moreover, a reluctance by periphery countries' leaders to admit to the core's influence for internal political reasons also muddies the water and prevents a clear cause-and-effect line to be drawn. Still, there is a palpable effect of influence from core countries that can best be explained through the concept of transnational governance.

The US and Mexico form a prime example of the influence a core country can exert on its peripheral neighbor. Internal changes in US laws and greater cooperation on the US-Mexico border have increased the relevance of such cooperation and funding to be applied to Mexico's southern border. Moreover, these collaborations and cooperations precipitated internal legal and policy changes in Mexico, which support the rights of migrants on paper, but follow the same restrictive notions of US policies in practice. Far from being an emigrant country only concerned with how the northern neighbor treats Mexican citizens, Mexico has become a transit and immigration country with a new migration law on the books. Its migration policy has developed alongside these collaborations and has the same goals as in the US: deterrence and containment. This change is not unusual when realizing that transnational governance methods are imbued with power imbalances that favor core countries. Still, it is somewhat astounding that peripheral countries adopts the same viewpoint as quickly as they have; leading to the conclusion that Mexico is slowly shifting its position and is becoming part of the core.

From a transnational governance perspective, this seems a success story: the system works as intended. Information-sharing, capacity-building, and ultimately transnational harmonization – all of the elements are present and provide a viable governance system of a transnational phenomenon. The question remains one of whether the system in place is one we want to have.

References

_____. 2012. 'Acciones para la consolidación de la relación estratégica con América del Norte 2006–2012: Libro Blanco', *Secretaría de Relaciones Exteriores*, https://sre.gob.mx/images/stories/doctransparencia/rdc/2lbrean.pdf

_____. 2018. 'Relación estratégica de México con América del Norte 2012–2018: Libro Blanco', *Secretaría de Relaciones Exteriores*. https://www.gob.mx/cms/uploads/attachment/file/426734/LB_Relaci_n_estrat_gica_AmNorte.pdf

_____. 2019. 'Immigration agents 'used excessive force' during Tennessee raid', *Aljazeera*. 29 September, https://www.aljazeera.com/news/2019/02/immigration-agents-excessive-force-tennessee-raid-190221180535570.html

_____. 2016. 'Mexico's Recent Immigration Enforcement Efforts', *CRS In Focus.* https://assets.documentcloud.org/documents/2842650/CRS-Report-US-Assistance-Mexico-Southern-Border.pdf

_____.2018. 'Mexico: Evolution of the Mérida Initiative, 2007–2019'. *CRS In Focus.* https://fas.org/sgp/crs/row/IF10578.pdf

_____. n.d. 'European Reintegration Instrument – Project Leaflet', *European Migration Network.* https://emnbelgium.be/sites/default/files/attachments/eri_project_leaflet.pdf

_____. The Immigration Policies in Comparison (IMPIC) Project. http://www.impic-project.eu

_____. The International Migration Policy and Law Analysis (IMPALA) Database. http://www.impaladatabase.org

Abrego, Leisy, Mat Coleman, Daniel E. Martínez, Cecilia Menjívar, and Jeremy Slack. 2017. 'Making Immigrants into Criminals: Legal Processes of Criminalization in the Post-IIRIRA Era', *Journal of Migration and Human Security* 5: 694–715.

Alba, Francisco and Manuel Ángel Castillo. 2012. 'New Approaches to Migration Management in Mexico and Central America.' Wilson Center/Migration Policy Institute. https://www.wilsoncenter.org/sites/default/files/new_approaches_migration_management.pdf

Alba, Francisco. 2013. 'Mexico: The New Migration Narrative', *Migration Policy Institute.* 24 April. https://www.migrationpolicy.org/article/mexico-new-migration-narrative

Alvarado Fernandez, Paulina. 2006. 'La Migración Centroamericana Indocumentada En Su Paso Hacia Estados Unidos: El Papel De La Iglesia Católica Y La Política De Regulación Migratoria En México'. Licenciada thesis, Universidad de Monterrey.

Arriola Vega, Luis Alfredo. June 2017. 'Policy Adrift: Mexico's Southern Border Program', Mexico Center, James A. Baker III Institute for Public Policy of Rice University https://www.bakerinstitute.org/files/11965/

Baker, Matt. 2011. 'Mexican migration, transnationalism, and the re-scaling of citizenship in North America', *Ethnic and Racial Studies* 34, no. 1: 1.

Beer, Rand. 2015. 'The Third Meeting of the U.S.-Mexico Security Coordination Group', White House – President Barack Obama (archived). https://obamawhitehouse.archives.gov/blog/2015/02/27/third-meeting-us-mexico-security-coordination-group

Betts, Alexander. 2011. 'Introduction: Global Migration Governance', in *Global Migration Governance*, edited by Alexander Betts, 1–33. Oxford: Oxford University Press.

Blakemore, Erin. 2018. 'The Largest Mass Deportation in American History', History.com. https://www.history.com/news/operation-wetback-eisenhower-1954-deportation

Brown, Aaron. 2018. 'The Militarization of the US-Mexico Border is Not a New Idea', *History News Network*. https://historynewsnetwork.org/article/170423

Bueno Pedraza, Alejandra. 2005. 'The US borders with Mexico and Canada after the Terrorist Attacks of September 11th 2001. A Comparative View', *Boletín Mexicano de Derecho Comparado* 113: 593–616.

Carrera, Sergio, Jean-Pierre Cassarino, Nora El Qadim, Mehdi Lahlou and Leonhard den Hertog. 22 January 2016. 'EU-Morocco Cooperation on Readmission, Borders and Protection: A Model to Follow?', *CEPS Papers in Liberty and Security in Europe*, No. 87. https://www.ceps.eu/system/files/EU-Morocco%20Cooperation%20Liberty%20and%20Security%20in%20Europe.pdf

Castillo, Alejandra. 2016. 'Programa Frontera Sur: The Mexican Government's Faulty Immigration Policy', Council on Hemispheric Affairs. http://www.coha.org/wp-content/uploads/2016/10/The-Mexican-Government's-Frontera-Sur-Program-An-Inconsistent-Immigration-Policy.pdf

Castillo, Manuel Ángel. 2002. 'The Mexico-Guatemala Border: New Controls on Transborder Migrations in View of Recent Integration Schemes?', *Frontera Norte,* 15: 35–64.

Castillo, Manuel Ángel. 2006. 'Mexico: Caught Between the United States and Central America', Migration Policy Institute. https://www.migrationpolicy. org/article/mexico-caught-between-united-states-and-central-america

Crépeau, François. 2018. 'Migration, Mobility and Diversity: New Horizons for Human Rights', Venice Academy of Human Rights, European Inter-University Center for Human Rights and Democratisation, Seminar, Venice.

Crépeau, François. 2013. 'Concluding Remarks', FRA-ECtHR Seminar on European Law on Asylum, Borders and immigration Conference, Strasbourg.

2011. Decreto por el que se expide la Ley de Migración y se reforman, derogan y adicionan diversas disposiciones de la Ley General de Población, del Código Penal Federal, del Código Federal de Procedimientos Penales, de la Ley Federal contra la Delincuencia Organizada, de la Ley de la Policía Federal, de la Ley de Asociaciones Religiosas y Culto Público, de la Ley de Inversión Extranjera, y de la Ley General de Turismo, Diario Oficial de la Federación, 25 de mayo de 2011 (Mexico) (Decree for Amendment).

den Hertog, Leonhard. 2017. 'EU and German external migration policies: The case of Morocco', Heinrich Böll Stiftung. https://ma.boell.org/sites/ default/files/eu_and_german_external_migration_policies_-_ceps.pdf

2019. Designating Aliens for Expedited Removal, Fed Reg 35,409 (23 July).

Faure, Aymeric. 2017. 'Why are bilateral agreements the most frequent form of cooperation in international migration?' *Open Diplomacy Blog.*

Fitzgerald, David. 2009. *A Nation of Emigrants.* Oakland: University of California Press.

Flynn, Michael. 2002. '¿Dónde está la Frontera?', *Bulletin of the Atomic Scientists*, 48: 24–35.

Galemba, Rebeccaa. 2015. 'Mexico's Border (In)Security', *The Postcolonialist.* http://postcolonialist.com/academic-dispatches/mexicos-border-insecurity/

Gammeltoft-Hansen, Thomas. 2011. *Access to Asylum.* Cambridge: Cambridge University Press

Gillespie, Patrick. 2018. 'Mexicans in U.S. send cash home in record numbers', *CNN*. https://money.cnn.com/2018/01/02/news/economy/mexico-remittances/index.html

Gonzalez-Barrera, Ana. 2015. 'More Mexicans Leaving Than Coming to the U.S.' Pew Research Center. http://www.pewhispanic.org/2015/11/19/more-mexicans-leaving-than-coming-to-the-u-s/

Gonzalez-Murphy, Laura Valeria. 2013. *Protecting Immigrant Rights in Mexico: Understanding the State-Civil Society Nexus*. Abingdon: Routledge.

Guild, Elspeth, Cathryn Costello, Madeline Garlick, and Violeta Moreno-Lax. 2015. 'Enhancing the Common European Asylum System and Alternatives to Dublin', *CEPS Papers in Liberty and Security in Europe*, No. 83. https://www.ceps.eu/system/files/CEPS_LSE_83_0.pdf

Gutiérrez, Ramón. 2007. 'George W. Bush and Mexican Immigration Policy', *Revue Française D'études Américaines,* 113, no. 3: 70–76.

Hathaway, James and Thomas Gammeltoft-Hansen. 2015. 'Non-Refoulement in a World of Cooperative Deterrence', *Columbia Journal of Transnational Law*, 53: 235–284.

Helbling, Marc and David Leblang. 2019. 'Controlling immigration? How regulations affect migration flows', *European Journal of Political Research*, 58, no. 1: 248–269.

Heschl, Lisa. 2018. *Protecting the Rights of Refugees Beyond European Borders.* London: Intersentia.

Heyman, Josiah and Howard Campbell. 2012. 'The Militarization of the United States-Mexico Border Region', *Revista De Estudos Universitários,* 38, no. 1: 75–94.

Hirschfeld Davis, Julie and Michael D. Shear. 2018. 'How Trump Came to Enforce a Practice of Separating Migrant Families', *New York Times.* https://www.nytimes.com/2018/06/16/us/politics/family-separation-trump.html

Holman, John. 2017. 'Mexico's "invisible wall", a migrant double standard', *Aljazeera.* https://www.aljazeera.com/indepth/features/2017/02/mexico-invisible-wall-migrant-double-standard-170214213612822.html

Horwitz, Sari and Maria Sacchetti. 2018. 'Sessions vows to prosecute all illegal border crossers and separate children from their parents', *Washington Post*. https://www.washingtonpost.com/world/national-security/sessions-says-justice-dept-will-prosecute-every-person-who-crosses-border-unlawfully/2018/05/07/e1312b7e-5216-11e8-9c91-7dab596e8252_story.html?utm_term=.102576372cc4

Illegal Immigration Reform and Immigrant Responsibility Act of 1996 (IIRIRA), Div. C, Pub. L. No. 104–208, 110 Stat. 3009-546 (1996).

Isaacson, Adam, Maureen Meyer, and Gabriela Morales. 2014. 'Mexico's Other Border - Security, Migration, and the Humanitarian Crisis at the Line with Central America', *Washington Office on Latin America*. https://www.wola.org/sites/default/files/Mexico%27s%20Other%20Border%20PDF.pdf

Jessup, Philip C. 1956. *Transnational Law*. New Haven: Yale University Press

Juárez, Melina, Bárbara Gómez-Aguiñaga, and Sonia P. Bettez. 2018. 'Twenty Years after IIRIRA: The Rise of Immigrant Detention and its Effects on Latinx Communities across the Nation', *Journal of Migration and Human Security*, 6: 74–96.

Keohane, Robert O. and Joseph S. Nye. 1974. 'Transgovernmental Relations and International Organizations', *World Politics*, 27 no. 1: 39–62.

Knippen, José, Clay Boggs, and Maureen Meyer. 2015. 'An Uncertain Path _ Justice for Crimes and Human Rights Violations against Migrants and Refugees in Mexico', The Washington Office on Latin America. https://www.wola.org/sites/default/files/An%20Uncertain%20Path_Nov2015.pdf

Koch, Wendy. 2006. 'U.S. urged to apologize for 1930s deportations', *USA Today*. https://usatoday30.usatoday.com/news/nation/2006-04-04-1930s-deportees-cover_x.htm

Koslowski, Rey. 2011. 'Economic Globalization, Human Smuggling, and Global Governance', in *Global Human Smuggling: Comparative Perspectives*, edited by David Kyle and Rey Koslowski. Baltimore: Johns Hopkins University Press.

Laessing, Ulf and Andreas Rinke. 2018. 'U.N. members adopt global migration pact rejected by U.S. and others', *Reuters*. https://www.reuters.com/article/us-europe-migrants-un-pact/u-n-adopts-global-migration-pact-rejected-by-u-s-and-others-idUSKBN1O90YS

Ley de Migración, Diario Oficial de la Federación, 25 de mayo de 2011, Art 2 (Migration Law).

Ley General de Población, Diario Oficial de la Federación, 7 de enero de 1974 (Mexico), Art 103.

Ley Sobre Refugiados, Protección Complementaria y Asilo Político, as amended, Diario Oficial de la Federación, 27 de enero de 2011 (Mexico).

Lundstrom, Kristi. 2013. 'The Unintended Effects of the Three- and Ten-Year Unlawful Presence Bars', *Law and Contemporary Problems*, 76, no. 3 and 4: 389–412.

Mann, Itamar. 2013. 'Dialectic of Transnationalism', *Harvard International Law Journal*, 54, no. 2 (Summer): 315–391.

Mann, Itamar. 2016. *Humanity at Sea*. Cambridge: Cambridge University Press.

Matalon, Lorne. 2016. 'The Costs Behind the Central American Migrant Crisis', *KPBS*. https://www.kpbs.org/news/2016/jun/07/costs-behind-migrant-crisis/

Mazzei, Patricia. 2018. 'Immigration Agents Target 7-Eleven Stores in Push to Punish Employers', *New York. Times*. https://www.nytimes.com/2018/01/10/us/7-eleven-raids-ice.html

McAuliffe, Marie and Martin Ruhs. 2017. 'Report overview: Making sense of migration in an increasingly interconnected world', *IOM World Migration Report 2018*. https://publications.iom.int/system/files/pdf/wmr_2018_en.pdf

Memorandum de Entendimiento entre los Gobiernos de los Estados Unidos Mexicanos, de la Republica de El Salvador, de la Republica de Guatemala, de la Republica de Honduras y de la Republica de Nicaragua, para la Repatriación Digna, Ordenada, Ágil y Segura de Nacionales Centroamericanos Migrantes via Terrestre, May 5, 2006.

Miller, Todd. 2014. *Border Patrol Nation: Dispatches From the Front Lines of Homeland Security*. San Francisco: City Lights Publishers.

Motomura, Hiroshi. 1999. 'Federalism, International Human Rights, and Immigration Exceptionalism', *University of Colorado Law Review*, 70: 1361–1394.

Nethery, Amy, Brynna Rafferty-Brown, and Savitri Taylor. 2013. 'Exporting Detention: Australia-funded Immigration Detention in Indones', *Journal Refugee Studies*, 36: 88–109.

Ngai, Mae M. 2004. *Impossible Subjects: Illegal Aliens and The Making of Modern America*. Princeton: Princeton University Press.

Nolen, Stephanie, 2016. 'Southern exposure: The costly border plan Mexico won't discuss', *The Globe and Mail.* https://www.theglobeandmail.com/news/world/the-costly-border-mexico-wont-discuss-migration/article30397720/

Olson, Eric L. 2017. 'The Evolving Mérida Initiative and the Policy of Shared Responsibility in U.S.-Mexico Security Relations', Wilson Center. https://www.wilsoncenter.org/sites/default/files/the_evolving_Mérida_initiative_and_the_policy_of_shared_responsiblity_in_u.s.-mexico_security_relations_0.pdf

O'Neil, Kevin. 2003. 'Consular ID Cards: Mexico and Beyond', *Migration Policy Institute.* https://www.migrationpolicy.org/article/consular-id-cards-mexico-and-beyond

Partlow, Joshua and Nick Miroff. 2018. 'U.S. and Mexico discussing a deal that could slash migration at the border', *Washington Post.* https://www.washingtonpost.com/world/the_americas/us-and-mexico-discussing-a-deal-that-could-slash-migration-at-the-border/2018/07/10/34e68f72-7ef2-11e8-a63f-7b5d2aba7ac5_story.html

Passel, Jeffrey S. and D'vera Cohn. 19 November 2015. 'U.S. Unauthorized Immigrant Total Dips to Lowest Level in a Decade', Pew Research Center. http://www.pewhispanic.org/2018/11/27/u-s-unauthorized-immigrant-total-dips-to-lowest-level-in-a-decade/

Pope, Amy. 2016. 'Partnering with Mexico to Combat Crime and Secure Our Borders', *White House – President Barack Obama (archived).* https://obamawhitehouse.archives.gov/blog/2016/11/07/partnering-mexico-combat-crime-and-secure-our-borders

Ribando Seelke, Clare and Kristin Finklea. 2017. 'U.S.-Mexican Security Cooperation: The Mérida Initiative and Beyond', CRS R41349. https://fas.org/sgp/crs/row/R41349.pdf

Rivers, Matthew. 2020. 'Why Trump? Why now? Behind Mexican President Andrés Manuel López Obrador's big trip to the US', *CNN*. https://edition.cnn.com/2020/07/07/americas/mexico-us-andres-manuel-lopez-obrador-analysis-intl/index.html

Rosenau, James N. 1995. 'Governance in the Twenty-first Century', *Global Governance*, 1: 13–43.

Sacchetti, Maria. 2018. 'ICE raids meatpacking plant in rural Tennessee: 97 immigrants arrested', *Washington Post*. https://www.washingtonpost.com/local/immigration/ice-raids-meatpacking-plant-in-rural-tennessee-more-than-95-immigrants-arrested/2018/04/06/4955a79a-39a6-11e8-8fd2-49fe3c675a89_story.html

Schmitt, Eric. 2001. 'Bush Aides Weigh Legalizing Status of Mexicans In U.S.', *New York. Times*. https://www.nytimes.com/2001/07/15/us/bush-aides-weigh-legalizing-status-of-mexicans-in-us.html

Sieff, Kevin and Mary Beth Sheridan. 2018. 'U.S., Mexico pledge billions to reduce migration from Central America', *Washington Post*. https://www.washingtonpost.com/world/the_americas/us-mexico-pledge-billions-in-program-to-reduce-migration-from-central-america/2018/12/18/22ecf7bc-02f4-11e9-958c-0a601226ff6b_story.html

Silva Quiroz, Yolanda. 2014. 'Transmigración De Centroamericanos Por México: Su Vulnerabilidad Y Sus Derechos Humanos'. DPhil Thesis, Colegio de la Frontera Norte.

Slaughter, Anne-Marie. 2005. *A New World Order*. Princeton: Princeton University Press.

Stankovic, Alma. 2018. '"Bad Hombres" and Such: Migration, Race, and the US', Conflict, Peace and Democracy (CPD) Policy Blog. https://policyblog.uni-graz.at/2018/10/bad-hombres-and-such-migration-race-and-the-us/

Sullivan, Kevin. 2002. 'U.S., Mexico Set Plan For a 'Smart Border', *Washington Post*. https://www.washingtonpost.com/archive/politics/2002/03/23/us-mexico-set-plan-for-a-smart-border/7f9927db-99f7-46f3-be7d-1f3e39cd471c/?utm_term=.c8339494e767

The Immigration Reform and Control Act (IRCA), Pub. L. No. 99–603, 100 Stat. 3445 (1986)

The Schengen acquis [2007] OJ L 239/19.

The Schengen Acquis. 2020. 'The Schengen area and cooperation'. https://eur-lex.europa.eu/legal-content/EN/LSU/?uri=CELEX%3A42000A0922%2801%29

Triandafyllidou, Anna and Angeliki Dimitriadi. 2014. 'Governing Irregular Migration and Asylum at the Borders of Europe: Between Efficiency and Protection' *Imagining Europe* (6), *Istituto affari internazionali*. https://www.iai.it/sites/default/files/ImaginingEurope_06.pdf

Triandafyllidou, Anna. 2016. 'Governing Irregular Migration: Transnational Networks and National Borders', in *Europe: No Migrant's Land?*, edited by Maurizio Ambrosini. Milan: Italian Institute for International Political Studies (ISPI).

Vivanco, José Miguel. 2020. 'Op-Ed: Mexico's president and Trump have this in common: They both trample human rights', *Los Angeles Times*. https://www.latimes.com/opinion/story/2020-07-07/andres-manuel-lopez-obrador-donald-trump-meeting-washington

Vonk, Levi. 2019. 'Mexico Isn't Helping Refugees. It's Depriving Them of Their Rights', *Foreign Policy*. https://foreignpolicy.com/2019/02/08/mexico-isnt-helping-central-american-refugees-its-depriving-them-of-their-rights-caravan-1951-refugee-convention-non-refoulement-honduras-central-america-turkey-syria/

Waslin, Michele. May 2003. 'The New Meaning of the Border: U.S.-Mexico Migration Since 9/11', Reforming the Administration of Justice in Mexico Conference, Mexico. https://escholarship.org/content/qt3dd8w0r6/qt3dd8w0r6_noSplash_a16a4441dccc5846bcee4834c0a59ccc.pdf

Weiss, Thomas G. 2009. 'UN Intellectual History Project', Briefing Note, No. 15. http://www.unhistory.org/briefing/15GlobalGov.pdf

Zelaya et al v Miles et al, 3:2019cv00062 (ED Tenn, Feb 21, 2019).

Zong, Jie and Jeanne Batalova. 2018. 'Mexican Immigrants in the United States', Migration Policy Institute. https://www.migrationpolicy.org/article/mexican-immigrants-united-states

20

Solidarity and Neoliberalism in the Implementation of Mexico's Refugee, Complementary Protection and Political Asylum Law (2014–2019)

GUADALUPE CHAVEZ AND ALEXANDER VOISINE

While much migration still tends to occur along a global south to global north axis, there has been an increase in south-south migration in a number of regions. Within this context of restricted entry, refugees have found it increasingly difficult to obtain asylum, with many states in the global north engaged in an 'illiberal turn' in their immigration policy (Cantor 2015, 189–193), electing to impose demarcations between political *refugees*[10] and economic *migrants* that have largely served to exclude the vast majority of forced migrants from receiving refugee status, a legal and political phenomenon that some scholars have called the *asylum-migration nexus* (Castles 2006). Zetter (2007), Landau (2008), and Bakewell (2008) have argued that the label 'refugee' itself is worth deconstructing and challenging in part because it disregards the multiple causes that compel people to be

---

[10]   The term refugee, derived from the Geneva Convention of 1951, refers to any person outside of their country of origin who 'owing to a well-founded fear of being persecuted for reasons of race, religion, nationality, membership in a particular social group or political opinion...is unable, or owing to such a fear, unwilling to avail himself [sic] of the protection of that country.' The Geneva Convention, and its 67 Protocol, have been signed by over 140 countries, and many exclusively use the Convention's definition in their domestic refugee law despite this definition's roots in a particular moment in history that differs categorically from the nature of contemporary forced migration.

unwilling or unable to return to their home countries, which has resulted in scholars and activists urging a reinterpretation of the conditions covered by the term 'refugee' (Shacknove 2017), the use of new concepts (Betts 2013, 26–28), and a reckoning with the hegemonic influence of the global north in the development and deployment of migration labels and categories (Chimni 2008).

There has been some legal progress in the effort to expand the term 'refugee' so that it corresponds with contemporary realities and more expansive sociological and academic definitions. However, this progress is regional and scarcely implemented in practice, as is the case in Latin America, where the 1984 Cartagena Declaration has substantially expanded the definition of refugee beyond the 1951 Convention Relating to the Status of Refugees. Despite this region's discursively progressive approach to forced migration and a recent increase in mass displacement in Venezuela and Central America that has rapidly converted countries that were previously sites of emigration or transit migration into destination countries (Gandini et al. 2019), much of the academic focus continues to center around the global north (Feline Freier 2015; Cantor 2015).

Mexico, as one of the few countries that has integrated the Cartagena Declaration into its domestic refugee law – the 2014 Law on Refugees, Complementary Protection and Political Asylum (LRPCAP) – offers an interesting and understudied case that provides insight into contemporary refugee reception beyond the global north. Over the last decade, Mexico has gone from being characterized as a country of emigration and migration *in-transit* to becoming a country of refuge for thousands of refugees from a wide range of Latin American and extra-continental countries. From 2013 to 2019, Mexico saw an increase of over 5,000 percent in applications for refugee status (COMAR 2019). With a long-standing, though numerically minor tradition of offering asylum to a wide range of refugees throughout the 20th century, Mexico has discursively presented itself as a devoted adherent to the protection of refugees (Ministry of Foreign Affairs 2011).

However, the recent arrival of large numbers of refugees to Mexico, political pressure from the US, and an inadequate implementation of the LRPCAP have hindered Mexico's ability to adhere to its discursive alignment with international standards. This chapter explores how Mexico has responded to recent arrivals of refugees after the passage of the LRPCAP, focusing on gaps between law and practice. Using over a year of participant observation and interviews at a refugee resettlement non-governmental organization (NGO) in Mexico City from 2018 through 2019 and an exhaustive review of reports by federal government agencies and local NGOs, we analyze how geopolitical pressure, extraterritorial expansion of US migration control, and the asymmetrical bilateral relationship with the US has conditioned the implementation of Mexico's refugee policy. We argue that Mexico's discourse, laws, and regional policies tend to reflect principles of state-state solidarity and a certain degree of solidarity with refugees. However, the implementation of these laws and policies represents a neoliberal model of migration governance that mirrors the global north's securitization schemes. In this context, translocal NGOs and grassroots groups are responsible for filling the gaps that the Mexican state is unwilling to address, employing transformative practices grounded in mobility, membership, and visibility that offer an alternative approach to the global north's migration governance frameworks. However, they are limited by the scarce support they receive from the state. Our fieldwork reveals that the lived experiences of refugees reflect not only the influence that the US exercises on Mexico's southern border, but also its influence on the implementation of Mexico's own refugee law.

Contemporary Migration Flows across Latin America, Regional Responses, and Extraterritorial Migration Governance

Traditionally characterized for its stable south-north economic and circular migration patterns, Latin America is shifting towards becoming a region of south-south forced migration (Feldmann, Bada, and Schütze 2019). People are fleeing particular parts of the region because of economic instability, corruption, climate change, state violence, and organized crime. However, as Délano Alonso (2020) argues, these root causes are not new. What is new in the region, however, is the multilayered (Miller and Mevin 2017) 'extra-territorial sprawl' of US migration control policies (Hiemstra 2017, 45) across Latin America. Within the last 10 years, the US has expanded its migration control policies outside its national borders through a process of extra-territorialization (Fitzgerald 2020), a strategy of deterrence disguised as national security aimed at preventing migrants and refugees from reaching its physical borders through regional 'collaboration'. Hiemstra (2017, 47–53) argues that the US has been successful in implementing its migration control policies across Latin America through regional 'partnerships' with transit countries and the international expansion of Department of Homeland Security (DHS) efforts to combat drug trafficking, organized crime, and 'irregular migration flows', thus 'stretching' the presence of US military across the region.

The US's extraterritorial extension of migration control policies has reshaped *how* people are moving across the region and *where* they are ultimately arriving and settling. Militarization and policing across the Central America-US corridor has forced migrants to forge new and dangerous paths *en route* to the US, putting them at a higher risk for assault, rape, kidnapping, and death (Martinez 2014). As survival strategies for overcoming these risks, asylum seekers and migrants are traveling together in larger groups as a method of survival, protection, and as a political act to visibilize the systemic violence they face in transit (da Silveira Moreira 2013; Rivera Hernandez 2017).

While scholarship has vastly examined how destination countries in the global north govern migration flows from the global south (Gibney 2004; Hollifield 2004) and how migrants and refugees experience and navigate migration policies in the global north (De Genova 2002; Mejivar 2006; Abrego 2012), scholars are beginning to analyze the challenges and opportunities that forced migration poses in the global south and unpack what factors, and at which level, shape how states frame and implement domestic refugee legislation. Although Latin America has a long tradition of acting as a region of asylum for political refugees (Gleizer 2011, 18; Grandi 2017, 4), the demographic profile of asylum-seekers in the region has changed, with an increasing number of asylum applications from extra-continental countries as well as from indigenous and lesbian, gay, bisexual, trans, and queer plus (LGBTQ+) communities (IOM 2019) posing social, linguistic, and legal challenges in countries unaccustomed to these demographic profiles.

According to Feline Frier (2015), Latin America is a distinctive region because it has discursively contested restrictive refugee law and policy grounded in national security. Refugee policy in the region has been characterized as leaning towards a 'liberal paradigm shift' – through adopting and implementing refugee policies centered on human rights, integration, and protection. Emblematic of this liberal paradigm shift is the development of the Cartagena Declaration of 1984, which arose as a response to mass displacement in Central America stemming from civil wars in Nicaragua, Guatemala, and El Salvador. Cartagena expands the definition of 'refugee' far beyond the 1951 Geneva Convention definition (Organization of American States 1984).[1] While Fischel (2019) argues that this represents an asylum regime change, Cartagena's limitations – being non-binding, validating sovereignty, serving largely as a conceptual framework – has meant that it is scarcely applied even by states that have signed it. Still, with the notable exception of the African Union's similarly expansive definition of refugee (Okello 2014), Cartagena and Latin America stand out globally as translating the humanitarian spirit of the Geneva Convention to contemporary contexts of forced migration.

---

[1]   In addition to containing the elements of the 1951 Convention and the 1967 Protocol, the Cartagena Declaration includes (among refugees) persons who have fled their country because their lives, safety, or freedom have been threatened by 'generalized violence, foreign aggression, internal conflicts, massive violation of human rights or other circumstances which have seriously disturbed public order'.

In addition to the Cartagena Declaration and likely as a result of its coalition building in the region, Latin American countries have adopted programs and initiatives with a focus on human rights to address forced migration regionally and sub-regionally. Among region-wide programs are the 1994 San José Declaration, the 2004 Mexico Plan of Action, and the 2014 Brazil Plan of Action. Among sub-regional collaborations are the Common Market of the South (MERCOSUR), which has created a free movement residence agreement between Argentina, Paraguay, Uruguay, and Brazil (previously Venezuela as well), and the Union of South American Nations (UNASUR), which has launched initiatives related to migration through the South American Conference on Migration (Pires Ramos et al. 2017). In Central America and Mexico, the 2017 Comprehensive Regional Framework for Protection and Solutions (MIRPS) and the 2019 Comprehensive Development Plan have taken a human rights-based approach to migration in the region, with collaborative resettlement plans and an emphasis on addressing the root causes of migration. Although there has been little indication as to the success of these last two initiatives, due in part to their relative novelty (Velázquez 2020, 43), in theory they represent a collaborative, transnational approach that contrasts sharply with the unilateralism and national security approach of the US, making these initiatives geopolitically significant.

Apart from multilateral collaborations, a number of countries have adopted refugee and migration laws that ostensibly prioritize human rights consider-ations over national security, with Argentina being the first in the world to recognize migration as a human right in 2003, followed by Colombia in 2004, and Ecuador and Uruguay in 2008 (Gandini et al. 2019). The Cartagena Declaration's wide framing of the definition of refugee has been adopted in domestic legislation by 15 countries in the region as well, lending a degree of credibility to its relevance (Fischel 2019; Cantor 2015, 196). However, despite the incorporation of the Cartagena Declaration into the domestic legislation of most countries in the region, Mexico remains the only country that has actually applied Cartagena *en masse*, and to this date it has only been applied to Venezuelans applying for refugee status in Mexico (Gandini et al. 2019). In the following sections, we analyze Mexico as a case study of a country that espouses the human-rights-centered principles enshrined in international and regional frameworks, exploring how the implementation of its refugee law coheres with and deviates from these frameworks under geopolitical pressures and the proliferation of extraterritorial bordering regimes.

Mexico's National Approach to Refugee Protection (2014–2019): Protection, Temporary Legality, and Deportation

Mexico's contemporary approach to refugee protection is grounded in three legal frameworks: the Mexican Constitution, the 2011 Law of Migration, and the 2011 Law of Refugees, Complementary Protection and Political Asylum[2]. However, Mexico's economic integration with the US (Delano 2011, 5), bilateral securitization agreements with the US related to the 2014 surge of unaccompanied Central American children, and the 2018 migrant caravans have pressured Mexico into implementing migration governance schemes grounded in border enforcement, deterrence, and removal, significantly affecting the process for seeking refuge in Mexico.

Since the early 2000s Mexico has entered a series of bilateral security agreements with the US on managing organized crime and migration flows across the Central America-US corridor. Through security partnerships, such as *Plan Sur* (2002) and the Merida Initiative (2008), Mexico has secured funding from the US[3] and has carried out its extraterritorial bordering schemes by implementing a series of law enforcement, militarization, and deportation procedures (Flynn 2002; Torre and Yee 2018) in cooperation with Central America and countries in the Caribbean. In effect, Mexico has become a fortress and a buffer zone for refugees and migrants, curtailing mobility towards the US.

This continued under former President Peña Nieto's implementation of the Southern Border Program (SBP) in 2014 after the surge of unaccompanied Central American children at the US-Mexico border. The purpose of SBP was to manage irregular migration flows with the aim of securing Mexico's southern border while protecting migrants entering Mexico. In practice, the Mexican government mobilized military and police presence in Mexico's southern border towns, establishing roadblocks and mobile checkpoints throughout highways from southern to east-central Mexico; constructed detention centers; and collaborated with officials from the National Migration Institute (INM) and local police enforcement to carry out raids and arrests (Arriola Vega 2017). As a result, Mexican apprehensions of migrants from Central America increased from 134,000 in 2014 to 173,000 in 2015, surpassing apprehensions by US immigration authorities; that same year, Mexico also carried out more removals at the Mexico-Guatemala border than the US-Mexico border (Selee et al. 2019). Furthermore, according to a 2017 survey conducted by Amnesty International with over 500 respondents including migrants and asylum seekers, 75 percent of individuals apprehended and detained by INM officials were not informed of their legal right to seek asylum in Mexico. In addition, 120 respondents seeking asylum were deported – violating the *non-refoulement* principle and thus domestic and international law (Amnesty international 2019). These policies have

---

[2]   In 2014, the Mexican Congress reformed this law to include political asylum.

[3]   As of March 2017, the US has delivered more than $1.6 billion to Mexico to carry out the goals of the Mérida Initiative. See Seelke and Finklea (2017).

expanded an 'architecture of repulsion' (Fitzgerald 2020) in Mexico, mirroring US interests, creating what some have called a 'vertical border' (Velázquez 2011; Torre and Yee 2018), and forcing migrants and refugees into more dangerous transit routes, leaving them more exposed to organized crime and harsh geographic and climate conditions (Martinez 2008; Hernández 2019). The human rights stipulations of the SBP were effectively ignored.

Paradoxically, at around the same time that the Mexican federal government implemented SBP, Mexico passed the LRPCAP, a transformative document that expanded the role and responsibilities of Mexico in receiving refugees. The law stands out not only for its incorporation of the Cartagena Declaration, but also for its inclusion of sexual orientation and gender identity (SOGI) based persecution as a grounds for refugee status, the figure of 'complementary protection', which offers a pathway to permanent residence, a relatively rapid time frame for resolving applications for refugee status (45 working days), the obligation of Mexico to facilitate access to rights and social services, and the requirement to collaborate with civil society organizations to combat xenophobia and address the protection needs of refugees and applicants for refugee status (LRPCAP 2014).

Aside from the LRPCAP, refugees and applicants for refugee status in Mexico are technically granted all rights accorded to Mexican citizens by the Mexican Constitution and are protected by binding international accords and conventions that Mexico has ratified. Recent policies have allowed for applicants for refugee status to access a civil registration document (CURP), a tax ID document (RFC), and a temporary residency card that can be renewed annually, together providing access to employment, healthcare, and education.

It is also important to note that Mexico's Commission for Assistance to Refugees (COMAR), which is responsible for processing applications for refugee status, is a decentralized humanitarian agency that ostensibly protects the needs of refugees and applicants and works closely with the United Nations High Commissioner for Refugees (UNHCR), unlike the INM, which is largely focused on detention, deportation, and national security. Despite the progress represented by the LRPCAP, recent surges in refugee arrivals in Mexico have put the LRPCAP to test. From 2013 to 2019, applications for refugee status in Mexico have increased by 5,000 percent (Government of Mexico 2019). The increase is particularly sharp following Donald Trump's inauguration in January 2017, as evidenced by Figure 1.

Mexico has dealt with the surge in applications for refugee status in conflicting ways, at times defying the rhetoric of the US and at other times acquiescing. Unlike his predecessor Peña Nieto, current President Andrés Manuel López Obrador has pledged to approach migration through a human rights, development, and regional framework to address the root causes of migration and transform migration into a choice rather than a necessity (Government of Mexico 2019). López Obrador has also stated that he would provide humanitarian protection to newly arrived migrants. In 2019, the López Obrador administration released a document titled the New Migration Policy of the Federal Government of Mexico 2018–2024. The document lists the administrative protocols that will be taken to address migration, including treating migration as a shared regional responsibility, establishing safe, orderly, and regular migration, strengthening migration institutions, the integration of foreign nationals into Mexican society, and fostering sustainable development, citing the 2011 Law of Migration, LRPCAP, and the Global Compact of Migration and Refugees.

In response to the arrival of Central American caravans in January 2019, the INM implemented the 'Emergent Program for the Granting of Visitor for Humanitarian Reasons Cards', or humanitarian visa program. These one-year visas provided both migrants and refugees with temporary mobility across the country, the right to leave and reenter the country, and work authorization – essential for local integration. However, the program ended on 28 January 2019 because, according to then-INM Commissioner Tonatiuh Guillen, the visa program was 'too successful' and overwhelmed the infrastructure of INM (Lin 2019) after more than 15,000 Central Americans applied for the humanitarian visa. Although this program was short-lived, it represented an alternative approach to the migration governance framework of the US, one centered on access to rights, mobility, and integration. However, in May 2019, the Trump administration threatened to increase tariffs on imported goods if the López Obrador administration did not reduce migration flows into US's borders, resulting in the López Obrador administration reneging on its original plans and further militarizing Mexico's southern border.

Gaps between Law and Practice: The Lived Experience of Refugees in Mexico

The lived experiences of refugees in Mexico deviate significantly from the protections the LRPCAP discursively offers, undermining what might have functioned as a counter-example to the illiberal policies of many global north countries, and in many cases replicating those same policies of exclusion against refugees crossing Mexico's southern border. One of the main sources of this deviation between law and practice is the scant funding appropriated to the COMAR, Mexico's humanitarian refugee agency. Despite a 5,000-percent increase in applications for refugee status from 2013 to 2019, the COMAR's budget has not increased anywhere near the same rate, with a 2020 fiscal year budget of just over $2 million, less than half of what was requested, to resolve a record high of refugee status applications (SEGOB 2020). The budget of the INM, which is largely focused on enforcement, is around $70 million; the increase in the INM budget from 2019 to 2020 alone was three and a half times more than the total budget of the COMAR from 2013 to 2019 (Soberanes 2019).

The meager budget of the COMAR is most directly experienced by refugees in the form of long application resolution wait times that far exceed the 45-day period outlined in the law, reaching close to two years for a little under half of applicants currently awaiting a resolution (Asylum Access 2020). Because applicants are required to sign in at the COMAR's office every week in person, these extensions are particularly prohibitive in terms of economic integration. During our fieldwork, many refugees recounted that they had to ask for time off to wait in the long lines at the COMAR to sign in, and in some cases, this limited their ability to get hired or maintain a job. For those who are held in detention centers while they await their application's resolution, this means weeks and often months living in degrading conditions that violate government human rights standards (Colectivo de Observación 2019), generating physical and mental health problems that follow detainees long after their release – according to representatives at Programa Casa Refugiados, a refugee resettlement non-profit based in Mexico City.

An analysis of favorable case resolutions also seems to imply that nationality and socioeconomic class may be factors that facilitate the application resolution process for some refugees. A lawyer at the Alaide Foppa legal clinic at the Ibero-American University in Mexico City explained in an interview that since 2016, when Mexico declared a situation of 'grave violations of human rights' in Venezuela, the Cartagena provisions in the LRPCAP have been nearly universally applied to Venezuelans, resulting in an acceptance rate of 99 percent (Colectivo de Observación 2019). Because Mexico has not applied the same standard for other countries – such as El Salvador, Honduras, Nicaragua, and Guatemala, where 'generalized violence' and 'grave violations of human rights' are arguably just as pervasive – the Cartagena provisions are less accessible, leading to a significantly lower acceptance rate for applicants from Central American countries (SEGOB 2020). It is important to point out that most Venezuelans arrive in Mexico by plane – which implies economic resources and the ability to obtain a visa in Venezuela before leaving – and predominantly have high educational levels (Gandini et al. 2019, 318.) While speculative, this may reflect, as Gandini et al. (2019) have suggested, a historical selectivity based on class and race that favors more socioeconomically advantaged groups (Wollny 1991; García 2006).

Due to the lack of a national resettlement program, refugees in Mexico are generally responsible for their own integration process, which disproportionately affects lower-income refugees. In our interviews with representatives from *Programa Casa Refugiados* and during our fieldwork, the local and federal government were scarcely presented as helpful or even involved in the integration process of refugees. NGO representatives that we interviewed cited a lack of financial resources, virtually no alliances between government institutions and refugee resettlement organizations, and insufficient sensibilization initiatives to combat xenophobia and educate employers about refugees' rights to work. All interviewees considered the government's response to be inadequate, and refugees consulted during our fieldwork had little confidence in the government, instead relying on shelters, NGOs, and the monthly $50–200 stipend provided by the UNHCR.

For vulnerable groups, including women and members of the LGBTQ+ community, the lack of government support combined with discrimination and violence makes for an even more difficult integration process. Many trans women and other members of the LGBTQ+ community often are obligated to perform sex work as a mode of survival, are unable to stay in most shelters due to discrimination, and also face discrimination within government institutions. Their difficulties integrating into Mexico reflect the violent limits of policies that not only fail to facilitate the integration process, but in many cases complicate it, especially in cases of institutional discrimination.

In the absence of state policies supporting refugees, NGOs represent the only source of material, affective, and informational support available to refugees, offering a wide range of services, including information about job openings, legal support, counseling, and social events. *Programa Casa Refugiados*, a particularly comprehensive organization, holds workshops about jobs, basic information about Mexico City, and legal processes, while also offering individualized case management and collaborations with other NGOs and the academic community to advocate for better refugee policies. Shelters like la 72 in Tabasco along with a number of shelters in Mexico City and border towns in the north of Mexico offer temporary housing, medical attention, and a sense of community. This 'grassroots' level support offers a minimum level of access to resources to refugees, but the organizations that provide these resources are generally under-resourced themselves, relying on private organizations, international NGOs, and unpaid volunteers. With an increase in applications for refugee status, these organizations have found themselves particularly strained, not least refugee and migrant shelters, which have had to turn refugees away because of a lack of space (Prensa Libre 2019).

Grassroots movements, such as the caravans of 2018 and 2019, have also emerged as a way of visibilizing the plight of refugees crossing through Mexico, collectively pooling resources, demanding fair treatment and appealing to the international community for support and sympathy (Valera et al. 2019). In a more global sense, as Varela argues (2017), these caravans also represent a reclamation of agency by their members, who demand an end to 'state, market, and patriarchal violence'. Interestingly, these demands are in line with Mexico's Comprehensive Development Plan mentioned above, which seeks to address the socioeconomic root causes of forced migration. Paradoxically, though, Mexico's foreign policy appears to be aligned with the demands of the caravans, Mexican authorities in 2018 and 2019 reacted with violence to the arrival of the caravans, detaining, summarily deporting, and tear-gassing its members, many of whom had expressed fears of returning to their home countries (Villegas and Yuhas, 2019; Averbuch and Semple, 2019; Pradilla, 2020).

Competing Agendas of Refugee Resettlement: The Neoliberal Model and the Solidarity Model

Mexico's progressive refugee law as well as the goals set forth in the regional compacts and development plans it has spearheaded and participated in contrasts with the reality lived by refugees in Mexico. We identify two models that Mexico has employed in its refugee resettlement strategies – a neoliberal model and a state-state centered solidarity model – which reflect the geopolitical balance that Mexico is tasked with navigating in its relationship with the US.

The neoliberal model of 'migration state policy' tends to view human rights in economic terms and in effect 'monetizes cross-border flows' and 'commodifies forced displacement' (Adamson and Tsourapas 2019). In the neoliberal model, the economically productive refugee – self-sufficient, not in need of state resources, able to facilitate their own integration process – has more market value' (Somers 2008; Adamson and Tsourapas 2019) than refugees who are in need of state protection or require state resources in order to socially and economically integrate into the host society. The neoliberal model of migration policy coincides with neoliberal state policies that seek to reduce the strength of the welfare state by disinvesting in public institutions and restructuring indebted economies through structural adjustment loans (Tobias 2012). The effects of neoliberal globalization have been especially acute in the global south, where state resources are inaccessible to many citizens, let alone refugees. In order to secure funding for refugee resettlement, states in the global south, like Mexico, rely on international organizations such as the UNHCR or funding from wealthier states, the latter of which is often earmarked for security and border enforcement, further eroding local human rights protections.

At the international level, solidarity entails processes of state participation and responsibility aimed at stabilizing social and political order (Weber 2007), grounded in national interests to protect sovereignty and the national community. The principle of solidarity at the state-state level in relation to contemporary forced migration privileges state-state relationships that encompass a series of state interventions based on responsibility, burden-sharing, and 'shared coercion' (Fitzgerald 2020) aimed at surveilling and curtailing the mobility of refugees. Nevertheless, these state-state oriented solidarity models produce multiple political configurations and implications across space and geographies. Although Mexico has seen a surge in refugee applications, it receives no support from neighboring countries in implementing regional refugee integration and protection programs, but instead has received solidarity from the US in the form enforcement 'aid' for further militarizing its borders and deterring mobility to protect the US's national borders from outsiders that fall outside its parameters of national membership. Mexico's replication of US border enforcement and coercion practices across its territory and its weak domestic solidarity model towards refugees indicates that Mexico continues to privilege state-state relationships over state-refugee relationships, thus failing to implement its discursively human-rights-based approach to forced migration.

As a result of Mexico's weak solidarity model at the domestic level, NGOs and grassroots collectives are filling gaps that the Mexican government is unwilling to address with regards to resettlement, such as *mobile solidarity*, which encompasses the protection and well-being of refugees in translocal spaces across the country, including offering refugees access to food and shelter along the Central American-Mexico-US corridor. Another important initiative is accompaniment programs where staff and volunteers accompany refugees to bureaucratic offices such as the INM to apply for identification documents necessary for accessing health, educational, and legal services, which are essential for facilitating the local integration of refugees. Such practices contest Mexico's state-based regional frameworks centered on securitization, which have had harmful and deadly consequences on the refugee population and represent an alternative approach towards refugee policy and, more broadly, migration governance frameworks because they are grounded in principles of mobility, membership, visibility, and close, empathetic contact with refugees, all of which have been minimized and criminalized by the Mexican state.

Although Mexico has adopted a discursively progressive approach to address the influx of Central American and extra-continental refugees through expanding the Geneva Convention of 1951 definition of refugees into its domestic refugee law, Mexico's day-to-day responses have been significantly shaped by geopolitics and bilateral economic and security agreements with the US. These factors have pushed Mexico to implement a neoliberal model in practice, despite laws and discourses that reflect a refugee solidarity model. The neoliberal model has left refugees in conditions of precarity – limiting legal routes to access refugee status and complicating their integration process.

Conclusion

Our case study of Mexico seeks to provoke further debate on how countries across the global south are responding to shifts in migration waves, unpacking which factors, and at what scale, shape their national responses. The case of Mexico reveals how the US supports and imposes a neoliberal model by earmarking much-needed funding for securitization schemes and refusing to financially support the Comprehensive Development Plan, the COMAR, and translocal initiatives premised on notions of refugee solidarity. Mexico, in turn, has increasingly acted in solidarity with the US's demands, at the expense of solidarity with refugees. In effect, the US has not only exported its southern border, but it has also conditioned Mexico's refugee policy to the extent that it scarcely reflects the law. As south-south and north-south migration waves continue to proliferate, new migration paradigms are needed to unpack the decisions, approaches, and implementation models that states are using to address these new challenges and opportunities, and how these models are conditioned by the demands of the global north.

Figures

Figure 1: Applications for Refugees Status in Mexico 2013–2019. Authors'
elaboration using data from the Government of Mexico (2019).

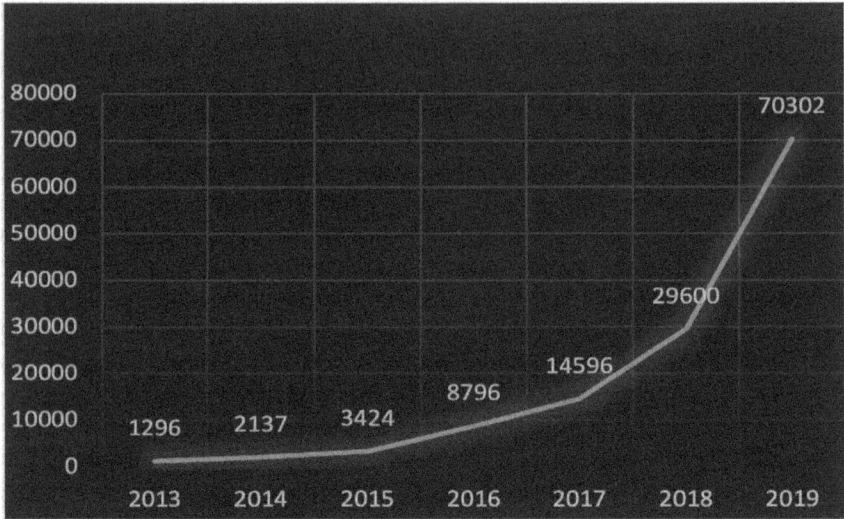

Figure 2: Percentage of Applications Granted Refugee Status by Nationality:
January 2013–June 2020. Authors' elaboration using data from the
Government of Mexico (2020).

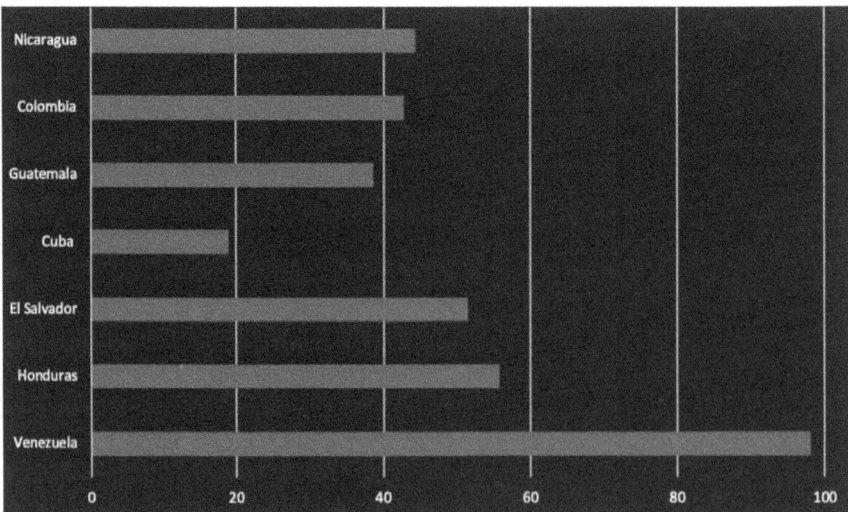

References

Arriola Vega, Luis Alfredo. 2017. 'Policy Adrift: Mexico's Southern Border Program', James A. Baker III Institute for Public Policy of Rice University. https://www.bakerinstitute.org/media/files/files/fa7ac127/MEX-pub-FronteraSur-062317.pdf

Averbuch, Maya, and Kirk Semple. 2019. 'Mexico's Crackdown at Its Southern Border, Prompted by Trump, Scares Migrants from Crossing', *The New York Times,* June 24. https://www.nytimes.com/2019/06/24/world/americas/mexico-guatemala-border.html.

Bakewell, Oliver. 2008. 'Research Beyond the Categories: The Importance of Policy Irrelevant Research into Forced Migration', *Journal of Refugee Studies,* 21, no. 4: 432–53.

Betts, Alexander. 2013. *Survival Migration: Failed Governance and the Crisis of Displacement.* Ithaca, NY: Cornell University Press.

Cantor, David James; Feline Freier, Luisa; Gauci, Jean-Pierre; Ceriani Cernadas, Pablo. 2015. *A Liberal Tide?: Immigration and Asylum Law and Policy in Latin America.* London:

Institute of Latin American Studies, School of Advanced Study, University of London.

Castles, Stephen. 2006. 'Global Perspectives on Forced Migration', *Asian and Pacific Migration Journal,* 15, no. 1: 7–28.

Chimni, B. S. 2008. 'The Birth of a 'Discipline': From Refugee to Forced Migration Studies', *Journal of Refugee Studies,* 22, no. 1: 11–29.

COMAR. Boletín Estadístico: Extranjeros presentados y devueltos. 2019. http://www.politicamigratoria.gob.mx/es/PoliticaMigratoria/CuadrosBOLETIN?Anual=2019&Secc=3

da Silveria Moreira, Julio. 2013. Migrant Routes Through Mexico and the Caravans of Mothers', *Voices of Mexico*, no 96: 23–27. http://ru.micisan.unam.mx:8080/xmlui/handle/123456789/19387

Délano, Alexandra. 2011. *Mexico and Its Diaspora in the United States: Policies of Emigration Since 1848.* New York: Cambridge University Press.

Délano Alonso, Alexandra. 2020. 'Time for an Alternative Politics of Migration', *Current Histories,* 119, no. 814: 73–76.

De Peña, Kristie., and Van Fossen, Emily. 2020. 'The State of Asylum: Changes Made to the Asylum System During the Trump Administration', *The Niskanen Center.* https://www.niskanencenter.org/the-state-of-asylum

De Genova, Nicholas. 2002. 'Migrant "illegality" and deportability in everyday life', *Annual review of Anthropology,* 31, no. 1: 419–447.

Diario Oficial de la Federación. 2014. Ley sobre Refugiados, Protección Complementaria, y Asilo Político. Articles 6, 13, 15, 36.

Diogo. 2017. 'Towards a regional agreement on environmental displacement', *Forced Migration Review,* no. 56: 65–67.

Espinosa Cantellano, P., Gómez Robledo Verduzco, J. M., Negrín Muñoz, A. 2011. *Informe de*

México: Avances y desafíos en materia de derechos humanos. Dirección General de

Derechos Humanos: México. Secretaria de Relaciones Exteriores.https://www.upr-info.org/followup/assessments/session17/mexico/Mexico-InformHR.pdf

Feldmann, Andreas E., Xóchitl Bada, and Stephanie Schütze, eds. 2018. *New migration patterns in the Americas: challenges for the 21st century.* Switzerland: Springer.

Fischel de Andrade, José H. 2019. 'The 1984 Cartagena Declaration: A Critical Review of Some Aspects of Its Emergence and Relevance', *Refugee Survey Quarterly*, 341–362.

FitzGerald, David Scott. 2020. 'Remote control of migration: theorising territoriality, shared coercion, and deterrence', *Journal of Ethnic and Migration Studies,* 46, no. 1: 4–22.

Flynn, Michael. 2002. '¿ Dónde está La Frontera?', *Bulletin of the Atomic Scientists,* 58, no. 4 25–35.

Freier, Luisa Feline. 2015. 'A Liberal Paradigm Shift?: A Critical Appraisal of Recent Trends in Latin American Asylum Legislation', in *Exploring the Boundaries of Refugee Law,* edited by Jean-Pierre Gauci, Mariagiulia Giuffre and Evangelia Tsourdi, 118–145. Leiden and Boston: Brill Nijhoff.

Gallemba, Rebecca. 2015. 'Mexico's Border (I)nsecurity'. *The Postcolonialist* 2, no.2. http://postcolonialist.com/academic-dispatches/mexicos-border-insecurity

Gandini, Luciana; Lozano, Fernando; Prieto, Victoria. (eds). 2019. *Crisis y migración de población venezolana. Entre la desprotección y la seguridad jurídica en Latinoamérica.* UNAM: Ciudad de México.

García, María Cristina. 2006. *Seeking Refuge: Central American Migration to Mexico, the United States, and Canada.* Berkeley: University of California Press.

Gibey, Matthew. 2004. *The Ethics and Politics of Asylum: Liberal Democracy and the Response to Refugees.* UK: Cambridge University Press.

Gleizer, Daniela. 2012. *El Exilio Incómodo México y Los Refugiados Judíos, 1933–1945.* México, D.F.: El Colegio de México/Universidad Autónoma Metropolitana.

Grandi, Filippo. 2017. 'Foreword: Regional Solidarity and Commitment to Protection in Latin America and the Caribbean', *Forced Migration Review* , no. 56: 4–6.

Guadarrama, Ricardo Domínguez. 2017. *Neoliberalismo: Treinta Años De Migración En América Latina, México y Michoacán.* Ciudad de México: Universidad Nacional Autónoma de México.

Hiemstra, Nancy. 2019. Pushing the US-Mexico border south: United States' immigration policing throughout the Americas'. *International Journal of Migration and Border Studies,* 5, no. 1–2: 44–63.

Hollifield, James. 2004. 'The Emerging Migration State', *International Migration Review*, 38 no.3: 885–912.

Huerta, Amarela Varela. 2017. 'La Trinidad Perversa De La Que Huyen Las Fugitivas Centroamericanas: Violencia Feminicida, Violencia De Estado y Violencia De Mercado', *Debate Feminista* 53: 1–17.

Huerta, Amarela Varela, and Lisa Mclean. 2019. 'Caravana De Migrantes En México: Nueva Forma De Autodefensa y Transmigración', *Revista CIDOB d'Afers Internacionals*, no. 122: 163–86.

International Migration Review. 2019. 'Extraregional Migration in the Americas: Profiles, Experiences and Needs'. https://publications.iom.int/system/files/pdf/extraregional-migration-report-en.pdf

Landau, Loren B. 2007. 'Can We Talk and Is Anybody Listening? Reflections on IASFM 10, "Talking Across Borders: New Dialogues in Forced Migration"', *Journal of Refugee Studies,* 20, no. 3: 335–48.

Martínez, Óscar. 2014. *The Best: Riding the Rails and Dodging Narcos on the Migrant Trail.* London and New York: Verso.

Menjívar, Cecilia. 2006. 'Liminal legality: Salvadoran and Guatemalan immigrants' lives in the United States', *American Journal of Sociology*, 111, no. 4: 999–1037.

Miller, Todd and Nevins, Joseph. 2017. 'Beyond Trump's Big Beautiful Wall', *NACLA Report on the Americas*, 59: 145–151.

Okello, J O Moses. 2014. 'The 1969 OAU Convention and the Continuing Challenge for the African Union', *Forced Migration Review*, no. 48: 70–73.

Pires Ramos, Erika, Cavedon-Capdeville, Fernanda, Yamamoto, Lillian and Andreola Serraglio, Pradilla, A. 2020. 'Opinión | México Insiste En Ser La Primera Línea Del Muro De Trump', *The Washington Post*. https://www.washingtonpost.com/es/post-opinion/2020/01/20/caravana-migrante-mexico-insiste-en-ser-la-primera-linea-del-muro-de-trump/

Prensa Libre. 2019. 'Albergues En México Se Desbordan Mientras Migrantes Esperan Respuesta a Su Solicitud De Asilo', *Prensa Libre*. https://www.prensalibre.com/guatemala/migrantes/albergues-en-mexico-se-desbordan-mientras-migrantes-esperan-respuesta-a-su-solicitud-de-asilo/.

Secretaría de Gobernación, 'Programa Frontera Sur: Proteger La Vida de Las Personas Migrantes y Fortalecer El Desarrollo Regional', May 11, 2015.

Selee Andrew, Silvia E. Giorguli-Saucedo, Ariel G. Ruiz and Claudia Masferrer. 2019. 'Investing in the Neighborhood: Changing Mexico-U.S Migration Patterns and Opportunities for Sustainable Cooperation', *Migration Policy Institute*. https://www.migrationpolicy.org/research/mexico-us-migration-opportunities-sustainable-cooperation

Shacknove, Andrew E. 2017. 'Who Is a Refugee?', *International Refugee Law*, 163–73.

Soberanes, Rodrigo. 2019. 'Gobierno Propone Aumento a Presupuesto Del INM Para Atender La Crisis Migratoria', *Animal Político*, September 9. https://www.animalpolitico.com/2019/09/gobierno-solicita-aumento-presupuesto-inm-crisis-migratoria/

Somers, Margaret R. 2010. *Genealogies of Citizenship: Markets, Statelessness, and the Right to Have Rights*. Cambridge: Cambridge University Press.

Rivera Hernandez, Raul Diego. 2017. 'Making Absence Visible: The Caravan of Central American Mothers in Search of Disappeared Migrants', *Latin American Perspectives*, 44, no.5: 108–126.

Torre Cantalapiedra, Eduardo, & Yee Quintero, Jose Carlos. 2018. 'México ¿una frontera vertical? Políticas de control del tránsito migratorio irregular y sus resultados, 2007–2016.' *Limina R. Estudios Sociales y Humanísticos*, 16 (2).

Tobias, Saul. 2012. Neoliberal Globalization and the Politics of Migration in Sub-Saharan Africa, *Journal of International and Global Studies,* 4.1: 1–16.

Velázquez Ortega, Elisa. 2020. *México como tercer país (in)seguro?* Opiniones Técnicas sobre Temas de Relevancia Nacional. Serie 13. Ciudad de México, DF: Instituto de Investigaciones Jurídicas.

Velázquez González, Eduardo. 2011. *Frontera Vertical: México Frente a Los Migrantes Centroamericanos*. Guadalajara, México: Centro Universitario UTEG.

Villegas, Paulina, and Alan Yuhas. 2019. 'Mexico Calls on U.S. to Investigate Use of Tear Gas at Border', *The New York Times,* January 3. https://www.nytimes.com/2019/01/03/world/americas/mexico-border-tear-gas-investigation.html

Weber, Martin. 2007. The Concept of Solidarity in the Study of World Politics: Towards a Critical Theoretic Understanding', *Review of International Studies,* 33, no. 4: 693–713.

Wollny, Hans. 1991. 'Asylum Policy in Mexico: A Survey', *Journal of Refugee Studies* 4, no. 3: 219–36.

World Health Organization. 2020. 'Refugee and Migrant Health', World Health Organization. https://www.who.int/migrants/en/

Zetter, Roger. 2007. 'More Labels, Fewer Refugees: Remaking the Refugee Label in an Era of Globalization', *Journal of Refugee Studies,* 20, no. 2: 172–92.

21

Aiding and Abetting: Assessing the Responsibility of European Union Officials for Crimes Against Humanity Committed Against Migrants in Libya

PAT RUBIO BERTRAN

The International Criminal Court (ICC) has had an open investigation in Libya since 2011, following a unanimous referral by the United Nations Security Council (UNSC) (ICC, 2011). The investigation has involved charges that include crimes against humanity (murder, imprisonment, torture, persecution, and other inhumane acts) (ICC, 2011). On 8 May 2017, the Prosecutor of the ICC, Fatou Bensouda, told the UNSC that her office was examining the feasibility of opening an investigation into migrant-related crimes in Libya (ICC 2017). Crimes against humanity, as per the Rome Statute of the International Criminal Court, means any of the following acts when committed as part of a widespread or systematic attack directed against any civilian population with knowledge of the attack: murder, extermination, enslavement, deportation or forcible transfer of population, imprisonment, torture, rape and other forms of sexual violence, persecution, enforced disappearance, the crime of apartheid, and other inhumane acts (ICC 1998).

In the context of widespread and systematic crimes committed against migrants in Libya, the European Union (EU) and its member states continue to collaborate with the North African country to stop migration to the EU via the Central Mediterranean. Since 2014, the EU has not had an active search and rescue mission for migrants at sea attempting to flee from Libya (Pillai 2019). Instead, the current policy consists of pushing migrants and refugees back to the North African country by training and funding the Libyan Coast Guard (LCG) to intercept migrants, which end up in detention centers in Libya (Pillai 2019). Scholars Itamar Mann, Violeta Moreno-Lax, and Omer Shatz have gone one step further and asked for the role of the EU to be scrutinized (Mann, Moreno-Lax and Shatz 2018). They state that 'assisting, training, or funding organs of countries that disregard human rights may trigger international responsibility'(Mann, Moreno-Lax and Shatz 2018). Moreover, they argue, no aid or assistance should be offered in a context of gross and systematic human rights violations if it can contribute to maintaining the status quo (Mann, Moreno-Lax and Shatz 2018).

So far, the issue of the EU and its member states' involvement in Libya has been mostly discussed in terms of state responsibility and human rights violations. However, influential observers, and even French President Emmanuel Macron, stated that trafficking in the North African country has become a crime against humanity (Mann, Moreno-Lax and Shatz 2018). Within this environment, claims demanding an investigation of the EU's involvement in crimes against migrants in Libya came to fruition with a Communication to the Office of the Prosecutor of the ICC in 2019 (Shatz and Branco 2019). Invoking Article 15 of the Rome Statute, relating to the initiation of *proprio motu* investigation, Omer Shatz and Juan Branco, lawyers and professors at the Paris Institute of Political Studies, also known as Sciences Po, alleged that thousands of deaths and other 'crimes against humanity' had been committed as a direct result of EU policy. In their communication, Shatz and Branco discuss several modes of liability that could emerge from the EU's policies in Libya and the Mediterranean (Shatz and Branco 2019). All the above calls for a need to assess the implications of the EU's collaboration with Libya, not as an international organization but as an individual agent.

The aim of this chapter is to assess if individual criminal responsibility can emerge as a result of border externalization policies in Libya, exclusively for aiding and abetting crimes against humanity against migrants. The first section of the chapter will look into the widespread and systematic crimes that migrants face in Libya and its alleged perpetrators. The second section will analyze the relevant legal aspects of aiding, abetting, and otherwise assisting crimes against humanity. The third section will critically analyze the EU's policies and collaboration with Libya, keeping in mind the two main elements of criminal responsibility: the mental and material elements. The last section will assess if those policies could trigger the ICC's jurisdiction and what challenges could arise.

Crimes against Migrants and Border Externalization Policies

As early as in 2011, when the ICC opened its investigation for crimes against humanity in Libya, the International Organization for Migration (IOM) issued an alarm after gathering testimonies of trafficking victims in Libya, which they defined as a 'torture archipelago' (UN News 2017). Also in 2011, the Panel of Experts on Libya, together with the United Nations Support Mission in Libya (UNSMIL), reported that from the moment migrants enter Libya, they become subjected to unlawful killings, torture and other ill-treatment, arbitrary detention and unlawful deprivation of liberty, rape and other forms of sexual and gender-based violence, slavery and forced labor, and extortion and exploitation by armed groups, traffickers, smugglers, private parties, police, the Libyan Coast Guard (LCG), and the Department for Combating Illegal Migration (UNSC 2017).

In August 2017, Agnes Callamard, United Nations Special Rapporteur on extrajudicial, summary, or arbitrary executions submitted a report regarding unlawful deaths of migrants and refugees (UNGA 2017). One of the violations Callamard addresses is the threat posed to migrants resulting from border externalization policies, which could amount to aiding and assisting in the deprivation of life and the failure to prevent foreseeable deaths or other violations (UNGA 2017, 2). In the same report, Callamard detailed how border externalization policies, including 'assisting, funding, or training agencies in other countries to arrest, detail, process, rescue, or disembark and return refugees or migrants' raised serious concerns where the recipient states are alleged to be responsible for serious crimes (UNGA 2017, 10–36). She goes on to remark that, by 'funding and training agencies that commit those abuses, funding States are potentially aiding and assisting loss of life' (UNGA 2017, 11–37). One year later, in 2018, Nils Melzer, the United Nations Special Rapporteur on torture and other cruel, inhuman, or degrading treatment or punishment echoed Callamard's findings and stated that 'for the most part, these violations follow a programmatic pattern that can be described as systematic' (UNGA 2017, 16–58).

Violeta Moreno-Lax and Mariagiulia Giuffré explain how the EU-Libya cooperation, both at sea and on land, and the Italy-Libya memorandum of understanding (MoU) are examples of those migration containment policies (Moreno-Lax and Giuffre 2017). Moreno-Laz and Giuffré define those policies as forms of 'contactless control' which, far away from continental Europe, present new challenges to determine responsibilities (Moreno-Lax and Giuffre 2017). The strategy launched in 2016 by the EU has transferred all effective management to Libyan agents, aiming to elude all possibilities of international legal responsibility (Moreno-Lax and Giuffre 2017). However, in his 2018 report to the UN Human Rights Council, Melzer affirmed that those policies of 'contactless control' might trigger the ICC's jurisdiction (UNGA 2018).

Aiding, Abetting, and Otherwise Assisting

Aiding, abetting, and otherwise assisting is a mode of liability in international criminal law, based on holding an individual criminally responsible for a crime, even if that individual is not directly responsible to having committed the act (Vij 2013). Whilst the Rome Statute does not strictly define aiding and abetting, *ad hoc* tribunals have unanimously defined an individual liable for aiding and abetting as 'a person who planned, instigated, ordered, committed, or otherwise aided and abetted in the planning, preparation, or execution of a crime' (United Nations 1993). 'Aiding' generally refers to physical assistance, and 'abetting' is used to refer to a form of encouragement or persuasion (Vij 2013).

The most challenging part of analyzing this mode of individual criminal responsibility is to determine its minimum requirements (Ambos 2013). There seems to be a universal agreement on two main requirements: *actus reus* and *mens rea*. *Actus reus* is the 'criminal act' (the physical/material element), while *mens rea* refers to the 'criminal intent' (the 'mental element') (Knoops 2014). Regarding the material element, jurisprudence under the International Criminal Court demands that the acts committed by the individual must be specifically directed to assist, encourage, or lend moral support to the commission of the crime (Vij 2013, 159). Most importantly, this support must be 'substantial' for the perpetration of the crime (Vij 2013, 35). In order to find the individual liable, the person must have aided or abetted before, during, or after the crime was being committed (Vij 2013, 35). It is important to highlight that the assistance can either be an act or omission, and there are no geographical or temporal limitations to it (Vij 2013, 35).

Under the jurisdiction of the International Court of Justice (ICJ), Article 16 of the draft articles of the Responsibility of States for Internationally Wrongful Acts of the International Law Commission (ILC) describes aiding and abetting as the following:

A State which aids or assists another State in the commission of an internationally wrongful act by the latter is internationally responsible for doing so if (International Law Commission 2001):

(a) that State does so with knowledge of the circumstances of the internationally wrongful act; and

(b) the act would be internationally wrongful if committed by that State.

Even if the ILC draft articles are not binding, scholars James C. Hathaway and Thomas Gammeltoft-Hansen argue that Article 16 has generated 'wide support as a matter of state practice and *opinio juris*' (Gammeltoft-Hansen and Hathaway 2014). While there is not exact definition of what an action must amount to for it to fit with the definition of 'substantial contribution', case law defines it as a 'contribution that in fact has an effect on the commission of the crime' (United Nations 2000). On the other hand, under ICC jurisprudence, there is no mention of a need for 'substantial' support for the perpetration of the crime. Subparagraph (c) of Article 25 (3) of the Rome Statute deals with the contribution that must exist for a person to be liable for aiding and abetting, and it defines it as a person that 'for the purpose of facilitating the commission of such a crime, aids, abets, or otherwise assists in its commission or its attempted commission, including providing the means for its commission' (ICC, 1998). According to scholar Kai Ambos, the fact that 'otherwise assisting' was added as a mode of individual criminal responsibility seems to entail an even lower threshold (Ambos 2013, 14). Still, Ambos concludes, one should consider the substantial effect of the assistance to the crime as an independent constituting element of modes of liability (Ambos 2013, 14).

The second requirement to assign liability is the mental element. In case law produced by the International Criminal Tribunal for the former Yugoslavia (ICTY), the *mens rea* for aiding and abetting cases has remained 'knowledge' (Vij 2013, 158). 'Knowledge' has been defined as being aware or having knowledge that the acts or omissions are indeed assisting in the commission of a crime by the direct perpetrator (Vij 2013, 158). Moreover, since *mens rea* is defined as knowledge, it is not even necessary for the aider and abetter to have the same intent as the main perpetrator (Vij 2013, 158). Generally, the aider-abettor must only be aware of the basic elements of the main perpetrator's crimes in order to satisfy the mental element (Vij 2013, 159). On the other hand, to be liable under the ICC's jurisdiction, the individual must act with the intent to facilitate the crime, know, or desire that his conduct will facilitate the commission of the crime (Vij 2013, 159).

Ambos explains that the wording in the Rome Statute suggests a threshold that goes beyond the ordinary *mens rea* requirement (Ambos 2013, 15). In Article 25(3) it says that the aider-abettor must act 'for the purpose of facilitating the commission of the crime' (ICC 1998). According to Ambos, the term 'purpose' extends beyond the mere definition of knowledge (Ambos 2013, 15). The world 'facilitating' though, confirms that substantial assistance is not an essential condition of the main crime (Ambos 2013, 53).

EU-Libya Cooperation: Externalizing Responsibilities

On 3 and 11 October 2013, two shipwrecks happened near Lampedusa, Italy, causing the death of 636 people (Tazzioli 2016). A few days after the shipwrecks, Italy launched a military-humanitarian operation called Mare Nostrum, with the main objective of rescuing migrants in distress at sea (Tazzioli 2016). Mare Nostrum managed to save over 150,000 people in one year and prevented 2,000 to 3,000 migrants from disappearing in the Central Mediterranean (Eisinger 2015). Italy then asked the EU to support their efforts and contribute to their life-saving efforts, but most nations refused because they considered Mare Nostrum a pull-factor for illegal immigration (Eisinger 2015). The Italian-led search and rescue mission officially ended in November 2014, when it was replaced by Triton, a joint EU operation coordinated by Frontex, the European Border and Coast Guard Agency (Tazzioli 2016). However, Triton changed its focus from rescuing refugees and migrants at sea to being solely about border control and preventing illegal crossings (Tazzioli 2016).

2016 marked a record of refugees and migrants attempting to reach Europe via the Central Mediterranean route (European Commission 2017). The year 2016 was also a record year for the number of lives lost at sea: over 4,500 people drowned in the attempt to cross (European Commission 2017). Since then, the EU has intensified efforts to prevent migrants and refugees from reaching Europe from Libya (Human Rights Watch 2019). EU institutions and member states have invested millions of euros to improve the capacity of the Tripoli-based Government of National Accord (GNA), to prevent migrants from fleeing Libya by boat and detain them in detention centres (Human Rights Watch 2019).

Italy has also taken the lead in providing material assistance and training to the LCG and have passed onto them the responsibility of coordinating rescue operations in order to increase the number of interceptions (Human Rights Watch 2019). However, the Panel of Experts on Libya explained in a report to the UNSC that the LCG has not been notified as part of the security forces under the control of the GNA, and the issue of control is further highlighted by multiple reports of criminal activities involving LCG (UNSC 2017, 41). Migrants have recounted dangerous, life-threatening interceptions by armed men believed to be from the LCG (UNSC 2017). After being brought back to Libyan shores, migrants are often beaten, robbed, and taken to detention centers or private houses and farms, where they are subjected to forced labor, rape, and other sexual violence (UNSC 2017).

In January 2017, the European Commission sent a communication to the European Parliament, the European Council and the Council titled 'Migration on the Central Mediterranean route: Managing flows, saving lives' (European Commission 2017). In that communication, the Commission set out the main goals to, firstly, ramp up training for the LCG to autonomously conduct search and rescue (including disembarkation) in Libyan waters and, secondly, to strengthen Libya's southern border (in the Sahara Desert) to hinder irregular movements through Libya and into Europe (Moreno-Lax and Guiffre 2017). The EU had already started a training program for LCG officers, with a focus on the interdiction of migrant boats (Moreno- Lax and Mariagiulia 2017).

In parallel, in February 2017, the Italian Prime Minister and the Head of the National Reconciliation Government of the Libya State signed an MoU to *inter alia* tackle border security and combat the steady rise of smuggling (El Zaidy 2019, 4). Under that framework, Italy's parliament approved the donation of 12 patrol vessels to the LCG to increase interceptions of migrant boats attempting to reach Europe (El Zaidy 2019, 10). Moreover, the EU trained 237 LCG officers to support Italian efforts (El Zaidy 2019). Danilo Toninelli, Italy's Transport Minister, stated in 2018 that the support to Libya given by Italy to prevent boats reaching Europe was worth €2.5 million and included the 12 boats and funds for training and maintaining the LCG officers (El Zaidy 2019). The parties to the MoU also agreed on the need to find rapid solutions to the problem of 'illegal' migration to Europe, while respecting international human rights treaties (Moreno-Lax and Guiffre, 8). Italy agreed to fund the establishment of 'reception' centers in Libya, where migrants and refugees will remain detained until they accept to be voluntarily returned to their home countries (Moreno-Lax and Guiffre, 8). Relying on EU funds, Italy agreed to provide technical and economic support to Libyan agencies in charge of the fight against 'illegal' migration, including LCG (Moreno-Lax and Guiffre, 8).

The training and assistance provided by the EU and Italy are aimed at enabling Libya to intercept boats of migrants and refugees attempting to reach Europe (Moreno-Lax and Guiffre, 8). Since all those measures were put in place, the amount of people reaching Europe via the Central Mediterranean lessened considerably (El Zaidy 2019, 11). Since then, migrants continue to attempt the crossing from Libya, but they are either intercepted by the LCG or pushed back by Italian or European authorities at sea (El Zaidy 2019). All migrants returned to Libya by the LCG encounter indefinite detention and other inhumane or ill treatment in detention centers (El Zaidy 2019, 15), as described in the introduction of this chapter.

Actus Reus: The Material Contribution

The EU's decision to end Mare Nostrum in 2014 led to a gross increase in drownings (Rettman, 2019). Triton covered an area up to 30 nautical miles from the Italian coastline of Lampedusa, leaving around 40 nautical miles of key distress area off the coast of Libya uncovered (Rettman 2019). The first mass drowning occurred in January 2015 and the overall death rate increased by 30 percent in the following years (Rettman 2019).

The EU also provides support to the LCG to enable it to intercept migrants and refugees at sea, after which they are taken back to Libya where they face arbitrary detention, inhuman, and degrading conditions and the risk of torture, sexual violence, extortion, and forced labor (Rettman 2019). According to Human Rights Watch, the increase in interceptions by the LCG led to an increase in the number of migrants and refugees detained in Libya (Human Rights Watch 2019). In July 2018, there were between 8,000-10,000 people in official detention centers, up from 5,200 in April 2018 (Human Rights Watch 2019). Despite the chaos and dangerous situation in the North African country, the EU's objective of returning migrants and refugees to Libya exposed a further 40,000 people to crimes amounting to crimes against humanity between 2016 and 2018 (Human Rights Watch 2019).

Mens Rea: The Mental Element

It is clear that EU agents have knowledge of the crimes to which migrants are exposed in Libya and are equally aware of the fact that those crimes are direct result of their acts and omissions. Concerning actions at sea, an internal report by Frontex in August 2014 warned that the withdrawal of naval assets from the area previously covered by Mare Nostrum would likely result in a higher number of fatalities (Rettman 2019). And still, Triton's objectives were never adapted to search and rescue. In addition, the humanitarian organization *Médecins Sans Frontières* (MSF), discussed in 2019 the consequences of European containment and pushback policies in the context of Libya. MSF argued that dismantling search and rescue capacities at sea and sponsoring LCG efforts to intercept migrants at sea and forcibly return them to Libya was resulting in an increase of people's chances of dying at sea as well as being subjected to trafficking, abduction, detention, and extortion (MSF, 2019).

The latest UNSC report from April 2020, clearly supports that statement (UNSC 2020). The Secretary-General states, 'Libya cannot be considered a place of safety for the disembarkation of refugees and migrants rescued at sea... However, refugees and migrants continued to be disembarked in Libya, mainly after interception by the Libyan coastguard'. The report reads that 'the continuing systematic and arbitrary detention of refugees and migrants who disembark in Libya is alarming' (UNSC 2020), and that 'conditions inside detention centres remain appalling' (UNSC 2020). UNSMIL has also documented the many ways in which the LCG poses a direct threat to migrants' lives by *inter alia* demonstrating reckless behavior, using firearms against migrants on boats and displaying physical violence (UNSMIL and OHCHR 2018). In the report, there are accounts of incidents, involving aggressive behavior against migrants and refugees, which 'are not isolated' (UNSMIL and OHCHR 2018).

Regarding the awful conditions in detention centers, senior EU officials are aware of the crimes migrants face when detained in Libya. In November 2017, Dimitri Avramopoulos, the EU's Migration Commissioner, said that 'we are all conscious of the appalling and degrading conditions in which some migrants are held in Libya' (Human Rights Watch 2019). According to Human Rights Watch, he and other senior EU officials have repeatedly asserted that the EU wants to improve conditions in Libyan detention centers in recognition of grave and widespread abuses (Human Rights Watch 2019). However, interviews with detainees, detention center staff, Libyan officials, and humanitarian actors revealed that EU efforts to improve conditions and treatment in official detention centers have had a negligible impact (Human Rights Watch 2019).

Besides the above reports from UN special rapporteurs, Frontex, and human rights organizations, the European Court of Human Rights (ECHR) also made clear its position to Italy regarding its policies towards Libya. In the case *Hirsi Jamma and Others v. Italy*, the Grand Chamber of the ECHR unanimously ruled that Italy's push back operations intending to return migrants and refugees at sea to Libya amounted to a violation of the prohibition of torture and other inhuman or degrading treatment under Article 3 of the European Convention on the Protection of Human Rights and Fundamental Freedoms (ECHR) because Italy 'knew or should have known' that migrants and refugees would be exposed to treatment in breach of the ECHR in Libya (Euopean Court of Human Rights 2012). On the other hand, that judgement has not deterred EU member states to continue implementing the same practices.

Conclusion

Nils Melzer detailed in his 2018 report that the widespread crimes against humanity committed against migrants in Libya have a causal connection to certain external policies (UNGA 2018, 16). The EU policies in Libya seem to fit that definition. By refusing search and rescue, and funding and training the LCG, EU agents are providing means for the commission of crimes against migrants in Libya. Therefore, criminal responsibility for crimes against humanity can emerge from those actions.

The investigation into the situation in Libya by the Office of the Prosecutor of the ICC focused on the crimes against humanity of murder, imprisonment, torture, persecution, and other inhumane acts, allegedly committed by Libyan agents (Mann, Morena-Lax, and Shatz 2018). However, for the ICC to properly address the systematic and programmed design behind the crimes against migrants, it cannot do so without examining the role of the EU and its officials (Mann, Morena-Lax, and Shatz 2018). Any investigation that fails to consider the role of the EU will only address the consequences rather than the cause of migrant's suffering (Mann, Morena-Lax, and Shatz 2018). Still today, almost on a weekly basis, we hear of incidents in the Central Mediterranean: European coastguards refusing to respond to distress calls at sea, leaving hundreds of people drifting at sea for several days, or secretly organizing privatized pushback operations to Libya (Migreurop 2020).

According to the case law and definitions of aiding and abetting, there is enough evidence to justify the emergence of individual criminal responsibility from the EU's collaboration with Libya. However, that does not mean that the Prosecutor of the ICC would carry out the investigation. Under the Rome Statute, the ICC would not have jurisdiction to investigate if EU member states decided to investigate domestically. Moreover, the Prosecutor could, under Article 53, decide not to pursue the investigation if there are substantial reasons to believe that it would not serve the interests of justice, even after taking into account the gravity of the crime and interests of victims (ICC 1998). If, on the other hand, the ICC decided to investigate EU officials, a wider scope and evidence would be taken into account, as well as other modes of liability, as described in Shatz and Branco's communication to the Prosecutor of the ICC (Shatz and Branco 2019).

Last but not least, as Mann, Moreno-Lax, and Shatz state, finding that 'European actors were involved in such crimes [...] would show that militia and trafficking agents are often working at the service (or for the ultimate benefit) of European principals, precisely for the purpose of preventing poor and black populations from access to European sources of wealth' (Mann, Moreno-Lax and Shatz 2018). Including EU officials in the investigation would also set a precedent for other cases of 'contactless control' or border externalization policies, like those of Australia and the United States (Ferlick, Kysel and Podkul 2016), showing that those policies can be deemed active forms of abuse where the end effect is the same (Mann, Moreno-Lax and Shatz 2018).

References

Ambos, Kai. 2013. 'Criminal Responsibility, Modes Of'. *Max Planck Encyclopedias of International Law [MPIL]*. https://opil.ouplaw.com/view/10.1093/law:epil/9780199231690/law-9780199231690-e1853?rskey=90xFeu&result=1&prd=MPIL.

Eisinger, Judit. 2015. 'Operation Triton: Europe Blind On Immigration Reality'. *Le Journal International – Archives*. https://www.lejournalinternational.fr/Operation-Triton-Europe-blind-on-immigration-reality_a2377.html

El Zaidy, Zakariya. 2019. 'EU Migration Policy Towards Libya: A Policy Of Conflicting Interests'. *Library of The Friedrich-Ebert-Stiftung*. https://library.fes.de/pdf-files/bueros/tunesien/15544.pdf

European Commission. 2017. 'Joint Communication to the European Parliament, the European Council and the Council Migration on the Central Mediterranean Route Managing Flows, Saving Lives'. *EUR-Lex*. https://eur-lex.europa.eu/legal-content/EN/TXT/?uri=JOIN%3A2017%3A4%3AFIN.

European Court of Human Rights. 2012. Case of *Hirsi Jamaa and Others v Italy* (Judgement) ECtHR 27765/09 (23 February 2012).

Ferlick, Bill, Ian Kysel and Jennifer Podkul. 2016. 'The Impact of Externalization of Migration Controls on the Rights of Asylum Seekers and Other Migrants'. Human Rights Watch.

Gammeltoft-Hansen, Thomas, Hathaway, James C.. 2014. 'Non-Refoulement in a World of Cooperative Deterrence'. *Law & Economics Working Papers*. 106. https://repository.law.umich.edu/law_econ_current/106

Human Rights Watch. 2019. 'No Escape From Hell: EU Policies Contribute To Abuse Of Migrants In Libya'. Human Rights Watch. https://www.hrw.org/report/2019/01/21/no-escape-hell/eu-policies-contribute-abuse-migrants-libya.

ICC. 1998. Rome Statute of the International Criminal Court (adopted 17 July 1998, entered into force 1 July 2002) 2187 UNTS 90 (Rome Statute).

ICC. 2011. 'Libya: Situation in Libya (ICC-01/11)'. 2011. *International Criminal Court*. https://www.icc-cpi.int/libya

ICC. 2017. 'International Criminal Court May Investigate Migrant-Related Crimes in Libya, Security Council Told'. *UN News*. https://news.un.org/en/story/2017/05/556872-international-criminal-court-may-investigate-migrant-related-crimes-libya

International Law Commission. 2001. 'Draft Articles on Responsibility of States for Internationally Wrongful Acts, With Commentaries'. *United Nations*. https://legal.un.org/ilc/texts/instruments/english/commentaries/9_6_2001.pdf

International Law Commission. 2010. Draft Articles on Responsibility of States for Internationally Wrongful Acts, November 2001, Supplement No. 10 (A/56/10), chp.IV.E.1.

Knoops, Geert-Jan Alexander. 2014. *An Introduction to The Law of International Criminal Tribunals: A Comparative Study*. 2nd ed. International Criminal Law Series, Volume: 7.

Mann, Itamar, Violeta Moreno-Lax, and Omer Shatz. 2018. 'Time to Investigate European Agents for Crimes Against Migrants In Libya'. *EJIL: Talk! Blog of The European Journal of International Law*. https://www.ejiltalk.org/time-to-investigate-european-agents-for-crimes-against-migrants-in-libya/

Médecins Sans Frontières (MSF). 2019. 'Trading in suffering: detention, exploitation and abuse in Libya'. Médecins Sans Frontières.

Migreurop. 2020. 'Deaths in The Mediterranean Are Not Inevitable!'. Migreurop, Observatoire Des Frontières. http://www.migreurop.org/article2984.html?lang=fr

Moreno-Lax, Violeta, and Mariagiulia Giuffré. 2017. 'The Rise Of Consensual Containment: From "Contactless Control" To "Contactless Responsibility"'. *SSRN Electronic Journal*.

Pillai, Priya. 2019. 'The EU and Migrant Detention In Libya: Complicity Under the Microscope Finally?'. *Opinio Juris*. http://opiniojuris.org/2019/07/05/the-eu-and-migrant-detention-in-libya-complicity-under-the-microscope-finally/

Rettman, Andrew. 2019. 'EU Guilty Of Libya Migrant "Tragedy", ICC Lawsuit Says'. *Euobserver*. https://euobserver.com/migration/145071

Shatz, O. and Juan Branco. 2019. 'EU Migration Policies in the Central Mediterranean and Libya (2014–2019)'. Communication to the Office of the Prosecutor of the International Criminal Court Pursuant to the Article 15 of the Rome Statute.

Tazzioli, Martina. 2016. 'Border displacements. Challenging the politics of rescue between Mare Nostrum and Triton', *Migration Studies*, Volume 4, Issue 1, March: 1–19.

UN News. 2017. 'African Migrants Reportedly Being Sold In 'Slave Markets' In Libya, UN Agency Warns'. *UN News*. https://news.un.org/en/ story/2017/04/555152-african-migrants-reportedly-being-sold-slave-markets-libya-un-agency-warns#:~:text=Hundreds%20of%20migrants%20along%20 North,of%20outrages%E2%80%9D%20in%20the%20country.

United Nations. 1993. Statute of the International Criminal Tribunal for the former Yugoslavia, 25th May 1993 (UN Doc S/RES/827[1993]).

United Nations. 1994. Statute of the International Criminal Tribunal for Rwanda, 8th November 1994 (UN Doc S/RES/955[1994]).

United Nations. 2000. Case of Prosecutor v. Dusko Tadić aka 'Dule' (Judgment) ICTY-94-1 (26 January 2000).

UNGA. 2017. 'Report of the Special Rapporteur of the Human Rights Council on extrajudicial, summary or arbitrary executions', Established by UNGA Res 71/198 (15 August 2017) 72nd Session (2017) UN Doc A/72/335.

UNGA. 2018. 'Report of the Special Rapporteur on torture and other cruel, inhuman or degrading treatment or punishment', Established by HRC Res 34/19 (23 November 2018) 37th Session (2018) UN Doc A/HRC/37/50.

UNSC. 2017. 'Final report to the Panel of Experts on Libya established pursuant to resolution 1973 (2011)', (1 June 2017) UN Doc S/2017/466.

UNSC. 2020. 'Implementation of resolution 2491 (2019), report of the Secretary-General'. UN Doc S/2020/275.

UNSMIL and OHCHR. 2018. 'Desperate and Dangerous: Report on the human rights situation of migrants and refugees in Libya' (2018) UNSMIL.

Vij, Vanshika. 2013. 'Individual Criminal Responsibility Under Aiding and Abetting after the Specific Direction Requirement in the Taylor and Perišić Cases', *Die Friedens-Warte* 88, no. 3/4: 157–75.

22

At the European Union-Turkey Border, Human Rights Violations are No Longer Clandestine Operations

MEREDITH VEIT AND FLO STRASS

The quaint and weathered island of Lesvos (also known as Lesbos), located in the far east of the Aegean Sea, is the third-largest of all the Greek islands. Lesvos is now home to 11 million olive trees, 86,000 Greeks, and over 14,700 asylum-seekers (Aegean Boat Report Data Studio 2020b; El-Rashidi 2019). Due to its physical proximity to Turkey, the island has a long history of transferred ownership – first the Anatolians, then the Byzantines, the Genoese, the Ottomans, and finally, the Greeks. An often-overlooked fact is that much of the current local population descends from refugees themselves, whose grandparents and great grandparents were forcibly displaced from Turkey in the aftermath of World War I.

Since 2014, more than 1.2 million migrants fleeing war, violence, and persecution have risked their lives crossing the northeast Mediterranean Sea en route to Europe, the majority of whom initially land on Lesvos (UNHCR 2020). They cross the deep and narrow strait on flimsy rubber dinghies – sometimes with duct-tape patchwork covering knife holes from previous crossings – typically carrying their lives on their backs, their children and babies, and a heavy-heart of tested faith, in utter contrast to their buoyant expectations.

Although the channel is narrow, its waves are unforgiving. Over 1,674 people have drowned in the Eastern Mediterranean (IOM 2020) in the past decade, a great deal of whom fell mercy to the sea's wrath when the humanitarian crisis first began over five years ago. Over recent years, the tides have turned for the worse as those in power have become as merciless as the sea. Since the signing of the European Uunion (EU)-Turkey Deal, hundreds of lives have been senselessly lost, and hundreds more have gone missing due to the steady amplification of draconian, anti-migrant immigration policies. Civil society organizations, including Mare Liberum, have been documenting and advocating against the politicization of human lives for years, regardless of the political climate, but as the situation worsens, we need more help. We are dismayed to report that 2020 has been particularly worrisome – though not for the reasons one might assume – and we urge that it is imperative that the international community take a stronger stance against the unveiled violations of human rights taking place at the EU border.

Mare Liberum is a non-profit human rights organization that monitors the Aegean Sea by boat along the EU-Turkey border. As a strong supporter of our goals, Sea-Watch e.V. donated what is now our ship at the beginning of 2018, and we have been sailing the coast of Lesvos ever since. We primarily serve as an independent observer and deterrent for violations of human rights by state authorities. Mare Liberum conducts research to document the current situation at the European border and to draw public attention back to this forgotten site of tragedies.

Greece acts as a migratory buffer-zone for the rest of the continent and has been largely abandoned by the EU. While locals, especially fishermen, have been rescuers and harborers of the weary travellers in the past, over recent years, some locals have grown highly intolerant of the situation.[1] Considering the economic effects of decreased tourism, high unemployment rates, and an increase in the rate of elderly poor, some are more vulnerable to absorbing the hate speech and false claims propagated by right-wing leaders such as Development Minister Adonis Georgiadis and Prime Minister Kyriakos Mitsotakis, who make statements like, 'Afghans are not refugees' and '93 percent are illegal immigrants'. According to the United Nations High Commissioner for Refugees (UNHCR), the overwhelming majority of sea arrivals to Greece in 2019 – over 90 percent – were from conflict zones (Keep Talking Greece, 2019), and the UNHCR Representative in Greece, Philippe Leclerc, has had to appeal politicians to refrain from such speech, predicting that it would trigger hate against refugees and volunteers (Leclerc 2019). Since the start of 2020, these feelings of anguish and intolerance began to manifest into outright acts of violence.

In January 2020, we witnessed thousands of anti-migrant islanders pouring

---

[1]   It is important to note that some locals also report being reported by the police for trying to help or rescue asylum seekers, with threats of smuggling charges. There seems to be growing polarisation on the island.

into the downtown streets of Mytilene in protest, demanding, 'We want our island back'. In February, local vigilantes began attacking the cars and homes of migrant aid workers and volunteers. In early March, the donation-based refugee school One Happy Family was burnt to the ground (Ng 2020). Right-wing groups began showing up at beaches along the east coast to threaten and insult migrants as they arrived on Lesvos' shores. Locals began distributing flyers directed at refugees that say, 'Don't come to our country, there is no money, we don't want you'. The Pikpa camp, which hosts the most vulnerable groups, including families, victims of torture, and lesbian, gay, bisexual, trans, and intersex (LGBTI) people, began receiving threats. Two German photojournalists were beaten for documenting violence between locals and refugee rights activists. Cameras and phones of non-governmental organization (NGO) employees were taken and thrown to sea. The Mare Liberum ship was doused with kerosene and was nearly set ablaze with the crew still on board. The match was lit, but the crew was able to set sail and pull away from the port just in time.

The effects of the pandemic took hold of the island towards the end of March 2020, but a plague of anti-migrant sentiments had already been festering for years. Even before the virus outbreak, the Greek government had implemented 'out of sight out of mind' tactics to remove refugees from their field of vision – setting up remote, closed-off detention centers, orchestrating clandestine pushbacks at sea, and executing mass-deportations. COVID-19 has closed borders across the globe, greatly fuelling nationalist agendas and furthering their respective 'national security' projects under the guise of reacting to a public health emergency. Lesvos, however, reached its tipping point before confinement measures were enacted. As a result, COVID-19 measures are being used as a rationalization for plans that were already in place. When the world's attention had been diverted elsewhere, the far-right Greek government was less afraid to take bolder actions.

Since migratory flows have slowed, authorities are now chipping away at civil society's capacity to monitor human rights violations, advocate for equality and justice, and even save human lives when coast guard ships act negligently. The situation has been dire for years, but the pandemic has been used as a flimsy justification for limiting civil society organization (CSO) oversight, segregating communities, and more openly violating international law.

What is Happening at Sea?

At least 8,697 asylum seekers have arrived on Greek shores as of 16 August 2020, which is a 66 percent decrease compared to 2019. This decrease can largely be attributed to migrants having been stuck at border closures along their journey; and fear of contracting COVID-19 may be acting as a means of self-hindrance for continuing along migration routes. As eyewitnesses on the ground, we have no doubt that this is also a result of the increasingly aggressive pushbacks[2] by the Greek authorities (Amnesty International 2020).

In February 2020, Turkey's President, Recep Tayyip Erdoğan, declared that he had opened his country's borders for all migrants to cross into Europe. Erdoğan announced that Turkey could no longer support the estimated four million migrants that are currently residing within its borders (Stevis-Gridneff and Kingsley 2020). In response, on 1 March 2020 Greece suspended all asylum application procedures for arrivals coming from Turkey (HRW 2020a) and began further militarizing the Aegean Sea. According to reports by local media outlets, 'more than 50 Hellenic Coast Guard vessels' were deployed 'in the eastern Aegean, along with 10 Navy vessels and 24 land, air, and sea craft provided by the European Union's border monitoring agency Frontex' (Souliotis and Georgiopoulou 2020). Our crew has noticed an increase in drone and helicopter presence. Many human rights organizations have been reporting a spike in violent pushbacks of migrants arriving in Greece via both land and sea (Bathke 2020; Cullum 2020; Deeb 2020; HRW 2020b). While there have been many testimonials of clandestine pushbacks in the past – even in 2013, pre-dating the media-acclaimed 'refugee crisis' (Pro Asyl 2013) – these illegal operations have now more openly become standard procedure, without regard to their illegality in the eyes of customary international human rights law.

As explained by one of the human rights activists currently aboard the Mare Liberum ship,

> the fear of perishing at sea and the fear of being violated at sea increased tenfold in 2020. Before, migrants were afraid of the sea itself, but now, they are afraid of the violent human behaviour at sea.

---

[2]   According to the European Convention of Human Rights: 'Push-backs are a set of state measures by which refugees and migrants are forced back over a border – generally immediately after they crossed it – without consideration of their individual circumstances and without any possibility to apply for asylum or to put forward arguments against the measures taken. Push-backs violate – among other laws – the prohibition of collective expulsions stipulated in the European Convention on Human Rights.' (ECCHR 2020).

Coast Guard practices of cruelty, violence, and humiliation

The purpose of any coast guard during peacetime is to carry out the enforcement of maritime law and the protection of life and property at sea. Under maritime law, it is the responsibility of the closest able vessel to 'render assistance and rescue those in distress at sea without any regard to their nationality, status, or the circumstances in which they are found' (IMO, ICS, and UNHCR 2020), which also applies to coast guard ships. Yet, to date, migrants continually testify to the violence they endure from the authorities that are tasked with saving them. They face a great risk of having their personal belongings thrown into the water by the coast guard, being physically injured by beatings, and being intentionally humiliated. The coast guard has become even more virulent since live videos have been posted on social networks showcasing these aggressions. Testimonials from recent arrivals have told our crew about how migrants have been stripped naked for body searches and sent back to sea in their underwear with no means of communication to call for help.

New pushback methods and public acceptance of refoulement

Fear of migrants bringing COVID-19 to the island has greatly facilitated the acceptance of immediate expulsion strategies. The Greek government has touted an approach of 'aggressive surveillance and deterrence' of migration without fully specifying what these methods will entail (The National Herald 2020). According to several reports from asylum-seekers over the past few years, the coast guard has been using unsafe pushback techniques, such as creating waves to further distress a migrant vessel, destroying or removing the dinghy engine to leave it floating at sea, firing bullets to deflate the dinghy itself, and even towing boats back across the unmarked 'border' line to be picked up by the Turkish Coast Guard and brought back to Turkey.

These operations, however, were always carried out in secret. The coast guard agents tried to destroy evidence by tossing migrants' cell phones into the sea, and they wore wear black ski masks and orchestrated the pushbacks by night. In some cases, it has been reported that the authorities confiscated all phones from the migrants. But now, it seems the virus is enough of an excuse to flagrantly exercise pushbacks using the boldest of colors. There have been numerous incidents where the Hellenic Coast Guard has forced refugees to board unsafe, orange tent-like life rafts at sea, or even after migrants have already arrived on the Greek islands, to then set them loose and leave them adrift at sea.

One of the best-documented life raft pushbacks happened on 28 April 2020. That day, people (including three children, four women, and 15 men) arrived on the Greek island of Samos, which is about 130 kilometers south of Lesvos. Instead of being brought to one of the refugee camps on the island, they were forced to board the Hellenic Coast Guard vessel, only to be taken back out to sea and stranded amongst the waves. A Turkish Coast Guard vessel was present as well, but only rescued the people in the life raft the next morning (Aegean Boat Report 2020b). Since March 2020, at least 1,336 people have been forced into life rafts by the Greek coast guard and left helplessly at sea (ABR 2020d; Kingsley and Shoumali 2020).[3] These are not isolated incidents. The Greek government denies that they are doing anything illegal (Hellenic Republic Ministry of Migration and Asylum 2020). In fact, the Greek Minister of Migration and Asylum, Notis Mitarachi, has boasted about how few arrivals have arrived on Lesvos recently without mentioning their tactics of abandoning men, women, and children at sea (ABR 2020d).

Once migrants are brought back or float back to Turkey, they are then likely to be sent to unsanitary, overcrowded Turkish prisons that are mal-equipped for combating the COVID-19 outbreak. Crossing the sea has never been riskier.

Frontex and the North Atlantic Treaty Organization (NATO) are present and watching these pushbacks. They neither rescue people from these floating tents nor actively push them back, but rather stand aside and observe silently. When asylum seekers are directly pushed back, they are not able to exercise their right to apply for asylum. Greece is not only in violation of the European Convention of Human Rights and the Charter of Fundamental Rights of the European Union, but also the international agreement on *non-refoulement* and the prohibition of collective deportations. Greece is actively putting refugees in perilous and inhumane situations, and the EU, as well as the United States, the United Kingdom, and other NATO member countries are acting as bystanders, and even accomplices due to the fact that they are actively not participating in human rights investigations. As governments work to further prevent human rights monitoring and watchdog NGOs, who will spearhead the investigations on the migrants' behalf?

Inhibiting and suspending NGO operations

NGOs are increasingly less able to intervene and prevent these human rights violations from taking place because their physical access to the spaces where incidents are occurring has been restricted. There are a select number

---

[3]   This number is in consideration of the *New York Times*' report from 14 August, as well as the reports from Aegean Boat Report from mid-August to September. What year?

of organizations, including Mare Liberum, Refugee Rescue, and Lighthouse Relief, that are alert and ready to respond to the sighting of an incoming migrant boat, working to assure everyone's safety. All organizations are required to report any first sightings to the Hellenic Coast Guard, which is charged with oversight of the Greek sea. In the past, it was more likely that the Hellenic Coast Guard would safely take the migrants to shore, especially while under the watchful eye of civil society. However, it is now more likely that they will perform a pushback, no matter who is watching. The Hellenic Coast Guard continues to violate human rights with unbridled confidence and impunity; they have not been given any incentives to abide by the law.

Meanwhile, human rights NGOs are being strong-armed into halting or even suspending their operations. On 19 August 2020, Mare Liberum (2020) received yet another detention order to prevent the crew from carrying out its human rights mandate, which is the third legal battle brought against us – even after winning the past two in court. 'We are furious and won't accept the blockade of our mission for solidarity and human rights', says Hanno Bruchmann, board member of Mare Liberum. These lawsuits are meant to drain small, donation-based non-profits like Mare Liberum of their financial capacity to fulfil their missions, as well as further criminalize those that aim to protect solidarity and human dignity.

On 29 August 2020, Refugee Rescue (2020) announced that it has also been forced to suspend its operations after five years of providing lifesaving search and rescue operations for people crossing the Aegean Sea to the northern shore of Lesvos. The NGO's press release cites criminalization as the main trigger for the need to cease its aid work: 'Unacceptably, the rising criminalization of humanitarian organizations in Lesvos and growing hostilities now pose an irrefutable threat to our staff, assets, and work – and we cannot in good conscience continue to operate if we cannot guarantee the safety of our team. Additionally, the unchecked impunity with which authorities now work has created a situation where we no longer trust that they will allow us to launch our independent rescue boat, Mo Chara. Make no mistake: our decision to suspend operations for the foreseeable future does not in any way mean that search and rescue is not still imminently needed off the North Shore of Lesvos. In fact, human rights violations on the Aegean have only intensified in the past few months – from authorities leaving people stranded at sea for hours, to illegal pushbacks on Greek waters – which have all made the journey from Turkey to Greece more perilous than ever for those seeking refuge' (Refugee Rescue 2020).

If the Hellenic Coast Guard is actively putting lives in danger, if NATO and Frontex continue to remain silent, and if human rights NGOs are unable to operate, what is preventing the Aegean Sea from becoming a more populous graveyard? And even more pressing of a question, how flawed is European domestic and foreign policy that humanitarian and human rights organizations are so desperately needed in the Aegean Sea? Why are resource-strapped non-profits filling the shoes of governments in protecting the most vulnerable in order to allow for a more prosperous society for all? We all need to be demanding more of our leaders. In a democracy, we have the power to put an end to government-funded xenophobia.

What is Happening on Land?

Inhumane activity is being reported at sea, and unfortunately the same can be said for the management of asylum-seekers on land. If and when asylum-seekers do make it to Lesvos' shores, processing procedures have been greatly altered due to the pandemic. While the low number of COVID-19 cases thus far on the island have been attributed to Greece's containment attempts, it is critical to note that not all lives are being held at equal value when quarantine measures are implemented. A spokesperson for the European Commission has noted, 'Quarantine and isolation measures must be applied in a reasonable, proportionate, and non-discriminatory manner. We have provided significant financial and operational support to member states, including Greece, to fight the coronavirus, and stand ready to provide further support if needed', but it is ultimately at the discretion of the Greek government to follow through with a human rights centric emergency response plan (Macej Kaczyński 2020). Rather than protecting the health of everyone, the Greek government is acting with distinction for how migrant lives and Greek lives are prioritized through its COVID-19 containment measures.

Discriminatory and unsafe quarantine practices

Beginning in late March 2020, the UNHCR and Greek police began setting up informal 'wild' beach camps at the landing sites where migrants would touch shore. These camps have no infrastructure, no access to running water, no toilets, and no showers. Since May 2020, people who have arrived in the north of Lesvos have been brought to 'Megala Therma', a temporary quarantine camp in the north, and those who arrive in the east and southeast are brought to the quarantine area of Kara Tepe. Both of these more 'formal' quarantine stations lack running water, sanitary facilities, medicine, and electricity. The loose policy has been that new-arrivals quarantine for two weeks before being transferred to Moria, however, some people have asserted, particularly from Megala Therma, that they are confined in these conditions for over a month.

While the UNHCR and Greek government may argue that they are working with limited resources to combat what could be an incredibly deadly situation, there is no justification for the reckless, indiscriminate mixing of potentially COVID-19-positive and tested-negative asylum-seekers. There is little or no separation between those who tested negative but remain in quarantine and the new arrivals that may be carrying the virus, which unnecessarily puts additional lives at extreme risk considering the quarantine camp's sordid conditions. The UNHCR protection unit added a line in the accommodation referral form for new arrivals to self-report any conditions that coincide with COVID-vulnerability, but there are no indications that this data collection is being used to improve preventative health protection for new-arrivals in practice. According to a contact we have from Médecins Sans Frontières (MSF), the hospitals on Lesvos are equipped with a total of 11 ventilators, none of which are provisioned for the camps. Would the hospitals be prepared to care for 60–100 cases from quarantined new-arrivals at any given time?

The double standard for implementing an effective quarantine response is duly noted by Lesvos' treatment of those arriving by dinghy versus those arriving by plane. During the strictest phase of the COVID-19 lockdown, everyone who entered Greece through the airport were immediately tested and received free accommodation and food until the test results arrived (Greek City Times 2020).

Restricting migrants' movement: Locking down Moria

Considering that the island's largest refugee camp, Moria, was built to hold 3,000 people, over 13,000 migrants have been forced to set up their tents in the peripheral area (referred to as the Olive Grove) in order to access what little goods and services are provided by shortlisted and government-approved NGOs. Certain travel and movement restrictions have been exclusively implemented for migrants, to the extent that those living in or around the camps have been rounded-up and herded closer together into an enclosed Moria. A team of volunteer lawyers from the organization Legal Centre Lesvos (2020a) noted that since 19 March 2020, migrants must obtain written permission from police or a security authority in order to leave the Moria or Kara Tepe refugee camps. On 30 March 2020, they posted on social media the following:

> Across Greece, those leaving their place of residence must carry a paper or send an SMS that indicates – from a set of reasons, including personal exercise, visiting the bank or going to the supermarket – why they are outside the house. Yet

reasons that are valid across the country are, unsurprisingly, abandoned in favour of far stricter rules for migrants...Only one member of each family can leave the camps per week, a measure that is strictly enforced – despite the fact that no such restriction exists for people living in towns and cities across Greece. Those without written permission will be blocked from leaving by police – either at the camps' exits, or at checkpoints on the roads that lead to the city of Mytiline – and will not be able to board public buses. An increased number of police units have been deployed around the camps to enforce these restrictions.

Locking down the camp has been posed as a necessary means of containing virus transmission rates, out of fear that new arrivals will bring COVID-19 with them, but in complete disregard for the social distancing needs of the camp's inhabitants. Most unfortunately, within the camp, not much has changed in regards to quotidian health and safety standards. Depending on the part of Moria in which one lives, refugees must share a toilet with 50–500 people. Social distancing is impossible when living in a tent with up to 12 other people, and when it is mandatory to go outside and wait in long lines in order to shower or receive daily meals. Attempting to fill the void of a properly implemented response, a group of refugees self-organized to create the 'Corona Awareness Team' to spread information about the virus and distribute masks.

From the start of the pandemic, the World Health Organization and United States Centers for Disease Control (2020) have made it clear that high concentrations of people within confined living spaces increases the likelihood of the virus spreading. According to an analysis by the International Rescue Committee (2020), the living conditions in camps such as Moria will prove to be more disastrous than the infamous Diamond Princess cruise ship case, where the transmission rate of the virus was four times faster than in Wuhan at the peak of the outbreak. Not only is the Moria camp over eight times more densely populated than the Diamond Princess, but there is little access to clean water, showers, toilets, and overall poor hygiene conditions and access to quality healthcare in displacement camps.

As many have feared, the first COVID-19 case from within Moria camp was just detected on 2 September 2020, and the entire camp will be under complete lockdown for the coming 14 days, meaning entry and exit will be prohibited (Panoutsopoulou 2020). This news comes approximately one month after MSF (2020) was forced to close their COVID-19 containment center within Moria. Local authorities imposed fines with potential criminal charges, citing urban planning regulations within an overpopulated Greek-run refugee camp that has had barely any planning in its development and maintenance. On 3 September 2020, the Greek Ministry of Immigration and Asylum announced that it will build a fence around Moria, costing €854,000, which will be immediately commissioned and completed within two months (ABR 2020c). COVID-19 has finally given Greece's far-right administration the excuse it needs to create the closed, highly-surveilled detention center for which it has been pushing since the elections.

Fear-mongering against the migrant populations

The Greek government has cited COVID-19 as a rationale for further investing in closed detention centers instead of migrant camps on the islands of Lesvos and Chios, feeding the vilified narrative that asylum-seekers are spreading the virus to local communities, even though these claims lack evidence (Trilling 2020). Certain nationalist politicians have never been shy about demonizing asylum-seekers, calling them 'cockroaches', for example, and now their stigmatization is being pegged to the spread of the virus (Sunderland and Williamson 2013). The public fear of infection is bringing out the racist undertones within local communities that may have always been wary about Lesvos' transition to becoming a transitory hotspot. Residents of Moria have reported to us that they are experiencing microaggressions and racism more frequently. For example, even after being granted permission to go to the supermarket, a storeowner will prevent them from entering the store.

'They are seen and treated as pariahs who can bring the virus to the island', reports an activist from Mare Liberum. The International Organization for Migration has warned that growing discrimination against migrants only impedes efforts to tackle the pandemic, as exclusion of any group from receiving the necessary goods and services will only prolong the virus' lifespan (UN Department of Global Communications 2020). In actuality, many of the cases that arrived in Lesvos were brought by Europeans coming from mainland Greece (Macej Kaczyński 2020). It was not until mid-August 2020 that the first migrant boat containing passengers with positive cases arrived in Lesvos.

Short and Long Term Implications

The measures being enforced on land and sea are not meant to protect the most vulnerable groups and save migrant lives. Rather, Greece is more focused on opening up to Europeans and re-starting the economy as quickly as possible. Restrictions on migrants' freedom of movement, the repression of solidarity NGOs, and the quelling of social movements will be difficult to undo. Migrants continue to be constricted and confined within the camp with only 70 permissions to leave the area being granted each day for a migrant population of over 13,000 (Legal Centre Lesvos 2020b). Meanwhile, tourist travel to the island began again on 1 July 2020, and without a vaccine, the risk of someone from Moria contracting the virus remains high (GTP 2020).[4] NGOs, particularly those that conduct human rights monitoring and migrant rescue operations, have been pressured to completely shut down their operations and stop any new volunteers from arriving to the island. Solidarity organizations are shrinking in size and capabilities, leaving asylum-seekers even more exposed while aid institutions are running at less-than-full capacity due to the pandemic.

The short-term impacts have proven to be swift and harsh, evidenced by the violent pushbacks taking place at sea. We are already seeing a hardening public discourse against migrants, which is having a tangible impact on the processing of identification documents and visas. Work visas for migrants have practically come to a halt, and the resettlement of refugees and asylum-seekers in third countries is becoming more difficult (SchengenVisaInfo 2020). There are more than 40,700 people applying for refugee status on the collection of Aegean islands, and thus far the European Commission has announced that 10 member states have agreed to accept the relocation of 1,600 children and teenagers from Greece (EU Commission Spokesperson's Service 2020). Greece has relocated about 13,657 people to camps on mainland Greece (Aegean Boat Report Data Studio 2020a), which provides little solace when coupled with the announcement that it plans to expel 11,000 refugees from government housing (Cossé 2020).

An immediate concern of Greece's COVID-19 response, perhaps the most overlooked, is the immense mental and physical impact that these extreme conditions of vulnerability and uncertainty have had on asylum-seekers. Mare Liberum has conducted numerous interviews with both long-standing Moria residents, as well as new arrivals to Lesvos, and all have experienced heightened stress, fear, and dejection. Social spaces where migrants can meet, socialize, and separate themselves from the horrors of the camp are now inaccessible. Any slight hint of normalcy amidst the exceptional life of an asylum seeker has now dissipated. The street-taverna right outside the camp gates where they could buy a cup of tea is now closed. The barbershop at the NGO-run recreation center is closed. It is more difficult to escape to immerse oneself in nature and breathe the fresh air. Children who were able to secure a coveted seat in a classroom will now go another year without education, seeing as most teachers were ex-patriate volunteers. The despair of further

---

[4]   Based on European Union guidelines, Greece was allowed to open its borders again for all types of air travel coming from EU states (GTP 2020).

prolonged asylum proceedings to determine one's legal status can prove dismal. They are stuck inside the camp, and inside their own minds, without proper mental health care.

It is also critical to remember the under-reported, gendered impacts of confinement in a refugee camp. When tensions are high, women may find themselves at greater risk of emotional, physical, and sexual abuse; and as reported by UN Women, domestic violence helplines and shelters across the world are reporting rising calls for help during the pandemic (Mlambo-Ngcuka 2020). The current confinement measures are further isolating migrant women from the people and resources that can best help them, further enclosing them in close quarters with their assailants.

One of the long-term impacts may be that more people will be forced to take dangerous routes, such as attempting longer or more treacherous passages across the Aegean Sea. Perhaps COVID-19 will further restrict the formal means by which refugees can seek protection and prosperity, and more people will be driven to impetuosity. As Erol Yayboke, deputy director at the Center for Strategic and International Studies wrote at the start of the pandemic, 'When combined, the economic, inequality, political, and displacement-related implications [of COVID-19] will only increase desperation at a time when fewer migration pathways exist. In such a scenario, those feeling compelled to move will do so increasingly using smugglers, traffickers, and other illicit groups. Migration will be increasing in and among developing countries with weaker health systems and rule of law'.

In the aftermath of crises, governments can garner more political will to exercise greater control for the purpose of protecting national security, or in this case, public health. Lesvos uniquely sits at the crossroads of a public health crisis, a humanitarian crisis, and a highly militarized border zone. Depending on how the EU and the rest of the world reacts to Greece's choices on its emergency relief response, we fear the normalization of taxpayer spending on a permanently hyper-militarized border patrol, the construction of dehumanizing and degrading closed detention facilities, as well as prolonged restrictions on access to sites for watchdog organizations.

If the Greek islands are closing down legitimate operations for both humanitarian assistance and human rights monitoring efforts, a sharp decline in transparency and all of its compounding effects will likely take a large toll on migrants and EU citizens alike. Rule of law is already gravely suffering, which is heart-wrenching to see knowing that Europe has the most advanced mechanisms and institutions for human rights anywhere in the world to date. What does this mean for accountability both in Europe and around the world?

To quote Albert Einstein, 'The world is a dangerous place, not because of those who do evil, but because of those who look on and do nothing'.

Conclusion

How Greece handles the first Moria COVID-19 case today and the ongoing pandemic will determine the spirit and soul of the island for years to come. The government must act now, pooling resources, knowledge, and assistance from the local, national, regional, and international community to protect the population of Lesvos no matter what their skin color, background, or citizenship status. If we have learned anything from this pandemic, it is that the virus does not discriminate. People do. Politics does. And because of that, many more innocent lives are needlessly lost.

We are calling on the community of Lesvos, the nation of Greece, the European Union, the United Nations, and the larger international community, to step-up and embody the values that we have established in our founding documents, treaties, and charters. As Germany holds the Presidency of the Council of the European Union for 2020, and touts the motto, 'Together for Europe's recovery', we are calling on the institution to take their role seriously and rectify the systemic issues that are preventing the EU from coming out of this pandemic as a more prosperous and equitable union. As Angela Merkel (2020) states, 'This motto is directed at us all... For Europe can only be strong if people have good prospects for the future, if they can see how important Europe is for them personally, and if they are committed to the European idea'. Now more than ever, we need to actively work towards re-building a society in which inclusion, tolerance, justice, solidarity, and non-discrimination prevail. We have a shared responsibility for how these human lives are being treated. Let the EU know that we, as a global community, will not stand for the degradation of human dignity taking place along its borders.

Figures

Figure 1: The scene after a boat of asylum seekers arrives on Lesvos during the COVID-19 pandemic. Non-governmental organizations are no longer able to participate in the assurance of a safe landing or clean-up efforts once the asylum seekers are transported away from the shoreline. Source: Mare Liberum (2020).

Figure 2: Lesvos is an island located in the Aegean Sea between Greece and Turkey. There are only about 10 kilometers between them at its closest point. Source: Mare Liberum (2020).

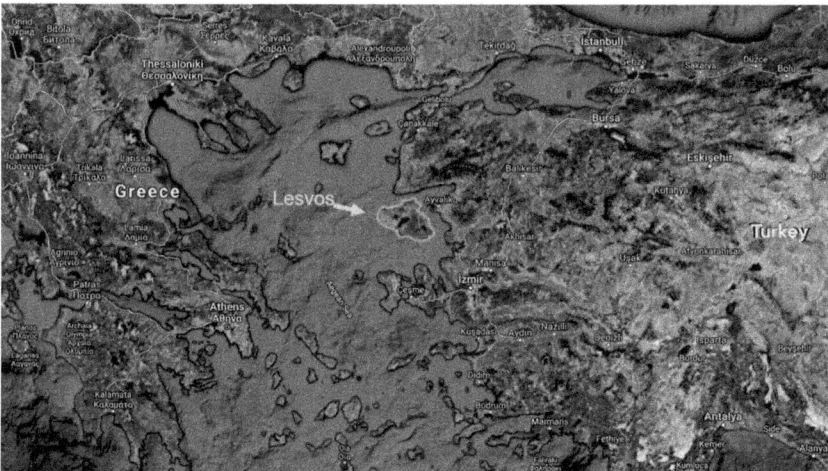

Figure 3: A volunteer and activist from Mare Liberum watches the shoreline for asylum-seekers travelling to Lesvos in inflatable rafts (dinghies). Source: Mare Liberum (2020).

Figure 4: The number of asylum seeker arrivals from 1 January 2020 to 16 August 2020. Source: UNHCR Statistics Portal (2020).

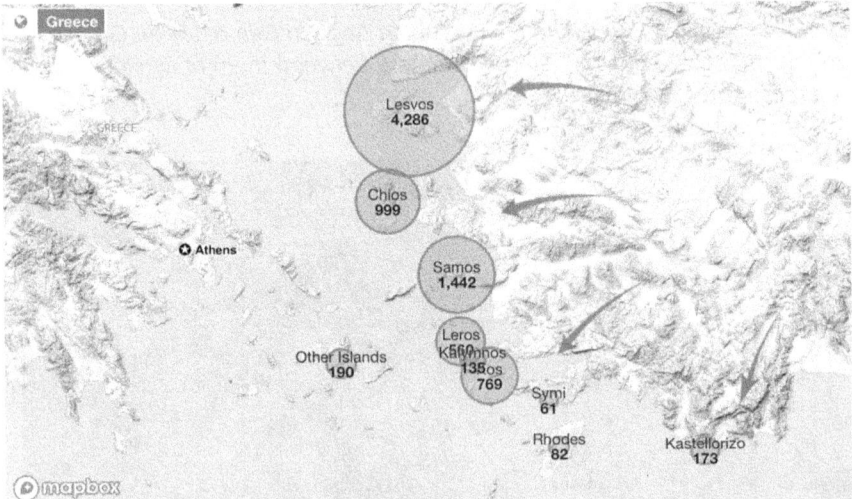

Figure 5: The number of asylum seeker arrivals from 1 July 2019 to 16 August 2020. Source: UNHCR Statistics Portal (2020).

Sea arrivals by day

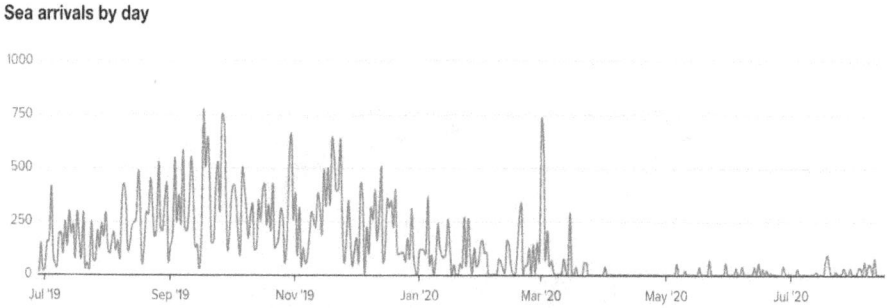

Figure 6: Flyers on the importance of hygiene in combating COVID-19 at Moria camp. Source: Mare Liberum (2020).

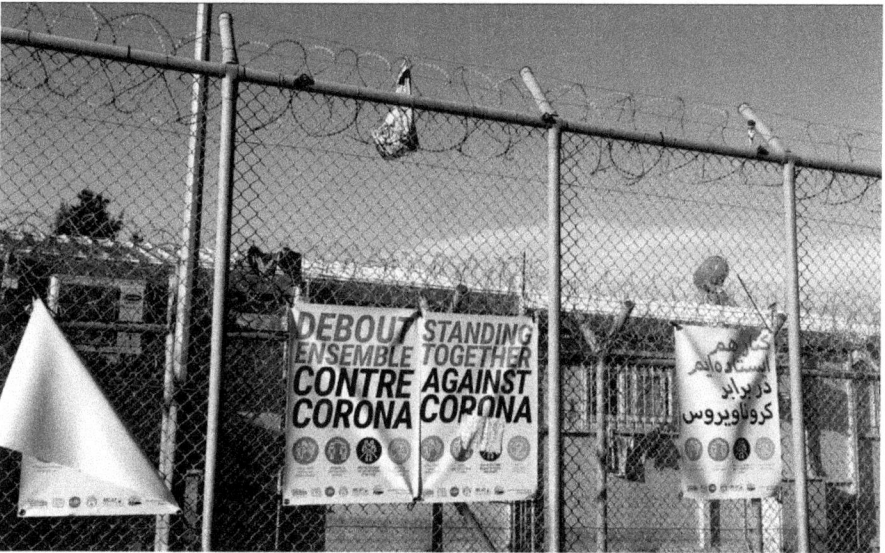

Figure 7: One of the 'wild' beach camps set-up to quarantine new arrivals on Lesvos. Source: Mare Liberum (2020).

References

Aegean Boat Report Data Studio. (no date). 'Aegean Boat Report: Page 1: Total Numbers', Aegean Boat Report. https://datastudio.google.com/reporting/1CiKR1_R7-1UbMHKhzZe_Ji_cvqF7xlfH/page/A5Q0

Aegean Boat Report Data Studio. (no date). 'Aegean Boat Report: Page 3: Numbers by island'. Aegean Boat Report. https://datastudio.google.com/u/0/reporting/1CiKR1_R7-1UbMHKhzZe_Ji_cvqF7xlfH/page/SfM0

Aegean Boat Report. 2020. 'Illegal deportations and pushbacks to Turkey, ordered by Greek government, executed by the Greek coast guard'. Facebook. April 6. https://www.facebook.com/AegeanBoatReport/posts/805700453286394

Aegean Boat Report. 2020. 'Pushback South east of Samos by HCG'. Facebook. May 11. https://www.facebook.com/AegeanBoatReport/posts/830301117492994?comment_id=840146463175126

Aegean Boat Report. 2020. 'The Greek government is taking the "pandemic excuse" even one step further'. Facebook, September 4. https://www. facebook.com/AegeanBoatReport/ photos/a.285312485325196/913366615853110/

Aegean Boat Report. 2020. 'The Greek minister of Migration and Asylum, Notis Mitarachi, is "celebrating" that there has been no arrivals on a Lesvos the last three weeks'. Facebook, September 1. https://www.facebook.com/ AegeanBoatReport/posts/910802526109519

Amnesty International. 2020. 'Greece/Turkey: Asylum-seekers and migrants killed and abused at borders'. April 3, https://www.amnesty.org/en/latest/ news/2020/04/greece-turkey-asylum-seekers-and-migrants-killed-and-abused-at-borders/

Bathke, Benjamin. 2020. 'Greece: Rights watchdogs report spike in violent push-backs on border with Turkey'. Info Migrants. May 11. https://www. infomigrants.net/en/post/24620/greece-rights-watchdogs-report-spike-in-violent-push-backs-on-border-with-turkey

Centers for Disease Control and Prevention. 2020. 'Social Distancing: Keep a Safe Distance to Slow the Spread'. https://www.cdc.gov/coronavirus/2019-ncov/prevent-getting-sick/social-distancing.htm

Cossé, Eva. 2020. 'From Chaos in Moria to Despair in Athens, Greece: Refugees Live Rough on the Streets of Central Athens'. Human Rights Watch. August 20. https://www.hrw.org/news/2020/08/20/chaos-moria-despair-athens-greece

Cullum, Barney. 2020. 'Boat Migration Push-back will never be the Asylum Solution'. *New Internationalist*. August 22. https://newint.org/ features/2020/08/22/boat-migration-push-back-will-never-be-asylum-solution

Deeb, Bashar. 2020. 'Samos And The Anatomy Of A Maritime Push-Back'. Bellingcat. May 20. https://www.bellingcat.com/news/uk-and-europe/2020/05/20/samos-and-the-anatomy-of-a-maritime-push-back/

El-Rashidi, Sarah. 2019. Stranded on the island of Lesbos, refugees remain in limbo'. Atlantic Council. November 25. https://www.atlanticcouncil.org/ blogs/menasource/stranded-on-the-island-of-lesbos-refugees-remain-in-limbo/

European Convention of Human Rights. (no date). 'Term: Push-back'. Glossary. https://www.ecchr.eu/en/glossary/push-back/

EU Commission Spokesperson's Service. 2020. 'Migration: First unaccompanied children relocated from Greece to Luxembourg'. European Commission. April 15. https://ec.europa.eu/commission/presscorner/detail/en/ip_20_668

Greek City Times. 2020. 'Greece vows to cover accommodation costs for tourists infected with coronavirus'. June 2, https://greekcitytimes.com/2020/06/02/greece-vows-to-cover-accommodation-costs-for-tourists-infected-with-coronavirus/

Greek Travel Pages. 2020. 'Greece Opens to Tourism: Who Can Come – Safety Rules'. 1 July. https://news.gtp.gr/2020/07/01/greece-opens-to-tourism-who-can-come-safety-rules/

Hellenic Republic Ministry of Migration and Asylum. 2020. 'Δελτίο Τύπου – Απάντηση σε δημοσιεύματα ξένου τύπου'. August 15. https://migration.gov.gr/deltio-typoy-apantisi-se-dimosieymata-xenoy-typoy/?fbclid=IwAR1enhTEieXHFZ0kPiveSQezrNlQgJajzttJUQSzm-YycmdJLSk84WSsAGE

Human Rights Watch. 2020. 'Greece: Grant Asylum Access to New Arrivals: Authorities Prevent Access to Services, Plan Transfers to Mainland Detention'. March 20. https://www.hrw.org/news/2020/03/20/greece-grant-asylum-access-new-arrivals

Human Rights Watch. 2020. 'Greece: Investigate Pushbacks, Collective Expulsions: EU Should Press Athens to Halt Abuses'. July 16. https://www.hrw.org/news/2020/07/16/greece-investigate-pushbacks-collective-expulsions

International Maritime Organization, International Chamber of Shipping, and United Nations High Commissioner for Refugees. 2015. *At Sea: A Guide to Principles and Practice as Applied to Refugees and Migrants*. https://www.unhcr.org/450037d34.pdf

International Organization for Migration. 2020. 'Total of Deaths Recorded in Mediterranean from 01 January to 31 August'. Missing Migrants. https://missingmigrants.iom.int/region/mediterranean?migrant_route%5B%5D=1377

International Rescue Committee. 2020. 'New IRC analysis reveals risk that coronavirus transmission rates in Moria, Al Hol and Cox's Bazar refugee camps could outpace those seen on the Diamond Princess cruise ship'. April 1. https://www.rescue.org/press-release/new-irc-analysis-reveals-risk-coronavirus-transmission-rates-moria-al-hol-and-coxs

Keep Talking Greece. 2019. 'Head of UNHCR-Greece appeal: Refrain from statements that would trigger hate against refugees'. October 4. https://www.keeptalkinggreece.com/2019/10/04/unhcr-greece-leclerc-government-refugees/

Kingsley, Patrick and Karam Shoumali. 2020. 'Taking Hard Line, Greece Turns Back Migrants by Abandoning Them at Sea'. *New York Times.* August 14. https://www.nytimes.com/2020/08/14/world/europe/greece-migrants-abandoning-sea.html?action=click&module=Top%20Stories&pgtype=HomepageHomepage.

Leclerc, Philippe. 2019. 'Responsibility and solidarity: Op-ed by Philippe Leclerc, UNHCR Representative in Greece'. United Nations High Commissioner for Refugees Greece. October 4. https://www.unhcr.org/gr/en/13090-responsibility-and-solidarity.html

Legal Centre Lesvos. 2020. 'Discriminatory Restrictions on Movement Further Contain Migrants in Unsanitary Conditions - and at Risk of COVID-19 Outbreak'. Facebook, March 30. https://www.facebook.com/LesvosLegal/posts/discriminatory-restrictions-on-movement-further-contain-migrants-in-unsanitary-c/3061323053906387/

Legal Centre Lesvos. 2020. 'Hostility towards migrants and those working to support them continues as state policy in Lesvos'. May 27. https://legalcentrelesvos.org/2020/05/27/hostility-towards-migrants-and-those-working-to-support-them-continues-as-state-policy-in-lesvos/

Macej Kaczyński, Piotr. 2020. '17 newly arrived migrants in Lesbos test Covid-19 positive'. *Euractiv.* August 14. https://www.euractiv.com/section/coronavirus/news/17-newly-arrived-migrants-in-lesbos-test-covid-19-positive/

Mare Liberum. 2020. 'Germany detains ships of human rights organization Mare Liberum'. August 19. https://mare-liberum.org/en/news/germany-detains-ships-of-human-rights-organization-mare-liberum/

Medicins Sans Frontiers. 2020. 'MSF forced to close COVID-19 centre on Lesbos'. July 30. https://www.msf.org/msf-forced-close-covid-19-centre-lesbos-greece

Merkel, Angela. 2020. 'Programme'. Germany's Presidency of the Council of the European Union. https://www.eu2020.de/eu2020-en/programm

Mlambo-Ngcuka, Phumzile. 2020. 'Violence against women and girls: the shadow pandemic'. UN Women. April 6. https://www.unwomen.org/en/news/stories/2020/4/statement-ed-phumzile-violence-against-women-during-pandemic

Ng, Kate. 2020. 'Greek refugee shelter in Lesbos engulfed in flames amid migrant crisis'. *Independent*. March 8. https://www.independent.co.uk/news/world/europe/refugee-shelter-lesbos-greece-fire-migrant-crisis-a9385116.html

Panoutsopoulou, Magda. 2020. 'Greece reports 1st COVID-19 case in Moria refugee camp: 40-year-old Somali national tests positive for coronavirus virus in overcrowded camp'. *Anadolu Agency*. September 2. https://www.aa.com.tr/en/europe/greece-reports-1st-covid-19-case-in-moria-refugee-camp/1960839

Pro Asyl, 2013. 'Pushed back – Systematic human rights violations against refugees in the aegean sea and the greek-turkish land border'. Frankfurt/Main: Pro Asyl, 2013. https://www.proasyl.de/en/material/pushed-back-systematic-human-rights-violations-against-refugees-in-the-aegean-sea-and-the-greek-turkish-land-border/.

Refugee Rescue. 2020. 'Statement: Suspension Of Operations'. August 29. https://www.refugeerescue.org/latest-news/statement-suspension-of-operations?fbclid=IwAR1dRxyCDOr2K-2pNcwbSQUiTcWjyN15r3tyFukZj1koFRSDcmiE0xm31Fl

SchengenVisaInfo. 2020. 'Greece Plans to Relaunch Its Golden Visa Program'. *SchengenVisaInfo News*. June 12. https://www.schengenvisainfo.com/news/greece-plans-to-relaunch-its-golden-visa-program/

Souliotis, Yiannis and Tania Georgiopoulou. 2020. 'Coast guard stops migrant arrivals by sea'. *Ekathimerini.com*. May 6. https://www.ekathimerini.com/252365/article/ekathimerini/news/coast-guard-stops-migrant-arrivals-by-sea

Stevis-Gridneff, Matina and Patrick Kingsley. 2020. 'Turkey, Pressing E.U. for Help in Syria, Threatens to Open Borders to Refugees'. *New York Times*. February 28. https://www.nytimes.com/2020/02/28/world/europe/turkey-refugees-Geece-erdogan.html

Sunderland, Judith and Hugh Williamson. 2013. 'Xenophobia in Greece'. Human Rights Watch. May 13. https://www.hrw.org/news/2013/05/13/xenophobia-greece

The National Herald. 2020. 'Migrants Landing on Lesbos Put in Quick Quarantine'. *The National Herald beta*. May 6. https://www.thenationalherald.com/archive_general_news_greece/arthro/migrants_landing_on_lesbos_put_in_quick_quarantine-284385/

Trilling, Daniel. 2020. 'Migrants aren't spreading coronavirus – but nationalists are blaming them anyway'. *The Guardian*, February 28. https://www.theguardian.com/commentisfree/2020/feb/28/coronavirus-outbreak-migrants-blamed-italy-matteo-salvini-marine-le-pen

Turkish Coast Guard Command. 2020. '25 Irregular Migrants Were Rescued Off the Coast of İzmir'. Republic of Turkey Ministry of Interior. May 15. https://en.sg.gov.tr/25-irregular-migrants-were-rescued-off-the-coast-of-izmir

United Nations Department of Global Communications. 2020. 'COVID-19: UN counters pandemic-related hate and xenophobia'. United Nations COVID-19 Response. May 11. https://www.un.org/en/coronavirus/covid-19-un-counters-pandemic-related-hate-and-xenophobia

United Nations High Commissioner for Refugees (no date). 'Mediterranean Situation: Greece' Operational Portal: Refugee Situations. https://data2.unhcr.org/en/situations/mediterranean/location/5179

Note on Indexing

If you are reading this book in paperback and want to find a particular word or phrase you can do so by downloading a free PDF version of this book from the E-International Relations website. View the e-book in any standard PDF reader such as Adobe Acrobat Reader (pc) or Preview (mac) and enter your search terms in the search box. You can then navigate through the search results and find what you are looking for. If you are using apps (or devices) to read our e-books, you should also find word search functionality in those.

You can download all of our books at: http://www.e-ir.info/publications